James Wills, Freeman Wills

The Irish Nation, it's History and it's Biography

Volume 1

James Wills, Freeman Wills

The Irish Nation, it's History and it's Biography
Volume 1

ISBN/EAN: 9783744717380

Printed in Europe, USA, Canada, Australia, Japan

Cover: Foto ©ninafisch / pixelio.de

More available books at **www.hansebooks.com**

THE IRISH NATION:

ITS HISTORY

AND

ITS BIOGRAPHY.

BY

JAMES WILLS, D.D.,

AND

FREEMAN WILLS, M.A.

VOLUME I.

A. FULLARTON & CO.
EDINBURGH, LONDON, AND DUBLIN.
1871.

have been compelled partially to advert in other lives. We may now proceed to its detail.

It will not be necessary to detail the incidents of Scottish history which led to Edward Bruce's descent on the Irish coast. The death of Edward I. freed the Scotch from the pressure of a formidable enemy. Robert Bruce, after a long struggle with adversity, was, by the issue of the battle of Bannockburn, placed in secure possession of the Scottish throne.

The Irish were also soon apprized of the feebleness of the English prince, and were seized by a strong desire to avail themselves of the opportunity to throw off the yoke. To effect such a purpose, it was, however, necessary to bring a force into the field adequate to struggle with the formidable power and valour of the English barons. Robert Bruce, who was at the time, without opposition, ravaging the northern frontiers of England, seemed an obvious resource upon such an occasion. To him, therefore, the chiefs of Northern Ulster applied. They represented the wrongs they had sustained, and were sustaining, from the inveterate enemies of his family, person, and nation; they must also have pleaded the ready assistance which he had in his own difficulties found from them; they reminded him of the near consanguinity of the two nations, and finally offered to receive a king from Scotland, should they first be liberated by his valour.

There were also reasons of a strong and peculiar nature, which operated to give ready effect to such an application. The juncture was seemingly favourable, and Robert Bruce was, by his nature, character, present situation, and tried experience, admirably adapted to succeed in such an enterprise. But other circumstances had been working, to prepare the way for the application made by the Irish, which gave a different turn to the event. The brave monarch to whom their offer was made had a brother, as enterprising and valiant as himself, to whose fiery and impetuous valour he had been indebted for success in many an arduous danger, and who had shared all his fortunes and sufferings, through the long and trying struggle which placed him on the throne. Edward Bruce was restless, violent, enterprising, and ambitious; a character which, though not unfitted to the nature of the warfare in which his youth had been passed, was scarcely compatible with the calm and peaceable subordination, which was so much the interest of his royal brother to preserve in his small and turbulent monarchy. Among the fiery, proud, and contentious elements of the Scottish aristocracy, a character like that of Edward was always to be feared. He was as rash and inconsiderate, as he was ambitious; and having so long been placed, by the emergencies of his brother's life, and the importance of his military services, in a station approaching equal command, he did not think it unreasonable to desire an equal share in the government of the kingdom. Such a proposal must have filled the breast of king Robert with disquietude, if not with alarm: however appeased by reason or concession, the wish itself was full of danger. King Robert, it is said, assured his brother of the succession, in case of the failure of issue male; but the proposal of the Irish chiefs came happily to relieve him from the difficulty, and he offered to place his brother at the head of an army, and to fix him on the throne of Ireland. The time was favourable to this undertaking; Ireland was seemingly defenceless; the English were divided and weakened by dissension; the Irish chiefs were favourable; and England not in a condition to offer any very efficient resistance. The great monarch, whose wisdom and valour would have made such an enterprise formidable, was succeeded by a feeble prince, whose incapacity was betrayed by the uncontrolled disorder and maleadministration of every province of his kingdom, which made him the subject of universal contempt. The project was full of golden promise, and Edward Bruce was easily tempted by the glittering bait.

Some historians speak of a premature attempt of Bruce's, the result of his impatience, which, not being proportionably seconded, was repelled. It will, however, be enough here, to detail the particulars of the main effort which worked so much woe in this island, and is connected mainly with the subject of this memoir.

It was in 1314, the seventh year of king Edward II., when lord Edmund Butler was deputy in Ireland, that Edward Bruce made his appearance with three hundred transports, containing six thousand Scots, on the north-eastern coast. Having effected a landing, he took forcible possession of the castle of Man, and took the lord O'Donnel prisoner.* Soon after, he landed his entire army, and was joined by the greater part of the native chiefs of Ulster, with such forces as they could command. They freely swore fidelity to his cause, and gave their hostages. He commenced hostilities without loss of time. It was thought necessary to begin by striking terror through the country; and his operations were of the most violent and desolating character: fire, waste, and a nearly indiscriminate slaughter were diffused among the northern settlements of the English. His barbarian outrages were heightened by the savage animosity of the natives. The castles of their English neighbours were levelled to the ground; their towns destroyed by fire; and the whole settlement depopulated. The terror of the spoilers went before them, and consternation was spread through every part of the English pale. Amongst the greater English barons disunion prevailed; and it is not improbable, that they were more intent on the consideration how this invasion might be made instrumental to their private animosities or cupidities, than on the means of averting the general calamity. As has been already noticed, De Burgo rose in defence of his own possessions, which were the first to suffer from the enemy's attack; but any force that De Burgo could command, was far below the demand of the emergency. The prince of Connaught was won from his alliance by the insidious flatteries of Bruce; and he was left to the support of his own proud and courageous spirit. The lord deputy came to his aid; but unwilling to be indebted to the English government, which he had always treated with contempt, for his safety, he declared his own forces sufficient to repel the enemy. The feebleness of the government is indicated by the fact, that the lord deputy yielded to this boastful rejection, and left him to a struggle for which he was manifestly unprepared. Bruce had advanced into Louth, but was compelled, by the scarcity of provisions, to fall back

* Cox.

into Ulster. De Burgo followed, and coming to an engagement, on the 10th of September, was defeated with great loss. This defeat was, however, not sufficient to paralyze the activity of De Burgo, and he was still enabled to harass the enemy.

The operations of Bruce were materially weakened and retarded by an inconvenience which was, in some measure, the result of his own improvidence. The waste committed by his army quickly made provisions scarce, and before long grew to a disastrous dearth, to which the failure of his enterprise is mainly attributable. He found it necessary to retire into Ulster, until he might make more efficient provision, and increase his force for an advance.

During this interval, a relation of Feidlim O'Conor's took advantage of his absence to usurp his rights. Feidlim was quickly re-instated in his possessions by Sir John Bermingham, but immediately after declared for Bruce. His example was followed by many other chiefs, who had till then rested neuter. The chiefs of Munster and Meath joined their forces. The clergy declared for Bruce, and loudly called to arms. Bruce was crowned at Dundalk; and to add to this formidable conjuncture, the king of Scotland landed with a fresh and powerful force in Ireland. This sagacious prince soon saw enough to damp his ardour for the field: the subsistence of an army, even under the most favourable circumstances, was at the time a main obstacle to such enterprises; the support of the Irish was little to be counted on; the resistance of the English, though tardy, would be formidable; and a sagacious eye could perceive, that while the Scottish force was daily becoming less efficient, the hostile power was slowly gathering from afar. The first step to be gained by the English was embarrassed by many difficulties: it was hard for the lord justice to bring an army into the field; but if this were once effected, the odds would be fearfully against any force that could be brought to oppose them. It was, besides, no part of king Robert's plan to waste his life upon an enterprise made painful by distressing dearth of means, and beset with incalculable difficulties and impediments. He was satisfied with having cheered his proud and hotbrained brother to perseverance, and having effected this purpose, he retired. He left his army with his brother, who was thus enabled to assume a more formidable posture. Among his adherents were many of the degenerate English, of whom the De Lacies and their numerous followers were the chief part.*

He laid siege to Carrickfergus. This town resisted to the most distressing extremities of weakness and famine; but the vast increase of the besieging force now rendered further resistance hopeless, and it was compelled to surrender. Bruce was next obliged to march southward.

The appearance of danger was imposing; a strong and numerous army, led by a renowned warrior and joined by the Irish nation, was not without extreme infatuation to be lost sight of in petty animosities. It became at last evident that the safety of the whole was at stake; and the common danger began to infuse unanimity and loyalty among

* Leland.

having disguised himself in a fool's dress, he entered the Scottish camp, and seeking out Bruce, he dashed his brains out with a leaden plummet. He was instantly cut to pieces. When Bermingham received intelligence of the event, he at once took advantage of the confusion it must have caused, and commanded an attack. Both accounts agree that Bruce was slain by Maupas, whose body was found stretched over him. This incident cannot be reconciled with the last mentioned accounts, as it seems to imply a state of confused resistance and hurried flight; for it is nearly impossible that the respect of the Scots would have suffered the body of his slayer to lie across that of their general, if there was a moment for the deliberate notice of such a circumstance. Maupas's heir was rewarded with forty marks per annum. Bruce's head was sent to king Edward by Bermingham, who was created earl of Louth, by a patent dated 12th May, 1319, with a grant of the manor of Atherdee in that county.

The same year he gained another victory, in Connaught, over O'Conor and MacKelly, in which 500 Irish were slain. In June, 1321, he was lord justice in Ireland, with a fee or salary of 500 marks. In 1322, he conducted a large force into England, to join the king in his intended war with the Scots.

In 1325, he founded the Franciscan friary of Thermoy. He was at length murdered by the Irish in Louth, on Whitsun-Eve, at Ballibeagan in 1329, with many of his kindred and name, to the amount of 200 persons. He was the most able leader among the Irish barons of his day. He was married to a daughter of the earl of Ulster, by whom he left three daughters.

ARNOLD DE LA POER.

CIRC. A. D. 1327.

AMONGST the most distinguished warriors who came with earl Strongbow to this island, none was more eminently distinguished for personal valour and the lustre of his exploits in the field, than Sir Roger le Poer, great-grandfather to lord Arnold. He had the government of the country about Leighlin, where he was assassinated. He left a son by a niece of Sir Armoric de St Lawrence, who was the grandfather of the subject of our present memoir. All the intermediate ancestors, from the first, were brilliantly distinguished in their several generations by those actions which, however illustrious, are unhappily the too uniform burthen of the page of our history. Lord Arnold's life presents an honourable variety of less conspicuous but more intrinsically noble distinction; he is here selected for commemoration on account of the creditable part he bore in resisting the power of a superstitious and persecuting church, and the honour of having been a martyr to the cause of mercy and justice. We shall therefore briefly notice the previous events of his life, in which he had his full share in those transactions of which we have already had, and still have, to detail so much, and hasten to the last melancholy tribute which is justly due to his memory.

The first remarkable event of his life was a single combat, in which he was, in his own defence, compelled to slay Sir John Bonneville, who was the assailant, as was proved at his trial before a parliament held in Kildare, in 1310, the year after the circumstance.

In 1325, he was made seneschal of the county and city of Kilkenny, an office of high trust and dignity in those days, though since degraded both in rank and functions, and in our own times existing as the foulest blemish on the distribution of justice in this country.

In 1327, he excited a tumultuary war in Ireland, by calling Gerald, earl of Desmond, a rhymer. Of this we have already taken notice in the memoir of that eminent person.

Among the gloomy characters which have appropriated to these periods in which we are now engaged, the name of "dark ages"—the most awful, both on account of its causes and consequences, was the cruel and arbitrary system of church despotism maintained by persecution. At a period when the original institutions of Christianity lay buried under a spurious superstition, developed out of all those very corruptions of human nature for which the gospel was designed to contain the remedy—the church, for the maintenance of its usurpations, had begun to protect its own groundless dogmas and spurious sanctity with an hundred-fold strictness. The primitive church was content to expel from its communion the idolater and the obstinate impugner of its fundamental doctrine: but the church of the darker ages, setting at nought this fundamental doctrine, yet assuming a character of more rigid and authoritative control of the conscience, guarded its own heresies with the rack and faggot of the inquisition. Opinion, reason, research, were hunted down with the cry of heresy and the bloodhounds of the hell-born inquisition; and a fearful tyranny, reared in moral and intellectual darkness and pillared by cruelty, was rapidly extending itself over all the kingdoms of Europe. Candour must admit that of the Popes, the majority would have restrained this horrid system within the limits which their own policy required; but the vindictive principle in human nature, when it becomes combined with either superstition or any other passion of a permanent nature, and capable of affecting the multitude, readily kindles into fanaticism. And an instrument of power will seldom fail to be abused for the purposes of individual resentment or ambition.

In Ireland, where the authority of the Roman see had received slow admission, and was not for a long time after this established, the prudence of the Roman cabinet would have refrained; but the rancour of the *odium theologicum*—a term which has survived its correct meaning—burned the more fiercely in the breasts of individuals. A bishop of Ossory, fired no doubt by the report of the portentous novelty of the continental institution of the *auto da fé*, seems to have conceived the liberal and patriotic project of introducing it into Ireland.

In the midst of its distractions, and amid the wild and sanguinary confusion of a state closely bordering on utter anarchy, the island was suddenly horror-struck with the cry of heresy. Alice Ketler, a lady of rank, was the first victim of a charge, which, notwithstanding some circumstances that seem to refer it to the bigotry of an individual, it is yet not easy to avoid regarding as part of a systematic contrivance.

The peculiar accusation was at least well adapted to the purpose of conciliating the sense of the multitude, ever easily brought round to any height of error or crime. A persecution for mere opinion is only popular when fanaticism has been fully kindled; but one for witchcraft, the horror of vulgar superstition, would be likely to win the support of opinion and public sentiment, and pave the way for the whole flagrant legion of St Dominic. Accordingly, this unhappy lady was accused in the spiritual court of Ossory, of the formidable crime of witchcraft; she was alleged to have stamped the sacramental wafer with the devil's name, and to have possessed an ointment to convert her staff into the flying broomstick of a witch. On this charge, one of her people was executed and her son imprisoned. The charge failed, but the accuser was resolved not to miss his object. The charge of heresy, which doubtless had been kept back to be an insidious aggravation, was brought forward, and Mrs Ketler was, on this charge, tried and condemned to the stake.

It was then that the lord Arnold de la Poer, being, as we have mentioned, the seneschal of Kilkenny, humanely interfered. The resource of bishop Ledred was prompt and terrible;—lord Arnold was himself assailed with the fatal charge. He appealed to the prior of Kilmainham, who was chief justice; the same accusation was extended to the prior. Lord Arnold, thus deprived of every resource, was left in prison in the castle of Dublin, where his death took place before he could be brought to trial. The prior of Kilmainham, Roger Outlaw, proved the falsehood of the accusation; but it is said that lord Arnold, having died "unassoiled," was left for a long time unburied.

As we shall not return to this disagreeable incident, we may here complete the account by adding that the archbishop of Dublin wisely and humanely determined to arrest in its commencement, the introduction of this new and fearful shape of calamity into Ireland. He assailed the fanatic of Ossory with his own weapon, and charged him with heresy. Ledred was obliged to fly, and made an impotent appeal to the Roman see.

ART M'MURROUGH.

DIED A. D. 1422.

Of the Irish chieftains at this period, any information to be obtained is unsatisfactory; and we are compelled to pass them in silence, from the very desultory nature of our information. We have already had occasion to name M'Murrough amongst those Irish chiefs who were knighted by king Richard.

It is unnecessary to detail the circumstances which so soon brought Richard back to Ireland, 1399; here alone he found even the shadow of honour or success. At this period, M'Murrough is represented as heading a strong force of his country against the English. His pride and sense of independence were deeply offended by the submissions he had been compelled to make; and neither the vows of allegiance and fealty, the pension of 80 merks, the honour of knighthood, nor even the

considerations of prudence, were sufficient to control his impatience to
fling off the imputation of a yoke, and wash out the stain of submission,
by the unconscious guilt of perjury and shame of falsehood.

For any open course of resistance on the battle-field, he had not,
however, sufficient means. He therefore had recourse to the well-
known system of light-heeled, though not unsoldier-like tactics of
flying and ambushed war that had so often perplexed and endangered
the soldiers of Fitz-Stephen and Strongbow. With a force of three
thousand men he took his post among the woods. The English, as
they approached, were surprised with the apparition of a well appointed
army drawn up along the forest edge, and seeming by their soldier-
like order, and intrepid front, prepared to offer immediate battle.
The appearance was illusory. As the English captains drew up their
troops in order of battle, their enemies melted away into the darkness
of the woods.

This incident elated Richard, who celebrated his triumph by the
creation of several knights; among whom was Henry of Lancaster,
whose father was at the moment preparing dethronement and disgrace
for the feeble Richard, while he was vapouring about the fancied dis-
comfiture of an enemy who despised him.

Richard ordered a large body of peasants to open a lane through the
impervious woods; and, when this insane order was executed, he had
the childish temerity to lead his army into a defile, aptly contrived for
the destruction of its designer. The English troops were soon
entangled in the miry passes of a labyrinth of thickets, lined with
invisible enemies—of hollow morasses and impeded ways, where it was
as hard to return as to proceed. At every point of disorder they were
assailed with sudden irruptions of the enemy, who rushed out into the
entangled and struggling crowd with astonishing force and noise, and
cast their darts with deadly effect. Under such circumstances, any force
of ordinary numbers must have fallen a sacrifice to the rashness of
their leader. The army of Richard was too strong to be beaten under
any disadvantage by a tumultuary crowd, whose strength was the concealment from which they made attacks which were rather directed
to cut off stragglers, than to make any impression on the main host.
There was, therefore, no hope of gaining any decided advantage;
and the chiefs of M'Murrough's army were most of them impressed with
a sense of the danger of provoking the hostility of the English to extremities. Many of them came of their own accord, to make their
peace with Richard; they appeared with halters round their necks and
threw themselves at his feet to implore for pardon and mercy.
Richard's anger was quickly appeased through the easy approach of his
vanity. M'Murrough was formally summoned to submit, but the summons was deprived of its authority and dignity by the accompaniment
of large offers. M'Murrough was, in his own way, as vain as his antagonist; and he saw the increasing distresses of the English. Richard
had, in his thoughtless impetuosity, neglected to observe, that the scene
of such long-continued wars and disturbances could not supply the wants
of his army. This oversight was not lost upon the sagacity of M'Murrough, who anticipated the sure consequences, and was thus encouraged
in the course of resistance he had pursued. There seems indeed to

have been throughout, a struggle between pride and prudence in the mind of this chief; he saw his advantages, but seems to have hesitated in their use—whether to obtain a beneficial compromise, or to win the name of a heroic resistance. The temptation to this latter vain course was very great. There was a dearth amounting to famine in Richard's camp: his men were perishing from want—the horses were become unfit for service—a general discontent possessed the army—the very knights complained of hardships unattended with the chance of honour. It became a necessity to change their quarters. M'Murrough saw the advantageous occasion which was unlikely to recur, as Richard's distresses must end with his arrival in Dublin. The plunder of some vessels, laden with a scanty supply of provisions, by his own soldiers, decided the king; and the Irish chief who wavered to the last moment, now sent in to desire a safe-conduct, that he might treat for peace. The duke of Gloucester was sent to meet him and settle the terms. The meeting has been described, by a historian of the time, with graphic precision; the description, though assimilated to caricature by some touches of grotesque truth, affords a curious gleam of the social state of the Irish of that generation, and is equally interesting for the lively portrait it gives of the ancient barbaric chief: the ostentatious and flourishing extravagance of barbarian vanity cannot be mistaken, and the portrait is altogether full of uncouth nature and truth. The Irish king darted forth from a mountain, surrounded by the forests which concealed his forces; he was mounted on a strong and swift horse, and rode without stirrups. A vast mantle covered his person with its ample folds, but did not conceal the strong mould of his tall and well-proportioned frame, "formed for agility and strength." As he approached with the rapidity of a warrior about to charge, he waved proudly to his followers to halt; and, darting the spear which he grasped in his right hand, with the display of much force and skill, into the ground, he rushed forward to meet the English knight, who stood more entertained than awed by this formidable exhibition of native energy.

The treaty ended in nothing; the prudence of M'Murchard was uncertain and wavering, his pride and prurient haughtiness were in permanent inflammation. The hero outweighed the statesman, and he could not resist the opportunity for a display of kingly loftiness. He offered submission, for such was the purpose of his coming, but he refused to be shackled by stipulation or security. His insolence quickly terminated a conference in which no terms could be agreed upon, and each party returned to their own camps.

M'Murrough had now plainly involved himself in a condition of which, in the ordinary course, ruin must have soon followed. The king was infuriated; and an adequate force, intrusted to a leader of ordinary skill and knowledge of the country, would soon have deprived him of every rood of territory. But circumstances, stronger than the arms and pride of M'Murrough or the anger of Richard, now interfered.

Richard remained in Dublin, and was engaged in the arrangements for the vindication of his authority, and the indulgence of revenge. But his power was come to its end; and he was already devoted to the hapless fate which he was meditating for an inferior. The continued prevalence of stormy weather had for some weeks prevented all intelligence from England; at length it came, and he learned that he was ruined.

The story of his return, and the sad particulars which followed, belong to English history, and are known to the reader.

Of the subsequent history of this chief we find but occasional tracks at remote intervals. In the following reign, during one of those occasional fits of vigour which a little retarded the decline of the English pale, his obstinate disaffection received a transient check. He exulted in the reputation of having alone, of all his fellow-countrymen, held out against the force and power of the English, and having foiled the power of the king at the head of thirty thousand men. This was the more galling to the English, as his territory lay within the pale. He was the only chief who refused to make submission to the duke of Lancaster; and as such submissions were in few instances more than nominal, he found no difficulty in seducing many of the others to join him. At the head of these he defied the government. Stephen Scrope, who was at the time deputy to the duke, called a parliament in Dublin, which was adjourned to Trim, to consider the best means for the defence of the country. The Irish barons Ormonde, Desmond, the prior of Kilmainham, and other nobles and gentlemen, joined such troops as they could collect, and marched against M'Murrough. The whole force of these leaders was but slight, and the Irish chief was enabled to present a formidable resistance. The first encounter was seemingly doubtful, and the little army of the English was compelled to give way before the impetuous onset of M'Murrough's host; but the steadiness of the English soon turned the foaming and roaring current of a tumultuous onset, and the Irish fled before them. O'Nolan and his son were taken, and many slain. But the English were prevented from following up their fortune. Accounts reached them on the field of other disturbances in the county of Kilkenny: they were obliged to make a forced march against O'Carrol, whom they slew, with eight hundred of his men; but M'Murrough was nothing the worse. A defeat was nothing to the Irish chief while he could save himself; his army was a mob that easily collected and scattered.

The power of the English was now far on the wane; their moments of vigour were desultory, and their effects were more than counteracted by the lengthened intervals of neglect and weakness. Henry IV. appears to have been both careless and ignorant about the interests of the Irish settlers; and the wisdom and valour of the best governors and deputies were unable to obtain more than a respite from the ruin that was coming on with uniform progress.

Talbot, lord Furnival, came over; and to show, in a very forcible point of view, what might be done by skill and prudence with adequate means, without any force but what could be raised among the inhabitants of the pale, he managed by judiciously directed and alert movements to repress the insubordination of the Irish chiefs. And there cannot be a more unequivocal test of the efficacy of his conduct, than the submission of M'Murrough, who gave up his son as a hostage.

The remainder of M'Murrough's life was probably spent in quiet.

SIR WILLIAM BRABAZON.

DIED A. D. 1552.

In August, 1534, Sir William Brabazon was appointed vice-treasurer and receiver-general of Ireland; and was for the eighteen years following the most distinguished person there for his eminent services, and his brave and steady conduct in various trying situations.

In 1535, he distinguished himself greatly by his resistance to the mad proceedings of Lord Thomas Fitz-Gerald, in the country round Naas. Allen and Aylmer, in a joint letter* to Secretary Cromwell, mention that but for Brabazon's conduct on that occasion, the whole country from Naas to the gates of Dublin, had been burnt; "which had been a loss in effect irrecuperable."

The following year, O'Conor Faly made a destructive inroad upon Carbery, in the county of Kildare, but was at once checked by Sir William Brabazon and the chancellor, who marched into Offaly, where they committed equal devastation in the lands of O'Conor who was thus compelled to return home, on which a peace was presently concluded.

In 1539, Brabazon was, with the chancellor and master of the rolls, appointed a commissioner for receiving the surrenders of the abbeys, and the granting of the necessary pensions for the maintenance of the abbots and fraternities by whom they were surrendered; and in 1543, he was appointed lord justice. At this time the king's style was altered from lord to king of Ireland, and the new official seals were sent through him to the respective officers by whom they were held.

He was again called to the government in 1546, and maintained his character by successful expeditions in which he reduced a dangerous combination of O'More and O'Conor Faly, whose territories he laid waste, forcing O'Conor to seek refuge in Connaught.

On the accession of Edward VI., being nominated of the Irish privy council, at the special desire of that king, who, at the same time, expressed his sense of his long and eminent service, Brabazon suggested the effective repair and occupation of the castle of Athlone, and had the charge of this measure, so important to the province of Connaught, committed to himself. The military importance of this place had been recognised so early as the reign of John, when the castle is said to have been built. Standing on the only part of the Shannon where this river is fordable for thirty miles, and commanding the territories on either side, this town obviously presented the most important advantages for a magazine, and central position in the western country. Under Brabazon, repairs were made, and additions, which were continued in the reign of Elizabeth. This service was rendered difficult by the strenuous opposition of the neighbouring Connaught chiefs.

In 1549, Brabazon was again called to the head of the Irish go-

---

* State Papers, Paper xcv. p. 260.

vernment by the election of the council, and during his administration performed many important and laborious military services, among which may be specified his expedition against Charles Kavenagh Mc-Art, whom he proclaimed a traitor, and having got £8000, and four hundred men from England, he attacked him in his own lands, and dispersed his soldiers with considerable slaughter; so that Kavenagh was soon after compelled to come to Dublin and submit himself to the council, publicly renouncing his title of M'Murrough, and surrendering large tracts of his estates.

Sir William Brabazon died at Carrickfergus in 1552. His heart was buried with his English ancestors in Eastwell, and his body in St Katherine's church, Dublin, where there was a long Latin inscription upon a monument, which has been removed in rebuilding the church; and an English inscription summing the above particulars, upon his gravestone. He was ancestor to the earls of Meath.

BERNARD FITZ-PATRICK, SECOND BARON UPPER OSSORY.

DIED A. D. 1550, OR A. D. 1551.

THE reader of ancient Irish history may recollect to have met the name of M'Gil Patrick, prince of Upper Ossory, among the most valiant opponents of the first settlers in the 12th century. A still earlier recollection carries us back to the famous field of "Ossory's plain," where the ancient warriors of Munster were crossed upon their homeward march from the battle of Clontarf, by Magilla-Patrick and his men, and subdued their generous enemies with the noblest display of heroism that history records.

The grandfather of the baron who is the subject of this notice, is also commemorated by an amusing anecdote, which is repeated by all the Irish historians. In 1522, this chief sent an ambassador to Henry VIII. with a complaint against Pierce, earl of Ormonde. The ambassador met king Henry on his way to chapel, and delivered his errand in the following uncouth sentence: "*Sta pedibus, Domine Rex! Dominus meus Gillapatricius me misit ad te et jussit dicere, quod si non vis castigare Petrum Rufum, ipse faciet bellum contra te.*"

The son of this chief, Barnard Fitz-Patrick, made his submission in 1537, to the commissioners of Henry VIII. They entered into indentures with him to make him baron of Cowshill, or Castleton, with a grant of the lands of Upper Ossory, at the annual rent of three pounds to the king, which agreement was carried into effect by a patent, dated 11th June, 1541. His first wife was a daughter of Pierce, earl of Ormonde, the "*Petrum Rufum*" of his father's complaint. By her he left a son, Barnaby, who succeeded him as second earl; and who was eminently distinguished for bravery, and for his prudent and honourable conduct as a public man.

This Barnaby was the distinguished friend and favourite of Edward VI., who wrote him many affectionate letters, still extant, while he was in France, where he served as a volunteer in the king of France's army. Afterwards, when he returned from France, he signalized his valour in England, in Wyat's insurrection; and in 1558 was knighted by the duke of Norfolk for his distinguished services at the siege of Leith.

An extract from a letter of the lord deputy Sidney to the Irish council, written while he was at Waterford, affords an honourable testimony of this lord: "Upper Ossorie is so well governed and defended by the valour and wisdom of the baron that now is, as—saving for surety of good order hereafter in succession—it made no matter if the county were never shired, nor her majestie's writ otherwise current than it is, so humbly he keepeth all his people subject to obedience and good order."* Under this impression, so honourable to the lord of Upper Ossory, the lord deputy made him lord lieutenant of the King's and Queen's counties, and the neighbouring country; throughout which the same good order was preserved, so that the turbulent chiefs of those districts were thoroughly repressed.

One of those chiefs whose insurrectionary sallies he had for many years controlled, Rory Oge O'More, having burnt Naas and other towns, was proclaimed by the government. As the baron of Upper Ossory was his most formidable foe, this chief made a characteristic effort to destroy him: he sent a person to the baron, who pretended to give him private information of the movements of O'More, and described the place where he might be surprised with a large prey and a small force, among the woods. The baron knew the rebel chief's character, and the ways of the country, and suspected the truth. The information was not, however, to be neglected, so he took with him a strong party, and when he approached the woods, he sent in thirty men to try the way. O'More seeing this, thought to mask his real force by appearing with an equal number, leaving the rest of his men in ambush. This well devised manœuvre was, however, defeated by the impetuosity of the baron's men, who instantly charged the enemy and scattered them; in the confusion O'More received a sword through his body, and was despatched. The reward of a thousand marks had been offered for O'More's head; this sum was offered to the baron by the council, but he refused to accept more than one hundred marks as a reward for his men. This occurrence happened in 1578.

In the following year, the baron attended the lord deputy into Munster against James Fitz-Maurice; in consideration of which, Lodge tells us, he received a pension with other compensations which showed a high sense of his services. Sir Henry Sidney, in his instructions to his successor, lord Grey, mentions the baron of Upper Ossory, with a few more, as "the most sufficient and faithful" persons he found in Ireland.

This baron died 1581, leaving a daughter only; on which his title and estates passed to his brother Florence, to whom he also left by will all his "wyle stoode," "his armour, shirts of mail, and other furniture of war, saving that which served for both the houses of Borriedge and Killenye, which, after his wife's decease or marriage, he wills to remain for the furniture of those two castles constantly. He leaves to him likewise half his pewter and brass; all his tythes in Ossory (except those of Aghavol bequeathed to his wife), all the plate left him by his father," &c., &c.†

* Quoted by Lodge. † Lodge.

SIR ANTHONY ST. LEGER.

DIED A. D. 1559.

The St. Legers were, for many generations, settled in the county of Kent; and several individuals of the family appear, during the course of the 15th century, to have held offices lay or clerical in Ireland.

Sir Anthony was sent over by Henry VIII. as one of the commissioners for setting the waste lands upon the marches of the English pale, for 21 years, to such tenants as would improve them, and on such rents as might appear fair to demand, &c., with certain conditions framed to extend the pale and preserve the English character of its inhabitants. This commission is historically important, for the distinct view which it affords of the state of the pale in the year 1537. We shall, therefore, have to notice it farther on in detail. It may be here enough for the reader to know, that the commission carried an inquest, by means of juries, into the several districts of the pale; from the returns of this the result is a most frightful picture of exaction and petty tyranny, under the odious names of Coyne and Livery, and other pretences of extortion all prohibited by law. Surveys were also made of several estates of the greater proprietors; regulations of the most judicious character were decided upon in conformity with these, and intrusted to this commission to carry into effect. For this purpose they were armed with very considerable authority, and executed their commission with vigour and effect. They made sufficient inquiries as to the parties concerned in lord Thomas Fitz-Gerald's rebellion to produce a salutary fear, while they refrained from an injudicious severity, which might excite disaffection. They let to farm the king's lands, reserving the annual payments due to the exchequer; and they reconciled the earl of Ormonde to the lord deputy.

Having executed his commission, St. Leger returned to England, where he remained till 1540. When he was sent over as lord deputy, and was sworn on the 25th of July, he brought over with him Commissioners, appointed for the further prosecution of the measures already mentioned, which they forwarded materially by a survey of the crown lands. An order was transmitted to the master of the rolls and the archbishop of Dublin, to have the goods of every description, which had been the property of the late lord deputy Grey, appraised and delivered into the custody of the new deputy, to hold for the king, and use during the royal pleasure. Grey, one of the ablest, most active, and in every way serviceable governors Ireland had yet known, was, on his return to England, by means of the malicious intrigues of his enemies and the reckless tyranny of Henry, most iniquitously accused, tried, and condemned. His conduct on the occasion was an instance of the difference between active courage and passive fortitude: so vigorous in military command, so brave in the field, his firmness was not of that high order that accompanies the hero into the horrors of captivity, and supports him against the wantonness of the tyrant's cruelty: his spirit sunk under the terror of Henry's brutality— which he had probably been accustomed to fear and shrink from; and he refused to defend himself. He was condemned and executed. He was more resolute to face death than the tyrant's bluster, and met his fate with heroic calmness. The principal charge against him was the suffering the son of Kildare, a youth of ten, to be saved from the general slaughter of his family.

St Leger successfully exerted himself to infuse activity, and control the direction of every department and functionary of the government. He sent the marshal of Ireland, Sir William Brereton, to receive the submission of the earl of Desmond. Brereton died at Kilkenny. But the earl came to meet the deputy at Cahir, in the following January, and tendered his submission which was accepted by St Leger. This submission was confirmed by the delivery of the earl's son, Gerald, as an hostage. This earl also renounced the privilege of the Desmond lords to absent themselves from parliaments, and not to enter walled towns: a privilege which, the reader may recollect, was granted in 1444, to James the 7th earl. This transaction had been a considerable time in agitation. Among the State Papers of the year 1538, a letter from St Leger, written during the time of his commission (already noticed), mentions that the earl had delivered a hostage and a written engagement. And another letter, written by lord Ormonde in the same year, mentions evidently with a view to injure the deputy, (Grey.) "And after my lord deputie of his own motion, went with four of his company to James, earl of Desmond, and perswaded him, after such a fashion, that he desired him for the love of God to deliver him the hostage, considering that he have written to the king's highness, that he had the same; otherwise, that he was like to be utterly undone, ... and hereupon he had the hostage given him, who promised, that after he had shewed the same, that he should be delivered (back) without any hurt, losses or danger, as he was true knight; which matter was done in Thomen, O'Brien's country."

On the 13th June, 1541, Sir Anthony summoned a parliament in Dublin, in which it was enacted that king Henry and his successors should from that time bear the title of kings of Ireland.* Several enactments were also made for the administration of justice in questions affecting property; and an application was made to the king for permission to hold the following session of the same parliament at Limerick, on account of the salutary effect its presence might have on the earl of Desmond and other chiefs in that vicinity.† At this parliament also, Meath was divided into East Meath and West Meath, for the convenience of county jurisdiction.

It was also in the same year, and in the administration of Sir Anthony, that O'Niall, and a number of other Irish chiefs, made their submissions, and swore fidelity to the English crown. In 1542, the king granted to Sir Anthony, in recompense for his many services, the site and precinct of the monastery of Grany, in the county of Carlow, with several other lands and profits in different parts of Ireland.

In 1543, Sir Anthony was summoned over to England to give a full account of his government, and of the state of Ireland. His account was considered so satisfactory, that he was created a knight companion

---

* This was followed by a coinage of groats, twopenny and penny pieces, for Irish circulation, having a harp on the reverse.—*Lodge.*

† State Papers, cccxlii. p. 311.

of the order of the garter, and sent back as lord deputy. After four months' stay in England, he landed in Ireland, June, 1544, and was received with every mark of the public regard which had been conciliated by the justice of his administration. It had been throughout his principle to support the weak against the injustice of the strong; and whenever the case admitted, he usually took occasion to dissolve every ancient convention which gave a pretext for tyranny: of this may be mentioned as an instance, his decision between O'Niall and O'Donell, by which he set O'Donell free from his oppressive subjection to O'Niall, substituting a moderate and defined annual rent.

Sir Anthony, in common with every other lord deputy, had to bear the vexatious consequences of the jealousy of the greater proprietors. Of these the earl of Ormonde was then at the head. The depression of the Geraldine faction, and especially of the house of Kildare, had given a great preponderance to the Butlers whose hereditary prudence had preserved them from the incitements by which other chiefs had been tempted into many a fatal step. Sir Anthony, feeling strongly the great want of means which limited and defeated his best efforts, seems to have determined to increase the revenue by tributes to be levied upon the country. The allowance from England* was quite inadequate, and the Irish revenue was insufficient to supply the deficiency. The means adopted by St Leger were, however, unpopular, and gave a handle to the factious hostility of the earl of Ormonde. This earl, after offering all the resistance in his power, at last accused the deputy of treason: the deputy retorted the accusation, and both parties were summoned over to England, and their accusations investigated by the privy council. But they were found to be vexatious, and both parties were dismissed.

Sir Anthony returned and resumed his government, which was continued to him at the accession of king Edward VI. In the following year his activity was employed by the restlessness of the Irish chiefs. These petty insurrections are in few cases worth detail. O'Conor Faly and O'More received a sanguinary overthrow from his arms, while they were plundering the county of Kildare; the O'Byrnes were attacked and dispersed. And some time after, receiving a reinforcement from England, of 600 foot and 400 horse, under captain general Bellingham, he invaded Leix and Offaly, and proclaimed O'Conor and O'More traitors. Their followers were routed and dispersed; and being left defenceless, these two powerful chiefs were reduced to the necessity of coming in with their submission. Sir Anthony took them with him to England, where, by his desire, they were pardoned, taken into favour, and had handsome pensions. The high sense entertained of these services of Sir Anthony was shown by large English grants: he received a grant of the manor-house of Wingham Barton, Bersted, an appendant to the manor of Leeds Castle, with the fee of one of the parks of Leeds Castle, with two manors, Eastfarbon and Bentley, in the county of Kent, where his own property lay.

In the mean time, Edward Bellingham, who had already distinguished himself in Ireland, was sent as lord justice; and St Leger

* £5000 per annum.

remained in England till 1550: he then returned to Ireland with instructions to call a parliament. On this occasion, the annalists mention one of those incidents which were at this time becoming more frequent, and which must impress the reader with a sense of the growing improvement of the condition of the settlement. Charles Kavenagh MacArt came before this parliament with his submission, consenting not only to renounce the title of Macmurrough, but giving up large tracts of land, and submitting to the limitation of his powers as chief or "captain of his nation."

On the 6th of February, an order for the reading of the liturgy of the church of England came over, in the name of Edward VI. On which the lord deputy convened an assembly of the Irish ecclesiastics of every order, to which he intimated the king's pleasure. To this announcement, Dowdal, the archbishop of Armagh, offered the most resolute opposition. The deputy, nevertheless, determined to carry the point: he was supported by Browne, archbishop of Dublin, and the other prelates; and on the following Easter Sunday, the English liturgy was publicly read in Christ Church. Dowdal was deprived, and withdrew from the kingdom, and the primacy was annexed to the see of Dublin.

Soon after, Archbishop Browne having some discontent against the deputy, had recourse to the common complaint of treason, which was then resorted to on the most frivolous grounds as the most efficient instrument of party hostility, and strongly indicates the weakness of government, and the low civilization of the aristocracy and prelacy of the time. St Leger was recalled to clear himself. And as he was again sent over by queen Mary, it is to be inferred that the charges of the archbishop were merely vexatious. He was not, however, allowed to hold the government long. Queen Mary, with a feeble intellect and a tender conscience, influenced by her own superstition and the craft of others, soon displayed that inflamed spirit of persecution which for a time filled the kingdom with horrors till then and since unknown: and a change of policy beginning in England, where it was opposed to the spirit of the nation, was quickly extended to Ireland where it was congenial. The Irish nation, the last to adopt the errors of the church of Rome, were as slow to turn from them at the dictate of a prince. And it is not likely that under the new government, a deputy, who, like St Leger, had mainly contributed to effect the changes of the last two reigns, could be acceptable to either queen or people. He had seized the abbey lands for Henry—carried into effect important regulations of church preferment—persuaded the Irish chiefs to renounce the church of Rome, and enforced the English liturgy. And such merits could not fail to be unfavourably recollected. His high reputation as a governor made it, however, inexpedient to remove him without some shadow of complaint. A complaint in keeping with the spirit of his accusers was found. It was represented that in the former reign he had aimed to ingratiate himself with the government by ridiculing the sacred mystery of transubstantiation. On this ground he was recalled in 1556. He defended himself so well, from various charges which his enemies brought against him, that his friends in Ireland looked for his return. But he adopted a wiser course. Having obtained a discharge from all future service in Ireland, he retired to Ulcomb in Kent, the seat of his ancestors, where he died in 1559.

THE O'NIALLS OF TIR OWEN, OR TYRONE.

HUGH O'NIALL OF TIR OWEN.

A. D. 1215.

Of the secondary class of Irish chieftains, who lived in this period, nothing is distinctly known, but as their names are occasionally brought into historical distinctness by their occurrence in the feuds, battles, and rebellions of the time. Amongst these casual notices there occurs much to excite regret that more abundant and distinct information cannot be found in any unquestionable forms; as it must be admitted that, unless in the point of military skill, the little we can discover of their actions may bear a not discreditable comparison with the most renowned and successful of their invaders. The characteristic features are, indeed, in some respects, so different, that such a comparison can hardly be made without the suspicious appearance of over-refining. But a closer inspection must remove something of this difficulty; because, when we scrutinize the conduct of our English barons to find the true indication of the virtues ascribed to chivalry, unfavourable allowances are to be largely made for the action of influences arising from their position as conquerors, holding their territories by continued violence, engaged incessantly in small yet irritating hostilities, possessed of enormous power, and tempted by constant opportunities to enlarge it. If, among the native chiefs, there occurs little that can be viewed with less reproach, equal allowances must be made on the score of the similar pernicious influences; while some indulgence must be thrown into the scale for the natural workings of pride and resentment. The comparison, indeed, has little to recommend it; its best points, on either side, are scarcely to be ranked under the predicament of virtues; but the lower the level on the scale of civilization, to which either side must be referred, the more signal are the examples of prudence and honour of which individual instances occur from time to time.

The main difference consists rather in the different means which we have of attaining to any thing of distinct knowledge of the personal history of the individuals of either class. The Irish chiefs have their record in a class of writers who, of all that ever held the pen of history, have left least information to after times. Barely confined to the dry mention of a fact, in the fewest words, and without description or detail, their accounts are nothing more than the brief entry of a chronological table. It is only incidentally that their names and actions occur in the diffuse page of Cambrensis, who, with all his misconceptions and prejudices, is the only historian from whom either the detail or colour of the time can be known, so far as regards Irish history. Of the English barons, we have abundant means of tracing the genealogy and verifying the biography in the more distinct records and documents of the English history of the same period; while of the Irish, we can only pretend to be so far distinct as their intercourse with the English barons places their names and actions in a clear point of view.

Such are the reasons why we have found it convenient to confine our plan, so far as respects these illustrious persons, to such of them as have a prominent place in the history of the English; and of these, to that portion of their history which thus appertains to the history of the settlement.

Among these, a prominent place cannot be denied to the O'Nialls of Tyrone. Of these, among the first whose names occur in this period may be mentioned that chief of Tyrone, Hugh, who had nearly fallen a victim to the cause of Cathal O'Connor, when he was deprived of his kingdom by De Burgo, in favour of his rival Carragh. To the circumstances of this part of his life we shall have to revert;—worsted in the field by De Burgo, he was deposed by his angry subjects, and another chieftain of his family elected.

This chieftain fell in the action, which soon followed, with the people of Tir Connel; but a considerable time elapsed before O'Niall regained his rights. In this he succeeded by means easily conjectured, but of which we have no detail; and some time elapses before we again meet him on the occasion of king John's visit to Ireland, in 1210. On this occasion, it is mentioned that he refused to present himself before the king, unless on the condition of being secured by two hostages for his safe-conduct. The terms of his submission to the English crown were then settled apparently to his own satisfaction, and he was peaceably dismissed; but, with the characteristic inconsistency of his countrymen, he no sooner found himself secure in his own territory, than he dismissed all idea of submission and spurned a demand of hostages from the king. The consequences of this boldness were averted by the timidity and feebleness of John, whose spirit was not roused by a bold defiance from the chief, as he marched through his territory. His chastisement was committed to the garrisons on the frontiers of the English districts, but the force, on either side, was too nearly balanced for any decided result; and this the more so, as the English, few in number and unprepared for extended operations, were confined to the defensive. O'Niall had the advantage of selecting the occasion and point of attack, and generally contrived to obtain some petty advantage, too slight to have any consequence, but sufficient to be exaggerated by the pride and jealous enthusiasm of his people and the magnifying power of report, into the name of victory. With the aid of the neighbouring chiefs, more decided results might have followed from the pertinacious hostility of this spirited chief; but the neighbouring chiefs were engaged in mutual strifes and animosities.

The next incident in which he is to be traced is in a combination with Hugh de Lacy, in which he gave assistance to that ambitious and turbulent chief, in his attempts to possess himself of some territory belonging to William, earl Marshall. Not many years after, his influence is apparent in the election of Tirlogh O'Connor, on the death of Cathal—an election which was defeated in favour of another brother, of which we shall have occasion to speak.

Of the death of Hugh O'Niall, we have no means of fixing the precise date; but from those we have noticed, the time of his appearance on the scene of Irish politics may be somewhat between 1190 and 1215.

There are some curious remains of the ancient rank and grandeur of this family, of whom we shall have to notice some of the descendants. The *Dublin Penny Journal*, to which we have already been indebted for valuable information on Irish antiquities, gives a woodcut of the coronation chair of one of the branches of this family—the O'Nialls of Castlereagh*; and in the same place mentions, that "there was, and probably still is, another stone chair on which the O'Nialls of Tyrone, the chief branch of the family, were inaugurated. It is marked in some of our old maps, under the name of the "stone where they make the O'Nialls." In the same page of this work, there is also a curious representation of the ancient arms of the family:—a "bloody hand, from an impression of the silver signet ring of the celebrated Turlogh Lynnoch. It was found, a few years ago, near Charlemont, in the county of Armagh."*

CON O'NIALL, FIRST EARL OF TYRONE.

DIED A.D. 1558.

THE name of O'Niall has a place of no mean distinction in every chapter of the history of Ireland. But it is the main difficulty of the present portion of our labour, that while events, scarcely historical in their nature, are crowded together on every page, we have, on the contrary, a lamentable absence of all the personal detail which might be looked for among records so minute and frivolous, that they seem rather to be the material for personal than for national history. The descendants of these renowned Irish kings, the heroes of the poets and chroniclers of our first period, appear in the subsequent periods as the actors in some slight transaction, or persons of some curious tale, and disappear without any satisfactory trace of their previous or subsequent course. It is mostly, only from the change of name, that it is to be inferred, that the father has died and the son succeeded. This obscurity, instead of diminishing, increases as we advance to later ages; so that it is easier to give the full details of the history of the hero of the nine hostages than of his descendant, who flourished among the sons of little men at an interval of thirty generations.

In every reign, the representative of the Tyrone O'Nialls is found among the more powerful opponents of the pale,—often the leaders of formidable insurrections of the native forces; often yielding and swearing fealty; often again in arms, and among the enemies or pensioned

* Vol. i. p. 208.—The monument here mentioned has been purchased by R. C. Walker, Esq. of Rath Carrick.

protectors of the pale. They assume, however, in the reign of Henry VII., a new character, by their alliance with the princely house of Kildare. As the authentic portion of the family history of this race is confined to notices insufficient for the purpose of biography, we shall here mention a few particulars about some of the immediate ancestors of the first earl of Tyrone. Con O'Niall was married to the sister of the eighth earl of Kildare; and, from the time of that great man's elevation to the administration of Irish affairs, he gave his powerful support to the English. He was, in 1492, murdered by his brother, Henry, who, in turn, was murdered, in 1498, by the sons of his victim, Con and Tirlogh. This Tirlogh was thus raised to his father's rights. In 1501, he had a battle with the Scots, near Armagh, whom he defeated, slaying about sixty soldiers,* and four captains. "A son," says Ware, "of the laird of Aig, of the family of the MacDonnels, and four sons of Colley MacAlexander." As this battle was on Patrick's day, it is doubtful how far it can be properly regarded as an affair of enmity. We find no account of the death of this chief: but he was succeeded, within a few years by Art O'Niall, whom we find receiving aid from the earl of Kildare, in 1509, when he was seized and imprisoned by the rival branch of the O'Nialls. Of Art we have nothing very memorable to tell: he died in 1519, and was succeeded by his brother, Con Boccagh, who was raised by popular election. This chief was not long at the head of his sept, when Thomas Howard, earl of Surrey, was sent to Ireland as deputy, in 1520. Con was, at the time, engaged in an incursion into Meath; but, hearing that Surrey was on his march against him with an overwhelming force—a thousand English, and the select men of Dublin—he became discouraged, and retreated into Ulster. Thither Surrey did not think fit to pursue him, as he was quite unprovided for so prolonged a campaign; and he therefore returned to Dublin. O'Niall, however, clearly saw, that he had not himself any force to be relied on, if the English governor should think fit to follow into the north; with this feeling, he sent letters to Surrey, offering entire submission, on the condition of being taken into favour; and offering to serve the king faithfully. To this Surrey agreed; he had, indeed, little if any choice. O'Niall was not aware of the penurious means allowed for the maintenance of the Irish government, by Henry VIII. The celebrated field of the cloth of gold was held in the same year, with all its well known circumstances of lavish cost; but the liberality of Henry was confined to his pleasures, and his love of ostentation. There was, however, good reason to fear the wisdom and military talent of Surrey, who, notwithstanding his difficulties contrived in August 1520 to march into O'Niall's country, on which O'Niall came in, with other Irish chiefs of the north, and submitted; or as king Henry describes it in his own communication to Surrey, "according to their natural duty of allegiance, have recognised us as their sovereign lord," &c. Sir John Wallop had been sent over with this intelligence to the king, who in answer states to Surrey, the advice of his council upon the government of Ireland, that the Irish chiefs should be dealt with by "sober waies, politique drifts, and amiable perswasions, rather than by

* Cox.

rigorous dealing, comminacions, or any other enforcement by strength or violence; and, to be plaine unto you, to spende so moche money for the reduccion of that lande, to bring the Irishry in apparannce oonely of obeisannce, &c., &c., it were a thing of less policie, less advantage, and lesse effect."*

It is more to our present purpose that we find in the same letter a direction to lord Surrey to knight O'Niall, "and other such lords of the Irishry, as ye shall thinke goode."† A complaint seems to have soon after (1521) been made to the English court, of O'Niall, representing him as engaged in a formidable conspiracy for the destruction of the English, by the aid of a Scottish force; and urging, as the only resource against this, the necessity of a strong English force being sent over. It was answered in the paper of instructions sent over by the king, that the king's engagements to foreign powers, and his "manifolde quarrels with France, made it inconvenient." This is, however, followed by a letter from the king, in which he states, that having caused all inquiry to be made in Scotland, and for other reasons assigned, there is no ground for any apprehension of immediate hostility from O'Niall. It appears certain from the same document, that O'Niall had expressed his gratitude to the king himself for the honours conferred upon him; and the probability, suggested by every gleam we can obtain of his personal conduct, is, that he became a true if not a zealous supporter of the English. In 1523, he appears bearing the sword of state before the lord deputy.

In 1525, O'Niall became involved in a war with Manus O'Donell; he was assisted by his kinsman, the lord deputy; but while engaged in an incursion in O'Donell's lands, his own were invaded by Hugh O'Niall, the chief of the rival house. On this they concluded a peace with O'Donell, and marched against Hugh O'Niall, whom they defeated and slew.‡

A very few years after, Con O'Niall seems to have been engaged in opposition to the English of the pale; and, in 1532, committed devastations which considerably injured his kinsman, the earl of Kildare, who was then deputy and was suspected of having countenanced his conduct. Two years after, he engaged in the disturbances, which are to be hereafter detailed in the life of the deputy's son—so well known under the appellation of Silken Thomas. By his conduct in the "Rebellion of Silken Thomas," he drew upon himself the especial attention of deputy lord Grey, in 1539, when his territories were invaded and sustained severe loss.

It was in the year 1538, that the peace of lord deputy Grey's administration was disturbed by the very energetic efforts of the Roman see against the progress of the reformation. Of these, we shall speak fully, under a more appropriate head. Our present purpose is to mention a communication from that see to O'Niall. A Franciscan friar, who was sent over for the purpose of exciting the native chiefs to arms, was seized. Among his papers was found the following letter written in the name of the council of cardinals by the bishop of Metz:—

* Letter from Henry VIII. to Surrey.—*State Papers.* † Ib. p 66.
‡ Cox. Ware.

"MY SON, O'NIALL,

"Thou and thy fathers were ever faithful to the mother church of Rome. His holiness, Paul, the present pope, and his council of holy fathers, have lately found an ancient prophecy of one saint Lazerianus, an Irish archbishop of Cashel. It saith, that the church of Rome shall surely fall when the Catholic faith is once overthrown in Ireland. Therefore, for the glory of the mother church, the honour of St Peter, and your own security, suppress heresy, and oppose the enemies of his holiness. You see that when the Roman faith perisheth in Ireland, the see of Rome is fated to utter destruction. The council of cardinals have, therefore, thought it necessary to animate the people of the holy island in this pious cause, being assured, that while the mother church hath sons of such worth as you, and those who shall unite with you, she shall not fall, but prevail for ever—in some degree at least—in Britain. Having thus obeyed the order of the sacred council, we recommend your princely person to the protection of the Holy Trinity, of the Blessed Virgin, of St Peter, St Paul, and all the host of heaven. Amen."

O'Niall, already irritated by the lord deputy's warfare upon his territory, and easily inflamed by representations so adapted to his character—which did not fail to reach him through many efficient channels—entered with violence into the views suggested by the Romish emissaries. He was joined by Manus O'Donell, and many other of the native chiefs. The clergy exerted themselves to the utmost of their power to inflame the pride of the chiefs, and the passions of all; and a strong confederacy was quickly raised. At the head of the formidable insurrection thus levied, Con O'Niall marched into the pale, committing ravage, and denouncing vengeance against the enemies of St Peter, and the chiefs of the holy island. Their hostilities terminated in destruction and plunder. Halting near Tara, O'Niall reviewed his numerous forces; after which they separated to their provinces congratulating themselves on an amount of spoil, which in their eyes constituted victory over their enemies.

In the mean time, lord Grey, though unprepared either to repel or take advantage of this inroad, was not idle. He collected his force, far disproportioned in number, but still more preponderant in material. He obtained a small reinforcement from England—the citizens of Dublin and of Drogheda flocked with ready zeal to his standard—and the inhabitants of the pale, whose resentment and scorn had been excited by the depredations and unwarlike conduct of O'Niall and his confederacy, showed more than their usual alacrity in contributing their exertions for their own defence.

When joined by Sir William Brereton, lord Grey led his army into Meath where he came up with a considerable body of the Irish insurgents, on the banks of a river at a place called Bellahoa. There was danger and difficulty in passing, but little in routing the host of Irish chiefs. The accounts of these encounters, though sufficiently authentic as to the main result, are yet too perplexed in most of their incidents to enable us to offer any detail that we feel to be satisfactory.

O'Niall appears to have pursued a temporizing course, the policy of which was to gain time and ward off immediate consequences, by professions, treaties, and pledges, to which he attached no weight and which deceived nobody who knew the Irish chiefs; they were yet entertained with some appearance of trust by the English court, and also gave a temporary pretext to his supporters and friends. When he possessed the means of resistance he respected no pledges; but when discomfited, his ready refuge was submission. Hence, the numerous treaties and the broken appointments, which it would be alike tedious and unprofitable to particularize. In the year we have been noticing, we are enabled to ascertain from the correspondence published by the State Paper committee,* that he occupied a large share of the attention of government, of which the above remarks will be found to be a faithful description. We, therefore, pass to the year 1542, when a more decided turn in the course of this powerful chief's life took place.

In a letter, dated the 24th August, 1542, the lord deputy and council acquaint the king that O'Niall had come to Dublin offering to go to England to visit the king, if they would supply him with money for the purpose; and affirming his own entire want of means, and adding, that " considering his good inclinations which were beyond all men's expectation," they would endeavour to supply him for this important purpose. O'Niall made his visit, and was most graciously received ; his arrival was, however, preceded by a communication, expressive of due penitence for all his past offences, with strong professions of submission for the time to come. Asking pardon, and " refusing my name and state, which I have usurped upon your grace, against my duty, and requiring your majesty of your clemency to give me what name, state, title, land, or living, it shall please your highness; which I shall acknowledge to take and hold of your majesty's mere gift, and in all things do hereafter, as shall beseem your most true and faithful subject."

King Henry created him earl of Tyrone, and gave him the " country of Tyrone." The patent limits the earldom to Con O'Niall for life, with remainder to his son Matthew intail male. Matthew was by the same instrument created baron Duncannon. This Matthew was an illegitimate son; and his right of succession was forcibly disputed by other members of the family, which disturbed the old age of his father, and renewed the troubles of the country. A paper written by the secretary Wriothesly, as quoted in the volume of *State Papers*, from which we have chiefly drawn this notice, gives some curious details of O'Niall's investiture. " A paper remains in the hand-writing of secretary Wriothesly, noting the presents to be made to O'Niall on this occasion, among which were robes of state, and a gold chain of the value of £100. And it appears by the register of the privy council, that the earl of Oxford was summoned to attend the king at Greenwich, on Sunday, 1st of October, to make a sufficient number of earls for O'Niall's investiture to that dignity; and, that as a further mark of favour, Mr Wiatt and Mr Tuke were, on the 3d of October, appointed to conduct the earl of Tyrone, [&c. &c.] on the morrow to do their duties to the young prince Edward." The earl, on this occasion, renounced the name and style of O'Niall, engaged that he and his

* State Papers, from 1538 to 1540, Vol. ii.—State Papers, vol. ii. Paper ccclxxix.

followers should assume the English dress, manners, customs, and language, and submit to English law. This arrangement may evidently be looked on as the commencement of a most important revolution in the state of Ireland; as it was followed by a like submission under all the same conditions on the part of other great chiefs, whom the gracious reception experienced by O'Niall encouraged to pursue a course, of which the honour and advantage was now becoming yearly more and more apparent. The course of events had been, during the whole of the reign of Henry, such as to show that sooner or later all pertinacious opposition to the progress of English dominion must be swept away; and although, as ever happens, the bulk of proprietors and petty chiefs looked no further than the shape and colour of the passing moment, sagacious or informed persons, whose means of knowledge were more extensive, saw and acted on the principle of securing themselves against changes likely to come. The dream of regaining a barbarian independence was roughly shaken.

The new earl—and he was at the time at the head of the native chiefs, for power and possession—was on his return sworn of the privy council in Ireland. O'Brien, O'Donell, Ulich de Burgho, and Desmond, soon followed, made the same renunciations, and received the same favours.

The next occurrence, of sufficient moment for notice, exhibits the advantageous operation of these arrangements upon the state of the chiefs who had thus submitted. The earl of Tyrone, and some others among the Ulster chiefs, having fallen into disputes amongst themselves, instead of entering on a brawling war to decide their difference by the plunder and murder of their dependents, they came up to Dublin to lay their complaints before the lord lieutenant and council.

The earl of Tyrone seems, however, to have fallen under suspicion not long after. In 1551 (5 Ed. VI.), he was detained in Dublin for some months by lord lieutenant Crofts, on the apprehension of disturbances in Ulster. It is evident that the ties of ancient habit and hereditary pride must have long retained an influence beyond the force of any other ; but the earl was now become an old man, and probably felt the civilizing influence of that prudent season of life. Younger hands, too, were already grasping for his honours and possessions; and the growing force of British law must have assumed the aspect of a shelter and security against the unregulated violence of native ambition and turbulence. The occasion of the earl's embarrassment with the lord lieutenant was in fact the result of contention among his descendants, and the unjust and dangerous disposition which he had made of the succession to the inheritance. Matthew, lord Duncannon, his recognised heir, was not only an illegitimate son; but common rumour, and the general opinion of the people, had long questioned his paternity, and it was said that he was the son of a smith. Indignant at a preference so questionable, the legitimate sons of the earl began to plot against the baron Duncannon, and partly succeeded in estranging from him the affection of the earl. Duncannon conceived the safest and surest resource would be to make common cause with the government. For this purpose he complained to the lord lieutenant, assuring him that his father and his brothers were leagued with the hope of throwing off their allegiance to the king, and re-asserting their independence. Upon this it was, that the earl was detained in close custody in Dublin. The other sons flew to arms, and attacked the lands of Matthew lord Duncannon, which they plundered and laid waste. Matthew was assisted by the English; but the deputy, in reliance upon the Irish lord's force, sent insufficient aid. The consequence was, a defeat sustained in an encounter with the brothers, John and Hugh, with a loss of two hundred slain. The war, (if we may so name it,) was, however, long kept up, and we shall have to notice its consequences under another head.

The earl of Tyrone does not further appear in any important transaction. This contention in his family clouded the prosperity of his latter days. He seems to have rested his affections on Matthew, baron Duncannon, who, it is probable, was not his son; and it was with impatient resentment he witnessed the successful encroachment of John O'Niall, whose active and turbulent disposition allowed no rest to Ulster. At length, having contrived to seize the person of Matthew, he put him to death. The old earl, whom he imprisoned, and who had put his whole heart into the contest, died 'of the shock.

JOHN O'NEALE.

KILLED A. D. 1567.

ALL history which bears any relation to the events of modern times, is apt to be popularly viewed through a medium coloured by party; and it cannot well be otherwise: for it is from this that principles of interpretation, and even habits of thinking, are mainly formed. In the history of Ireland, the difficulty arising from this cause is much increased by the fact, that the broad principles of human nature, and of the constitution of society, have been dismissed from political speculation, and replaced by the specious but most illusory adoption of a mode of appeal to facts, and reference to states of society, which, however important they are, as furnishing subjects of investigation, and as illustrative of principle, have not the *direct connexion*, which is but too often implied by party, with any thing at present existing. So far as party politics are directly concerned, the evil, if such it may be called, is of small moment; it little matters under what pretensions the game of faction is played on either side, by those who, on the pretence of reason, are only anxious to find the most effective weapons. But in the composition of a work such as the present, this evil is great and not to be disguised. However cautiously stated, the fact cannot fail to be regarded according to its weight as a political fact stated with a political view. This difficulty is again augmented by the circumstance, that in every statement of the facts of Irish history, this very bias is in a high degree observable, and more especially in those which are the produce of modern literature. They alone who are by their habits of study enabled to test the various notices of the Irish events of Elizabeth's reign, by the most authentic authorities, can imagine the extent to which, without any direct falsehood being told, a totally opposite view of the same events and characters can be dressed up for the use, or to satisfy the prejudices of either of the two great parties which occupy the stage of political life.

When such is the fact, it is but too easily shown that while an unprincipled writer who can consent dexterously to turn his narrative according to the views of a faction, will incur the certain reprehension of those who think and feel in opposition; the unbiassed statement which is made, as all such statements should be made, in an impartial disregard for both, must alternately give offence to each. The view by which this position is illustrated must be entered upon more at large hereafter, in the prefatory portion of our next period. It is briefly this: that, in the continued struggle between human beings, in no very high stage of moral or intellectual culture, and actuated by the deepest passions of human nature, there was generated a vast complication of errors and wrongs on either side. That usurpation, violence, fraud, rapine, murder, breach of treaties, perfidiousness, and generally a disregard for all the principles of equity, and humanity, and good faith, find instances enough on both sides. From this general truth, and from the "mingled yarn" of human virtues, vices, and motives, it is easy, by seemingly slight omissions, to draw a coloured view of persons or events.

This slight sketch of some of the leading views of our historical creed, has been prompted by the revisal of our chief materials for the few important lives with which it is our design to conclude this period.

John O'Neale, more familiarly known by the Irish name Shane, was one of the most remarkable persons of his time; and occupies a principal position in the history of Ireland during the first years of Queen Elizabeth's reign. We have elsewhere had occasion to notice the particulars which involved his early years in anxiety and contention. The influence of an illicit union had usurped the favour and regard due to legitimate offspring; and the earl of Tyrone had set aside the claim of Shane, his eldest son by his lawful wife, for one who was known to be the offspring of his kept mistress, and on specious grounds affirmed to be the fruit of her clandestine intercourse with some low artizan. After frequent renewals of the family contention, which was the natural consequence of such arrangements, Shane, who had for some years occupied a leading position in the affairs of Tyrone, and in the civil feuds of the neighbouring chiefs, caused the lord Dungannon to be slain, and threw his father into confinement. The old earl sunk under the vexation and impatience excited by this undutiful, yet looking to the customs and spirit of that age of lawless violence, not quite unwarranted action. If his allegations are to be admitted, Shane had sustained a wrong, not likely to be meekly submitted to in any state of human polity. The lord justice Sidney having marched to Dundalk, sent for Shane, who was six miles off, to come and answer for himself.* Shane did not think it consistent with his safety to obey,

---

* Ware. Cox.

and it was unsafer still to refuse. In this dilemma he took a prudent middle course: he begged to be excused from immediate attendance, and invited the lord justice to be his gossip, on the faith of which tie he would come and submit to do all that the queen's service might demand. The compliance of a man like Sidney with this irregular proposal, may show the real power and danger attributed to Shane O'Neale. Sidney was entertained with the barbaric magnificence of an Irish prince, and stood sponsor to the child of Shane O'Neale. After the ceremony was completed, a conference was held between the Irish leader and the lord justice: and Shane justified his conduct, and asserted his pretensions with temper and clearness.

He affirmed that the lord Dungannon was not the son of the late earl, but that he was well known to be the son of a smith in Dundalk, by a woman of low degree, and born after the earl's marriage, of which he was himself the eldest son. It was objected that he had, notwithstanding, no right to assume the title, as the earl had surrendered his territories to the king, and that under that surrender, the settlement had been made. To this it was replied by Shane, that according to the institutions still existing amongst the Irish, his father had no power to make such a surrender, having but a life-right to the title and territories of O'Neale; that his own claim was by election according to the law of tanistry. He went on to argue, that by the English law the letters patent were illegal, as no inquisition had been or could be made, as the country should for this purpose be made shire ground. The deputy, referring probably to the recent tumults in Tyrconnel, complained of his assumption of a right of oppressive interference in the affairs of the northern chiefs; to this it was frankly replied by Shane, that he arrogated nothing beyond the lawful rights of his ancestors, who were the acknowledged superior lords of the northern chiefs. By the advice of his council, the deputy answered that he was sure the queen would do whatever should appear just; and advised O'Neale to continue quiet, until her pleasure should be known. He then departed, and O'Neale remained at peace during his administration.

This period was unfortunately of no long continuance. Sussex came over to take the administration into his own hands, and held a turbulent parliament, in which the regulation of ecclesiastical affairs was to some extent effected, and the sovereignty of Elizabeth, as queen of Ireland, affirmed by statute. The opposition met by Sussex in this assembly was, however, enough to deter him from remaining, and he returned to England, leaving Sir William Fitz-William deputy. The change was unfavourable; the times required a person of more weight. The efforts which had been recently made, and were still in progress, to introduce the reformation—now happily established in England, where the soil had long been prepared—into Ireland, where all was opposed to the introduction of any change founded on the advance of civilization, caused a violent excitement of popular feeling, and a dangerous activity among the priesthood of the Romish communion. Emissaries from Rome were at work in every quarter among the chiefs; and the king of Spain was already entering on the course of successful cajolery, by which, during the greater portion of the reign of Elizabeth, he contrived, with the least conceivable sacrifice of means, to keep up a delusive reliance on his power and assistance among the refractory chiefs, whose eagerness for small advantages, and blindness to remote consequences, were the result of their rude state; though the credulity with which they listened to all illusive promises has been proved by time to have in it something of national temper.

Shane O'Neale, surrounded by dependants and flatterers, by nature disposed to insubordination—strongly urged by these underhand agencies, and seeing the general ferment of the people, soon resolved to take advantage of the weakness of the administration. His first demonstrations were directed by keen and cherished animosity; the occasion which gave latitude to turbulence was favourable to revenge. Recollecting the humiliation which he had so recently met from the arms of O'Donell, he made a sudden inroad upon the territory of that chief, whom he seized, with his family. The chief himself he cast into prison, and only released him at the ransom of all his moveables of any value. When released from durance, Calvagh O'Donell had to learn that his cruel enemy had reserved a more galling humiliation for him than the chains redeemed so dearly; his son was retained for an hostage, and his wife for a mistress. Shane O'Neale, notwithstanding his ability and intelligence, is said to have been coarse and brutal in his habits; and this cruel and ungenerous conduct is quite reconcileable with the general descriptions of his character preserved by the old historians, and repeated more doubtfully by the ablest moderns, by all of whom he is described as one addicted to gross debauchery and beastly excess, the fever of which he was often fain to allay by having himself buried up to the shoulders in the earth. This account has been questioned on the specious ground of not being consistent with the other ascertained features of Shane's character—his subtilty, cautious policy, his polished manners, and the great ability shown in conference with the lord-justice. But this is the reasoning of men who are more conversant with books than with life. There is a latitude in human character that cannot be found in annals, or in the necessarily contracted record of men's deeds. Any one who is conversant with mankind, in any class of society, can easily recall greater contrasts than that presented by the cunning and sensuality—the wit and brutality—the politeness and cruelty—the prudence and the drunken intemperance of Shane O'Neale; these qualities scarce afford materials for the characteristic antithesis of Irish eloquence. O'Neale's native intelligence and subtilty of understanding were in no way inconsistent with the simplicity of a barbaric chief, and still less so with the want of that steady regard for the principles of truth, and the strict duties of mercy and humanity, which scarce can be said to have belonged to his age; still less again with the existence of fierce passions and appetites. He was not without native virtues, which are indicated in many of his actions, but cannot be quoted in disproof of vices, which have been charged on strong authorities, and denied upon none.

It may be admitted that the disaffection of Shane O'Neale was the result of injuries real or apprehended; it was at least increased and matured by views of policy, and by the influence of flatterers and advisers. His pride made him keenly alive to the appearance of slight or favour, and in his intercourse with the queen or her deputies, the influence of this sentiment is easy to be discerned. But new instruments, not quite so clearly traceable, were also at work; and however he may have contracted an occasional sense of regard for the queen, a constant current of opposite causes was still controlling this inclination, and bringing him back to the level and direction of the dispositions of an opposite tendency, which were the air in which he breathed. Having once taken a determined step into rebellion, he was quickly led to extremities which were equally pointed out by inclination and caution. From the government he could only expect severe justice; but it was whispered by pride, and echoed by a thousand flatterers, that the prince of Tyrone might safely hold out for higher indulgence from an enemy which seemed unable to carry its anger to extremities, and even showed itself ready to purchase peace on the easiest terms of compromise. Thus impressed, Shane O'Neale began to breathe defiance and revenge against the English. His determination appeared in manner, conversation, and in the ferocious zeal with which he vindicated his hate against the slightest disposition or act which savoured of English. This may be illustrated by several instances: one of his followers he caused to be hanged for eating English biscuit, which he considered as a base instance of unpatriotic degeneracy.

The queen ordered Sussex to lead his army to the north; and O'Neale, who had carried fire and sword through the pale, now lent a docile and pliant ear to his kinsman, the earl of Kildare, who represented in strong terms the hopeless character of the contest in which he was about to embark. Shane was not on his part wanting in plausible allegations to give a colour to his repentance and justify the past; and, such was the policy of the time, his excuses were allowed. Sussex advised submission, and as before, promised justice. It was arranged that O'Neale should be suffered to retain his possession of Tyrone, until the parliament should have examined and decided on the validity of the patents granted to his father and supposed brother; if they should be declared void, that he should then receive possession of his lands by tenure from the crown, and be created earl of Tyrone. To this O'Neale consented, and repaired to Dublin, where he was honourably received, and made his submission in due form. While remaining in Dublin, he received intimation of a rumour that he was to be sent over to England, under a guard. Alarmed at this report, he took ship and passed over to England himself, where he presented himself before the queen, with a gorgeous train of his followers, arrayed in the rude magnificence of ancient Ulster. His guard of gallowglasses are described by Camden, as having their long curled locks hanging from their uncovered heads, their shirts stained with saffron,* having ample sleeves, over which were short tunics, and hairy cloaks, which, says the annalist, were objects of wonder to the English, not less than

* The curious reader may desire to see the original description. "Ex Hiberniajum venerat Shanus O'Neale, ut quod ante annum promiserat, præstaret, cum securrigo *galloglassorum* sattellitio, capitibus nudis, crispatis cincinnis dependentibus, camisiis fluvis croco, vel humana urina infectis, manicis largioribus, tuniculis brevioribus et lacernis billosis." Camd. ad. an. 1562.

Chinese and Americans are in the present day. He was received with courtesy, and is described as having cast himself on his knees before the queen, and with a loud and wailing voice begged pardon for his rebellion. He was then interrogated upon the murder of the baron of Dungannon, and the seizure of Tyrone, to which he replied by the explanation already given in his meeting with Sir Henry Sidney; on which he was honourably dismissed, and returned to Ireland, and landed at Howth on the 25th of May.

When Shane O'Neale went to England, lord Sussex had been sent for by the queen, to give a distinct account of Irish affairs, and Sir William Fitz-William was sworn in to govern during his absence. Sussex returned in July, and again took the oaths in St Patrick's church, the roof of Christ church having fallen in two months before, on the 3d of April, 1562. As O'Neale continued quiet, he was for some time enabled to attend to the execution of various measures for the improvement and security of the country. Among the chief of these may be mentioned the division of the reduced districts into counties; Annaly was called Longford; and Connaught was divided into Clare, Galway, Sligo, Mayo, Roscommon, and Leitrim.*

Things could not continue long in this quiet state. O'Neale was little the wiser for the lessons he had received from experience and a life of struggle. He was surrounded by followers, kinsmen and friends, still ruder than himself. The general atmosphere of boasting and barbaric pride in which he breathed, may be feebly illustrated by a story from Ware. "A kinsman of his (O'Neale's) named Hugh O'Neale, drinking in company with the collector of the archbishop of Armagh's revenues, at Drogheda, was heard to swear by his soul, that his cousin was a patient fool, and so were his ancestors, in taking an earldom from the kings of England, when by right themselves were kings. He further added, by way of question to the bishop's servant, 'Is it not so?' The man was glad to comply, and say it *was so*, seeing six of the Irish in the room, with their skeans by them. But as soon as he came to his master, Adam Loftus, he cried out, 'Pardon me, master.' The archbishop asking him, 'Why, what hast thou done?' he told him the whole story; whereupon he wrote to the lord lieutenant of it." From this apparently trifling incident, a suspicion was strongly excited against O'Neale; on which the lord-lieutenant began preparations for an expedition into the north, which he made in April, 1563. He was not far on his way, when he had the good fortune to detect an ambuscade contrived by Shane O'Neale, whose party he quickly put to flight with the loss of many lives. Lord Sussex took a prey of four hundred black cattle, and for several days pursued his march, visiting Dundalk and Dungannon, till the 2d June, when he came to Tullahogue. Here he had an encounter with O'Neale's people; but they did not venture to stand the shock of the English, and scattered away before them into the woods. A few slight successes followed, until the 6th of June, when lord Sussex came upon and took three thousand cattle and fifteen hundred horses, with which he marched to Drogheda. Such a loss induced O'Neale

* Ware, ad. an. 1563.

to listen to the voice of moderate counsel from the emissary of his kinsman, Gerald, earl of Kildare. He then sent to the lord-lieutenant his proposal of submission, and offered again to appear before the queen.* His submission was allowed, and once more he appeared with his retainers before the queen, to whom he repeated his submission in the presence of the ambassadors of Sweden and Savoy. Without placing any faith in his professions, the politic Elizabeth allowed her personal vanity to be soothed into complaisance by his flattery, and dismissed him with favour and presents, which she knew must have some influence upon the minds of himself and his turbulent allies and followers. Nor did she form a mistaken estimate of the influence of her munificent generosity on the mind of a barbarous chief, who with all his native subtilty, was a child in the ways of courts. Among other favours, she lent him a sum of £2500, and ordered her commissioners, Worth and Arnold, to inquire into his complaint against a person of the name of Smith, whom O'Neale accused of an attempt to poison him.

The favour of the queen was loudly boasted by Shane, and gave him increased dignity in the eyes of his followers, who nevertheless regarded the affair rather in the light of a treaty of alliance than a submission. Shane's new-born zeal, though of brief duration, gave a strong impulse while it lasted, to his impetuous character. His fidelity was shown by an expedition against the islanders from the Hebrides, who had long infested the north, and were in possession of some towns. Coming to an encounter with these, he routed them, and slew their general. This exploit, though not perhaps without a touch of the double policy that looks for the promotion of self-service in the pretext of duty, was received as a grateful and deserving service. Sir Thomas Cusack was appointed to draw up and execute an instrument of agreement on the terms previously offered by lord Sussex. This was confirmed by letters patent from the queen, in which his services were recorded, and his former failings extenuated.

This exaltation to the pride of O'Neale soon made him troublesome to his neighbours, over whom he asserted and exercised a tyrannical jurisdiction, under the pretence of preserving the peace of the north. Many complaints of this nature reached Dublin, and there began to prevail a strong sense that he was only waiting for a favourable opportunity to break out into rebellion. The lord-lieutenant wrote an account of these reports to the queen, and informed her also of the sedulous care with which O'Neale strengthened and disciplined his military force. From Elizabeth he received the following answer:—
"As touching your suspicion of Shane O'Neale, be not dismayed, nor let any of my men be daunted. But tell them that if he arise, it will be for their advantage; for there will be estates for them who want. Nor must he ever expect any more favour from me."†

Lord Sussex sent a messenger to demand an explanation. O'Neale was prepared with a reply which indicates the secret which governed alike his loyalty and his disaffection. Under the declared pretext of

---

* Leland appears to confound the two submissions here separately noticed, on the authority of Camden, Ware, &c.

† Ware's ad. an. 1564.

serving the queen against the Scots, the wily barbarian covered his real design to maintain his claim to Ulster by force. Lord Sussex was too clear-sighted to be deluded by the pretence, and began at once to put the northern borders of the pale in a state of defence. He issued a proclamation forbidding all military service under unauthorized persons, and commanding all so engaged to come in on an appointed day, under the penalty of treason. He also increased the pay of the soldiery on the northern border. He was, however, recalled into England, where more pressing services demanded his presence, and an English knight, Sir Nicholas Arnold, was sent over; but great complaints arising from his want of influence, and other causes, and the aspect of Irish affairs beginning to look alarming, it was thought advisable to send over Sir Henry Sidney, who had already been distinguished for his successful administration of Ireland. It was high time indeed to take the most active and wise precautions. Various disorders had broken out in every part of the country, and no common means of prudence and alertness were required to restore even the usual state of order. Among the precautions now taken, an English officer, with a strong garrison, was stationed in Derry, to curb the disaffection of O'Neale, whose intentions were not concealed. He felt resentment rather than alarm, and his pride was more roused than his confidence shaken, for he yet rested in ignorant reliance on the force he had about him, and the great deference he had received from friend and foe. It was at this period that his pride sustained a violent check from the earldom of Clancarthy being conferred on M'Carthy More. He told the commissioners of the queen, "that though the queen were his sovereign lady, he never made peace with her but at her own seeking;" and that "she had made a wise earl of M'Carthy More; but that he kept as good a man as he; he cared not for so mean a title as earl; his blood and power were better than the best, and therefore he would give way to none of them; his ancestors were kings of Ulster, that he had won Ulster by the sword, and would keep it by the sword." On the report of Sidney, the queen sent over her vice-chamberlain to confer with him on the best means for the suppression of a rebel so daring and incorrigible. They agreed that this service should be prepared for during the summer months, and carried into effect during the following winter.

Shane O'Neale fully resolved on trying the fate of war, yet cautiously avoided all appearance of open rebellion. His plan was, however, artless to a degree not in our own times easily conceived; it was to provoke hostility by appearing in arms before fortified places; and he seems to have formed the notion that thus he need not be involved in war with the queen until he had first gained a victory. This expedient was more dangerous than he imagined. After some mischievous irruptions upon the borders of the pale, and a feeble demonstration of force in an unsuccessful attempt on Dundalk, he marched and encamped near Derry, in the month of October, with two thousand five hundred foot, and three hundred horse. Without attacking the town, he aimed by every insolence to draw out the garrison. So far he was successful. Colonel Randolph issued forth at the head of three hundred foot and fifty horse, and a battle took place, in which O'Neale was defeated and put to flight, leaving four hundred dead on the field. This victory was dearly purchased by the death of the brave Randolph. O'Neale had the assurance to complain: he remonstrated as an injured friend, against an attack which no direct hostility had provoked, and demanded a conference with Sidney, at Dundalk. The lord-deputy granted his desire; but before they could meet, an accidental circumstance gave a new turn to the mind of Shane O'Neale. By some unlucky accident, the powder magazine was blown up in Derry, and the provisions of the garrison, as well as their means of defence, being thus destroyed, the soldiers were obliged to embark for Dublin. The means of transport were at the time so defective, that one of the consequences of such a step was, that it became expedient to destroy the horses that they might not fall into the hands of the enemy. To avoid this disagreeable resource, Captain Harvey and his troop resolved to brave the dangers of a long and circuitous route through many hostile regions to Dublin. This they effected, and after being four days pursued by native parties through an enemy's country, they gained their destination without loss.

The accident which occasioned this retreat changed the purpose of O'Neale. A notion was circulated which Cox thus relates from Sullevan. "Mr Sullevan," says Cox, "makes a pleasant story of this, and tells us that St Columbkill, the founder and tutelar saint of Derry, was impatient at the profanation of his church and cell by the heretics, the one being made the repository of the ammunition, and the other being used for the Lutheran worship; and therefore, to be revenged on the English for this sacrilege, the saint assumed the shape of a wolf, and came out from an adjacent wood, and passing by a smith's forge, he took his mouth full of red hot coals and ran with it to the magazine, and fiercely spit the fire into the room where the ammunition lay, and so set all on fire, and forced the heretics to seek new quarters!"

Shane O'Neale felt the advantage of being freed from the constraint of the garrison, and was perhaps as forcibly actuated by his superstition. He was expected in vain by Sidney, who waited for him six days at Dundalk.

O'Neale was at the same time strongly encouraged by the troubles which started up in other quarters, so as to draw away the attention and divide the forces of the deputy. It was reported that the earl of Desmond had taken the field with the intention of joining O'Neale: on further inquiry the report was found incorrect. Desmond was at war with the earl of Ormonde and other noblemen, and on the deputy's summons, attended on him in Dublin, and took his station with one hundred horse to protect the borders of the pale. The deputy was nevertheless compelled to march through Connaught and Munster, as O'Neale took occasion to invade the pale, in which he destroyed some castles. He next attacked Armagh, which was unprotected, and burned the church; he entered Fermanagh and expelled the M'Guires, who had rejected his claim of sovereignty. Further, to place beyond doubt the nature of his designs, he again sent emissaries to Spain, at that time the hope of Irish insurgents. While engaged in these seemingly unequivocal proceedings, he not the less preserved the language of fair purpose, and endeavoured to amuse Sidney with assurances of loyalty and invitations to meetings at which he never meant to attend.

Sidney, of course, could not be imposed upon by a game so flimsy. Politics had not at that time reached the high perfection which omits to take facts, conduct, and the known character of men into account. Sidney was on the watch, and with a full comprehension of the character of Shane, and of his real strength, was exerting his vigilance and sagacity to counteract him. While Shane imagined that he was amusing the deputy, he was simply imposing on himself. Sidney conciliated those whom the exactions and tyrannies of O'Neale had offended, restored those chiefs whom he had unjustly deprived, and re-assured those whom his menaces had terrified. He thus restored Calvagh O'Donell, lord of Tirconnel, and M'Guire, lord of Fermanagh. He received the free submission of O'Conor Don, and O'Conor Sligo, &c., and soon contrived to draw round O'Neale a strong circle of enemies. Shane O'Neale, in whose character desperation and pride outweighed prudence, became furious, and vented his ill temper so freely, that his followers presently began to desert; and in one way or other, between desertion and slaughter, his force became reduced to a mere handful of ineffective followers.

In this dreadful extremity, he consulted with his faithful secretary, Neale MacConor, on the prudence of presenting himself to the lord-deputy with a halter round his neck, and throwing himself on his mercy. To this proposal it was replied by MacConor, that it would be time enough to try so dangerous an experiment when no other resource should be left; and advised that he should first endeavour to gain the Scots to his aid. Shane was persuaded. He issued letters proposing a general rising of the Irish chiefs, and was immediately proclaimed a traitor, and a day set for his adherents to surrender under the same penalties.

Shane O'Neale then repaired to Clandeboy, where Alexander MacConell, whose brother he had slain, was encamped with six hundred Scots. To conciliate the favour of this chief, he liberated his brother Surley Buy, whom he had detained in captivity since the victory which he had gained over his countrymen. The Scots were not to be conciliated by favours which were too evidently the resource of desperation, and simply saw the occasion for revenge. They, however, received their victim with apparent welcome, and Shane was deluded with all the pomp and circumstance of a reception suited to his pretensions. He had with him his secretary MacConor, and his mistress, the wife of Calvagh O'Donell, and a few soldiers. At the feast which was prepared for their entertainment, all went smoothly for a while, until by degrees, as the usquebagh or wine went round, the conversation gradually stole into the language of boast and accusation, and as confidence grew firm, in the heat of wine, more sore and delicate subjects were as if by accident introduced. At last, a nephew of MacConell accused MacConor of having been the author of a foul and calumnious report that his aunt, James MacConell's wife, had offered to marry Shane O'Neale, the slayer of her husband; the secretary replied that if his aunt had been queen of Scotland, there could be no disgrace in such a marriage. Shane himself, heated with wine, boastfully maintained the assertion of his secretary. The dispute grew loud, clamorous, and reproachful, and the soldiers of Shane who were present, took an angry part in it, till all became a scene of uproar and wild confusion. From words they soon came to blows, and the Scots rushing in, Shane and his secretary were slain. They wrapped their victim in an old shirt, and cast him into a pit; but four days after, captain Pierce cut off his head and brought it to the lord-deputy, by whose command it was set up on a pole in Dublin.

THE FITZGERALDS.

The House of Kildare.

GERALD, NINTH EARL OF KILDARE.

DIED 1534.

This earl, it has been already mentioned, was, in 1503, during his father's life, appointed treasurer in Ireland, but did not succeed to the earldom till 1513, when his illustrious father died. He was the only son of his father's first marriage with the daughter of lord Portlester.

His father's death caused much perplexity; it removed the terror and authority of his great name: excited the hopes of the enemies of the pale, and threw a damp over the courage of its friends. The force too which he had collected, at once melted away. Under these discouraging circumstances, no expedient seemed to offer so ready a prospect of relief, as the nomination of his son and successor, Gerald, now lord Kildare. He was nominated lord justice by the council, until the king's pleasure should be known. The king appointed him lord deputy. He followed the active example of his father, vindicating the peace of the country by prompt and successful expeditions into each district in which any demonstration of a hostile character called for his interference. He drove the O'Mores into the woods in 1514, and on his return attacked the O'Reillys, who had made an excursion against the English—he slew Hugh O'Reilly, and razed the castle of Cavan. In the following year he went over to England, leaving lord Gormanston deputy in his place. On his return he convened a parliament. At this, it appears that the bills thought necessary were prepared in England, and sent over with directions that no other business should be entered upon by this parliament. The discussion of these bills, the preparation of which seems to have been a chief object of Kildare's visit to England, occupied a considerable time—at least the parliament was continued to 1517, by successive prorogations.

In 1516, this earl passed a year of signal activity. He invaded Imaly, slew Shane O'Toole in battle, and sent his head, after the manner of the time, a barbarous trophy to the lord mayor of Dublin. Ware mentions one of the numerous prophecies which, from time to time, have amused the native credulity of the simple, but imaginative Irish. This old prophecy foretold, that in the year 1516, the Irish nation, being at the lowest ebb of its prosperity, was to become then powerful and warlike. "The author of a book," writes Ware, "called the *People's Welfare*, gives a touch of this prophecy; it is extant under the title of *Ireland's Pandar*."* Ireland has had Pandars enough to administer such illusions in the same name, and under a like pretence:† but this was a work of great research and practical knowledge, of which the views were founded on extensive and just observation, and quoted as of considerable authority. We shall have to notice Panderus again. He is supposed to have lived from Edward IV. to Henry VIII.

In 1517, Kildare pursued his successes in Ulster, in battle, foray, skirmish, and siege; discomfiting the Magennises, taking Dungannon, and bringing back an ample spoil to Dublin. These successes were sadly qualified by the loss of his countess, the lady Elizabeth de la Zouche, who died soon after his return. This lady is mentioned by Ware as "commendable for her excellent qualities." She was interred at Kilcullen, near her lord's mother, (Alison Eustace.)

Many circumstances, seemingly slight in their nature, were working to the disadvantage of this earl. The great rival family of Butler were again represented by a person of ambitious and intriguing temper. We have already mentioned, in our notice of Sir James Ormonde, how Sir Pierce Butler, having been excluded from his rights, recovered them by the assassination of the wrongful occupant. This Sir Pierce, now the earl of Ormonde, with the usual policy of his courtly race, pursued his ambition more by cultivating the grace of the English monarch and his minister the great Wolsey, than by playing the more dangerous and uncertain game of provincial hostilities and alliances pursued by his rivals. He stood high with the king and his minister, and was, it is mentioned, strongly instigated by his wife— herself a Geraldine, and probably opposed to her kinsman with the implacable animosity of family hate—to undermine the favour of Kildare. This earl was, like most of the lords of his race, more apt to lead his faction to the field, than to bow with supple grace before the tyrant of the English court, or administer dexterous flatteries to the accessible infirmity of Wolsey.

To Wolsey, the character, conduct, and services of Kildare, were represented unfavourably; the representations were, it is likely, not without truth, but they were one-sided and partial. The services of Kildare were probably regulated on the common principle of public service, as it was understood in those days—that is, with great latitude. In performing their public duties, the Irish barons did not lay aside their private interests: nor indeed was this quite possible. The whole tissue of the affairs of the island were interwoven with those of the leading barons of this great family. Nor could the earl of Kildare, without a political suicide, separate his interests as chief from his duties as viceroy. It must, therefore, have been easy for factious hostility to find matter for charges like these—1st, "That he had enriched himself and followers by unjust seizure of the king's revenues and

* Ware's Antiquities. † Panderus "Salus Populi."

crown lands; and 2d, That he had alliance and correspondence with divers of the Irish, enemies to the state."*

Though the earl was acquitted of the express charges, when in 1519 he was summoned over to England, yet the work of enmity was not the less effective; for by means of the exposure of the policy by which Ireland was governed, and the confused state of its interests, it was made plainly apparent to the English council that there were great objections to the administration of any Irish baron. It was, therefore, now resolved to send over Thomas, lord Surrey, lord high admiral of England, with a sufficient armed force to subdue and awe the insurgent chiefs.

During his stay in England, the earl married the lady Elizabeth Gray, daughter to the marquis of Dorset. This match secured him a powerful influence at court, and had long the effect of counteracting the hostility of his enemies. He was directly taken into the king's favour and accompanied him into France, where he was present at the celebrated field of the cloth of gold, held between the French and English kings in the same year.

To pursue the remainder of his political course, without a violent interruption to the history of the country, we must now state some particulars concerning the administration of lord Surrey. He was the son of the first duke of Norfolk, whom he afterwards succeeded as second duke. He came to Ireland on the 23d of May, 1520, with an army of a thousand men, and a lifeguard of one hundred. His first contest was with Con O'Niall. O'Niall had probably a natural sense of hostility towards the successor of his kinsman, Kildare, and acted with the design to make him uneasy in his seat, and by raising as much disturbance as he could, help to work out the proof of the useful proposition, that none but the earl of Kildare could preserve the peace of the country. It seems to have been his hope to take the new governor by surprise; but the alertness, and military promptness of Surrey prevented him, and he felt it necessary to retreat into Ulster. His conduct is traced to the suggestion of Kildare, and the correspondence of this earl's enemies is filled with such complaints. It is indeed evident, that this was the interest of the earl at the time, and there is sufficient proof that he thought so himself. In common with the other great lords of the pale, he derived much of his power, and all his political weight from the cultivation of alliances of this nature. The English of the pale were protected, governed, and oppressed, by means of a power which, while it was wielded by their own lords, was yet thoroughly Irish in its composition. They were, consequently, become unwarlike in their habits, and unprovided with proper arms. Their great barons, holding, in fact, the place and power of great Irish chiefs, and regarded in this light by the natives, contrived to avail themselves of the double advantages of this twofold position. Their power and possessions had a foundation, in a great measure, independent of the English interest. The armies they led, like those they opposed, were tumultuary; they were sufficient to collect the plunder of a district, and to neutralize hostilities for the moment, and they sought no more.

* Lodge.

In the confusion thus preserved, lay the secret of their strength: the individual was above the law. An English force adequate for the purpose, and adequately maintained, would quickly end this state of turbulent confusion and arbitrary licence. Thus, while the prospect of such an interference could not fail to be welcomed with delight by the large class which was altogether dependent on tranquil industry, and subject to the varied eddies of this whirlpool of perpetual movement, it could not be regarded with any complacency by the earl of Kildare. It may therefore be admitted, on the ground of such documentary or inferential proofs as have been advanced by historians, that he adopted, at once, the obvious, yet rash and dangerous course of exciting hostility against Surrey's government. Accordingly, this nobleman soon found sufficient indications of this influence. His time and resources were lamentably wasted in enterprises which had no important result. At considerable cost, and frequent danger of his life, he traversed hostile provinces, and pursued the insurgent chief to his tower; but a submission and an empty pledge ended the affair, until it next became the marauder's convenience or pleasure to ride out on a party of plunder. The king had exhausted his father's accumulated hoards, on the gorgeous tinsel of the fields of Ardres, and wrote to his lieutenant in Ireland, that "Considering the scantitie and dearthe of vitailles in those parties, the horsemen cannot conveniently live upon their wages at the said rate, [the allowance of government for their support,] therefore be he contented that ye suffer them to take *cune and livery*, after the ancient accustumable manner there used, &c."* Such was the oppressive, unpopular, and illegal resource on which the government was thrown. From the same document it appears, that the complaints against Kildare had formed the chief substance of the representations of the Irish government. The king acknowledging the complaint, tells the lord lieutenant and council, that, "as touching the sedicious practisis, conspiracies, and subtle driftes of the erle of Kildare, his servantes, aiders, and assisters, we have committed the examinacion and trial of that matier to the moost Reverend Fader in God, our right entierly beloved Counsaillour, Chancellour, Cardinal and Archbishop of Yorke, &c., &c."†

The whole interval of Surrey's administration was a succession of perplexing alarms, and fatiguing, and often dangerous marches, in which the object to be attained was by no means adequate to the fatigue and danger. In one of his expeditions, lord Surrey had the vizor struck off from his helmet by a shot fired from a thick wood as he passed; and he was perhaps soon anxious to escape from a warfare in which fatigue and danger were to be thus endured without fame or honourable success. The greatest success was to bring the insurgents to the encounter; dangerous in the lurking places, into which they seemed to melt away at the approach of an English force; if they were caught in the field, it was but the slaughter of a barbarous rabble, and had no consequence. The war was one of depredation and burning, and not of arms. The chiefs had comparatively little to lose; hostilities began on their side with a knowledge of the consequences.

* Letter from Henry VIII.—*State Papers.* † *State Papers.*

and a sufficient preparation to save themselves from them. They could drive away their cattle at the approach of the enemy; and, when any serious danger appeared, it was time enough to propose peace, swear allegiance, and observe the engagement so long as was convenient. Many of these chiefs excused their hostilities by pleading the influence of Kildare; and there is much reason to suspect, that the excuse was not without better proofs than mere assertions. A letter from Kildare to a chief of the name of O'Carrol is quoted by Leland, as having been given to Surrey in proof of this earl's practices. It does not, however, bear the degree of evidence which the historian's statement seems to imply. The letter was not itself forthcoming when demanded by Surrey; but after much pressing and urgent persuasion, the contents of the letter were recollected and sworn to by Donogh O'Carrol. The following is the form of this person's deposition:—" He [Donogh O'Carrol] saith that in Easter week last past, the abbot of Monastricow, called Heke, brought a letter to O'Carrol, out of England, on the behalf of the earl of Kildare, wherein was written these words: ' There is no Irishman in Ireland I am better contented with than you; and whenever I come into Ireland I shall do you good for any thing that ye shall do for me; and any displeasure that I have done to you, I shall make you amends therefor. Desiring you to keep good peace to Englishmen, till an English deputie come there; and when any English deputy shall come thither, do your best to make war upon Englishmen there, except such as be towards me, whom ye know well yourself.' "*

Surrey's representations, founded mainly on such evidence, had the effect of prepossessing the English monarch and his minister against Kildare; and when this lord lieutenant was recalled, after two years' continuance in the country, he was commanded to commit the administration to the earl of Ormonde, the rival and enemy of Kildare. Surrey's government had been productive of much good; for though he had not been enabled to remedy the vicious state of the country's laws and customs, or to put a stop to the numerous abuses which depressed and retarded the prosperity of the pale, still the mere abstinence from wrong, and the cessation of partiality, oppression, and misgovernment in the seat of administration, were felt as great and rare blessings, which shed lustre on his government, and caused regret at his departure.

The elevation of an inveterate enemy to a position which empowered him to encroach on his rights, and endanger his power, made Kildare's presence in Ireland necessary. Ormonde had the will, and many pretexts for the persecution of the Geraldine faction; and there were even territorial questions liable to be raised between these powerful earls, which it would not be well to leave undefended. Kildare returned; his influence was increased by the unpopularity of his rival. The government of Pierce earl of Ormonde was unpopular, and Kildare soon found that he might, with safety, avow his enmity. At first, he had evidently resolved to preserve appearances. His character had been shaken by the complaints of Surrey, but Ormonde was himself

* State Papers, Vol. ii. Part III. p. 45.

involved in the whispers of faction, and liable to be denounced by his victims or his enemies. Having begun, therefore, by efforts to support the deputy, Kildare soon began to enter on the more congenial course of factious underworking, so familiar to the time.

The dissensions between the earls were brought to an issue by an accidental circumstance. James Fitz-Gerald, a relation and friend of Kildare, meeting a favourite servant of Ormonde's on his way to Kilkenny, slew him. The earl of Ormonde, in his anger, transmitted a complaint to the English court, which was retaliated by the complaints and accusations of Kildare. Commissioners were appointed to try the merits of the allegations on both sides in Ireland. Here Kildare had, however, a twofold advantage; his faction in Ireland, and his wife's powerful relations in England, combined to turn the scale of judgment. By the first, the selection of the commissioners was influenced; and by the second, if necessary, the representations and testimonies must have been affected. The commission decided for him. His triumph was completed by the recall of his adversary, in whose place he was appointed as lord deputy. The whole of this transaction was evidently preconcerted in England; the commission was managed by the marquis of Dorset, and the commissioners, Sir Ralph Egerton, Sir Andrew Fitz-Herbert, and James Denton, dean of Litchfield, were appointed, and their instructions provided for the event by directing that Kildare, on his acquittal, should be named deputy in place of his accuser. This view is confirmed by the fact, that the indenture between the king and the earl bears date prior to this transaction.*

The triumph of Kildare was swelled by the joy of his numerous and powerful faction; but circumstances soon arose which involved him in trouble and danger. The earl of Desmond, whose remote position, rather than any inferiority of power, kept him apart from the main course of Irish affairs, had, it is stated by all the old historians, entered into a treasonable correspondence with the king of France, who was at the time at war with Henry; but peace being made between the kings, this correspondence was thus exposed. Kildare was ordered to march into Munster, and to apprehend Desmond. This was, however, a command opposed to all Kildare's principles of action and politics. Desmond was his kinsman, his ally, next to himself too, the most powerful and popular chief in Ireland. Formal obedience could not be avoided; he marched against Desmond, but there was a secret understanding between these great chiefs, and nothing was done in earnest. Kildare turned on his march to assist his kinsman O'Niall, against O'Donell. He also attacked the Birnes to serve Desmond. A letter of his to Desmond had been intercepted by his sister, the wife of Ormonde, and is said to have been used against him.† The recent publication of the state papers of this reign by government, has placed before us a more detailed and expanded view of these transactions than we can allow ourselves to enter upon, or than the interest of the period would justify. The principal charges occupy mainly

* Cox.
† This is verified by Kildare's own admission. See State Papers, Vol. III. Part ii. p. 121.

the several representations on either side; forming alliances with the king's enemies, seizing on the king's land, or withholding his rents and subsidies. These statements were such as to have inevitably prejudiced both parties, and it is probable that the king and English council were fully impressed with a conviction which had so often before been the inference from similar brawls, that the country should be governed by an English governor only. Kildare's account of the letter represents it as written and intercepted long previous to the recent transactions with Desmond. He asserts that it had been seized by his own sister, Ormonde's wife, on the occasion of his messenger, a Fitz-Gerald, having slept at her house; that lord Ormonde had used it against him on the commission, when the commissioners had set it aside as proceeding " of no evil intent." This account may be the truth, but it is also very likely that the letter had a distinct bearing which cast an unfavourable light on the recent accusation. The earl was recalled to answer the charges against him. From the mass of letters and articles of charge against Ormonde, we will extract a portion of one short letter, less formal and more characteristic than the long documents which precede it.

" Kildare to Henry VIII.*

* * * * * * * * " In my most humble maner beseeching your grace not to regard such untrue surmises of myne adversaries, till the truth bee tryed; trusting, and knowing right well, that I never did bethought any thing whereby I should deserve your moost drad displeasure, where unto I was not only bound by my duty of allegiance, but also for that in my youth I was brought up in your service, and when I came to discretion, it pleased you to make me your tresurer, and consequently [subsequently] your deputie, and gave me landis to the yearely value of 100 markes. My first wife [Elizabeth Zouch] was your poor kinswoman; and my wife now [Lady Elizabeth Gray] in like maner. And in all my troubles before this, by untrue surmises against me, ye were good and gracious unto me, which ought enough suffice to bind, to owe unto your grace, my true and faithful service. And though there were no such cause, yet could I find in my heart to serve your grace before all the princes in the world, as well for the great nobleness, valiant prowess and equity, which I ever noted in your most noble person, as also for the vertuous qualities wherein ye excell all other princes. And besides that, I do know right well, if I did the contrary, it shulde bee the distruccion of me and my sequel for ever. As knoweth Almighty God, who ever have you in his tender tuicion. From my manor of Maynoth, the 17th daye of August [1525]."

Kildare was called to stand his trial in the following year (1526), and had a narrow escape. The articles of his impeachment were, that 1st, He had disobeyed the king's command by not taking the earl of Desmond. 2d, That he had contracted alliances with Irish enemies. 3d, That he had caused certain good subjects to be hanged, for no other reason than they were friends or favourites to the family of the

* State Papers, Vol. iii. p. 125.

Butlers; and lastly, that he held private intelligence with O'Niall, O'Conor, and other Irish lords, to make an inroad into Ormonde's territories.* In spite of the very strong and numerous charges contained in the letters and memorials of Ormonde, some of these charges impress the idea, that evidence of any very serious delinquency must have been wanting. The charges, most of them appear to be revivals of accusations long disposed of by the commission already mentioned. On these charges, Wolsey contrived to obtain a sentence of death against Kildare. Kildare, however, knew the true source of this decision. The lieutenant of the Tower was his warm friend, and it was agreed that he should repair to the king, as if to take his commands on the affair. There was little time to lose; Kildare was, most probably, to be beheaded in the morning early. It was late, and there was perhaps much uncertainty as to the king's being reached at the hour of midnight. Fortunately for Kildare, no such difficulty occurred: his friend stated the fact, and asked the king's pleasure. The king was much affected and surprised; the cardinal, to make the matter sure, had kept it from his knowledge, and this malicious privacy was now favourable to his intended victim; Henry might easily have been talked into a very opposite feeling; his tyranny was the result of deliberation, his better feelings were the impulse of the moment; these were now quickened by indignation, for he saw through the conspiracy, and his arbitrary temper, prompt whether in good or evil, suggested a decided course. He forbade the execution, and prohibited any further proceeding against the earl. He took off his ring and gave it to the lieutenant to bear to Wolsey as a token of his authority. The interposition of his friends had now time to work, and the earl was liberated on their security, that he would appear when called upon to answer such charges as should be made against him. His securities were the marquis of Dorset, the countess dowager of Dorset, and several members of the family of Grey, with Sir Henry Guilford, John Abbott, and Sir John Zouch. Cox gives a curious and highly characteristic report of the speeches of Wolsey and Kildare, on the trial above referred to; but as they seem altogether unauthentic, and still more because they are too long, we omit to extract them. Cox doubts this whole account of the earl's condemnation, and he may be right enough. He asserts that there is no authority for it.

It is certain that Kildare was taken quickly into favour with the king. An extract from a letter, written by archbishop Inge and lord chief justice Birmingham, to Wolsey, dated 3d February, 1528, throws some additional light on the king's great partiality towards this earl. It also exhibits the strength of his party, and his great power in Ireland. "Thabsence of thise bothe lordes hathe greatlie enhaunsed and couraiged our soveraine lordes Hirish and Englisshe rebelles; whereby the londe is alway in danger, and wolde be ferr more, werr nat the foree of their retourn.

"And now, within this thre or foure daies, there is privey reaporte, that therll of Kildair, for som his mysdemeanours of late, is committed unto the tour. If it so be, the seid erll is mervellous, and hathe

* Ware.

been unknowen to us and other divers the kinges true subjectes, of this his londe. In consideration wherof, it was never so great nede to provide for defens of this poor londe, in our daies as nowe; for the vice deputie* is nat of power to defend the Englisshrie; and yet the poor people is ferr more chargid and oppressed by hym, than they have been, th erll of Kildair being here. He hathe no great londes of his owne, and the kinges revenues, besides the subsidie, is skante ynowe to pay the kinges officers ther ordinarie fees; and the subsidie may nat be hadde, till it be grannted by parliament, without the whiche the deputie hathe full litle to manteyn his chargies. Th erll of Kildair coude help hymself, in taking advantage of Hirishmen, better then any other here."

The state of affairs in Ireland was such as to cause serious alarm in the pale and among the members of the administration. On his departure, the earl had committed the government to his brother, the lord Thomas Fitz-Gerald of Leixlip: the annalists briefly tell us that he was removed; and his removal may be regarded as a fresh demonstration of the enmity of the faction opposed to the earl. Richard Nugent baron Delvin was substituted; but he was soon found to be unequal to the difficulties of a situation, which demanded at the time extensive power and influence. O'Conor Fally, the ally and kinsman of the Geraldines, made an irruption into the pale, and carried off a large prey into Offaly: on receiving information of this, Delvin ordered the stoppage of his pension, claimed by O'Conor as due upon certain plough-lands in Meath. A meeting was proposed at Sir W. Darcy's castle, near Ruthven; but O'Conor, whose real object was far from a desire of accommodation, contrived an ambuscade, by which he intercepted the deputy, and made him a prisoner. The historical writers on this period state, that lord Ossory (Ormonde) was now appointed in place of the imprisoned lord, and that he used every effort for his deliverance, but without effect. It is certain that considerable efforts were made by the earl of Ossory and his son, for the deliverance of Nugent; and we think it likely, that the correspondence from which this fact appears must have misled the historians; they inferred the appointment of lord Ossory from the authoritative position in which he appears during the transaction of so important a negotiation. But it seems nearly certain, from a letter of the Irish council to Wolsey on the occasion, that Thomas Fitz-Gerald was appointed by them; and it is also little probable that he would enter with any sincerity into the negotiations for the liberation of Nugent; O'Conor having probably acted as the friend of the earl, and partisan of the Geraldines.

O'Conor's claim is mentioned in the letter of the Irish council, from which our information is drawn; and from this document it appears, that they had urged the payment of his pension. This claim is also mentioned by Inge and Birmingham, in a letter to the duke of Norfolk, in which they state, that there had been continual contention on the point, "sithe the earl of Kildare left this."† Lord Butler, son to lord Ormonde (Ossory at the time), mentions in a letter to archbishop Inge, his own visit to O'Conor's house, where he slept and was,

* Richard Nugent, lord Delvin.   † State Papers.

with some difficulty, permitted to speak to Nugent, in presence of the O'Conors. He then mentions, that he contrived to bring away Cahir O'Conor (who was " to be the next O'Conor"), as a protection, and that he brought him with him to his father; at his father's, they prevailed on him to promise to join their party, if his brother would not " be conformable to reason:" O'Conor's chief stipulation was, that the king should not suffer the earl of Kildare to take revenge on him for taking part in the king's quarrel. Lord Butler adds, " surely, my lord, many great wise men that I have spoken with, since this misfortune happened, think precisely that it comes through the abetment of the earl of Kildare, his counsellors and band; and that they look for much more mischief, if that you see not this substantially ordered. Therefore, my lord, at the reverence of God, look substantially at this matter, and beware whom you trust that you have trusted of this band [party]. I have many things to say to your lordship, that I dare not write," &c. It would be a vain accumulation of parallel authorities to extract the abundant passages of an authentic correspondence which exhibit the sufficiently evident state of party feeling on either side. One sentence from a letter written at this time by the duke of Norfolk, probably contains the most important commentary upon the whole of these transactions. " The malice between the earls of Kildare and Ossory, is, in my opinion, the only cause of the ruin of that poor land." It is also obvious, from another letter written to Wolsey, by the same nobleman, that his opinion was for sending over Kildare, as the best course under the circumstances.*

Wolsey's own opinion seems to have been formed on something of a compromise between the extreme opinions of the opposite parties; he advised the committal of the administration to the Butlers, but still so as to communicate the impression to the Irish, that Kildare, who was nominally still deputy, should soon be sent over. For this reason, also, he would not advise that this earl should be discharged of the office; and further, that he thought it expedient to impress him with a sense of responsibility. It is evident through the entire of the long paper,† from which this opinion is taken, that he attributes the main disturbances to the influence of Kildare. The following extract may satisfy the reader:—" Thies folowing bee the causes, whiche movethe the saide lorde cardinall to thinke, in his pore judgement, that the erle of Kildare shuld not bee put from his rome at this tyme, but the same to bee deferred, untill a more mature consultation were takene and had therein; soo that, upon his discharge, substanciall direction ymmediately moght bee takene for the defence of the said lande, in thavoiding of suche perill and dannger, as mought folowe.

" The firste cause is, that syns the harveste and collecte is nowe at hande, by reason thereof, no provision canne bee sente from hens, in tyme for the withstanding thereof, but that it suld bee in the powro of the Irishe rebelles, combined to gidder, to distroye and devaste the hoole Englishery, if, by good wisdome, dexteritie, and pollicie, they bee not conteyned by dulce and faire meanes, and somme hope of the erle of Kildares retourne: for it is greatly to bee fered, that the said

---

* Letter to Wolsey. *State Papers*, Ib. p. 135.   † State Papers, Ib. p. 136.

erle of Kildares kynnysfolkes, servanntes, and suche other wild Irishe lordis (with whome the said erle hathe, and hathe had, intelligence), if they shall perceive that he is clerely excludid from his office, and in the kingis displeasure, they shall peradventure, for revenging thereof, seeing they may nowe commodiously, in maner without resistence, doo the same, over ronne the hoole Englishe boundes and pale, and doo suche high displeasure, as woll not, withoute an army royall, and mervaillous great expensis, bee redubbid or repayred hereafter; where as they, being in somme hope, and not in utter disperation of the said erles retourne, there is some apparence that they woll forbere from doing the said extreme hurtis, and soo, by such meanes, the said danngers maye bee wisely put over, till other better provysion shall bee made and devised for withstanding of their malicious attemptates.

"The second cause, why there shuld bee none other deputie made at this tyme thene, is, that as long as the said erle of Kildare is not dischargid of his rome, he shalbe aferd that any thing shuld bee done or attemptid, to the great hurte of the Englishery, by those that he hathe intelligence with, or any others, supposing that the same mought be layed and arrected unto his charge; forasmoche as he standeth onerate, as yet, as the kingis deputie of that lande: where as he, being thereof discharged, shall litle or nothing care, what may comme of the said land, or what hurte or dammage bee inferrid thereunto."

Lord Ossory was soon after sent over as deputy; and the lord chancellor having died of the sweating sickness, which was this year (1528) very prevalent and fatal in Ireland, a creature of Wolsey's was appointed, with the well understood purpose of giving all annoyance possible to the earl of Kildare. The earl on his part, sent over his daughter, lady Slane, to stir up O'Niall and O'Conor, his friends and kinsmen, to oppose and thwart the lord deputy. She was, as Cox observes, "unhappy in being successful;" having thus caused great confusion and devastation,* which ultimately told with nearly fatal weight against the earl himself.

For the present, however, affairs began to wear a favourable aspect for Kildare. For although his practices were thoroughly known to all parties, and fully understood by the king, they had not the effect of prejudicing his reputation with the council, or of causing any serious displeasure in Henry's mind. His misdeeds were consistent with the principles of the age, and practised by his rivals and opponents according to their power. The one question looked upon was expediency, and Kildare's great power for good or evil, suggested the trial of making him a friend, and securing his good offices by favourable conditions. In pursuance of this object, the king determined to liberate the earl, and send him over with Sir William Skeffington, who was in 1529 appointed deputy to the duke of Richmond. The duke was made lord lieutenant, and held the office for life. Though it was thought inexpedient to intrust the earl with the government, or in any way to increase powers already too large for the peace of the country, yet his

* Letter from Ossory to Wolsey.—*State Papers*, p. 143. See also the letter which follows from lord Butler, and the Paper of Instructions from the deputy and council, p. 145.

pride was to be conciliated, and his good offices secured. The instructions to Skeffington were prepared accordingly; particular stress is laid upon the importance of keeping the peace between "the king's well beloved cousins, Kildare, Desmond, and Ossory," as a principal means to preserve the peace of the country, and consult its interests. Amongst these instructions in which the deputy is desired to call a parliament—to get a subsidy before its sitting, to charge the lands of the clergy, to repress military exactions—he is also specially desired to assist the earl of Kildare in his enterprises.* The paragraph is worth extracting. " And whereas therle of Kyldare hath made faithfull promise unto the kynges highness to employe and endeavor hym selfe, to the uttermost of his power, for the annoyance of the kynges sayd rebellious subjectes of the wyld Irishry, as well by makyng excourses upon them as otherwise; farasmuche as the men of warre, now sent oute of this realme with the sayde deputie, shall move in suche case, doo right good stede to the sayd erle, in such exployttes as he shall make, whene the sayde deputie shall not fortune to procede therunto hym selfe, shall, at the requisicion of the sayd erle, send unto hym the sayd men of warre, or as many of them as he shall requier for makyng of suche exployttes, reserving a convenient nomber of them to remayne and attend upon hym selfe; and the proffyttes of suche imposicions, that is to say, of bestes or other thyng, that at an entre or exployte shalbe imponed or had, by way of patysment or agreement upon thenemyse, to be alwayese the moyte answered to the kynges highnes, to thandes of the sayde undertresawrer, and the other moyte to renue to therle of Kyldare, yf he shall make thexploite, and putt the imposicion, and to his company not havyng the kynges wages, to be ordred and divided by his discrecion, as hath bene accustomed."†

The arrival of Kildare excited among his friends and powerful party, a sensation of great joy. He was, together with the deputy, received by a procession of the citizens, near St Mary's abbey.‡ His conduct was, for some time, conformable to the expectations of the government. He probably aided the deputy in an invasion of the O'Mores; and in the following year (1531), he certainly accompanied him in an expedition into Ulster.

The habits of Kildare were factious; he was not likely to submit with much patience to have his predilections and animosities curbed by one whom he must have regarded as an inferior: it was not long before ill-will began to grow up between him and the deputy, who appears to have soon entered into a friendly understanding with the earl of Ossory. The death of Wolsey, which occurred in the year at which we are arrived, gave also an impulse to the ambition of Kildare. Both he and the deputy now commenced their efforts to undermine each other in the favour of the king. With Skeffington was joined the Butler faction, and their various correspondence, which, if quoted here, would appear as the repetition of the same characteristic complaints and charges of which the reader is now fully aware, must have at length produced a strong prejudice against the earl in the English council. He became at last so impatient, that he could no longer be

* State Papers.   † Ib., Vol. ii. p. 150.   ‡ Ware.

content to suffer their efforts for his overthrow to pass unresisted. His enemies were superior in the game of intrigue, cabal, and private diplomacy: his character was framed for less artificial courses, and in going over to speak for himself, Kildare undoubtedly best consulted his own interests; with the warm and arbitrary temper of Henry, which often led him to act with independent decision on the impulse or conviction of the moment, the frank and hardy simplicity of the earl was likely to have more influence than those refined and courtly arts, of which experience had taught him the true value.

He went over in 1532, and so managed matters at court, that with the help of his English friends he prevailed to have Skeffington removed, and himself appointed deputy in his place. He was as usual welcomed with acclamations in Dublin, when he received the sword from the hands of his enemy. Instead, however, of recollecting the example of his father, and the experience of his own life, and confirming the advantages he had gained by a prudent self-control, and by conciliating enemies for whom he was no match at their own game, the earl acted with precipitate rashness, and only recognized his character as governor, as the means of success in the party hostilities into which he threw himself with increased infatuation of spirit. He made a furious incursion into the districts of Kilkenny, and committed devastation on Lord Ossory's lands; he encouraged the O'Nialls in an attack on the English villages in Louth. The clamour of an irritated and increasing faction grew louder, and their accusations more weighty. Against this menacing juncture of affairs, Kildare's power and spirit rather than his discretion maintained him for a while. He was not solicitous to gain friends, and carried all his objects with a high hand. He married his daughters to O'Conor Faly, and to O'Carrol, and the alliances which thus strengthened him in the country, helped to confirm the reports of his accusers.

He called a parliament in Dublin, in the May of the next year 1533. Its acts were not important; when it was over he invaded the country of Ely O'Carrol, at the desire of his son-in-law, Ferganim O'Carrol, who asserted himself to be the chief of that district. In this affair Kildare received a bullet in the thigh. Ware tells that on this occasion, a soldier who was standing near observed the earl show some signs of pain, and said, "My lord, why do you sigh so, I was myself thrice shot with bullets, and I am now whole." "I wish," replied the earl, "you had received the fourth in my stead." A letter in the state papers from "Cowley to Cromwell," adverts to a report prevalent at this time that the "lord of Kildare was shot with a hand gun through the side under the ribs, and so lyeth in great danger."

In the year 1533, a deputation was sent over to England, from the Irish council, with representations of the state of the country, and private instructions to lay every thing amiss to the charge of Kildare. This commission was trusted to John Allen, Master of the Rolls. The written instructions are published in the *State Papers*, and convey a just notion of the low state of the pale at the time. We shall therefore enumerate the heads of complaint, from that document. It begins by stating that "the lande" is fallen into such decay, that the English language, dress and laws are not used, except within a compass of about twenty miles. This evil is attributed first and chiefly to taking of coyne and livery, "without order, after men's own sensual appetites;" also "cuddies' gartie, taking of caanes for felonies, murders, and all other offences." Secondly, the disuse of arms among the English, who formerly practised archery, and kept stout English servants able to defend them; instead of which they had now in course of time fallen into the custom of employing native servants, who could "live hardily without bread and other good victuals;" they also preferred Irish tenants, because they could make them pay higher rents, and submit to "other impositions," which English husbandmen could not afford to give. Thirdly, it is alleged, that the lords of the pale, instead of retaining soldiers in their castles at their own cost, for the defence of the pale, that they kept them at the expense of the king's poor subjects, on whom they were a severe burthen. Fourthly, they complain of the "liberties," kept by the great lords, by which the king was defrauded of his revenues. A still more injurious abuse, was the payment of "black rent," to the native chiefs for their forbearance and protection, by which they were encouraged in violence, and enriched at the expense of the English. To this complaint it is added, that when they committed their robberies on the king's subjects, and were pursued by an English force, the lords deputy instead of restoring the property thus recovered to the people who had been plundered, kept it to enrich themselves. Fifthly, they attribute these evils to the appointment of Irish deputies, and also to the frequent change of deputies. Sixthly, the negligence in keeping the king's records. Seventhly and lastly, they complain of the king having lost and given away his manors, lordships, &c., so that he had not left any resources in the country for the maintenance of his government. This paper of instructions is signed by the bishops of Armagh, Dublin, Meath, Kildare, the abbots of St Mary's abbey, and Thomas' court, and by lords Gormanstown, Trimleston, &c. In an annexed paper, they propose answerable remedies for all these abuses; and among other things state, that "there is grown such a rooted dissension between the earls of Kildare and Ossory, that in our opinions it is not likely, and the experience of many times proved manifesteth the same, to bring them to good conformitie, especially if either of them be deputie, or aspire to that roome." Such was probably the hint on which Allen was to speak; and such were the various topics on which the earl was assailable.

These representations were backed by an ample correspondence in which the same complaints and suggestions were urged with the added weight of private communication. Among the documents appertaining to this time, is a lengthened statement not inappropriately called a "boke," by the writer, which sets the disorders of the period in the strongest light. Amongst other things, it states with considerable force the evils arising from the great power acquired by Kildare. We shall have to recur to this document hereafter.

The result of all these representations to Kildare was unfortunate. He received an order to go over into England, that he might answer the charges against him. Kildare was alarmed; he sent over his wife to stir the zeal of her own powerful kindred in his behalf, to have the order revoked. In the meantime he found some pretence in the disordered state of affairs to delay his own journey. The subterfuge was however of no avail; he was again ordered over, and directed to commit the government during his absence to some one for whose conduct he could be answerable. Even in his fear, the habitual care of his own power was uppermost in Kildare's mind: he garrisoned his castles and armed them from the king's ordnance, in defiance of an express prohibition. His greatest and most fatal error, was the committing the government to his own son, the lord Thomas Fitz-Gerald, a youth without experience, and not above twenty-one years of age. The fatal consequences to the earl, the numerous members of this great family, and to the unhappy youth himself, must be separately related. Excited to rebellion by the artifice of his father's enemies, a few months closed his rash career. The earl died of grief in the Tower, in the chapel of which he was buried, 12th December, 1534.* An act of attainder was passed against him and his family, but his son Gerald was afterwards restored to the title and estates.

The college of Maynooth was founded by this earl in 1521.

LORD THOMAS FITZ-GERALD.

BORN A. D. 1513.—BEHEADED, A. D. 1536.

As the best continuation of the history of the events mentioned in the previous memoir, we shall here subjoin some account of the brief and tragic career of the unfortunate Thomas Fitz-Gerald, son to the powerful earl last noticed.

On the earl's departure for England, he committed the government to lord Thomas, his eldest son, not yet more than twenty-one years of age. The act was in the highest degree rash and fatal; but the earl did not neglect to give his son such prudent advice, that if it be not recollected how wide is the distinction between sensible reasoning and prudent conduct, one may wonder that the giver had not acted more prudently himself.

This imprudent commission might have been attended with no ill consequences, if the youthful deputy had no enemies to deal with, but those of the pale; for he was brave, alert, and possessed of no small military talent. But the danger of his situation arose from those who should have been his friends and trusty advisers; the powerful faction which had undermined the earl, were now prepared to follow up the blow, by taking advantage of the inexperience and impetuosity of his son. They began with artful attempts to provoke his temper by petty slights, and it became evident to the youth that there was a cabal raised against him in the council. A few trivial anecdotes are told by Cox, which have their place at this stage of his history. At a banquet, he met with Allen, Master of the Rolls, a bitter enemy of his father's; the conversation turned upon heraldry: in its course, Allen turning to the deputy, said, that "his lordship's house gave a marmo-

* State Papers, lxxxvi.

set, whose property it was to eat her tail; to whom the deputy replied, that he had been fed by his tail, and should take care that his tail did not eat him." On another occasion he kept the council waiting for some hours, when the archbishop of Dublin at last grew impatient, and asked if it were not a pretty matter that they should stay so long for a boy. Lord Thomas who was at the moment entering the room, overheard the remark, and told the council that "he was sorry they should stay so long for a boy."*

It did not require much observation to apprise lord Thomas that he was surrounded by watchful and malignant enemies, who would let pass no occasion to injure him. His father's strong injunctions, might nevertheless have restrained him within the path of prudence, had not his enemies, or indiscreet friends originated a false report, that his father was put to death in the Tower. It was added, that his five uncles were also to be seized and executed, and that the same fate was designed for himself. To favour this report, it is affirmed, letters were written and sent in different directions, and it was perhaps by contrivance, that one of these fell into the hands of Deluhide, lord Thomas's confidential adviser. The young Geraldine rushed into the snare, if such it was, and at once flinging aside deliberation and every purpose but revenge, he associated himself with O'Niall and O'Conor the fast friends of his family, and resolved on the most violent and immediate measures. Summoning together such of his followers as could be collected, he rode through the city at the head of 140 armed cavalry (in shirts of mail), to Dame's gate, where he crossed the river, and proceeded straight to Mary's abbey, where the council were sitting at the moment. Attended by these followers, he entered the chamber and sternly took his seat, his disordered appearance indicated repressed passion and an angry purpose; and as the foremost of his followers were pressing into the chamber, the members of the council began to shew signs of alarm. Lord Thomas sternly commanded his followers to be silent, and addressed the council with a fierce calmness of tone and manner. He told them that notwithstanding his wrongs, he would act as a soldier and a gentleman, and that he did not mean to use to their hurt the sword that had been intrusted to him. That he now came to return it. That it had a pestilent edge bathed in the blood of the Geraldines, to whom it now menaced farther injury. That he came to resign it, and would thenceforth use his own. That he warned them that he was become their enemy, and the enemy of the king, whom he renounced and declared war against from that moment. "I am none of Henry's deputies," he concluded, "I am his foe, I have more mind to conquer than to govern, to meet him in the field than to serve him in office: if all who have been wronged by him, would unite, as I trust they will, he should learn of the treatment due to tyranny and cruelty, such as never have been exceeded by the most infamous tyrants in ancient history."† Some such step was expected from lord Thomas, and it is possible that the consternation produced by this speech, was nothing more than the anxiety which some present may have felt for their personal safety. And the historians who

* Cox. † Cox, Holinshed.

describe the scene, appear to agree, that the speech which is attributed to Cromer, the chancellor, was insincere. It was perhaps, partly fear, and partly policy, that suggested the answer of the chancellor, when lord Thomas returning him the sword of state was turning to depart: but it is to be recollected, that Cromer had been the friend of the Geraldines. We are therefore not inclined to set down altogether to political finesse, the affecting appeal which this state officer is said to have addressed to the rash youth. Catching the young lord by the wrist, with streaming eyes and affectionate emphasis Cromer reminded him of the affectionate terms on which they had ever been. And then solemnly warned him against the rash delusion of imagining that any force he could bring together and support in the field, could avail against the strength of the kingdom and the power of the king. He suggested the uncertainty of the report of the earl's death. He urged the sacredness of the kingly character, and reminded him of the uniform fate of rebellion.

These obvious suggestions had little effect on the young lord, though urged with great force of language, and earnestness of manner.

While the chancellor was thus addressing the impatient young lord, his rude followers who did not understand the English language, looked with wonder at the speaker, and listened to his oration "which he set forth with such a lamentable countenance, as his cheeks were all blubbered with tears."* Some of them supposed he was preaching, others that he was spouting heroic verse in praise of lord Thomas, the pride and glory of the Geraldines. No sooner was the supposed song or sermon ended, than Donolan, lord Thomas's bard took up the strain, and thundered out the praises of his lord, in all the sounding modulation and figurative affluence of the Irish tongue. He celebrated his courage and high blood, his personal beauty and magnificent appearance, calling him by the popular name of silken Thomas, from the richness of his attire, and that of his train whose armour was embroidered with silk, and concluded by telling him significantly, that he delayed too long then. Lord Thomas was more alive to flattery, and the sense of admiration than to fear or reason: but it is not necessary to assume with some writers, that his purpose was in any way affected by this uncouth stimulus. His high-flown confidence in the power of his family, was enough to repel reasons grounded on their insufficiency for rebellion: he knew the insincerity of those before whom he stood, and felt that he had gone too far to retract with safety: scorning to be cajoled, he made a brief and stern reply, and flinging the sword on the council table, he left the chamber with his followers. The chancellor who had been so pathetic in attempting to dissuade him, now lost no time in writing and despatching an account to king Henry, by his own servant Thomas Brode, as we learn from a letter of baron Finglas, written to Cromwell at the same time.† Orders were also sent to the mayor to seize him as he passed through the city. But this was a command which there was no force to execute: the city had been nearly depopulated by the plague. The archbishop Allen, and baron Finglas took refuge

* Cox. † Finglas to Cromwell.—State Papers, Let. 75.

in the castle, and lord Thomas proceeded to raise the surrounding country, with the resolution to make himself master of Dublin. He next looked round for allies, and endeavoured to strengthen his cause to the utmost. He sent an ambassador to the Pope, and one to the king of Spain, he also wrote a pressing letter to lord Butler, son to Lord Ossory, and his cousin, to engage his assistance. To this young lord he proposed, that they should conquer the whole island, and share it between them. Lord Butler wrote him in reply, a letter of friendly but yet rough rebuke. Saying, that in such a quarrel, "I would rather die thine enemy, than live thy partner," and advising him, that "ignorance and error with a certain idea of duty, have carried you unawares to this folly, not yet so rank but that it may be cured." On receiving which letter, lord Thomas immediately proceeded to invade his lands about Kilkenny. In this district he committed much destructive ravage, and then returned toward Dublin. It was his design to lay siege to the castle. The inhabitants of the city were far from being favourable to his cause: they largely contributed to supply the castle with provisions. Lord Thomas in his resentment, directed Fingal, from which they drew their chief supplies, to be plundered. The citizens attempted to rescue the prey, as a party of the marauders passed by Kilmainham. But they were worsted in the attempt, with the loss of 80 citizens. Availing himself of the consternation thus produced, lord Thomas sent word to the city, that though he could destroy them, he would be content to spare them, if they would allow him to besiege the castle. The mayor and corporation were perplexed, they had no desire to yield, but the danger of resistance seemed rather formidable. In this strait they sent information of their condition to the king, and advised with the constable of the castle. This officer did not think they could prevent the siege, and stipulated for a liberal supply of men and provisions. The mayor sent in 20 tons of wine, 24 tons of beer, 2000 dried ling, 16 hogsheads of beef, 20 chambers, and an iron chain for the drawbridge.

The possibility of falling into the hands of the lord Thomas, awakened the fears of his enemy the archbishop Allen. Should the castle be stormed, his life might be seriously endangered in the insolence of victory: little moderation was to be anticipated from the late scene in the council chamber. Under this alarming impression, Allen resolved to escape into England, where alone he could find security from the threatened danger.

Awaiting the concealment of darkness, on the evening of the same day, Allen got on board a vessel near Dame's gate, and as he felt himself on the waters perhaps gratulated himself on his escape from the fiery Geraldine and his ruffian band. He was roused from his dream of security, by the information that his vessel was stranded, and could not be disengaged from the sands, near Clontarf. A fact which may indicate the precipitation of the fear which had urged him to sail without the tide. It is, however, said that the pilot was a Fitz-Gerald, and it is probable that the mishap was contrived. Allen was highly alarmed, his enemies were not far off, and while he calculated the probability of falling into their hands, he thought with regretful longing of the castle, from the shelter of which he had rashly fled. The only resource left, was a village called Artayne,* not far from the shore where he was forced to land. There he might still hope for a short concealment, until the means of escape should offer. But unhappily for this hope, the report of his being there was straight conveyed to his enemies. Early the next morning, the lord Thomas with two of his uncles, John and Oliver, were at the door of the hut in which he lay. Two men, John Zeling and Nicholas Wafer, were sent in for him. These ruffians found archbishop Allen on the bed where he lay trembling in the agony of a terror which but too justly estimated his danger; and seizing him with savage violence, dragged him out in his shirt upon the road. Naked and trembling, he threw himself on his knees before his enemies, and with a suppliant voice and countenance, begged pity for the love of God on a Christian and an archbishop.

What followed has received different constructions. The lord Thomas turned away, saying to his followers "take away the clown," on which they fell upon the poor old man and beat his brains out.

Such was the end of this unfortunate prelate. To suppose that his murder was intended by lord Thomas, is hardly consistent with the impression made by his general character; though proud, impetuous and rash, he was not without generosity, and the common sense of humanity. Yet the combination of circumstances is such as to suggest a less favourable decision: it is hard to believe that he did not know his followers well enough to be aware of the consequence of his own words and actions; or, that they would have had the gratuitous audacity to murder an old priest, before their chief, without any order or distinct understanding to that effect. If the lord Thomas's manner was sufficiently equivocal to countenance the mistake of his meaning, we should be inclined to call the ambiguity intentional. Nor should the aggravating circumstances, of the age, rank, profession and helpless condition of the sufferer, weigh so far as to repel these suspicions. Against this, it is enough to recollect the cause of the young Geraldine's resentment: the supposed execution of his father had driven him into rebellion, and he probably saw in Allen the chief instrument of his death. If such was his impression, revenge would appear a sacred duty, and the terrors of the victim were but the needful demands of vindictive feeling. This is a true, though fearful aspect of human nature. We are still, however, not compelled to have recourse to this conclusion. The two uncles, whose characters we know not, may have given the private order or signal. Nor is it quite impossible, that the impression that Allen was the cause of their lord's death, may have induced the murderers to imagine that the service would be acceptable, and they knew that it could be done with impunity. The following is the statement of Robert Reilly, who assisted in the murder, made on his examination when he had delivered himself up to government. "The lord Thomas, accompanied by J. Fitz-Gerald, and about 40 others, went to Artayne, where the archbishop lay, at the house of Mr Hothe, and there the prelate was murdered. But whether it was by lord Thomas's command or not, he

* State Papers.

could not say. But he admits, that on the same day, he was sent by Fitz-Gerald to Maynooth, with a casket which his master had taken from the bishop. And that lord Thomas afterwards sent one Charles his chaplain to the bishop of Rome, to the intent (as he had heard) of obtaining absolution for killing the bishop."

The murderers were excommunicated, and a copy of the sentence was sent to aggravate the suffering of the unhappy earl of Kildare in his imprisonment. It is published at full length in the *State Papers*, from a copy addressed for "Mr Lieutenant, at the king's Tower, London."*

Lord Thomas's party next took lord Howth and Mr Luttrel prisoners in their own houses; and being permitted by the mayor, according to the arrangement already mentioned, he proceeded to besiege the castle. For this purpose he detached 600 men, under the command of Field, Zeling, Wafer, &c., who planted two or three small cannon (called falcons) near Preston's inns, against the castle. Having obtained possession of many of the children of the citizens, they threatened to expose them in their trenches, if the castle guns should be turned that way.

It was in this interval that lord Thomas himself, with O'Niall and others, went to fulfil his menace to lord Butler, by invading the county of Kilkenny, which they laid waste to Thomastown. We have already mentioned the result. The Butlers were defeated, and lord Butler wounded.

In the mean time, alderman Herbert, who had been sent over by the corporation of Dublin to the king, returned with an assurance of immediate aid. On this, the citizens took courage, and ordered their gates to be shut. The rebels, whom they had admitted in their fears, now attempted to escape. Some swam the Liffey, but the greater part were secured.

On hearing this, lord Thomas left Kilkenny and summoned the force of the pale. He seized on many children of citizens who were at school in the country.†

He also sent an expostulation to the city, reproaching them with their breach of agreement and demanding the liberation of the prisoners. But his reproaches and demands met with equal disregard. He, therefore, attacked the castle from Ship Street, but was repelled by the fire of its battery. He then moved his position to Thomas Court, where he pulled down the street and made a gallery for the protection of his men. He burnt the New Street, and planted a gun against Newgate, which shot a man inside through the gate. His men were, in turn, severely cut up by the enemy's fire, and they were very much irritated by the success with which their fire was returned by Staunton, the gaoler of Newgate. An instance is mentioned of the skill of Staunton. Seeing one of the enemy taking aim at the loop-hole, from which he had been firing, he shot him through the head before he had time to fire; then rushing out by a postern, he brought in the gun of the fallen rebel before any attempt could be made to prevent him. This so enraged the troop of lord Thomas, that they brought fire and attempted to burn the gate.

* State Papers, lxxxi. p. 217. † Cox.

The citizens, after a little, began to perceive that lord Thomas was not sincerely supported by his men, who had been most of them compelled into the service. Headless arrows were shot over the walls, and other signs of remissness appearing, a sally was resolved. A report was first spread that succours had arrived from England; and before the artifice could be detected they rushed with sudden impetuosity through the burning and smoking ruins on the enemy. Fitz-Gerald's army scattered away before the attack. One hundred were slain and his cannon taken.

After this misfortune, it is likely that lord Thomas had not much confidence in the result of a message to the city, proposing "that his men who were prisoners should be enlarged; that the city should pay one thousand pounds in money, and five hundred in wares; to furnish him with ammunition and artillery; to intercede with the king for his pardon, and that of his followers." To these demands, of which the last should of itself have made the rest seem frivolous, the city answered by its recorder, "that if he would deliver up their children they would enlarge his men; that they were impoverished with his wars, and could not spare either wares or money; if he intended to submit, he had no need of artillery and ammunition, if not they would not give him rods to whip themselves; that they expected he would request good vellum parchment to engross his pardon, and not artillery to withstand his prince; that they promised all the intercession they could by word or letter."*

Lord Thomas agreed with the citizens on these terms.. It was all he could do at the moment. He thus recovered his men. Having given and received hostages, he raised the siege, and sending his men and military stores to Howth, he went to Maynooth, and left directions for the storing and fortifying the castle against a siege: and then speedily returned to his little army near Howth. In the meantime a landing had been effected by a party of English, who, with an imprudence not easily accounted for, had been separated from the main detachments under Sir William Brereton and Skeffington, who were then entering the bay with a sufficient, though small force, sent over in aid of the pale and city. The small party, commanded by two captains Hamerton, amounted to 180 men; on their way to Dublin they were met by the lord Thomas, and a sharp encounter took place, in which they were all slain or taken. Lord Thomas was wounded in the forehead by one of the Hamertons. Encouraged by a success, from which considering the disparity of numbers and arms, no very satisfactory inference could be soberly drawn; he now led his men to the heights of Howth in the vain hope to prevent any further landing of the English by a feeble cannonade from a scanty and inefficient battery. He seems to have forgotten the other coast of the bay: the firing only served to prevent Sir William Brereton from attempting a useless and dangerous collision, and probably informed him of the fate of the previous party. It is mentioned that Rouks, Fitz-Gerald's pirate, took one ship laden with English horses: but he could not prevent the English from landing at several points. Sir William Brereton and Skeffington landed without

* Cox.

opposition, and marched into Dublin, where it is needless to describe how gladly they were received. Their arrival was felt on both sides to amount to a decisive change of their respective positions. Lord Thomas must have felt his hopes expire when from the height on which he stood, he caught the distant acclamations of the city, which in its weakest moment had defied him.

Many circumstances, however, were unfavourable to the active exertions of the deputy Skeffington, and protracted the rebellion. Skeffington was himself ill—the winter was at hand—it was late in October—and the present state of the rebels required more distant and extended operations than the season or the strength of the English force permitted. Under these circumstances the deputy confined his operations, and awaited further supplies of men. He only marched to Drogheda, on the report that it was besieged by lord Thomas; and remained there about a week.

The winter passed without any decided event; but the suffering of the pale was unusually severe, from the activity of the rebels, to whom no adequate resistance could be made. Lord Thomas, himself, went into Connaught, to engage the aid of the western chiefs.

It is said that the citizens of Dublin and the English troops were much discontented at the inactivity of Skeffington, whose illness produced debility of mind and body. Early in March, however, active steps were resolved on, and Sir William Brereton was appointed to command a party against the strong castle of Maynooth. On his way he had an encounter with the rebels, and defeated them with great slaughter; and on the 16th March he invested Maynooth. He raised a strong battery against the north side of the castle, and sent in a summons to the garrison to surrender, with offers of pardon and reward. His summons and offers were rejected with scornful derision, and he opened his fire upon the walls. The castle was well supplied and garrisoned, and fortified with walls of immense solidity. The artillery of the time was comparatively inefficient, and that of Brereton not of the best. A fortnight passed, and no considerable impression was made; so that it became a matter of doubt and strong apprehension that the lord Thomas might be enabled to relieve the castle before they could obtain possession of it. Fortunately a result which must have led to a continuance of this pernicious war, and to a vast increase of slaughter, was prevented by an act of perfidy, which, if it has seldom been paralleled, has never been exceeded.

The castle was commanded by Christopher Parese, the foster brother of lord Thomas, and bound to him not only by the common pledges of important trust and obligation but by every tie of gratitude and sacred understanding of affection and duty. This base wretch, with a cowardice or venality disgraceful even in a bad cause, had conveyed to Skeffington an intimation that he would put the castle in his hands for a sum of money and certain other stipulations. Skeffington consented, and came off to the besieging army to take possession. Parese took advantage of a small success gained in a sally of the garrison, and probably preconcerted, to make them all drunk at night; and while they were in this condition, he gave the signal to the English, who, meeting no resistance, scaled the walls and took possession without resistance.

The spoil of the castle was very rich, for it was the best furnished castle in the island. Brereton planted his standard on the turret, and in the afternoon Skeffington entered the walls. It now remained to discharge his obligations to the traitor. Parese, triumphant in success and solicitous to receive his reward, was not slack to present himself before the lord deputy. A few minor matters were first attended to. Two singers came and "prostrated themselves, warbling a sweet sonnet, called *dulcis amica;*" their harmony won the favour of the chief justice Aylmer, at whose request they were pardoned. The deputy next addressed himself to Parese, and told him, that the service he had done in saving charge and bloodshed to the English was so great, that he thought it should be taken into consideration; and for this purpose, it was desirable first to ascertain what benefits he received in the service of Fitz-Gerald; Parese in his eagerness swallowed the bait; only intent on magnifying his own merits and importance, he detailed the advantages he had reaped from a long course of unremitting generosity, kindness, and affectionate confidence, and unconsciously unmasked the heartless baseness of his conduct and character, to his revolted and loathing hearers; he was lord Thomas' foster brother, he owed his whole importance and all he possessed to his munificence, and was placed by his confiding regard in the first place of trust and honour among his people; "and how Parese," said the deputy, "couldst thou find it in thy heart to betray so kind a lord?" Parese stood confounded—he had forgotten himself too far—he felt the load of contempt that breathed around him, and perhaps, for there is pride without honour, he wished so foul a deed undone. He was not long allowed to ponder on his position. "Go," said the lord deputy to an officer, "see him paid the price of his treachery, and then, without a moment's delay, see his head cut off." Parese had the coolness to say, "Had I known this, your lordship should not have had the castle so easily." "The deputy was silent, but a person who was present exclaimed, "Too late," and this exclamation passed into a popular saying, "Too late, says Boyce."*

Of this latter incident, the official account of the lord deputy and the council take no notice. It is not unlikely that, considering the game of complaint and misrepresentation which seems to have been so deeply played on either side, that it was deemed expedient to sink an incident that lowered the honour of a success which was necessary as a set off against the charge of dilatoriness and inefficiency. The description contained in this despatch, may be received as a correct outline of the facts of the siege. The deputy only forgot to mention that the garrison was drunk while he was performing his gallant *coup de main.* For the same reason he denied himself the honour of his severely equitable dealing with the traitor. But we see no reason to doubt the story of the annalists. The reader is fairly entitled to both. Here is the official account.

* Cox.

"The lord deputy and council of Ireland, to king Henry VIII.

"May it please your moost excellent highness to be advertised, that I, your deputie, with your armye in thes parties, the 14th day of Marche last past, beseaged the castell of Maynuth, which by your traitor and rebell, Thomas Fitz-Geralde, was so stronglie fortified, booth with men and ordenannce, as the liek hath not been seen in Irelonde synes anny your moost nobell progenitors had furst domynion in the lande. Ther was within the same, above 100 habill men, whereof wer 60 gonners. The 16th day of the said monith your ordenannce was bent upon the north-west side of the dungeon of the same castell, which ded baitter the tope therof on that wise, as ther ordenannce within that parte was dampned; which doone, your ordenannce was bent upon the northe side of the base corte of the said castell at the north-east ende wherof ther was new made a very stronge and fast bulwark, well garnisshed with men and ordenannce, which the 18th, 19th, 20th, 21st, and 22d dayes, of the said monith, ded beat the same, by night and daye, on that wise, that a great batery and a large enterie was made ther; whereupon the 23d day, being Tewsday next before Eister day,* ther was a Galiarde assaulte gyven betwixt fower and fyve of the clocke in the morning, and the base corte entered. At which entery ther was slayne of the warde of the castell aboute 60, and of your grace's armye no more but John Griffen yemen of your moost honorable gaurde, and six other, which wer killed with ordenannce of the castell at the entree. Howbeit, if it had not pleased God to preserve us, it wer to be mervelled that we had no more slayne. After the base corte was thus wonne, we assaulted the great castell, which within awhile yielded; wherin was the dean of Kildare, Cristofer Parys, capitaine of the garysone, Donough O'Dogan, maister of thordenannce, Sir Symon Walshe, priste and Nicholas Wafer, which tooke tharchbishop of Dublin, with dyvers other gunners and archers to the nomber of 37; which wer all taken prysoners, and ther lifes preserved by appoyntment, untill they shulde be presented to me, your deputie, and then to be orderid, as I and your counsaill thought good. And considering the high enterprise and presumption attempted by them ayenst your grace's crowne and majestie, and also that if by anny meane they shuld escape, the moost of theym beyng gunners, at some other tyme wold semblablie elliswhear, aide your traitors, and be example and meane to others to doo lykewise, we all thought expecient and requisite, that they shulde putto execution, for the dread and example of others. According wherunto, the Thursday following, in the morning, they wer examyned, and ther depositions written; and after none the same day arrayned before the propheest marshall, and capitaines, and ther, upon ther awne confessions, adjudged to die, and ymmediately twenty-five of them heeded, and oon hanged. Dyvers of the heedes of the principalles, incontynentlie wer put upon the turrettes of the castell. We send your highness here inclosed theffect of ther depositions, amonges which there is a priste, which was privay with the traitor, deposeth that the Emperor promised

* In 1535, Easter day fell on the 28th of March, which fixes the date of this despatch.

to send hether, against your grace, 10,000 men, by the first day of Maye. And the kinge of Scottes promised to yeve aide to your rebell lykewise. We doo advertise your highnes therof, in discharge of our duties, to thintent serche may be made of the furder circumstance therof; not doubting but if anny soche thinge be intendid by themperor, or kinge of Scottes, your highnes hath some intelligence therof, and will provide for it accordingly; for onles aide be sent hither from owtward parties, this traitor shalbe pursued to his adnoyannce and destruction, to the best of our powers we trust to your grace's honor. Albeit thenhabitanntes of this lande have an imagination and doubt, that he shulde hereafter obteyne your grace's pardone, as his antecessors, dyverse tymes, in lyke caases ded, which if, at anny tyme, he shulde, wer ther undoyng, as they say. The same causeth dyverse of theym to adhere to hym, and others not to doo soche service, as they ells wolde."*

The capture of Maynooth decided the fate of lord Thomas. By the aid of his friends in the west, he had collected a force of seven thousand men. Immediately on the report of this important success of the English, this army began to fall away, and he was soon reduced to a few hundreds: a force insufficient for any purpose but pillage. Even with this handful of men, the young Geraldine's spirit of infatuation did not yet desert him; obstinate to the last, he came into the vicinity of Clare. The lord deputy advanced to Naas: there he took one hundred and forty of the Irish. Presently being apprized that the lord Thomas was on his march to meet him, he very cruelly ordered them to be put to death. The rebels soon came in sight, but as a marsh, not to be crossed in the presence of an enemy, lay between, he directed a hot fire of artillery, which soon dispersed the remnant of their force. It was the last the unfortunate lord Thomas could bring together. Still, however, with a pertinacity which strongly shows the rashness and infatuation of his disposition, he persevered in hostilities which could have no object unless the pride of constancy in ill. He exerted himself to collect small parties, and carry on a desultory and marauding hostility. At Rathangan he caused a drove of cattle to be driven near the town to draw out the English: they fell into this trap. Believing the cattle to be a fair booty, numbers of the garrison came out unarmed to drive them in. The Geraldine party awaited their approach, until they came near their place of concealment, when they leaped forth, and few of the English escaped. On another occasion, he sent some of his people, disguised in the dress of English soldiers, to give information that his party were burning a village near Trim. On which the garrison in Trim sallied out, and, falling into an ambush, prepared for them, the greater part were slain.

The unfortunate youth soon retired into Munster; the pale and its vicinity were fast becoming unsafe for him. Lord Grey was sent after him; but no result could be looked for, from the weekly skirmishes in which a few rebels or soldiers were slain. Lord Thomas easily kept himself out of the reach of seizure, but it was become difficult for him

* State Papers, No. 87, page 236.

to live; and the crisis was arrived when he should either yield on terms, or be a hunted robber without means, or the prospect of a termination to his misfortunes. Under such circumstances, a parley was proposed, and lord Thomas surrendered to lord Grey at discretion, but implored his good offices with the king. Lord Grey carried him to Dublin, from whence he was embarked for England. He was confined in the Tower, where, it appears from the following letter that, his sufferings were very severe.

" Lord Thomas Fitz-Gerald to Rothe.

" My trusty servant, I hartely commend me unto you. I pray you that you woll delyver thys othyr letter unto Obryen. I have sent to hym for £20 starling, the which yff he take you (as I trust he woll), than I woll that you com over, and bryng it onto my lord Crumwell, that I may so have ytt. I never had eny mony syns I cam in to pryson, but a nobull, nor I have had nothyr hosyn, dublet, nor shoys, nor shyrt, but on; nor eny othyr garment, but a syngyll fryse gowne, for a velve furryd wythe bowge, and so I have gone wolward, and barefote, and barelegyd, dyverse tymes (whan it hath not ben very warm); and so I should have don styll, and now, but that pore prysoners, of ther gentylnes, hathe sumtyme gevyn me old hosyn and shoys, and old shyrtes. This I write onto you, not as complaynyng on my fryndes, but for to show you the trewthe of my grete nede, that you shuld be the more dylygent in going onto Obryen, and in bryngyng me the before said £20, wherby I myght the soner have here mony to by me clothys, and also for to amend my selender comyns and fare, and for othyr necessaryes. I woll you take owte of that you bryng me for your costes and labur. I pray you to have me commendyd onto all my lovers and frendes, and show them that I am in gude helthe.*

" By me, THOMAS FITZ-GERALD.
(Superscribed) "To my trusty and well loved servant, John Rothe."

It appears that lord Thomas confidently anticipated mercy. But this anticipation must seem weak to the reader of the foregoing detail: his rebellion was sadly aggravated by the combination of circumstances. His father's character cast an unlucky reflection on the crimes and follies of a son who had thus impetuously rushed into rebellion. The monarch, who was justly incensed against the conduct of his father in a place of high authority and trust, was not likely to look with much indulgence on the commission of this trust to a rash youth of twenty-one; and from the frantic folly with which this youth flung all consideration of fidelity and duty aside, and rushed from the seat of honour, authority, rule, protection, and justice, to the downright betrayal of his father's honour, and his own trust, he could not be a safe person to represent the most powerful house in Ireland, nor would his pardon be the best example of royal mercy in such a time. Further, whether or not lord Thomas was a consenting party to the foul murder of archbishop Allen, so it was believed, and so ran the sentence of the Roman see, pronouncing him accursed for the crime. There were some high features of gene-

* State Papers, letter clviii. Vol ii. p. 502.

rosity and heroism in his character, but he was a traitor in the eyes of justice, which does not, and cannot dive into men's motives, or weigh their secret virtues in the balance against their crimes perpetrated in the eye of day. In those evil times, in which the license of great Chiefs was the main cause of the sufferings of the pale, it was rather the error of justice to be lenient; and the impunity of outrages like those of this unfortunate young lord, would be a fatal precedent in a country which had still to learn that murder and rebellion were not virtues but crimes.

The Lord Thomas had been arrested on his way to Windsor, by the king's order, and sent to the Tower. After a short confinement, he was beheaded in Tyburn, with his five uncles, on the 3d February, 1537.

In denying that his suffering has any claim on the historian's compassion, we must add, that the justice of that execrable tyrant by whom he was ordered to his fate, was probably the result of no purer principle than revenge. We cannot demand much of the reader's "valuable indignation" in behalf of good men who were hurried to an ignominious and unworthy end, four hundred years ago; their account has long been balanced, and posterity has troubles of its own. But nothing can throw a clearer light on the furious and bloodthirsty violence of Henry VIII., than the indiscriminate murder of five noble Geraldines, brothers to the ninth earl of Kildare. Of these, two were unquestionably guilty and met a just death, had it not been inflicted by the foulest treachery; but the other three were notoriously innocent, and opposed to the whole proceedings of their nephew. These lords were taken by a detestable artifice, and executed without trial, or even the form of inquiry Lord Grey was commissioned to take them, he invited them to a feast, and from the feast they were transferred to the bloody scaffold. Three of them in the confidence of innocence, and the unconsciousness of a charge; all thinking the blow past, and the tyrant's vengeance appeased. The tyrant may, it is true, be said to have had some forecast in his fury; he asked his council if he might not now seize all the lands of the country into his own hands, and conquer the whole of it for himself. Fortunately, for the descendants of many a noble house, he was better advised. But his rage against the Geraldine branch of Kildare had been long kindling, and was not to be appeased by a sacrifice less than extermination. A young brother of twelve years, escaped, and with difficulty was saved from the vengeance of Henry. As this youth lived to act a very distinguished part in his own generation, we shall have to notice him further on.

GERALD, TENTH EARL OF KILDARE.

BORN A.D. 1525—DIED A.D. 1585.

WE concur with Lodge in reckoning this nobleman the eleventh earl of Kildare. The reason is sufficiently conclusive. The attainder which for a time extinguished the title and honours of this illustrious branch of the Geraldines, was not passed for a year and a half after the death of the ninth earl; during which time the young lord, his eldest son, though in rebellion, was not yet attainted, or by any legal act deprived of his rights.

Gerald was yet but ten (Cox says thirteen) years of age at the time of the execution of his half-brother, the lord Thomas. As the rage of Henry VIII. blazed with indiscriminate fury against the family of Kildare, there could be no doubt that the seizure of this youth would at the least be attended with serious danger. The oblivion and secret miseries of a dungeon was the least to be expected from a king who had butchered his five uncles, of whom three were notoriously innocent of the crime alleged. Gerald was, fortunately for him, at the habitation of his nurse at Donoure, in the county of Kildare, and lying ill of the small-pox. The nurse, apprized of his danger, committed him to the zeal of Thomas Leverous,* foster-brother to his father, who carefully conveyed him in a basket into Offaly to lady Mary O'Conor, his sister. There he remained until his recovery. The search after him had, however, begun, and his continuance there might be dangerous to his protectors; concealment was rendered difficult by the system of espial and tale-bearing which characterized the intriguing chiefs of the time. The child was removed upon his recovery to Thomond, then least accessible to the English, and from thence to Kilbritton, in the county of Cork, to his aunt, Eleanor Fitz-Gerald, who had married Macarthy Reagh, and was at the time a widow. To ensure protection for her nephew, this lady consented to marry O'Donell, chief of Tyrconel, in 1537, who was himself a widower, and had that year succeeded his father Odo in the chieftainship. With this chief the aunt of Gerald stipulated for the protection of her nephew. But O'Donell was not to be trusted: his lady soon discovered that he was fickle in his politics, destitute of affections, and that he was engaged in secret negotiations with the English government. It is probable that she was enabled to discover some proof of an actual design to betray her nephew; but it is certain that there was enough of ground for such suspicions, to satisfy her that it was no longer safe to continue in his power. She therefore sent Gerald away privately into France, having given him 140 pieces of gold, for his travelling charges. Having thus secured his safety, she had no longer any reason to remain with the unworthy husband she had married solely for Gerald's sake, and

---

* Afterwards bishop of Kildare.

consulted her indignation and contempt by leaving him: O'Donell never saw her more. Her nephew was long and anxiously sought for, though after the first burst of king Henry's fury, it is unlikely that any harm would have happened him. On this point, the following extract is at least worth notice. It is taken from a paper written by St Leger and the other commissioners joined with him in 1537, and we should think speaks from authority:—

"Item, whereas young Fitz-Gerald, second sonne to the late earl of Kildare, hath withdrawn himself from the king's majesty without ground or cause, his grace nothing minding, to the said Gerald Fitz-Gerald, but honour and wealth, and to have cherished him as his kinsman, in like sort as his other brother is cherished with his mother in the realm of England: we require the said lord James of Desmond to write unto the said Gerald Fitz-Gerald, advising him in like sorts, as his uncle the lord deputie hath done, to submit himself to the king his sovereign lord. And if he will not do so at this gentle monicion, then to proceed against him and his accomplices as against the king's rebels and disobedaunntes. Item, if the said Gerald Fitz-Gerald do at the monicion of the said lord James of Desmond, submit himself and come to the said lord James of Desmond, upon certificate thereof to the said commissioners made, we the said commissioners concede, that the said Gerald Fitz-Gerald shall have the king's most gracious pardon for his said absenting, and for all other offences done to our said sovereign lord, and to be from thenceforth taken as the king's true and loving subject."*

From this document it should be inferred, that the course most obvious, safe, and beneficial for young Gerald, then about fifteen years of age, would be a surrender of his person. The first fury of the king's resentment had, in the course of two intervening years, been cooled; and a youth who could have as yet incurred no personal hostility, might have reckoned with certainty on the just indulgence thus held out in a formal and public pledge. But he was in the hands of advisers and protectors who saw the whole matter in a different light, and who had other views for him. His situation made him the subject of political intrigues, and his own friends were also strongly actuated by religious feeling in refusing to submit him to the tuition of Henry.

Fitz-Gerald arrived safely at St Maloes,† and was from thence sent to the king of France. There had lately been a peace concluded, and it was probably according to some of the articles of a treaty that Sir John Wallop, the English ambassador, demanded that he should be delivered up. The king of France, unwilling to comply with this demand, temporized with the ambassador, and suffered Gerald to escape towards Flanders. The ambassador received some immediate intimation of this, and lost no time in having him pursued. He was overtaken by Sherlock, the person thus employed, at *Valenciennes:* but the governor of the town, made aware of the king's favourable intent, and probably acting upon instructions, arrested Sherlock. Gerald thus escaped to Brussels. Here, too, he was pursued, and claimed by

* State Papers, vol. ii. † Cox.

the messengers of the same ambassador; he was therefore compelled to make his escape to Liege. At Liege he was befriended by the emperor, who granted a hundred crowns a-month for his expenses, and recommended him to the bishop's protection.

At Liege he remained safely for half-a-year, at the end of which time he had the good fortune to be placed in security from all further attempts on his freedom. Cardinal Pole, his kinsman, and the enemy of Henry VIII., sent for him and had him conveyed to Rome, where he took every means to have him educated according to his rank and future expectations. It is mentioned, that he placed him under the care of the bishop of Verona, the cardinal of Mantua, and the duke of Mantua, in succession, and gave him an allowance of three hundred crowns a-year, to which the duke of Mantua made the like addition. At about the age of seventeen, he was removed by his friendly protector to his own immediate superintendence, and had apartments in his palace in Rome. "The cardinal," writes Hooker, "greatly rejoiced in his kinsman, had him carefully trained up in his house, interlacing, with such discretion, his learning and studies, with exercises of activity, as he should not be after accounted of the learned for an ignorant idiot, nor taken of active gentlemen for a dead and dumpish meacocke. If he had committed any fault, the cardinal would secretly command his tutors to correct him; and all that, notwithstanding he would in presence dandle the boy, as if he were not privy to his punishment. And upon complaint made, he used to check Fitz-Gerald his master openly, for chastising so severely his pretty darling."*
Here, his education being completed, when he was twenty years of age he was allowed to enter the service of the knights of Malta, in which he quickly obtained military distinction. The knights of Malta were engaged in continual war against the Turks, and were in the habit of making frequent descents on their coasts, from which they often carried away plunder to a considerable amount: in this service young Gerald not only won great distinction, but also much wealth. The cardinal rejoiced in his success; made a large addition to his allowance, and recommended him to the service of Cosmo, the duke of Florence, by whom he was appointed master of the horse. His conduct and character recommended him to the great duke of Tuscany, from whom he received a similar appointment, which he held for the following three years.

Holinshed mentions, that while he was in this service, he met with an accident which harmonizes well with the vicissitudes of his life. Having made a visit to Rome for his amusement, he was hunting in company with the cardinal Farneze, when his horse came suddenly upon a concealed pit, twenty fathoms deep, and, with his rider, plunged headlong down and fell to the bottom. Fortunately for young Gerald, he was light, alert, and self-possessed. After going down to a great depth, the fall of the horse was slightly impeded by some bushes or roots, or perhaps creepers, which had, during the lapse of ages, grown down to that depth: he had the thought to grasp at them. The horse reached the bottom with full force, and was killed instantaneously by the

* Sup. to Holinshed's Chron. vol. vi.

shock: Gerald held fast by the roots, until his arms grew so weary that he could hold no longer: he then let himself down, little hoping to escape the fall; fortunately he had not far to go, and lighted safe on the dead carcase of his horse. The situation was still unpromising enough. There was no possibility of ascending; and he stood there, up to his ankles in water and in a hopeless condition, for about three hours. Providentially he had taken with him a dog, which, after hunting about for him a long time to no purpose, at last traced him to the chasm into which he had fallen. Stopping there, the faithful and sagacious creature set up a long howling, and never stopped until he drew the attention of some hunters of the same company. Being thus discovered, he was soon extricated by a rope and basket. Cox, who tells the story from Hollinshed, rejects it as "a little monkish." It may be in a great measure fictitious, but has assuredly nothing otherwise monkish in its object or construction.

While such was the course of his life abroad, he seems to have been the object of continued anxiety and unremitting contention both among friends and foes at home. The O'Donells, O'Nialls, and other Irish chiefs, were loud in menace and expostulation; and a letter from John Allen to Cromwell, in 1539, mentions the threat of these chiefs, "that if the king's majestie will not restore young Gerald to all the possessions and pre-eminence that his father had in this land, they will do what they can, if they may have opportunity, to put him in by force."*
By a letter from Brabazon, of the same date, it appears as if there then existed a suspicion that Gerald was actually in the kingdom, and consequently a strange ignorance as to his real place of abode; though, if we do not impute the same ignorance to nearly all Irish historians of this period, there is no reason to suppose that he returned to Ireland for many years from his first escape, until long after the death of king Henry. One thing is certain, that his capture was considered as an object of the first importance, not only, as Brabazon expresses it, "lest this said Gerald Fitz-Gerald may play the like part (with others of his party and kinsmen) when he may," but also, on the ground that if he were once taken, their power would cease. These notices, and many other to the same effect, which from time to time occur through the correspondence of the chief Irish officers with the English court, indicate undeniably that an importance was attached to this young nobleman, which by no means appears in Ware, Cox, Leland, or any others of the various historical writers whom we have had occasion to consult.

In 1544, five years after the mention above referred to, this impression seems to be much augmented, and a long letter, exclusively on the subject, is written from the Irish lord justice and council to king Henry. It informs him, that by letters from Waterford, the council is informed that young Gerald is at Nantes, on his way from Italy to invade Ireland, and that he was there awaiting a navy and army, to be supplied for the purpose by the French king. This information evidently occasioned great alarm to the council, who express their conviction of the inadequacy of any means of resistance in their power, or that of

* State Papers, vol. iii.

the city of Waterford, against which the expedition was supposed to be directed. This report seems at the same time to have been transmitted to the English council, whose communication to the Irish council seems to have reached Ireland before the despatch here noticed had been sent off. The information appears to stand chiefly on the authority of W. de la Cluse, a person dwelling in "Bridges," whose father seems to have kept a house of entertainment for the Irish resorting thither; and also certain Wexford men, who being prisoners, were offered their freedom on the condition of joining in the service of Gerald Fitz-Gerald. The Irish council express their opinion that the invasion would be more likely to take place in the country of the Macarthies, near the city of Cork; not only of its being more directly in their course, but also on account of the circumstance of one of the Macarthys being son to his aunt Eleanor.*

From the whole tenor of the government correspondence, during the latter years of Henry VIII., it is certain that Gerald was for a considerable time the subject of much anxious fear, expectation, and vigilance both to his friends and enemies; but, notwithstanding a few doubtful affirmations to the contrary, we should infer that he prudently kept aloof, and avoided committing himself in any proceeding which must have had the sure effect of barring for ever the remotest possibility of his restoration to his family honours and possessions. The death of Henry VIII., in 1546, must have been felt to be the promise of better days to this young lord. But we cannot, with any certainty, trace the favourable turn which his affairs may have taken from this time till 1552, when he was taken into royal favour, and restored to very considerable portions of the estates of his father. In two years more he was created earl of Kildare and baron Offaly; and is from this date found taking an active part in the various measures of the English government for the reduction of rebellious chiefs, and the pacification of the country.

In 1557 he is mentioned as having joined with the lord lieutenant, Sidney, in his campaign against Mac Donnell, a Scot, who had invaded the north of Ireland at the head of a strong party of his countrymen. Besides the earl of Kildare, the lord lieutenant was accompanied on this expedition by the lords Ormonde, Baltinglass, Delvin, Dunsany, and Dunboyne. There was no engagement, as the Scots scattered before them, and took refuge in the woods.

In 1561 he persuaded his kinsman O'Neale, then engaged in rebellious proceedings, to submit to the queen; and generally conducted himself with a prudent regard to the interests of the government. The events of the remainder of his life are, however, such as to fall more appropriately under other heads, as at this time the troubles of the pale rose to a dangerous height, and long continued, during the restless life of the celebrated Shane O'Neale, and the rebellion of the sixteenth earl of Desmond, both of whom we must notice at some length. Though Gerald's lands were restored, and his titles conferred anew by creation, yet it was not till 1568 that the act of attainder against his father's blood was repealed, in a parliament held in Dublin. He was

* Married to Macarthy of Carbery.

at this period of his life frequently intrusted with the defence of the pale, especially in 1574. In 1579 he joined Sir William Drury against the Spanish force which landed in Kerry, to support the earl of Desmond's rebellion; notwithstanding which services, he was, in the following year, arrested on suspicion of corresponding with the Leinster rebels, and sent with his son, lord Henry Fitz-Gerald, to England, where they were thrown into the Tower. On trial, he was fully acquitted. He was one of the lords present in Sir John Perrot's parliament, in 1585, in which year his death took place.

His eldest son, Gerald, left a daughter, Lettice, who claimed the barony of Ophaly as her father's heir. It was after a time adjudged to the earls of Kildare. She had married Sir Robert Digby, and was created by James I. Lady Digby Baroness Ophaly. We shall notice her further in a future page.*

The House of Desmond.

JAMES, ELEVENTH EARL OF DESMOND.

DIED A. D. 1529.

OF this powerful nobleman it will be enough to mention, that he lived in great power and wealth, apart from the politics, and remote from the power of the English government. These circumstances naturally operated on a proud and insubordinate spirit, and he entered into two treaties with the foreign enemies of England, which would have been fatal in their consequence to any nobleman of the Pale; but from the penalties of which, Desmond was protected by his remote southern position, which reduced the power which the English deputies could exercise over his conduct, to something merely nominal. Of these rebellions, the first was in conjunction with the king of France, in 1523, and was terminated and detected by a peace made between Francis and Henry. The second was a similar correspondence with the emperor Charles V., who sent an ambassador to him to move him to rebellion. This embassy was, however, rendered abortive by the earl's death, in August 1529. He was succeeded in the earldom by an uncle.

* " Nothing can better show the extreme difficulty of writing, even now, on the subject of Irish Peerage descents, with any degree of documentary certainty, than the following piece of evidence brought forward during the progress of the above family contest. It is part of a Chancery pleading wherein it is alleged, and was not denied or disproved, that no less than four sets of daughters or co-heirs had occurred in the family of Kildare, previous to that time, and that none of them had inherited the title or dignity of the Parliamentary Barony belonging to the Earls of Kildare, which, it seems, always devolved on the next heir male: 'That the said title or name of dignity of *Offaley* is not due, or ought not to be due, to the said Lady Lettice, although the same had been fee simple in the ancient Earls of Kildare, yet indeed it was not, for that there had been several women-heirs-general of that family which ought to have had that title had it been in fee simple, 1. namely *Annabell* and *Julian*, daughters and heirs to Maurice Fitzgerald, and *Julian*, daughter to Gerald Fitzgerald, and *Elizabeth*, daughter and heir to Gerald Fitzgerald, ancestor to Gerald, grandfather to the Lady Lettice, which Elizabeth was married to the Earl of Ormond; and lastly, *Katherine*, sister and heir of Thomas, late Earl of Kildare, who have heirs yet living.'—BURKE.

JAMES, FIFTEENTH EARL OF DESMOND.

DIED A.D. 1558.

THIS earl succeeded his father Thomas, who died of extreme old age in 1536. It is perhaps a just inference which we have no means to verify, that this earl was himself far advanced in life at the period of this event. Immediately on his accession he followed the example of his illustrious ancestors by attempting an insurrection in Munster. James, viscount Thurles, (afterwards 9th earl of Ormonde,) was immediately dispatched against him by lord Grey, and soon reduced him to submission—wasting his lands, and seizing on his castle of Lough Gur, which, as we have already mentioned in our notice of that nobleman, he fortified and garrisoned against its lord. Desmond submitted, and gave pledges to be a faithful servant to the king, and to do right to the rival claimant of his earldom. He had strongly, on this occasion, expressed to Grey his wish to submit and his fear of the consequence. The lord James Butler, it seems, pretended a claim in right of his wife Joan, daughter and heir to the 11th earl of Desmond. On this account it was, that in the correspondence of James Butler, this earl of Desmond is always called "the pretended earl." On the subject of this claim, Desmond observes that it was to be apprehended, lest by a submission to English law his enemy's claim might be unjustly preferred, "lest by the favours of the other, he and his blood shall be put from their inheritance, which they have possessed, he saith, from the conquest."* The deputy in the same communication recommends Desmond to favour on strong prudential grounds, both as the best means of repressing the natives, and also as a counterbalance to the growing power of the house of Ormonde, now freed from the rivalship of the other great branch of the Geraldines, by the recent hapless events in that family.

This view is corroborated strongly by part of a letter afterwards written 1542, by lord deputy St Leger to Henry. We extract the passage which is interesting for the authentic sketch it presents of the actual state of these parties in the reign of Henry VIII.:—"It may also please your majestie, that where it hath been to me reported, that the said M'Cowley, lately the master of your rolls here, should article against me that I went about to erect a new Geraldine band (probably here referring to lord Thomas's rebellion); meaning the same by the erle of Desmond. The truth is, I laboured most effectually to bring him to your perfect obedience, to my great peril and charge; and this, gracious lord, was the only cause. I saw that now the erle of Kildare was gone, there was no subject of your majestie's here meet nor able to way (weigh) with the erle of Ormonde, who hath of your majestie's gifte, and of his own inheritance, and rule given him by your majesty, not only 50 or 60 miles in length, but also many of the chief holds of the frontiers of Irishmen; so that if he or any of his heirs should swerve from their duty of allegiance, (which I think verily that he

* Gray's letter to Cromwell. State Papers, clx.

will never do,) it would be more hard to daunt him or them than it was the said erle of Kildare, who had always the said erle of Ormonde in his top, when he would or was like to attempt any such thing. Therefore I thought it good to have a Rowland for an Oliver, (&c., &c.)"

It was probably on these grounds that Desmond was encouraged to look for favour and protection from the king. He sailed from Howth in the summer of 1542, bearing recommendatory letters from the lord deputy St. Leger; and was received with great honour by the king. On the same occasion he was also appointed lord high treasurer in Ireland, and enjoyed the post during this and the two following reigns. He was sworn of the privy council, and deputy St. Leger by the king's authority, granted to him and his heirs male St. Mary's abbey to hold by the fifth part of a knight's fee: with the condition of forfeiture in case of rebellion.

From this he remained in prosperity and honour till his death in 1558, at Askeaton, where he was buried in the Franciscan Friary.

GERALD, SIXTEENTH EARL OF DESMOND.

DIED A. D. 1583.

GERALD, the sixteenth earl of Desmond, "was," as the letter of queen Elizabeth expresses it, "not brought up where law and justice had been frequented." On his father's death, a violent controversy, which had to be determined by arms, arose between him and an elder half-brother, Thomas, who, from the colour of his hair and complexion, was called "the red," and is spoken of under that name by the Irish annalists. Thomas was the son of earl James by his first wife, the daughter of lord Fermoy, from whom, soon after the birth of this son, he had procured a divorce on the pretence of too near a consanguinity. Thomas's claims to the earldom were supported by Thomas, lord Kerry, and by the distinguished branches of the Geraldine family, who bore, and whose descendants still bear, the romantic titles of the White Knight, and the Knight of the Vallies, or as it is now more frequently called, of the Glen. In spite of this formidable opposition, Gerald succeeded in establishing his claim—was styled and acknowledged earl of Desmond, and as such sat in the parliament held in Dublin, in January, 1559. Thomas, after his unsuccessful attempt, retired to Spain, where he died, leaving a son, whose fortunes we shall have to record in a later period of our history. The disputed claim to the earldom threw Gerald into the hands of his Irish followers, and though his rights seem to have rested on grounds familiar to English law, yet the necessity of sustaining them by the aid of armed retainers compelled him to adopt the wild and lawless life of an Irish chieftain. The exigencies of a turbulent life forced him to impose exactions on his dependents and neighbours. This course of ruin is one that it is painful to relate, as it involves the destruction of the illustrious house which he represented. In his extravagant ambition, in his desperate defiance of the power of England, and in his traitorous intercourse with foreign states, he appears to have been inspired with a wild spirit of rash adventure, which exhibited itself in his early contests with the powerful family of Ormonde. His first recorded acts were acts of aggression upon the Butlers. He sought to charge the Decies in the county of Waterford with *coigne* and *livery, black rents* and *cosheries,* according to the Irish usages which had become almost the law of the Anglo-Irish of the remoter districts. The claim, which even his own clansmen resisted as they best could, was sought to be enforced by him on the lands of the earl of Ormonde. The retainers of the two earls resorted to arms, and a pitched battle was fought between their forces at Affane, in the county of Waterford, on the 15th of February, 1564, where Desmond lost two hundred and eighty of his men, and was himself wounded and taken prisoner. As the exulting followers of Ormonde conveyed him from the field, stretched upon a bier, they exclaimed with natural triumph, "Where is now the great earl of Desmond?" "Where," replied the captive, "where but in his proper place? Still upon the necks of the Butlers."*

The dissensions between the Butlers and Geraldines kept Munster in such a state of utter lawlessness, that in the course of the next year both earls were summoned to London to account for their unwarrantable conduct. They were examined before the privy council, where their narratives of the disputes between them were so wholly irreconcilable that no order could be made, and under the circumstances the case was referred to the privy council of Ireland. While the earls were engaged in mutual accusations in England, their followers in Ireland did not cease to carry on hostilities. The lands of Ormonde were invaded by John, a brother of Desmond's; villages were burned, and a brother of Ormonde's slain. This did not interrupt the adjustment of the differences between the rival earls. The privy council of Ireland shrank from deciding the matter, and urged both to submit to the queen's award, to which they agreed; and for their obedience thereto, and preserving peace, they entered into recognizances of twenty thousand pounds each. A commission under the broad seal of England was thereupon directed to Sir Henry Sidney (who had been lately sent over as lord-deputy) to take their examinations, and the queen wrote a private letter to Sidney, which is still preserved. This extraordinary document, amid much that is obscure, and much that is susceptible of more than one interpretation, contained passages that show decided hostility to Desmond. She tells Sidney to "make some difference betwixt tried and just, and false friends; let the good service of well-deservers never be rewarded with loss; let their thanks be such as may encourage new strivers for the like; suffer not that Desmond's dinning deeds, far wide from promised words, make you trust for other pledge than either himself or John" [his brother, afterwards styled Sir John Desmond] "for gage. He hath so well performed his English vows, that I warn you trust him no longer than you see one of them. I pray God *your old strange sheep, late as you say, returned into the fold, wear not her wooly garment on her wolfy back.*" Sidney, who appears to have felt what was the duty of an arbitrator better than his royal mistress, when he saw how strongly she was affected

* Lelund.

against Desmond, declined to undertake the investigation of a case thus prejudged, unless other commissioners were sent from England to assist him. His letter to Cecil is manly and memorable: "I assure you, sir, if I served under the cruellest tyrant that ever tyrannized, and knew him affected on the one side or the other side, between party and party, and referred to my judgment, I would rather offend his affection, and stand to his misericord, than offend my own conscience, and stand to God's judgment. Therefore, I beseech you, let me have others joined with me." His request of additional commissioners was complied with. One of the points in controversy was the right to the profit of prize wines at Youghal and Kingsale, which both earls claimed under grants from the crown. Another subject of litigation was the boundaries of their respective estates. In enforcing their respective demands, many outrages had taken place: seizures of cattle had been made, which in a peaceful state of society, and with courts of law competent to decide between the parties, might have been but a mode of asserting a right to property in the ground on which they pastured, but late acts of the Irish parliament had made such seizures punishable as treason; blood had been frequently shed in the violent altercations between the clansmen of the mighty rivals, and each had a long catalogue of inexpiable offences to charge against the other. Ormonde took the bold ground of defending the affray at Affane, by pleading that he had levied his forces for the defence of the country against Desmond; that having gone, at Sir Maurice Fitz-Gerald's request, into his country, and travelling quietly within a mile of Drumana, Sir Maurice's residence, the earl of Desmond, accompanied by numbers of proclaimed traitors and Irish rebels, set upon him, and that he was obliged, in self-defence, to kill several of Desmond's people. The commissioners sought to effect a reconciliation. The question of boundaries they determined in favour of Ormonde. A part of their award required the contending earls to shake hands, and they met for the purpose in the chapter-house of St Patrick's church, Dublin, where two centuries after, an aperture in the old oak door was still shown as cut on the occasion for the purpose of enabling them with safety to perform this part of the award, each fearing to be poignarded by the other.

A reconciliation such as this did not promise much for the future harmony of the newly-made friends. A year of quiet followed, and if depredations were committed, they have not been recorded by our authorities. The villages of Ormonde had to be rebuilt before they could be again burned; and the Abbè M'Geogeghan, the historian who most loves to dwell upon the exploits of Desmond and his followers, leads us to think it not unlikely that for about a year and a half the lands of Ormonde were allowed to remain undisturbed. Desmond, however, was not idle. An expedition of his is mentioned with no measured terms of praise, against M'Carthy Riogh, and the M'Carthys of Duhallow, in the county of Cork; and he was next engaged against Edmond M'Teague, the son of M'Carthy of Muskerry, by whom he was taken and kept in prison for six months.

The M'Carthys were at this time in rebellion, and it is not improbable that Desmond made a merit of these services against them to the

English government. He no sooner was released from prison, than we find him, at the head of an army of two thousand men, encamped on the frontiers of Ormonde's county. The lands of Ormonde's friends, the lords Barry and Roche, and Sir Maurice Fitz-Gerald, and the Decies, were plundered for the supply of his men. Sidney, who was then engaged against O'Neale in the north of Ireland, could not undertake an expedition to Munster, to quell these disturbances. Desmond's pretence for keeping such an army on foot was his private quarrel with Ormonde; but the deputy had strong reason to fear that he was preparing to act in concert with O'Neale. He dispatched Captain Herne, the constable of the castle of Leighlin, to learn from Desmond his objects, and to remind him of his duties to the queen. Desmond proposed as a proof of his allegiance, or Sidney demanded it, that he should attend him into Ulster with all his men, or remain upon the borders of the pale, for its defence, with a party of horse, during the deputy's absence. Desmond did not hesitate to obey—he marched with his brother John of Desmond to the frontiers of Leinster.

In the beginning of the following year, 1567, Sidney made a progress through Munster and Connaught. The chief object of his journey was to hear the respective complaints of the earls, who were still at war—Ormonde continuing to urge upon the queen complaints of Desmond's violence and Sidney's partiality. At Youghal, Sidney examined into some late acts of depredation, and ordered Desmond to make reparation for a prey of cattle which he had taken on Ormonde's lands. Desmond replied with violence, and was told that, by this breach of the peace, the recognizance which he had entered into for twenty thousand pounds was forfeited. The affront, as he esteemed it, was resented by Desmond, who did what he could to prevent the leading persons of the district from attending the deputy during his progress. Sidney heard of Desmond's outrages, and saw vestiges of ruin wherever he went. One of his letters says, "that the county of Cork was the pleasantest county he had ever seen, but was most miserably waste and uncultivated; the villages and churches burned and ruined, the castles destroyed, and the bones of the murdered and starved inhabitants scattered about the fields;" he adds that "a principal servant of Desmond's, after he had burned down several villages, and destroyed a large tract of the country, put a parcel of poor women to the sword, and that soon after this cruel fact the earl feasted him in his house." M'Carthy More, who had, two years before, been created earl of Clancare, and Sir Owen O'Sullivan, were among those whom Desmond persuaded to refuse paying any civilities to the deputy. Desmond himself was compelled by the nature of the investigation which brought Sidney to the country, to attend him in his progress, but he seems to have lost no opportunity of expressing the scorn with which he regarded, or tried to regard him. "For every Irish soldier that he now kept," he proudly boasted "that before long he would maintain five; and that before midsummer he would take the field with five thousand men." Such was the haughty reply of Desmond, when questioned on the ravages which were exhibited on every step of the deputy's progress.

This bickering altercation could not last long, and it is probable that some violent attack upon Sidney was meditated. When they approached Kilmallock, one of the earl's principal strongholds, the deputy was startled at hearing that all Desmond's people were up in arms. The earl was at no loss for an excuse, when the cause of this sudden rising was enquired into. He said it was for the purpose of seizing O'Brien O'Goonagh and the White Knight, two of his followers, who had committed some outrages and whose persons the deputy had demanded. The calmness with which Sidney had hitherto listened to all Desmond's grievances, and the forbearance with which he endured his repeated insults, seem to have misled the earl into the notion that such easy credulity could be imposed upon to any extent, for the White Knight and O'Brien were at the head of the tumultuary hands. When this was stated in reply to Desmond's pretences, he threw himself upon his knees—he asked pardon of the deputy, and offered to disperse them with a word. Sidney, whose temper had been tried beyond endurance, could no longer disguise his loathing and contempt for the suppliant whom he saw fawning at his feet. He told him, " disperse them or not as you please; my men are two hundred, and if one act of mine be interrupted by this army of your's, I shall give them battle;—but know, you are my prisoner; your life shall be the instant forfeit of any hostile movement of theirs." The earl was removed from his presence, was instantly confined, and in the same hour sent prisoner to Limerick, from thence to Galway, and, under a charge of high treason, to Dublin.

Sidney appears to have found himself in some difficulty from the very extensive rights granted in former reigns to the ancestors of Desmond. Desmond was an earl palatine, and as such had privileges which made him little less than a sovereign, and which, within his palatinate, rendered almost every act which was requisite for the purpose of good government illegal, or of doubtful legality. This difficulty seems to have been Sidney's best excuse for appointing John of Desmond, whom he knighted on the occasion, seneschal of Desmond. He associated with him an old soldier of high character, Henry Davern, or Davels, for the name is differently written, and Andrew Skiddey. Their commission was to govern the counties of Cork, Limerick, and Kerry, during the earl's imprisonment. The earl was soon after sent into England, and Sidney pressed upon the government the necessity of appointing a president of Munster. "Desmond," said the deputy in an official letter, " is a man both void of judgment to govern, and will to be ruled. The earl of Clancare is willing enough to be ruled, but wanted a force and credit to rule." In the same communication he condemns the absurd system of keeping up dissensions among the Irish, the miserable policy which had hitherto been pursued, and which English statesmen justified to themselves by their fear that union among the Irish would lead to universal revolt.

Sir John Desmond did not disappoint the confidence which the deputy placed in him. During the few months for which he was left in power, he made reparation to the amount of three thousand pounds for injuries done by the earl. Ormonde, however, who feared that John would soon prove as troublesome as his brother, and whose interest with the queen was undiminished, found means to make such representations of Sidney's conduct in the contests and negotiations with the Desmonds, that no notice was taken, in the public dispatches addressed to him, of the victories in the north of Ireland. The war with O'Neale in Ulster was regarded in England as but a scuffle with a beggar and an outlaw, unworthy of attention. The public letters to Sidney, written under the influence of Ormonde's representations, were filled with reprimands for his endurance of the insolence of Desmond. Sidney, whose services, more particularly in his repressing the Ulster disturbances, were valued in Ireland, where the good effects of his government were felt, was offended, and earnestly entreated to be recalled;—he at length, with great difficulty, obtained permission to return to England to explain the character of his government in Ireland. He presented himself at the court of Elizabeth, attended by his prisoner the earl of Desmond, by the son of the late baron of Dungannon, by O'Conor Sligo, O'Carroll, and other chieftains of Irish birth, whom he had reduced, or won into allegiance to the queen. Dungannon and O'Carroll were favourably received, their submissions accepted, and they were permitted to return to Ireland. O'Conor was for a while confined in the Tower; but the difficulties which prevented his immediate release seem to have been merely with regard to the form of his submission, for he was soon after set at liberty. The chieftains of Irish blood and birth were in all cases distinguished from the descendants of English settlers—and O'Carroll and the others were regarded by Elizabeth as conquered enemies, or princes of barbarous tribes, negotiating with a state to which they owed no natural allegiance. The law of England was, properly speaking, the law but of the English colonists in Ireland. Even in the theoretic view of lawyers, it did not apply to any of the Irish blood, except such as from time to time purchased letters of denization, or executed deeds of submission. Thus the submission of an Irish chieftain,—his acceptance of a grant of his lands from the crown, or of an English title of honour, was in substantial effect an extension of the power of England. The English settlers and their descendants were, on the contrary, in the eye of the law, subjects of England,—colonists, who received protection from the parent state, and owed it allegiance. The Geraldines of Desmond, though in every thing they adopted the manners of the Irish among whom they lived, till they were regarded as "more Irish than the Irish," were viewed in England as rebellious subjects whom no ties of gratitude could attach—as wily traitors, who but watched their moment to disown all dependence upon England. John of Desmond was arrested and brought to London—he, with the earl, was sent to the Tower, where they endured a tedious imprisonment of two years. On the 11th July, 1570, Desmond's submission to the queen was accepted; "he laid his estate at her feet, promised to convey what parts she pleased to accept of," and acknowledged his recognisance of £20,000 to be forfeited. He and his brother were remanded to Ireland.

During Sidney's absence the disturbances in Ireland increased. Butlers and Geraldines were at their unceasing work of mutual outrage and depredation. O'Mores and O'Conors brought into the field a thousand gallowglasses, and threatened to burn Kilkenny, O'Carroll's country. The lords justices, who held the sword of state in Sidney's absence, deceived themselves by thinking they were acting with vigour in issuing proclamations against the insurgents. The proclamations but increased the evil—the government thus provoking into desperation those whom it was too weak to punish. M'Carthy, who had but lately submitted to hold his lands on an English tenure, and to accept an English title, seems to have repented him of the appearance of submission, and his acts appear almost to have been inspired by the intoxication of sudden madness. Desmond's imprisonment led him to arrogate for himself the dominion of the south of Ireland. He styled himself king of Munster, and right royally did he use his power. Assisted by O'Sullivan More and the M'Swineys, he invaded, in warlike array, and with banners displayed, the territory of the Roches. The records of the period tell of his burning the country before him, and destroying all the corn therein—of his slaughtering great numbers of men, women and children—of his returning in triumph with a prey of seven hundred sheep, fifteen hundred kine, and a hundred horses. Fitz-Maurice of Desmond was at war with Fitz-Maurice of Lixnaw— a private quarrel, but one which involved a district. In Cashel there were two competitors for the archbishoprick, and each had his advocates. James M'Caghwell had been placed there by Elizabeth— Maurice Gibbon Reagh challenged the see as appointed and consecrated to it by the pope. The Romish bull, aided by the Irish dagger, was nearly successful. Maurice,—of Cashel, that would be,—when his right was denied by the occupant of the archiepiscopal throne, rushed upon the bishop with an Irish skean or dagger, and so wounded him that his life was for a while regarded as in danger.

On Sidney's return to Dublin he convened a parliament. On the 17th of January they met. Hooker, who sat in that parliament, tells us that the scene was more like a bear-beating than a parliament of wise and grave men. The great object of assembling the legislature was to do away with the ancient customs and exactions which had for ever interfered with the influence of the English crown, and to extend the English law to districts of Ireland in which it had not yet been received. The ecclesiastical reformation of the country was also an anxious object with the government. Fierce opposition was anticipated, and means were taken to secure a majority in the lower house, which gave the opponents of the measures of government strong grounds on which to place their resistance. Writs had been directed to towns not corporate, and which had never before been summoned to return members to parliament. In many places the sheriffs and mayors of corporate towns returned themselves. A number of Englishmen were also returned, who were totally unknown to the corporations which they were said to represent; the law, it was insisted, required that they should be residents.

The country party, as they called themselves, succeeded in the two first objections. The third was, after taking the opinion of the judges, determined against them, and this left the government a sufficient number to carry their measures.

These measures appear, like all those of Sidney, to have been conceived with wisdom. The lands of O'Neale, forfeited by late treasons, were declared to be vested in the crown—many of his followers were pardoned and suffered to retain their lands, but with the incidents of English tenure. The chancellor was empowered to appoint commissioners for viewing all territories not reduced to English counties, and the deputy authorized, on their certificates, to reduce them into shires. It was also enacted, that no person should assume the Irish title or authority of chieftain or captain of his country, but by letters patent from the crown. The chief governor and council were also empowered to grant letters patent, whereby all those of the Irish or degenerate English race, who were disposed to surrender their lands, might be again invested with them, so as to hold them of the crown by English tenure. Other acts of great importance, and which prepared for the gradual civilization of Ireland, were passed in this parliament, but the distractions of the country prevented their having any immediate effect.

We pursue our narrative of the fated house of Desmond.

The early years of Elizabeth's reign were distracted by numberless conspiracies. The sentence of Rome had been twice solemnly pronounced, deciding against the validity of Henry's marriage with the mother of Elizabeth, and by necessary consequence denying her legitimacy. Elizabeth, on her sister's death, wrote to Sir Edward Carne, the English ambassador at Rome, to communicate her accession to the pope. The pontiff's reply was haughty and intemperate. He told Carne that "England was a fief of the Holy See;—that, being illegitimate, Elizabeth could not possibly inherit." Elizabeth instantly recalled her ambassador. Negotiations, however, to which England was no party, but in the result of which the fate of England and Elizabeth was supposed to be deeply involved, continued to be carried on at the papal court. The sovereigns of France and of Spain were at the time engaged in a game of diplomacy, and England was the stake for which they played. On the supposition of Elizabeth's illegitimacy, Mary Stuart, (queen of Scots,) who had been lately married to the French Dauphin, was the rightful queen of England; and on Mary of England's death, the queen of Scots and her husband assumed openly the arms of England. In this assumption they were countenanced and supported by the king of France, who was secretly soliciting a bull of excommunication against Elizabeth. Philip of Spain, the consort of the late queen of England, immediately upon her death, made proposals of marriage to Elizabeth, which it was Elizabeth's policy to allow her Roman Catholic subjects to believe were not altogether unfavourably received; and Philip had such hopes of ultimate success, that his agents were actively engaged at Rome in endeavouring to procure a dispensation to enable their master to marry his deceased wife's sister. The ecclesiastical state of England was such as to leave serious grounds of anxiety to the favourers of the doctrines of the Reformed Church. The bishops had been for the most part appointed during the reign of Mary, and so powerful was the effect of the sentence of Rome, denying the validity of Henry's marriage with Anne Bullen, that no archbishop would assist at the ceremonial of Elizabeth's coronation. It was a time when men's minds were violently agitated by controversies on subjects, the deep importance of which can never die away; and it would be injustice to the actors in the scenes which we relate, to suppress the mention of the feelings by which they were inspired, and which give their true interest to what, in the language of Milton, would otherwise be of as little moment as an account of "the battles of kites and crows." The court of Rome acted, during the pontificate of Paul and of his immediate successors, in the feeling that England might be recovered to the Catholic church. Pius IV. sent two of the order of Jesuits into Ireland as his legates, besides those whom the general of the order had already placed there. Those whom Pius chose for this delicate mission were men of opposite characters: Paschase Broet was remarkable for serenity of temper, great cheerfulness, open candour, and steady prudence—qualities which had won the regard of Loyola, who named the young enthusiast his angel; Alphonso Salmeron was the other, described as powerful of voice and pen—a fiery champion of the church. These missionaries are described as acting with the enthusiasm of young and ardent devotees against the efforts of the English to introduce the doctrines of the reformation into Ireland. In a plausible document which praises their zeal, they are described as exciting insurrection wherever they went; "their exertions," it is mildly said, "became dangerous to those whom they attached to their cause." The view which was taken of their conduct in England is thus recorded in a document of the state council of the period: "What an abuse is this to bear us in hand that no harm is meant by the pope, when already he hath done as much as in him lieth to hurt us; the pope, even at this instant, hath his legate in Ireland, who is already joined with certain traitors there, and occupied in stirring a rebellion."*

We have already described the distractions of the south of Ireland. In such circumstances as Munster was now placed by the absence of Desmond, and by the want of any effective power of control in the lords justices, it is not astonishing that the disaffected there, having strong bonds of union with the continental states in their common hostility to the doctrines of the reformation, should look abroad for assistance; and accordingly we find swarms of Irish adventurers, at this period, in every court in Europe. France, Spain, and Rome, seemed to listen to every tale that gave them the hope, with Irish aid, to recover England to the Holy See. In addition to the military adventurers, whom the love of excitement, and the hope of interesting foreign powers by the proofs which they were able to bring of the certainty of support from Ireland in any meditated invasion of the British dominions, the state of ecclesiastical affairs in Ireland created another body of residents from that country in the courts of every country which remained united to the Papal See. As soon as Elizabeth had declared for the reformation, the bishops appointed in Mary's reign, who refused to conform to the new arrangements, were displaced. Their ecclesiastical title of bishops still remained, and they continued to style themselves bishops of the sees to which they had been consecrated, but from which they were forced to remove. As

* Sharon Turner's Elizabeth. Lord Somers's Tracts.

vacancies in church dignities occurred by death, Elizabeth filled the places with churchmen favourable to the reformed doctrines; and the papal court, denying her right, appointed to the same dioceses bishops of its own. The Romish claimants of episcopal rank and authority resided abroad, and were active agents of the disaffected in Ireland. While Desmond was still a prisoner in the Tower, the earl of Clancare, James Fitz-Maurice, M'Donough Carthy, and others, held a meeting in Kerry, from whence they dispatched their bishops of Emley and Cashel for aid to the king of Spain, "to reform religion," and the immediate result of the mission was a supply, from the king of Spain, of a thousand targets, a great number of sword-blades, harquebusses, and other weapons.* The insurrections in Ireland during the early years of Elizabeth's reign, frantic as they may seem, if regarded as the rebellion of Irish clans against the sovereignty of England, were far from being such rash enterprises. Ireland was but one of the fields of battle, on which the great powers of Europe seemed disposed to try the question of the right to the crown of England. The bull of excommunication which all Catholic princes were invited to execute, had been already issued against Elizabeth. The same policy, which in a few years after fitted out the Armada, from the moment when Philip had lost all hopes of obtaining England by marriage, animated the counsels of Spain. Looking at the history of those times from the vantage-ground of the present, we feel that the heart of England being with Elizabeth, there could have been but little chance of a successful invasion; but, dignified as her bearing was, and well calculated to inspire the continental nations with that awe of England which they have since learned, there was much at the moment to alarm—much to create great doubt as to the event. The interests of religion at stake gave a character of sublimity to the contest, not less likely to affect those who regarded the reformation as a violent disruption of Christian unity, than the advocates of the reformed doctrines. The language of detestation in which Elizabeth is spoken of, both in the papal bulls and in the writings of the Roman Catholics of the period, is evidence of the intensity of feeling under which men acted at the time.

The agents of Spain practised successfully on the mind of James Fitz-Maurice, whom the imprisonment of his kinsman, the earl, had at once irritated, and inspired with the hope of succeeding to the vast estates and power of the family. James Fitz-Maurice O'Desmond, as his name is sometimes written, was the son of Sir Maurice Fitz-Gerald, *the Black*, as he was called, or more often *the Murderer*, from his having slain James, the thirteenth earl. Between Fitz-Maurice and the title of Desmond, according to the English laws of succession, there were none except the earl and his brothers. In more peaceful times, wilder dreams of succeeding to property less important have been indulged and realised. Fitz-Maurice, a faithful clansman, was yet one of a family seeking to assimilate themselves to Irish habits and manners, and if the law of tanistry, which on the vacancy of the chieftainry by death or otherwise, gave the sovereignty over the family to

* Sidney's Letters.

the most worthy of the name and blood, suggested to him the hope of attaining this honour; and even before the death of Desmond, it was but the natural suggestion of the circumstances in which he was placed. He was a man of popular talents, and as it answered his purposes, he courted popularity; "a deep dissembler, passing subtile, and able to compass any matter he took in hand, courteous, valiant, expert in martial affairs," ardently attached to his views of religion. Such is the character which Hooker, a writer not willing to allow any merit to the unhappy Geraldines, gives to this distinguished man, who squandered his talents and his life in these miserable wars.

The communications of the insurgents in the south of Ireland with Spain were soon learned by the government. The lord-deputy at once proclaimed them traitors, and prepared for an expedition against them. Sir Peter Carew, who commanded at Kilkenny, made the first assault against the insurgents by taking Cloughgrennan, a castle of Sir Edmond Butler's, which he gave to be plundered by his soldiers. He returned to Kilkenny, and was not many days there when, as he was walking in his garden, he was fired at by a man of the earl of Ormonde's. More surprise is expressed at the incident than ought to have been felt. While Carew remained at Kilkenny, news was brought him that the rebels were encamped in great numbers three miles from the town. Carew held a council with his officers, and they agreed to send out to ascertain the truth of the matter. Henry Davels, an "honest and a valiant English gentleman,"* who had served long in Ireland, and whose marriage connected him with Kilkenny, was appointed to this service. From an eminence near the town he espied a company of about two thousand men resting upon a little hill in the middle of a plain, being all armed and marching in battle array. When he returned with this report, Carew directed Captain Gilbert to charge them. Gilbert, with Davels and twelve others of the company, galloped before the rest and gave the charge. Carew followed so near "that all the company, even as it were at one instant, gave the like charge." Four hundred Irish soldiers were slain in the first onset; most of the remainder were butchered in their flight to the neighbouring mountains—" of her majesty's side no one man was slain."

Sir Peter Carew returned to Kilkenny exulting in this victory. Hooker describes every captain and soldier of his company as carrying two gallowglasses' axes in his hands, which they brought home as the spoils of a vanquished enemy. " The townsmen of Kilkenny were very sorry for the slaughter of so many men." It seems difficult to believe this utter destruction of nearly two thousand men in arms without the loss of one man on the part of the conqueror. That many of the Irish were surprised and slaughtered appears certain, and the maddened natives were, ere long, in the field seeking bloody revenge. They besieged Kilkenny. The town was garrisoned and well defended, and the disappointed insurgents burned and plundered the small towns and villages in the open country. They overran and spoiled the county of Waterford, and even of Dublin. After "they had taken

* Hooker.

their pleasure in this country," they went to the county of Wexford. Ruffian outrages, committed at the fair of Enniscorthy, are particularly recorded—violation of women, and unsparing slaughters—from thence they went into Ossory and the Queen's County, and ravaged the country. In Ossory they met with the earl of Clancare and Fitz-Maurice, with whom they combined. They made arrangements for procuring aid from Scotland, and sending new messengers to the pope, and the king of Spain. All Ireland, with the exception of the English pale, is described as "imbrued and infected with this rebellion."

The earl of Ormonde, who was in England during the commencement of these disturbances, did what he could to satisfy the queen that the danger was not so great as it appeared; his own high sense of loyalty was deeply offended by his brothers' participating in the outrages; he pleaded for them with the queen, and besought her permission to serve in Ireland against them, if he could not otherwise reclaim them to allegiance. Elizabeth, who doubted not the good faith of the earl, confided to him the important trust which he sought. He arrived at Wexford on the 14th of August, 1569, the very day on which the frightful outrages were committed at the fair of Enniscorthy. Sidney had already gone down to the south, by his presence "to encourage the well affected, and to terrify the enemies of government." Ormonde found him encamped near Limerick, and brought with him his brother, Edmond Butler, in bonds. The first show of activity on the part of government was sufficient to disunite the insurgents. The earl of Clancare, who had so lately styled himself king of Munster, falling upon his knees, acknowledged his treason, and prayed her majesty's pardon, and surrendered his eldest son as a hostage to insure his fidelity. O'Brien, earl of Thomond, still held out; but on hearing of the approach of Ormonde's army, he fled to France. Through the intervention of Norris, the English ambassador at that court, he afterwards obtained his pardon.

In 1570, presidency courts of Munster and Connaught were established, in pursuance of Sidney's earnest recommendation. Sir John Perrot was the first president of Munster. He was reputed to be the natural son of Henry VIII., and to have inherited much of his father's character. From whatever source he may have derived his blood, he inherited from the Pembrokeshire family, whose name he bore, considerable revenues;—he was not only wealthy, "but" says Hooker, "valiant and of great magnanimity, and so much the more meet to govern and tame so faithless and unruly a people as those over whom he was made ruler." The president's authority was, in his own district, all but absolute. He had power of life and death, was attended with armed guards of horse and foot, and his patent gave him the command of all the military forces in the province. Like the viceroy, he could confer the honour of knighthood. With the assistance of his chief justice and second justice, he had authority to hear and determine all complaints, to hold commissions of oyer and terminer and gaol delivery, and to hold his courts where he thought proper. All persons who had not freehold property worth five pounds a-year, or personal property of ten pounds, might be tried for any offence with which they were charged, by martial law; and the president had authority to call on any loyal subject to assist him in prosecuting rebels with fire and sword. He could hear and decide all complaints against officers, civil and military, throughout his province, and punish the offenders at his discretion. His authority extended to putting persons, accused of high treason, to torture for the purpose of extracting confessions of guilt or accusations of their accomplices. He had also the right of reprieving all condemned persons. In short, in his own district, he had all the powers of viceroy. Like the viceroy, he had his council and his staff of officers, civil and military.* Perrot, says Hooker, was well acquainted with the character of the people among whom he was to serve; he knew that he " had to do with a sort of nettles, whose nature is, that being handled gently they sting, but being hard crushed together, they will do no harm." " The sword, and the law," he adds, " were the foundation of his government: by the one he persecuted the rebel and disobedient, and by the other he ruled and governed in justice and judgment." The reduction of the rebels was necessarily the first of these duties, and never were unfortunate men followed by keener bloodhounds than those that pursued the wretched inhabitants of Desmond's territories. Perrot followed and chased them through all their hiding places: " in the bogs he pursued them, in the thickets he followed them, in the plains he fought with them, and in their castles and holds he besieged them." Fitz-Maurice, at last, tired and wearied out with this unremitting chase, was obliged to surrender. He flung himself at the feet of the president in Kilmallock, which town he had a few months preceding burnt and plundered, having executed the sovereign and several of the townsmen.† He made his submission in the church, in the sight of all the people, kneeling before Perrot, who held the point of his sword to Fitz-Maurice's heart. This painful humiliation was intended to express that he owed his life to the mercy of the queen. Perrot, though he held out hopes of pardon to Fitz-Maurice, retained him as a prisoner—his followers he executed in great numbers. When order was in some degree restored, he made circuits through Munster, and held sessions and courts, and in a short time restored such confidence or inspired such fear that, " whereas, no man could before pass through the country without danger of being robbed or murdered, and no man durst turn his cattle into the fields without

* We transcribe Fynes Morrison's statement of the expense of the presidency of Munster in the year 1598. The scale of expense in Perrot's time was not probably materially different:—

President's salary	£133	6 9
His diet with the Council at his table	520	0 0
Retinue of 20 foot and 30 horse	803	0 0
Chief Justice	100	0 0
Second Justice	66	13 4
Queen's Attorney	13	6 8
Clerk of Council	20	0 0
Clerk of Crown	20	0 0
Serjeant-at-Arms	20	0 0
Provost Martial	255	10 0
	£1951	16 6

† Smith's History of Kerry.

watch; now every man with a white stick only in his hand, and with great treasures, might, and did travel without fear or danger where he would, and the white sheep did keep the black, and all the beasts lay continually in the fields without any stealing or preying."*

Among the more anxious cares of the president, it is not without surprise that we find his attention directed to assimilating the dress of the Irish to English forms and patterns. If the cloak of the Irish peasant could be converted to one-half the uses which Spenser ascribes to it: a bed by night—a tent by day—and defending the wearer alike from the inconveniences of heat and cold—we are not surprised that all the efforts of legislation failed to make the Irish give up a garment so suitable to their uncertain climate, and to their mode of life, which exposed them with little other shelter to its many changes. The war against their costume, and their modes of wearing the hair, which afterwards occupied the statesmen of James the First's time, was now earnestly fought by Perrot. He dealt with the disobedient in such matters as with traitors against the queen; and though in the parts of the country where his authority was absolute, in spite of a thousand capricious changes of fashion among the higher classes, the dress of the peasant still exhibits traces of the proscribed costume, yet he was for the time delighted with the effect of the reformation which he introduced;— " he suffered," says Hooker, " no glibs nor the like usages of the Irishry to be used among the men, nor the Egyptiacal rolls upon women's heads to be worn, whereat, though the ladies and gentlewomen were somewhat grieved, yet they yielded, and giving the same over, did wear hats after the English manner."

Soon after the establishment of this presidency court in Munster, Sidney was succeeded as deputy by Sir William Fitz-William. The favourite project of the age was the plantation of English settlers in such lands as by forfeiture became vested in the crown. A settlement of this kind had been attempted with strong prospects of success, at Ardes, in the county of Down. The appearance of prosperity was such as for a while to deceive the colonists; but the project was abandoned in consequence of the assassination of the son of Sir Thomas Smith, the originator of the plan. A more extensive effort at colonisation was soon after undertaken by Walter Devereux, lately created earl of Essex, on the district of Ulster, called Clan-hu-boy, which became vested in the queen by the forfeiture of the O'Neale's. Jealousies between the lord-deputy and Essex delayed and finally defeated this proposed settlement. The Irish chieftains were maddened by the fear of projects which seemed to aim not alone at the diminution of their power, but at the utter extirpation and very extinction of their race; and the country, which Sidney had left in seeming quiet, again exhibited every where turbulence and disaffection. At this eventful moment the earl of Desmond, and his brother Sir John of Desmond, who had been sent from England as prisoners of state to Dublin, contrived to escape from their imprisonment. After being detained for several months in the castle of Dublin, they were given to the custody of the mayor. Their custody was not strict, and in a hunting party they contrived to distance mayor, aldermen

* Hooker.

and constables, and make their escape into Munster. The mayor described them as having broken their parole of honour. They had a story of their own: they said, and possibly believed, that it was intended to waylay and murder them,—that flight was their only security.

On Desmond's escape, a proclamation was issued, declaring him a traitor—a reward of £1000 with £40 a-year was offered to any one who should bring him in alive, and £500 and £20 a-year pension to him who should bring in his head.

Immediately on his arrival in Munster, a confederacy was entered into between him and his principal adherents, who bound themselves by oath neither to spare life or fortune in his defence. They signed an engagement to this effect on the 18th of July, 1574. Letters too were about this time intercepted from the pope, exhorting the Irish to persevere in their opposition to the government of the heretical queen, promising supplies of arms and money, with such plenary indulgences to the champions of this holy war, as were usually granted to the armies of the faithful warring against infidels, and promises of absolution to themselves and their posterity to the third generation.* Desmond, however, found the means of quieting the suspicions of the government as they felt themselves unprepared for active measures against him. He was permitted to renew his engagements of submission and allegiance, and on Perrot's being recalled from the presidentship of Munster, he was appointed one of the council to assist his successor, Sir William Drury. Fitz-William was now recalled, and Sidney again bore the sword of state with increased powers, and with an assurance of an annual remittance of twenty thousand pounds in aid of the ordinary revenues of Ireland. A plague which raged in Dublin, and the disturbances in Ulster, made him proceed to that province before going to the capital. His presence restored tranquillity. He continued his circuit through the other provinces, and, with a force of but six hundred men, without encountering the slightest opposition, suppressed all appearances at least of disaffection. In his progress through the south he lodged three nights at Dungarvan castle, to which place the earl of Desmond came to him and humbly offered him any service he was able to do the queen. From Dungarvan, Sidney passed into Sir John of Desmond's country, in the county of Cork. From Sir John of Desmond's he arrived at Lord Barry's; and, on the 23d of December, reached Cork, where he was received with every demonstration of joy. The earls of Desmond, of Thomond, and of Clancare, waited upon him in Cork, with the bishops of Cashel, Cork, and Ross; viscounts Barry and Roche; the barons de Courcy, Lixnaw, Dunboyne, Power, Barry-Oge, and Lowth; Sir Donald M'Carthy, Reagh of Carbery, and Sir Cormac Teige M'Carthy of Muskerry; the latter "the rarest man for obedience to the queen, and to her laws, and disposition for civility, that he had met among the Irishry."

He was also attended by Sir Owen O'Sullivan, and the son and heir of O'Sullivan More, his father being too old and infirm to attend; by O'Carroll of Ely O'Carroll, and M'Donough, each of whom, he, says, might for his lands rank with any baron of England or Ireland.†

* Leland.—Phelan. † Colins's State Letters.

O'Mahon, and O'Driscol, each of whom had lands enough to live like a knight in England, attended, and the sons of M'Auliffe and O'Callaghan represented their aged fathers. Sir Maurice Fitz-Gerald of the Decies, and Sir Theobald Butler of Cahir, were there. Some worthies of more doubtful character and aspect made their bow at these crowded levees. Five brothers, and three sons of two other brothers, all captains of gallowglasses, armed in mail and bassenet, holding in their hands weapons like the axes of the Tower,* the M'Swineys, whose enmity was dreaded, and whose friendship was courted by the greatest men of the province, stood like Indian warriors offering the service of their axes to the deputy. In the same circle stood Arundels, Rochforts, Barrets, Flemings, Lombards, Terrys, eyeing the M'Swineys with well-merited distrust. These were men of English descent, whose ancestors had lived like gentlemen and knights, but who were ruined by the oppressive wars of the greater potentates and the plunders of the M'Swineys. All spoke with detestation, real or affected, of their barbarous mode of living. They offered fealty to her majesty, surrendered their lands to her, and agreed to hold them by English tenure. All these lords, with their ladies, attended Sidney during the Christmas at Cork, and "kept very plentiful and hospitable houses." It was a period of confidence and festivity. Sessions of gaol delivery were held from the morrow after twelfth day to the end of January. The dignity of the law was sustained by the execution of several notable malefactors, and the attainder of some of the principal persons engaged in the late disturbances. Sidney next visited Limerick, where he was received with greater magnificence than he had before witnessed in Ireland. Numbers of the principal inhabitants of Limerick and the neighbouring counties, both those of English descent and the aboriginal Irish, repaired to meet him. They complained of the waste and misery occasioned by their great men; they entreated him for English forces to protect them, and English sheriffs to execute the laws. They also sought permission to surrender their lands and to hold them of the queen. The counties of Kerry and Tipperary, being palatinate counties, he did not visit; but in the letter from which we make these extracts, he states, in the strongest manner, his conviction that no perfect reformation could exist in Munster till the privileges claimed by the earls palatine were abolished, and the grants resumed.

Drury did not wait for the slow process of legislation, or for any formal resumption of the grants; he disregarded the old patents under which Desmond claimed his privileges, and determined, as lord-president of Munster, to hold his courts within the privileged territories, which had become a sanctuary for every malefactor who sought to escape justice. Desmond resisted, and with warmth pleaded his palatine rights. When he found resistance useless, he spoke of an appeal to the lord-deputy, and still protesting against the usurpation, said, that as the lord-president was determined to hold his court in Kerry, it was his duty respectfully to submit, and he invited Drury, when his progress led him through that part of Kerry, to reside in his castle at

* Sentleger.

Tralee. Drury was unsuspicious, and he travelled through the country with an attendance of but six or seven score men. As he approached the castle of Tralee, he was astonished to behold a body of seven or eight hundred armed men, who shouted violently as the president's little party approached. It was a moment of serious alarm, and the president, having consulted with his company, charged the armed party, who in the instant retired and dispersed among the woods, without returning the charge. The countess of Desmond soon after approached. She assured the president that the body of men whom he supposed to be enemies had never intended hostilities, that the shouts which he mistook for battle-cries were the national mode of welcome; that the earl had assembled his principal friends and retainers to greet the lord-president; and that they were assembled to entertain him with the sport of hunting—the favourite pastime of the country. Drury believed, or affected to believe this account of the matter, which was probably true. He accepted the hospitality of the earl, but pursued his determination, and held his courts and sessions through the whole of the earl's palatinate.

Desmond's complaint had the show, perhaps the reality, of right, though in favour of Drury it must be said that in the original patent creating the palatinate certain pleas were reserved to the crown, and only cognizable by the king's judges. Desmond, too, on his late submission, had made an absolute surrender of all his lands to the queen, with promises to execute any conveyances she might direct of them. Fierce hostility, however, against Drury, was the result of the experiment made of invading the earl's territory.

The negotiations of the discontented in Ireland with the continental states, did not cease during this troubled time. Stukely, an adventurer of English birth, a man of profligate habits and desperate fortunes, was actively engaged at the court of Rome, and the writers who relate the events of this period tell us that he succeeded in persuading Gregory the XIII., who was then supreme pontiff, that nothing could be easier than to obtain the throne of Ireland for an Italian nobleman, the nephew or son* of Gregory. The invasion and conquest of Ireland was to be the work of Spain. When this island was won, the rest of her dominions might soon be torn from Elizabeth, and the crown of England was to be Philip's reward. Eight hundred Italians were raised for this service, and placed under Stukely's command. They were to be paid by the king of Spain. Gregory, who seems already to have regarded Ireland as his own, had the audacity to confer upon Stukely the titles of Marquis of Leinster and earl of Wexford and Carlow. The impression of Stukely's military talents was such as to occasion considerable alarm to the government. All danger, however, from that quarter was soon at an end. He had embarked at Civita Vecchia, and arrived at Lisbon at the time when Sebastian was setting out on the romantic African expedition which had such a disastrous termination. Sebastian succeeded in persuading him to join him in this expedition, promising that on their return he would assist in the invasion of Ireland. The consent of the king of Spain was easily obtained to this arrangement. Stukely fought gallantly at

* Hume calls him his *nephew*, Cox, Leland, Phelan, and Sharon Turner, *his son*.

Alcazar, holding in his hand the banner of Portugal; but was, on the day of battle, murdered by the Italian soldiers whom he had involved in this unfortunate adventure.* A cloud which has never been dispersed rests upon the fate of Sebastian.

At the same time that Stukely was engaged in his negotiations with Rome, Fitz-Maurice, burning with indignation at the humiliating condition to which he had been exposed by Drury, repaired first to Spain, and afterwards to the court of France, and urged upon Henry with anxiety the invasion of Ireland. After two years of lingering expectation he was contemptuously dismissed by the king with a promise that he would intercede with the queen of England for his pardon. He left France and returned to Spain, where his communications were better received. Philip sent him to the pope. Saunders, an English ecclesiastic, distinguished for his hatred of the reformed doctrines, and Allen, an Irish Jesuit, were able to satisfy the pope of the probable success of an Irish insurrection. A banner exhibiting the arms of the holy see, was consecrated with many religious ceremonies, and delivered to Fitz-Maurice. Proclamations were issued, addressed to the people of Ireland, in which Elizabeth was described as "that evil woman who has departed from the Lord, and the Lord from her."† An expedition was resolved upon at once. About fourscore Spaniards, and some English and Irish fugitives, with Allen and Saunders, embarked with Fitz-Maurice. Saunders was appointed legate by Gregory. They landed in the beginning of July, 1579, at Smerwicke, or St Marywicke, on the western coast of Kerry, and built a fort in the west side of the bay. "The two doctors," says Hooker, "hallowed the place" after the manner of their religion, and assured the invaders that no enemy should dare to come upon them, "and yet," he adds, "they were beguiled." A ship of war, commanded by a Devonshire man, Thomas Courtenay, was at the time lying in the bay of Kinsale. Henry Davels, a name that has before occurred and must again be mentioned in this narrative, suggested to Courtenay the practicability of taking the three vessels in which the Spaniards had arrived, which were at anchor near Smerwicke. The wind was favourable. Courtenay doubled the point of land and succeeded in taking the vessels, thus cutting off from the invaders all power of retreat. Intelligence of their landing was soon communicated to John and James of Desmond, the earl's brothers, and through them to the whole country. They had looked for the return of Fitz-Maurice, and immediately repaired to him with all their tenants and retainers. The earl, on hearing that the Spaniards had landed, made immediate preparations to resist them, and wrote to the earl of Clancare to assemble such forces as he could command, and join him in attacking the enemy at Smerwicke. M'Carthy came, but seeing reason to distrust the earl's sincerity, he ceased to act with him, and dismissed his company.

Sidney had left Ireland in the May of the preceding year, and Drury, the late president of Munster, held the office of lord-justice. As Sidney entered the vessel which was to convey him to England, he was heard to recite, in a lamenting tone, the words with which the hundred and fourteenth Psalm commences:—" *When Israel went out*

---

* Evans's old ballads, vol. ii. † Phelan's Remains, Vol. ii.

of Egypt, the house of Jacob from a people of a strange language," &c. A wiser or a better man than Sidney never held in Ireland the perilous and thankless office of viceroy. But our immediate task is the biography of Desmond, and other opportunities will occur in the course of our work to exhibit the sound policy of the course of government which he sought to establish. "The Romish cocatrice," says Hooker, "which had long sat upon her eggs, had now hatched her chickens." By this metaphor does he describe the religious insurrections in the south of Ireland. When Drury learned that Fitz-Maurice had landed with his Spaniards, he ordered Henry Davels to summon Desmond and his brothers to prepare themselves to assist him in attacking the fort at Smerwicke. Davels, after an interview with the Desmonds, inspected the fort, and returned to the earl endeavouring to persuade him that it could be easily taken. The earl's heart, it would seem, was with the Spaniards, and on one pretence or another he declined the service. "My shot," said the earl, "is more meet to shoot at wild fowl, than to adventure such a piece of service. My gallowglasses are good men to encounter with gallowglasses, and not to answer old soldiers."

Davels and Carter, the provost martial, who accompanied him on this errand, took leave of the earl on their return to the lord-justice. They rested for the night near Desmond's castle of Tralee, in a victualling-house or wine tavern; the house being strong and defensible.* Their servants were dispersed wherever they could find lodgings in the adjoining town. John of Desmond had secretly followed Davels to Tralee, and bribed the person in whose house he lodged to leave the gates and doors open. Davels and Carter, suspecting nothing, retired to their beds. At midnight they were suddenly awakened from sleep by the glare of lights, and the voices of men in their chamber, with swords drawn. When Davels recognised John of Desmond, his confidence was for a moment restored—for he and John of Desmond had been for a long time to all appearance attached friends. During the earlier part of the earl's imprisonment, Davels had been associated with Sir John in the temporary government of the earl's territories. He had assisted him in the various exigencies in which his turbulent spirit for ever involved him—had with his money released him from prison more than once, and was even the means of saving his life when charged with capital crimes. The relation between them seemed to be that of father and adopted child, "*My son,*" said Davels, "what is the matter?" The answer of Desmond was, "no more of *son,* no more of *father;* make thyself ready, for die thou shalt;" and immediately he and his men struck at Davels and Carter, and murdered them. The strange motive assigned for this fiendish atrocity, by all the writers who record it, is that the Spaniards were distrustful of the sincerity of the Desmonds—and that John committed this dreadful act to prove to them that he was pledged to their cause, as far as utter hopelessness of reconciliation with the government, which such an act would render impossible, could pledge him.

* Hooker. Other writers describe the murder as taking place in the castle of Tralee.

Fitz-Maurice, when he heard of the manner of Davels' death, was shocked. To murder a man naked in his bed, "when he might have had advantage of him, either by the highways or otherwise, to his commendation," was not consistent with Fitz-Maurice's notions of fair dealing with either friend or enemy. The earl, too, was grieved and offended, and it was thought that this act would separate him for ever from his brother; but the earl was the weakest of men, and seems to have been a mere instrument in the hands of others. At this time there was with him an Englishman, Applesby, whom the fate of Davels taught apprehension for himself. He succeeded in persuading the earl to retire to his castle of Askeaton, in the county of Limerick, there to wait the lord-justice's arrival, and to join with him in serving against the insurgents. The earl followed the advice so far as removing to Askeaton, where "he lay close and did nothing." He affected to disapprove of Fitz-Maurice's doings, but did nothing to discountenance his followers from joining his standard. The Spaniards, in spite of numbers of the country people repairing to Smerwicke, felt that they were not supported as they had been given reason to hope—and Fitz-Maurice found some difficulty in keeping them together. He determined to see what his own presence would do in rousing the disaffected in Ulster and Connaught, and with this view left the fort, telling the Spaniards that he would first go to Holy Cross, in Tipperary, to perform a vow made by him in Spain. Journeying with three or four horsemen and a dozen kernes, he passed through the county of Limerick and came into the country of Sir William de Burgo, his kinsman, and who had joined actively with him in the insurrection of a few years before. Fitz-Maurice's horses were fatigued, and could go no farther; he seized some which he saw ploughing in a field and pressed them into his service. The horses were De Burgo's, whose sons, as soon as they heard of this depredation, pursued Fitz-Maurice's party. A quarrel ensued, and the skirmish became earnest and furious. Two of the De Burgos were slain—and Fitz-Maurice, shot with a bullet through the head, shared their fate. The loyal indignation of the lord-justice was wasted on the corse of Fitz-Maurice. The dead body was exposed on a gibbet, and the head set over one of the town gates of Kilmallock. The queen wrote to Sir William de Burgo a letter of thanks and of condolence—and created him baron of Castle Connell. De Burgo was old and feeble; and the emotion of these events was more than he could bear. He fainted while reading the queen's letter, and died soon after.

On the death of Fitz-Maurice, Sir John Desmond assumed the command of the Spaniards at Smerwicke—and soon afterwards had letters from Rome, appointing him general in the place of Fitz-Maurice. Drury, on hearing of the murder of Davels, marched to the south. His whole disposable force was four hundred foot, and two hundred horse. He had with him of Englishmen, Sir Nicholas Malbie; Wingfield, master of the ordnance; Waterhouse, Fitton, and Masterson. Some of the Irish lords, who brought forces of their own, accompanied him. They were the earl of Kildare; Sir Lucas Dillon, chief baron; lord Mountgarret, the baron of Upper Ossory, and the baron of Dunboyne. They brought about two hundred horsemen, besides footmen and kernes. They marched by as rapid journies as they could till they came to Kilmallock, where they encamped. Drury wrote to the earl of Desmond and the chief persons in the neighbourhood, calling upon them to assist him.

The earl came to Drury's camp, with a formidable company of both horse and foot. Suspicions, however, of his loyalty arose of such a kind, that Drury committed him to the custody of the knight marshal. He made new protestations and promises, and was released from custody.

The earl was scarcely at freedom, when news was brought to Drury that John of Desmond was encamped with a great company of rebels, upon the borders of Slievelogher. For nine weeks he left the royal army no rest either night or day, and on one occasion succeeded in cutting off two parties of one hundred men each, under the command of Captains Herbert and Price; Price and Herbert were both slain. Additional forces arrived from England, and Sir John Perrot, the late president, landed at Cork, with six ships of war to guard the coast, and deprive the rebels of all foreign assistance. The earl of Desmond no sooner obtained his liberty, than he separated from Drury, sending occasional letters, but avoiding to give any assistance. The countess of Desmond waited upon Drury, pleading in behalf of her husband, and she placed in his hands her only son, as a hostage for the earl's fidelity. This campaign was too much for Drury's health; he placed the command of the army in the hands of Sir Nicholas Malbie, and went by easy stages to Waterford; Drury felt that he was dying; his last act was an effort to serve the queen by encouraging as far he could the officers sent with Perrot to active exertion. At Kilmallock he had bestowed the honour of knighthood on Bourchier, Stanley, Carew, Moore, and he now almost at the moment of death gave the same honour to Pelham, Gorges, Thomas Perrot, son and heir of Sir John Perrot, and to Patrick Welsh, mayor of Waterford.

Malbie's first act, after Drury's retirement to Waterford, was to send for the earl of Desmond, who received his letters, and on one frivolous pretence or another, refused to leave his castle of Askeaton, whither he had again retreated. Malbie, on finding all applications to the earl were worse than fruitless, abandoned him to his inevitable fate. Malbie had great experience in military affairs, "having served under sundry kings and in strange nations." A student—a traveller, and an observer—how contrasted with the feeble and irresolute Desmond, who thought that his shallow artifices were deceiving him! His forces consisted of one hundred and fifty horse and nine hundred foot. He sent Bourchier, Dowdal, and Sentleger, to Kilmallock, with three hundred foot and fifty horse, to garrison that well fortified and well situated town, the importance of possessing which was felt alike by both parties; with the rest of his company he marched to the city of Limerick, to recruit his harassed soldiers. He again sent to Desmond, but with the same unsatisfactory result. The same shallow duplicity still marked all the earl's answers.

Malbie was encamped in the fields near Limerick, when intelligence was brought him that the rebel camp was at Connillo, some eight or nine miles off; he marched towards them, and "being come to an abbey called Manisternenagh, seven miles from Limerick, there appeared a great company in a plain field, both of horsemen and footmen, in estimation two thousand or thereabouts, marching in battle array, and had cast out their wings of shot, and placed every thing very well and orderly." Malbie soon made his disposition to give them battle. John of Desmond, who was at the head of the insurgent's army, wished to avoid an engagement, but the ecclesiastic Allen, encouraged him with assurances of miraculous aid and certain victory. Sir John displayed the papal banner, placed his men, horse and foot, to the best advantage. In disposing his men, and making arrangements for the battle, he was assisted by the experience of the Spanish officers, who had by this time abandoned their fort at Smerwicke, and were employed in fortifying Desmond's castles, and disciplining his army for the field.

"The governor," we borrow Hooker's language, "setteth onwards and giveth the onset upon them with his shot, who valiantly resisted the first and second volées, and answered the fight very well, even the couching of the pikes, that the matter stood very doubtful. But the Englishmen so fiercely and desperately set upon them with the third volée, that they were discomfited, and had the overthrow given them, and fled. John of Desmond put spurs to his horse, showing a fair pair of heels, which was better to him than two pair of hands." Two hundred of his men were slain, and among them Allen.

The earl of Desmond, and the baron of Lixnaw, viewed the engagement from a wooded eminence, which, in memory of the day, with reference to the original meaning of the word Tory, is called Tory Hill.

The patience of the English government with individuals seems as remarkable as their determination to rule the nation according to their own notions of policy. For certainly the engagements made by the Irish nobles, whether of English or native descent, were seldom entered into with good faith. Lixnaw's son had an office in the court of Elizabeth, and was now in Ireland on a visit to his father. His assistance was given to the rebels. We preserve the language of provocation into which one of the historians of the period is excited. "He was no sooner come home, than away with his English attire, and on with his brogs, his shirt, and other Irish rags, being become as very a traitor as the veriest knave of them all, and so for the most part they are all, as daily experience teacheth, dissemble they never so much to the contrary. For like as Jupiter's cat, let her be transformed to never so fair a lady, and let her be never so well attired, and accompanied with the best ladies, let her be never so well esteemed and honoured, yet if the mouse come once in her sight, she will be a cat and show her kind."

The earl, when the victory was decided, wrote letters of congratulation to Malbie, which were coldly answered; a personal interview was requested, which Desmond still evaded. In a few days he learned that papers had been found on Allen's person which left no doubt of the earl's participation in the treason of his brothers. Detection rendered him desperate. He attacked the English camp at Rathkeale, in person, on two successive nights, and lost several of his people. Even after this, Malbie wrote to him, conjuring him to return to his allegiance. He replied, "that he owed no allegiance to the queen, and would no longer yield her obedience," and proceeded to fortify his castles of

Askeaton and Carrigfoile. Malbie garrisoned Rathkeale, and proceeded to attack Askeaton, when news was brought of Drury's death, which terminated Malbie's deputed authority.

Sir William Pelham succeeded Drury as lord-justice. The earl of Ormonde was appointed governor of Munster. Pelham immediately proceeded to the disturbed districts, and summoned Desmond to meet him at Cashel. Desmond did not attend, but sent his countess with some vague excuse. A council was called, and it was agreed that Ormonde should confer with the earl, and require his distinct answer to the following propositions:—

1st, That he should deliver up Doctor Saunders and the Spaniards.

2d, That he should deliver up either the castle of Askeaton, or of Carrigfoile, as a pledge of his good behaviour.

3dly, That he submit himself and his cause to the judgment of her majesty and council in England, or to the lord-justice and council in Ireland.

4thly, That he assist and aid the earl of Ormonde in prosecuting the war against his brothers and other traitors.

The interview was unavailing. Desmond's replies were evasive, and his only object seemed to be delay. Pelham then published a proclamation, declaring Desmond a traitor; lords Gormanstown and Delvin refused to sign the proclamation, for which they were afterwards severely reprimanded by the government of England.* Within an hour after the proclamation was issued, the countess of Desmond came to the camp, but the camp was already broken up, and Ormonde's soldiers were destroying before them whatever fire and sword could consume. The day the earl was proclaimed, he had already set up his standard at Ballyhowra, in the county of Cork. This place, which we call by its Irish name, is part of the mountain range which Spenser, who came over as secretary to lord Grey of Wilton, the next lord-deputy, has rendered familiar to the English reader by the name of *Mole*. Desmond attacked and plundered Youghal, which he kept possession of for five days. The Irish annalists, disposed as they are to defend every act of his, describe him as not sparing even the churches; they tell of his soldiers "polluting and defiling whatever was most sacred, bringing every thing to utter confusion and desolation, and making havoc as well of sacred vestments and chalices as of any other chattels." The Spaniards in Desmond's army were shocked at this wicked exploit, perceiving by the furniture and ornaments of the churches that the townsmen were all Catholics. They refrained from plunder, and were reproved by their Irish companions in arms; they answered, that they ought not to rob better Christians than themselves. "One of the Spaniards cut his cloak as St Martin did, in five parts, and distributed the same on five children that were stripped of their cloathes, and left naked by some of the kernes."† The subsequent calamities that befell Desmond and his illustrious house, are referred by the authorities to whom we owe these details, to the judgment of heaven against this sacrilege.

Whatever plunder the town afforded, was carried off to the castles

* Cox. † Theatre of Catholic and Protestant Religion. Curry's Civil Wars.

of Strangically and Lisfineen in the county of Waterford, which were garrisoned by Spaniards. Desmond himself returned to his old haunts in the county of Limerick. Ormonde, in a skirmish at Newcastle in that county, lost some of his men under circumstances that increased his fury against the earl. The policy of destroying every thing belonging to the earl or his retainers, was now relentlessly acted on. Houses, towns, and villages, were everywhere devastated and destroyed. The mayor of Youghal, whose treachery or cowardice had surrendered that town to Desmond, was taken in Cashel, brought to Youghal, and hanged before his own door. On the entrance of the queen's army into Youghal, they found it all desolate, no one man, woman, or child, within the walls, except one friar. We regret that the friar's name is not preserved, for in those dreadful days he ventured upon what must have been a dangerous act of humanity. He was at Tralee during the dreadful tragedy of Davels' murder, and he brought the body of Davels to Waterford, that it might receive the rites of Christian burial.

Desmond had now so openly connected himself with the rebellion, that his sending an arrogant letter to the lord-justice, stating that he and his followers had entered into the defence of the Catholic faith, with authority from the pope, and in concert with the king of Spain, and calling on Pelham to join them, can scarcely be regarded as an aggravation of his treason. The lord-justice and Ormonde, early in the year 1580, entered Kerry, burnt the country up to the mountains of Sleevelogher, and slew four or five hundred men. Pelham then besieged Carrigfoile which was garrisoned with nineteen Spaniards and fifty Irish, commanded by Julio, an Italian engineer. The castle was taken, after considerable resistance, and the whole garrison put to the sword or hanged.

Askeaton castle was, at the same time besieged. The garrison, fearing the fate of that at Carrigfoile, contrived to evacuate the castle. They abandoned it at night, leaving a train of powder to set it on fire. Great part was consumed, but the principal towers remained uninjured.

Every one of Desmond's castles were soon taken and garrisoned by the queen's forces. His vast estates were one wide scene of devastation. He himself, with his countess and with Saunders, wandered from one mountain fastness to another, in momentary fear of being taken. His youngest brother, James of Desmond, whose birth had but three and twenty years before been celebrated with unusual rejoicing, and at whose baptism lord-deputy Sussex had attended, was seized in the act of carrying off a prey of cattle from the lands of Sir Cormac M'Carthy. The party who assisted him in this plunder must have been considerable, for an hundred and fifty of them are said to have been killed on this occasion by the M'Carthys. James was mortally wounded, taken prisoner, and executed with every circumstance of cruel indignity, in the city of Cork. The misfortunes of the surviving parties were aggravated by mutual recrimination, and John of Desmond and Saunders left the earl in the hope of being able to join lord Baltinglass, who, with one of the Fitz-Geralds of Kildare, was in arms in Kildare. The garrison at Kilmallock intercepted their little party, which consisted but of four. Sir John and Saunders succeeded in escaping the immediate danger; but being unable to elude the vigilance of the English so far as to make their way to lord Baltinglass's army, returned to their haunts in the mountain fastnesses of Aherlow. Of the others one was slain, and the fourth, a friar named Hayes, was taken, and supplied his captors with evidence of the earl's connexion with the treasons of his brothers, so far back as the time of Fitz-Maurice's landing with the Spaniards. This was felt of moment, as at the very date of the proclamation declaring him a traitor, there was but little evidence of any overt act of treason against him.

Lord Grey of Wilton, the newly-appointed viceroy, had already arrived in Dublin with orders to spare no resources of the government in order at once to crush the rebellion in Ireland, and he was impatient of an hour's delay. Even before Pelham, the lord-justice, could return from the south to deliver to him the sword of state, he ordered the officers who waited upon him at his arrival, to proceed to dislodge from their haunts in the Wicklow mountains the formidable body of insurgents whom we have before mentioned, as under the command of lord Baltinglass. With Baltinglass was Phelim Mac-Hugh, chief of the sept of the O'Byrnes, and one of the Leinster Fitz-Geralds, a kinsman of the earl of Kildare. They were encamped in what was then called "the fastness of the glen," the valley of Glendalough, about twenty miles from Dublin. The valley was one of considerable length, lying among lofty and abrupt hills, the soil marshy and sinking under the foot; and where a firmer footing could be obtained, perplexed with rocks which could not be passed without great difficulty even by men unencumbered with arms; the sides of the steep mountains, through which the valley wound, were dark with ancient forest and underwood. The officers whom Grey ordered to this service, knew that he was leading them to almost inevitable destruction, but did not venture to remonstrate.

When Fitz-Gerald heard of this determination, he concealed himself and his men among the trees on both sides of the valley, and when the English had advanced about half-a-mile, at one of the most entangled parts of the valley, they were fired upon with murderous execution; Moore, Audley, Cosbie, and Sir Peter Carew, distinguished officers, were slain. George Carew, whom we shall have occasion to mention in the after wars of Ireland, was forcibly prevented by his uncle, Wingfield, the master of the ordnance, from joining his brother in this day's rash service. The party in advance, both officers and soldiers, were almost to a man slain; the rest retreated as they best could, scrambling over rocks and sinking amid marshes. The Irish commenced a pursuit, but retired into their woods on the approach of the deputy, who, with his staff and a party of horsemen, was stationed on the side of the mountain. He returned to Dublin, dispirited, and awaited the return of Pelham from the south of Ireland to be sworn into office.

This success of the insurgents in Wicklow, gave the disaffected in Munster momentary hope, which was increased by the circumstance of vessels from Spain finding an opportunity of baffling the vigilance of admiral Winter, and landing at Smerwicke seven hundred Spaniards, with arms for five thousand men. They brought cannon, ammunition, and money, which they were directed to deliver to the earl of Desmond, his brother John, and Saunders. They added new works to the fort which Fitz-Maurice had begun, and called their fortress the *Fort del ore*, or Golden Fortress. Ormonde marched against the invaders. On hearing of his approach, they fled to the neighbouring woods of Glanigalt, a fastness resembling in many points that of Glendalough, and equally dangerous to an invading enemy. Ormonde did not think of pursuing them to the desolate glens and precipitous hills, whither the greater part of them, led by the country people, escaped. While Ormonde rested for the night, a party of Spaniards, about three hundred, returned to their fortress, and re-occupied it. After sallies from the fort, and some skirmishes between the Spaniards and Ormonde, he retired to Rathkeale, where he was met by the lord-deputy.

Sir William Winter had now returned. Grey encamped as near the fort as he could, and Winter, with his vice-admiral Bingham, besieged it at sea. After considerable resistance, the fort, which the Spaniards described themselves as holding for the Pope and the king of Spain, was taken. The garrison sought to obtain terms: Grey would grant none. He was fighting, he said, against men who had no regular commission either from the king of Spain, or from the Pope, and who were but private adventurers giving their assistance to traitors. They surrendered at discretion—Wingfield disarmed them, and an English company then took possession of the fort. The commander, and a few of the officers, were made prisoners of war. The garrison were put to the sword. This execrable service was executed by Raleigh. Grey is said to have shed tears at the determination of the court-martial; and Elizabeth, to have expressed pain and displeasure at the event. On the continent, where a false statement was circulated of Grey's having made terms with the foreigners that they should be permitted to depart in safety, and with all the honours of war, the account was received with horror.*

With the destruction of the Spanish fort, Desmond's last hope expired. His extensive territories were one wild solitude—and he himself a houseless fugitive, sheltering with a few of the humblest of his retainers among the woods. Famine and disease now came to add to the inflictions of war. Spenser has given a picture of the scene which, though often quoted, we cannot omit:—" Out of the corners of the woods and glens the natives came creeping forth upon their hands, for their legs could not bear them; they looked like anatomies of death; they spoke like ghosts crying out of their graves; they did eat the dead carrions, happy when they could find them, yea, and one another soon after; insomuch as the very carcasses they spared not to scrape out of their graves; and if they found a plot of water-cresses or shamrocks, there they flocked as to a feast for the time, yet not able to continue therewithal, that in short space, there was none almost left, and a most plentiful and populous country suddenly left void of man and beast."†

A yet more shocking account is given by another faithworthy writer

* Leland. Camden. † Spenser. State of Ireland.

We feel it a painful duty to transcribe the loathsome details, that the horrors which accompany civil war may be if possible fully felt. We slightly abridge the language of our authority:—" Famine followed; whom the sword did not destroy, the same did consume and eat out. They were not only driven to eat horses, dogs, and dead carrion, but also the carcasses of dead men. In Cork, a malefactor was executed, and left on the gallows. The poor people came secretly, took him down and ate him. A ship was wrecked at Smerwicke, and the dead bodies which were washed on shore, were devoured greedily. The land itself, which before these wars, was populous and well inhabited, was now become barren both of man and beast. From one end of Munster to another, from Waterford to Smerwicke, a distance of one hundred and twenty miles, no man, woman, or child was to be met except in the towns, nor any beast but the very wolves, the foxes, and other like ravening beasts."*

Several narrow escapes of Desmond from the parties in pursuit of him and his brother, are recorded. The movements of John were betrayed by one of his associates to Zouch, a distinguished English officer, who succeeded in coming up with him. He was killed by Zouch's party. His head was sent to Dublin—his body to Cork, where it was exposed hanging by the heels over the north gate of the city. His head was placed on one of the turrets of Dublin castle. We wish that we could suppress all record of such acts as these. Their effect is to create ferocity, demoniacal cruelty, and burning revenge. Saunders sunk under the fatigues of a wandering life—he was found dead in the woods—his body mutilated by wolves and birds of prey.

The earl had now survived all his brothers—his son was in the hands of Elizabeth—his countess, occasionally sharing his abject fortunes, occasionally seeking interviews with such of the court as she thought would assist her in obtaining any terms for her unhappy husband. Allen and Saunders were both dead. The unhappy earl had none to advise with, but some hunted priest, or poor gallowglass, or woodkerne. In his misery he wrote to Ormonde a letter, which we transcribe.—" My lord, great is my grief, when I think how heavily her majesty is bent to disfavor me; and howbeit, I carry the name of an undutiful subject, yet God knoweth that my heart and mind are always most loyally inclined to serve my most loving prince, so it may please her highness to remove her displeasure from me. As I may not condemn myself of disloyalty to her majesty, so I cannot excuse my faults, but must confess I have incurred her majesty's indignation; yet when the cause and means which were found to make me commit folly shall be known to her highness, I rest in an assured hope that her most gracious majesty will think of me as my heart deserveth, as also of those who wrong my heart with undutifulness. From my heart I am sorry that folly, bad counsels, slights, or any other things, have made me forget my duty; and therefore, I am most desirous to get conference with your lordship, to the end I may open and declare to you, how tyraneously I was used; humbly craving that you will appoint some time and place, when and where I may attend your honour; and

* Chronicles of Ireland in continuation of Holinshed.

then I doubt not to make it appear how dutiful a mind I carry; how faithfully I have, at my own charge, served her majesty before I was proclaimed; how sorrowful I am for my offences, and how faithfully I am affected ever hereafter to serve her majesty: and so I commit your lordship to God.   (Subscribed)   GIRALD DESMOND."

This letter was disregarded. We approach the termination of this tragical story. Desmond continued to hide himself in woods and bogs, shifting his quarters often, both for the purpose of concealment, and because his whole means of subsistence was derived from the success of his followers in taking preys of cattle. In the earl's better days, such exactions were not unknown, and the customs of the country clothed them with some pretence of right, when the demand was confined to the cattle of his own vassals. In the present exigencies of the earl, the same acts were felt as plunder. In the autumn of 1582, the earl had his retreat in the mountains above Gleneefy, and in the fastness of Aherlow; in the winter "he kept his christmas" in Kilquieg wood, near Kilmallock. His hiding place was discovered by the garrison at Kilmallock, and an effort made to surprise and take him was nearly successful. A wide river, swelled at that time by the winter rains, between Kilquieg and Kilmallock, must be crossed before the earl's cabin could be reached. The party who thought to have taken him crossed the river on rafts made of hurdles. At break of day they were at the earl's cabin, but the underwood grew so close round this miserable place of shelter, and the ground at the side of the house was so miry that the military party moved at a few spears' paces from the walls; before they reached the door the earl was alarmed by the noise of their approach, and ran into the river that flowed by the cabin. He was accompanied by the countess, and the soldiers searched the place in vain. Dowdal, the captain of the garrison at Kilmallock, led the party engaged in the pursuit of Desmond.

The earl, driven from Kilquieg, returned to the Aherlow mountains. Some three score gallowglasses now joined him. Their mode of sustenance was by such plunder of cattle as we have before mentioned. "Like a sort of deer," says one of the old chroniclers of the period, "they lay upon their keepings, and so fearful were they, that they would not tarry in any one place any long time; but where they did dress their meat, thence would they remove and eat it in another place, and from thence into another place to lie. In the night they would watch, in the forenoons they would be upon the hills and vallies to descry the country, and in the afternoon they would sleep." A detachment from the garrison at Kilmallock surprised them in the night, when some were asleep, and some feeding upon a horse which they had just stolen, for they were without other food. Most of them were slain. When this party of gallowglasses was destroyed, the rest of the Irish rebels were so dismayed that all disturbances ceased in Munster.

The earl, thus hunted from the mountains of Limerick and Tipperary, repaired to Kerry, and was discovered by lord Roche's men, and Dowdal, his indefatigable pursuer, to be lurking in the woods near Dingle. Goron M'Swiney, one of the captains of gallowglasses, who, a few years before, had made his appearance at Cork to welcome Sidney in his viceregal progress, was, with his brother Moyle Murrough M'Swiney, still with Desmond, and by plunders of cattle supported their little company. Goron was slain in one of those marauding expeditions by some of the country people, whose cattle he was driving away. No garrison was yet placed at Dingle, and the earl continued to take, as he best could, cattle in the neighbourhood, chiefly from such as had forsaken his cause, and placed themselves under the protection of the English.

Desmond, on one of these occasions, sent two horsemen and one of his wood-kernes to take a prey of cattle from the neighbourhood of Castlemagne, on the strand of Tralee. Among the cattle taken were those of a poor woman, of the name of Moriarty. The cattle were her only property, and she and her brother followed the track of the plunderers. At Castlemagne the constable of the castle gave them the assistance of some ammunition and a few wood-kernes. The party was in all three and twenty—one of whom, Kelly, an Irishman by birth, but who had in these wars served under the English, they made their captain. Moriarty, who was well acquainted with the country, undertook to be their guide. They followed the track of the kine till they came to the side of a mountain, and a winding path led them to the deep and wooded valley of Glanikilty. It was now night, and they thought to have rested for the night in the shelter of the wood. The glimmering of a fire among the trees at a little distance attracted their notice, and one of them cautiously approached and saw through the windows of a ruinous old house five or six persons sitting by a wood fire. The party immediately determined on ascertaining whether these were the men in pursuit of whom they came. They retired for a moment to consult how their object might best be effected. Before their return all had departed but one man of venerable appearance, who lay stretched before the fire. Kelly struck the old man with his sword, and almost cut off one of his arms; he struck at him again, and gave him a severe wound upon one side of the head. The old man cried out " spare me, I am the earl of Desmond." The appeal was one which he knew was not under any circumstances likely to be made in vain. If no feeling of compassion for fallen greatness could be expected to stay Kelly's hand, still his avarice or ambition might be interested, for though large rewards were offered for Desmond's head, yet the great object of the government was, as all their proclamations expressed, to take him alive. The appeal was unfortunately too late. He was too severely wounded to be easily removed, and Kelly was perhaps afraid of the arrival of some of his retainers. Kelly bade him prepare himself to die, and smote off his head. It was brought to Ormonde—sent by him to the queen—and impaled on London bridge. His body was concealed by his followers; and after several weeks interred in the little chapel of Killanamanagh, not far from Castle Island.

For many a long year after the earl's death there was a popular belief that the place where he died was still red with his blood.*
The persons instrumental in his death were the object of detestation to the Irish, and in every unfortunate incident that from time to time

* O'Sullivan.

occurred in their families, there was a disposition to read judgments inflicted upon them by heaven for the destruction of this champion of the faith. Kelly had his reward. For some thirty years he continued to receive a pension from the government; but the detestation of his own countrymen rendered it necessary for him to live in London, and the Abbé M'Geogeghan, with evident delight, tells of his being at last hanged for highway robbery.

Desmond was attainted, and his vast estates vested in the crown by act of parliament. That act was obtained with difficulty. A feoffment of his lands, made by him several years before, to one of the Munster Geraldines, was produced for the purpose of defeating the forfeiture. As proof, however, was given of this Fitz-Gerald being himself implicated with the earl in treason before the date of the conveyance, the houses of parliament, in the excitement of the moment, disregarded the instrument, and no longer hesitated to pass the acts of attainder and forfeiture. The lands thus forfeited included almost the entire of four counties, and contained 574,628 acres.

JAMES, THE SUGAN EARL OF DESMOND.

THE fifteenth Earl of Desmond having divorced his first wife Joan, daughter of Lord Fermoy, on the plea of consanguinity, and married a second; the title and inheritance were transferred by settlement from Thomas, his son by the first wife, to his son by the second, Gerald, the unfortunate earl, whose history has already been given at length in this volume. In the mean time, the son thus set aside, grew up and obtained possession of a sufficient inheritance in the county of Cork, where he built the castle of Conoha, in which he spent his life in quiet; prudently forbearing to entangle himself in the sea of disturbance, in which so many of his race had been wrecked. He married a daughter of lord Poer, by whom he had three sons and a daughter.

On the attainder of his unfortunate uncle, the sixteenth earl, James, the eldest of these, was induced to plunge into the troubles which were beginning to rise to an unprecedented height, and to menace destruction to the English possessions in Ireland. It was a subject of deep irritation to see an inheritance to which the obstruction to his own claim was now removed, in the hands of the English undertakers, and his last hope of obtaining redress, was reduced to the chances of rebellion. These chances seemed now to multiply in appearance; rebellion was beginning to assume a more concentrated form; the discipline of the Irish was increasing under the ceaseless activity of Hugh O'Donell, the cautious policy of Tyrone, which matured rebellion on a broad basis; and the enmity of Spain against the queen, which promised effectual aid. Such were the motives which led this claimant of the earldom to join Tyrone, of whose rebellion, his will be found to form the regular preliminary; so that we are led to pass in the natural order of events, from one to the other.

In 1598, he was raised by Tyrone's authority to the title of earl of Desmond. The earl of Tyrone, whose history virtually comprehends that of all the other insurgent chiefs of his time, had first sent Owny

M'Rory, with captain Tyrrel, and a considerable body of men, into Munster, for the purpose of awakening and giving a strong impulse to rebellion in that quarter. And, according to the account of the earl of Totness, who conducted this war to its conclusion, he shortly followed himself. Those whom he found in rebellion he confirmed, and from those who were doubtful he took pledges. But of all those whose influence he courted, as the most efficient in the south, the heir of the estates and principles of the princely and ever rebellious house of Desmond stood foremost in his estimation. From the white knight he took pledges; Donald M'Carthy he deposed, and in his place raised Florence M'Carthy to the title and authority of M'Carthy More. On good subjects he inflicted the punishment of fire and sword: but the Sugan earl was his chief object and hope in Munster.

The Sugan earl began his career by a descent on the estates of the brave and loyal lord Barry, with a small tumultuary force of 100 kerne, and drove away 300 cows and 10 horses.

The lord-president early adopted a system of action, which in the Munster rebellion he found in a considerable degree available. The operation of fear and self-interest had a material influence with its leaders, who were not like those of the north, strengthened in the secure and unshaken hold of their vast possessions:—Desmond and M'Carthy were scarcely seated in their authority; and Dermond O'Conor was a soldier of fortune, whose reputation as a soldier, along with his marriage with a daughter of the old earl of Desmond, were in reality his chief claims to authority. These were, nevertheless, the heads of the rebellion, and if allowed, likely to gather a degree of power, which might, considering the state of Ulster, become difficult to cope with. The president therefore tried the effect of separate treaties, and had the address to divide these shallow but dangerous spirits. Florence M'Carthy was awed into a temporary neutrality, and O'Conor was easily detached from his rebel kinsman.

Dermond O'Conor had been appointed by Tyrone to the command of his men, whom he left in Munster; and being retained for pay, was therefore considered by the president as a fit person for his purpose. For this and other considerations, he assailed O'Conor through his wife, who, being a sister to the son of the late earl, at the time confined in the Tower, would be the more likely to take a strong part against the pretender. It was through this lady settled with O'Conor, that he should take Desmond prisoner, and deliver his person up to the president, for which service he should receive £1000, and be appointed to a company in the queen's service. Dermond also stipulated for hostages, which were granted. The lord-president selected four persons who were likely to be safe in his hands, and to prevent suspicion they were met taken as prisoners by a party of Dermond's men sent to meet them for the purpose.

In the mean time, each party pursued its preparation. The president contrived to spread a premature alarm, which brought together the rebel forces in the forest of Kilmore, between Moyallo and Kilmallock, where they waited for ten days in daily expectation of the enemy: after which, having consumed their provisions and wearied conjecture, they were forced to separate. By this contrivance the president was enabled to scatter the rebel force, and at the same time ascertain its extent. The following letter, from Desmond to Florence M'Carthy, was written 17th May, and may serve to give a view of his condition at the time, as well as of the motives which he thought most likely to be influentially put forward.

Letter to Florence M'Carthy.

" After my very heartie commendations, having received inteligence of your happie escape out of Corke, it was very joyfull to mee and many other your cosens and adherents heere; the fruite of your conference with the president, and the rest, I hope shall purchase ripe experience, and harvest of further knowledge, to cut off the cruell yoke of bloody enemies, who daily studie to worke our perpetuall destruction and exile: I am given to understand, that they pretend a journey towards the countie of Limerick, I am gathering the best force, and rising out of these parts to resist their wicked desires: Redmond Burke is bordering on the confines of Ormonde, expecting to heare from me, if occasion of important service should require. I have the other day received his letters signifying his constant service, to be ready whensoever I shall send to him, what news you have with your best advice in all causes tending to our generall service, I expect to heare, and if the president doe rise out (as it is thought), I pray you goode cosen slacke not time, with your best force and provision of victuals to prosecute him freshly in the reare-ward, as you respect me, the exaltation of the Catholike faith, and the case of our countrey: I looke no excuse at your hands, which I pray to lay apart, wherein you shall further the service, and bind me with all my forces to second you at your need. I have retained Dermond O'Conor in Kerry, two hundred souldiers this quarter, besides the Clanshikies and other borroghs with the rising out of my country, so as I think, I shall make up sixteen or seventeene hundred strong, well appointed, together with the force of Redmond Burke. Thus for the lacke of farther novelties, I commit you to the blessed guiding of God. From Crome the seventeenth of May, 1600.

" I am credibly informed, that five Spanish ships are landed in the north, with treasure, munition, and great ordinance, with a competent number of three thousand soldiers, pioneers, and religious persons, I expect every day advertisement in writing, and the coming up of captain Ferrell, with the munition sent me by O'Neyle. I appointed your cosen Maurice Oge, Fitz-Maurice Gerald, to have the charge of Keirrycorrie, I pray you afford him your lawfull favour.

" Your most assured cosen,
" JAMES DESMOND."

Previous to Dermond O'Conor's attempt on the Sugan earl, another plan of the same nature was tried to be executed against his brother, John of Desmond. A person of the name of Nugent, who had been a servant to Sir John Norris, had on some real or imaginary grievance joined the rebel party, and, being a person of great valour, and activity, and resolution, became quickly very formidable in Munster. About the time in which we are now engaged, he saw reason to return to the English, and came to the commissioners St Leger and Power, who sent him to the president. The president informed him, that after his great crimes, he could only expect to be taken into favour by the performance of some good service, in consideration of which he might expect pardon and recompense. Nugent offered to "ruine within a short time," either the pretended earl or John his brother. The president, relying on the plot already prepared for the earl, accepted his offer for the other. To prevent suspicion, he was brought before the council and reprimanded with great severity, his petition for mercy rejected, and himself only dismissed on the faith of the queen's word.

John Fitz-Thomas, as he is commonly named, was keeping possession of an island in Lough Gur, on which there was a strong castle, well garrisoned, and from its position till then impregnable. This place the president considered it to be of the first importance to reduce, as it rendered the way unsafe between Kilmallock and Limerick. Hither on the 25th May, 1600, the president marched from Brough, and made all necessary preparation for the siege. But the cost and delay of this difficult undertaking were saved; the person to whom John Fitz-Thomas gave the charge of the castle, delivered it up for the sum of £60. On receiving possession of this castle, the president marched on, and John Fitz-Thomas came from the island towards the "fastnesses of Arlough," where most of his men were. Nugent followed at some small distance, accompanied by a person named Coppinger, whose aid he had, as he thought, secured. Approaching gradually to his intended victim, he came within pistol shot. He then drew out a pistol charged with two bullets, and was raising it to take aim, when unexpectedly the pistol was wrested from his grasp by his companion, who at the same instant shouted "treason." Nugent turned to escape, but in turning too sharply his horse fell, and he was taken and hanged next day.

The effect of this incident was to put John of Desmond in continual fear, and as Nugent before his death mentioned, that it had been his intention to have immediately repaired to the earl, and under pretence of giving him the account, to have also killed him: the same fear was communicated to the earl, who afterwards acknowledged to the president, that he and his brother never durst lodge together in one place, or even serve at the head of their troops, for fear of being shot by some of their own men.

The execution of Dermond O'Conor's stratagem was now to be furthered by a movement of the president. As the capture of the Sugan earl was rendered both difficult and dangerous by the presence of his army, it was thought advisable to induce him to dismiss it by the division and separate cantonment of the English, who were for the purpose ordered to several garrisons in possession of the English. It fell out accordingly, when the president had, to the great surprise and dissatisfaction of his officers, thus distributed his troops, the Irish were allowed to scatter away to their homes. Shortly after, all being prepared, O'Conor sent a messenger to the Sugan earl, desiring a conference on the 18th June, to arrange some operations for the conduct of the war. The earl accordingly came; his suspicion had been slightly roused by some secret intelligence, which he did not, however, credit; he came nevertheless attended by 200 foot: O'Conor brought with him 150. A quarrel seemingly accidental, was easily excited, and under the pretence of interference quickly spread until the tumult became confused enough to afford a pretext for any construction: O'Conor easily found an excuse to be angry, and to affect the suspicion of some treasonable intention. Unsuspicious of design and only desirous to appease him, the Sugan earl offered to dismiss his kernes. The offer was insidiously accepted, and they were at once removed to some distance from the place of parley. This having been adjusted, the bonnoghs or men of O'Conor drew round the place where they stood, and O'Conor laid hold of the Sugan earl, and told him he was his prisoner. The earl expressed surprise, and asked for whom and what cause. "For O'Neale," answered O'Conor, "and I purpose to detain you till his pleasure shall be known, as you have conspired with the English, and promised the president, to deliver me alive or dead into his hands;" in confirmation of which he drew forth and read out a letter which he pretended to have intercepted, but which was really contrived for the purpose. This letter has been preserved by the president himself in the account which he left of the transaction.

Pretended letter from the Lord President to James Fitz-Thomas.

"Sir,—Your last letters I have received, and am exceeding glad to see your constant resolution of returne to subjection, and to leave the rebellious courses wherein you have long persevered, you may rest assured that promises shall be kept; and you shall no sooner bring Dermond O'Conor to me, alive or dead, and banish his bownoghs out of the countrie, but that you shall have your demand satisfied, which I thanke God, I am both able and willing to performe; beleeve me you have no better way to recover your desperate estate, then by this good service, which you have proffered, and therefore I cannot but commend your judgement in choosing the same to redeeme your former faults: and I doe the rather believe the performance of it, by your late action touching Loghquire, wherein your brother and yourselfe have well merited; and as I promised, you shall finde mee so just, as no creature living shall ever know, that either of you did assent to the surrender of it; all your letters I have received, as also the joynt letter, from your brother and yourselfe; I pray loose no time; for delayes in great actions are subject to many dangers. Now that the Queenes armie is in the field, you may worke your determination with most securitie, being ready to releive you upon a dayes warning: so praying God to assist you in this meritorious enterprize I doe leave you to his protection this twentie nineth of May, 1600."

This specious imposture reconciled the minds of the persons present. But to ensure their satisfaction, O'Conor gave three other gentlemen whom he took at the same time to his chief captains to keep them for their ransoms. The Sugan earl was then, with the other prisoners, mounted on some lean hacks, and conveyed through Coumlogh to castle Lyshin, where O'Conor's wife and family with the English pledges were. From thence he went and took the castle of Ballianinan, belonging to Rory Macshihy, father to two of his prisoners; and having done so, he sent for his wife, family, and the English pledges, leaving at castle Lyshin sixteen trusty persons to guard the earl and his companions. O'Conor's fear of a rescue caused him to divide his prisoners and pledges thus. He then sent John Power, one of the English pledges, to apprize the president of his success, and to beg of him to draw towards Kilmallock with such force as he could muster, where his wife should meet him to receive the thousand pounds and to deliver the prisoner.

The president had about one thousand foot, and two troops of horse, having sent the rest of his army under captain Flower, to the earl of Thomond, on whose lands O'Donell had made a sudden descent. With this force he drew toward Kilmallock, in the hope of receiving there a prisoner of such importance. There however, he was delayed nearly six days, without any account from the lady Margaret, who was detained by the danger of the way, but at last brought an account that castle Lyshin was besieged by the people of Connaught. The president ordered a march to raise the siege, but had not gone a mile when a messenger brought word of the escape of the earl.

Dermond O'Conor soon found himself compelled to enter upon terms with his country, who ever after held him in distrust. A letter from the rebel chiefs of Munster to O'Donell, inviting him to their assistance in their attempts to rescue the Sugan earl, was intercepted and brought to the president. He, on his part, having received Dermond's letter, that he was besieged in Ballyaninan, marched that way by Conniloe, and the town of Killingery, to relieve him. But when he arrived within three miles of Ballyaninan, the rebels being unwilling that a person so dangerous as Dermond should be leagued with the English, resolved to treat with him. Dermond, perhaps unaware that relief was so near, and also uncertain as to his reception from the president, consented, and surrendered the castle and himself on terms more favourable than he had reason to expect.

The lord president now directed his march to the Glynne castle, belonging to O'Conor Kerry, in the county of Limerick. On his way he took Crome castle, at the entrance of Conniloe; and on the 30th June, came to Askeaton, where he continued a few days in expectation of supplies. On the 4th of July, he continued his march west from Askeaton, while during the entire day, the enemy to the number of 3000, continued marching in sight. It seemed to the president, that they were all the time on the watch for some occasion of advantage for an attack. There was, however, division in their camp; they were composed of two classes, the provincials and the hired troops, who entertained a mutual jealousy of each other. The bonnoghs or mercenaries from Connaught began to perceive that they were likely to be disappointed in their sanguine expectations of plunder, and the situation of the earl was such as to make their hire itself precarious. This was made apparent by several letters from some of the leaders, who desired safe conducts from the president to retire with their people.

A letter written at this time, from the Sugan earl, to Florence M'Carthy, explains his position and gives some additional interest to these movements.

THE FITZGERALDS.

Letter from James Fitz-Thomas to Florence Macarthy :—

"MY VERY GOOD LORD,

"I was driven through the treacherous dealings of Dermond O'Connor, to let the president and the English armie pass into Glenne, without any resistance; and yet they are but thirteene hundred foote, and one hundred fiftie horse; Dermond O'Connor did undertake that the Connaght men should not medle with them, nor take our parts, being the only encouragement of the English, to venter this enterprise: but now God be praysed, I am joining my forces with them, and doe pray you to assist mee with your forces, for now is the time to shew ourselves upon the enemy, for they are but very few in number, and destitute of all reliefe, either by sea or land: if your lordship bee not well at ease yourselfe, let your brother Dermond, and the chiefe gentlemen of your forces come without any delay; assuring your lordship, that I will, and am ready, to shew you the like against your need: beseeching your lordship once againe, not to faile, as you tender the overthrow of our action; even so committing your lordship to the tuition of God Almighty I end. Portrinad the fifth of July 1600.

"Your honours most assured friend and cosen,
"JAMES DESMOND."

On the 5th of July the lord president sat down before the castle of Glynn, the army of the Sugan earl and his allies looking on from a hill, in reliance on the great strength of the castle. By engaging the besieged in a parley, the president contrived to plant his two cannon within battering range without any resistance. The attack seems to have been delayed for one day more by different parleys and negotiations both with the besieged and with the chiefs of the rebel host. Of these latter, the Knight of the Valley sought and obtained a safe conduct to confer with the earl of Thomond; through this lord, he conveyed his demand of an audience from the lord president, who refused to see him, unless on his absolute submission. This condition he rejected, and was commanded to depart; "he saw," writes the president, "the cannon already planted, and his son, then a child, in the president's hands ready to be executed, being by himself formerly put in pledge for his loyaltie." The sight for a moment shook the resolution of the knight, and the conference was renewed, though in vain; ambition, resentment, or partizanship, were stronger than the parental tie, and frustrated every attempt to bring him to yield, and in the evening of the same day, he was dismissed. The constable of the castle came to the same earl under a safe conduct, and represented the danger of the attack; as he assured him the earl of Desmond would attack the English and drive them into the Shannon.

The earl of Thomond laughed at the threat, and in return advised the surrender of the castle, assuring him that the lives of the garrison should be spared; this, however, he would not hear of, and a little after, as he was departing, he received a message from the lord president, "that since he refused the earl of Thomond's favourable offer, he was in hopes before two days were spent, to have his head set upon a stake."*

On the following day, the president ordered his battery to be opened, but the cannon on which their dependance was placed, was found to be so clogged at the touch-hole, that it could not be freed. The lord-president, by a curious expedient, which he records for the instruction of posterity, contrived to remedy this obstruction. He ordered the gun to be raised on its carriage, as nearly as possible into a vertical position; then "he willed the gunner to give her a full charge of powder, and roule a shot after it, whereby the touch-hole was presently cleared, to the great rejoicings of the armie."† The president then ordered the knight of the valley's child to be placed on one of the gabions, and sent word to the castle, that "they should have a fair mark to bestow their small shot upon." The constable, in terms not sufficiently decorous to be repeated, answered that the knight of the valley might have more sons, and that they should not spare their fire on account of the child. On this the president ordered the child to be removed and the cannon to be discharged against the walls. A fire commenced on both sides, and before long a breach was made into a cellar under the great hall of the castle.

Into this breach a party, led by captain Flower, entered, and forced their way into the hall, driving the garrison before them into a neighbouring tower which opened from it. Here four of the English were slain by shots from a spike-hole. Captain Flower then led his men up the narrow spiral stairs, which led to two turrets, on the top of the castle; these they gained with the loss of an inferior officer, and planted the English ensigns upon them.

By the time the last-mentioned service was effected, it had grown quite dark, and as it was impossible to make any further progress, captain Slingsby was ordered to maintain the position already won till morning. During the night, there was some firing on both sides within the castle, each party being kept in apprehension of the other. The constable, seeing that he was unlikely to save himself by any other means, thought to escape during the darkness under cover of a sally. The English guard was too alert; his party was repulsed and himself slain. In the morning, it was found that the Irish had retired into the tower of the castle. The stone stairs, which were the only ascent, were so narrow that one only could mount at a time: this difficult ascent was guarded by a strong wooden door, to which the assailants set fire. By this means the narrow way became so filled with smoke, that a considerable time elapsed before any further step could be taken; when the smoke was cleared away, several English officers, followed by their men, ascended in single file; they met no resistance; the Irish had made their way out on the castle wall. An offer to surrender, on condition of their lives being spared, met with no answer, and they then resolved to sell them dearly. The English, led by captains Flower and Slingsby, rushed out through the door which led to the battlements, and a rough and desperate but short struggle took place in the gutters, between the battlements and the

* Hiber. Pac.   † Ibid. Pacata.

roof of the castle: here many fell on both sides—mercy was unthought of, and the narrow gutters ran with blood; eleven English soldiers were killed and 21 wounded. Of the Irish, fell 80 in all; some were slain on the battlements; some who hoped to escape by leaping over into the water below, were killed by the English who surrounded the castle.*

The earl of Desmond had not resolution to offer any interruption to the taking of this castle, the importance of which was very considerable. It had served the Irish as a secure factory, from whence, by means of a Limerick merchant, all their wants had been supplied.

The Sugan earl in the meantime seemed to be content with the show of war. With a force in general nearly triple that of the English, he was content to hang at a safe distance on their march and observe their movements, or seize occasion to show hostility by some small depredations or assaults on straggling parties. The president pursued his operations, very much as if there was no hostile force in the field.

The county of Kerry had until recently been untouched by these military operations, and abounded with men and provisions. In the heart of this district lay the strong castle of Lisaghan, an object of the utmost importance, and presenting no small obstacles to any hope of successful attack. The enterprise was however undertaken by Maurice Stack, a gentleman in attendance upon the lord president, and highly reputed for his conduct and valour. He was probably favoured by the tranquil and isolated position of the place, for he contrived to take the castle by surprise. The loss was felt by the rebel chiefs to be a serious blow, and all means for its recovery were put in motion; force and fraud were tried in turn and failed. The siege was repelled, and the rebel army compelled to retire with some disgrace from before the walls. A little after, while the brave Stack was away, and the command entrusted to Walter Talbot, Florence M'Carthy, whose conduct seems to have been curiously temporizing, and ordered very much with a view to avoid committing himself, came to Talbot, and endeavoured to cajole him into a surrender. Such efforts were little likely to succeed; but when reported to the lord president, he thought it prudent to visit him, and accordingly took with him 1000 foot, and 75 horse, and in five days came to Kilrush; when by the aid of the earl of Thomond, he had his troops ferried across the river.

In the meantime these movements were not unobserved. A letter was written by the Sugan earl to Florence M'Carthy, which was, we presume, intercepted by the lord president, on whose authority it is given.

Letter from James Fitz-Thomas to Florence M'Carthy.

" Cousen,
" Yesterday I came over the mouhtaine, and brought with mee the Bonnaghs of Conelloe, the residue and force of the countery I have left to keepe their Crets. I understand since my comming, that Sir Charles Wilmott, with six hundred foot, and fiftie horse, are come

* Pacata Ibid.

to Clanmorris, and this night pretend to be at Tralee. I have sent to the knight, and all the countery presently to meet mee to-morrow, to resist their determination; and for your better furtherance and accomplishment of our action, I am to entreat your lordship, as you regard your own quiet, and exaltation of the service, to make what haste you may, and speedily to yeeld us your helping assistance, for which, will rest thankfull and most readie to answere your lordship at your need: and thus referring the consideration hereof to your lordship, I commit you to God. Primo Augusti, 1600.

"Your lordship's very loving cousen,
"JAMES DESMOND."

Thus was the wave of destruction rolled into this hitherto unmolested district. On reaching Carrigofoyle, the president obtained information that the Irish had come to a determination to destroy their castles in Kerry; on which he sent Sir Charles Wilmot to prevent them. Sir Charles made a rapid march and came by surprise on several castles—Lixnaw, which had been undermined by its lord, who afterwards is said to have died of grief, for this work of his own folly: Tralee the house of Sir Edward Denny, which 150 soldiers of the Sugan earl were in the very act of destroying; while these were yet busy in the completion of this exploit, the noise they made in the vaults which they endeavoured to undermine, prevented them from hearing the approach of Sir Charles and his troop of fifty horse, who killed 32 of them, and seized the arms of a hundred men.

We have already mentioned the very peculiar position which Florence M'Carthy was all this time endeavouring to maintain; in which it seems obviously his object was to keep fair with either party, and finally to attach himself to the stronger. The league which was at the time in the course of progress against the English, was such as to raise strong hopes of their entire subversion; when the concentrated forces of the northern and southern chiefs, strengthened by the men, money, and arms of Spain, should be brought to bear upon them. But the vast superiority of the English force, in point of efficiency in the field, was still such as to cast a strong doubt on the success of any numerical superiority which could be brought against them. The best indication for the Irish, was the caution they had learned; they now evinced a strong sense that their only safe tactics consisted in vigilant observation for the moment of advantage. Hence it may be observed by the reader, that such was the conduct of Desmond's army; with all his numerical superiority, he was contented with such a course that while the utmost activity was maintained on either side, the English appear, by all statements, to have moved in a perfectly unobstructed course to the execution of their objects. Such was the state of things at a juncture, which actually constitutes the turning point of the fortunes of the pale. And which may without great rashness be taken as the cause, which suggested so much doubt, and caused such continual wavering among the native chiefs. It was a question, whether they were to embrace safety or irreversible ruin, and the grounds of decision presented as yet no very decisive aspect, to the subtile yet circumscribed observation of these barbarous leaders.

Of these, the most curious instance of conduct, rendered perplexed and vacillating from indecision of character, together with embarrassment of position, was that of Florence M'Carthy. This chief, sincere to neither party, and keeping on doubtful terms with both, presents us with that species of general illustration which is sometimes to be found in an extreme case: steady only in availing himself of all circumstances, which could for the moment render him important to either party— or gain an object, or divert a suspicion. Still, though an anxiety for his own safety was uppermost in his wavering counsels, he undoubtedly preferred the rebel cause. It was at the period of his arrival at Kerry, that the lord-president, hearing that this chief was near, and having strong reasons to suspect him, sent to desire his presence at Carrigofoyle. M'Carthy sent excuses joined with oaths of fidelity. Another message was dispatched with a safe-conduct, but all was of no avail. This confirmed the suspicions of Carew, who a little before had received information, that Florence M'Carthy was engaged in the negotiation of a marriage between Desmond and the sister of Cormac M'Carthy of Muskerry. As this alliance was if possible to be prevented, the lord-president resolved to exert himself for the purpose. With this in view, he committed the military operations in Cork to Sir Charles Wilmot, and repaired to Kerry to counteract the subtile underplotting of M'Carthy, of whom he was accustomed to say, that he saw him, "like a dark cloud over his head, threatening a storm to hinder and disturb his proceedings."* The apprehended marriage was prevented by a negotiation with M'Carthy of Muskerry, who by dint of threats and promises, was induced to undertake for his sister's appearance on the summons of the lord president or the council.

While this point was in course of attainment, many incidents of less moment marked the slow progress of the war in Munster. A detachment, commanded by captain Harvey, was passing through a village belonging to the white knight. One of the houses was unthinkingly set fire to by a few of his men, who mistook their position, and by a very pardonable error thought themselves in an enemy's country. The outrage was instantly arrested in its commencement; but a party of 160 foot and 18 horse was drawn together by John Fitz-Gibbon, the knight's younger son. Captain Harvey explained the error of his men, and promised satisfaction. But the inexperienced youth, relying on the numerical superiority of his force, conceived the unlucky notion that the English were in his power, and only saw the tempting occasion to perform an exploit of arms: giving no answer to captain Harvey, he ordered a charge upon the English. His party came rapidly up to the charge, but stopped short when close to the enemy's line, and stood surprised at the tranquil aspect with which their rush was awaited. Seeing that they hesitated, Harvey ordered his men to charge. Fitz-Gibbon's troop gave way at once, and left nearly half their number dead or wounded on the field. The white knight, on being informed of this affair, condemned the rashness of his son; and the guide, who, on enquiry, was discovered to have set on the English

* Pacata Hib.

soldiers from a malicious motive, was, by order of the president, hanged.

The president, aware of the enthusiasm of the Kerrymen for the Desmond family, caused a person in the livery of the young earl of Desmond to be shown in several places, and a report spread, that the earl himself was soon to make his appearance in the country—an expedient at this time actually entertained, and soon after tried. The Sugan earl had with him five hundred mercenaries, together with such forces as the chiefs of his party could draw together. But the activity of Sir Charles Wilmot, to whom in the interval the main operations, consisting chiefly of detachments, had been committed, brought over the minds of many, and among these of Fitz-Gerald the knight of Kerry—so that he not only professed his desire to become a British subject; but on Desmond's coming to Dingle, refused to give him entrance to his castle. In return, the Sugan earl destroyed as much as he could, and went on to Castlemagne. Not long after the knight made his submission, and was accepted in form; and the Sugan earl, with Pierce Lacy, entering his country with a view to plunder, he gave them battle, and routed them with a loss of sixteen of their men and two officers of mercenaries.

The affairs of the Sugan earl were gradually drawing to a point. The lord president, unable to carry matters by a decisive action, had contrived to make the most judicious arrangements, securing the country every where as he advanced his line of operation. He carried the war into the disaffected parts, and placed his garrison in the most commanding positions in the countries of his chief opponents. Above all, he had at an early period of the year occupied Askeaton and Kilmallock with strong garrisons, which were productive of more decisive advantages as the rebellion approached nearer to its crisis.

The garrison of Kerry at the present period, (the beginning of September, 1600,) distressed the Sugan earl so much, that he found it difficult to maintain his force. In this juncture he wrote the following letter to Florence M'Carthy:—

"MY LORD,

" Your letter I have received, and the present time of service is now at hand, which by letters, nor any excuse so ineffectual ought to be delayed; and whereas you write, that you intend to confer with the president and the earl of Thomond, I marvel that one of your lordship's acquaintance with their proceedings, doeth not yet know their enticing bayts and humours to entrap us all within the nets of their policies; your vow to God and this action for the maintenance of the church and defence of our own right, should not for any respect be unregarded: you know that of long time your lordship hath been suitor to the queen and council, and could not at any time prevail nor get any liklichood of your settlement. And now, being duly placed by the assent of the church, and us the nobilitie of this action, your lordship should work all means possible for to maintain the same. You know the ancient and general malice that heretofore they bare to all Irish birth, and much more they rave at the present, so as it is very bootless for any of us all to seek their favours or countenance, which were but a mean to work our total subversion. Write me effectually your lordship's mind, and what resolution you purpose to follow, whereby I may proceed accordingly. This armie is but very slender, for they are but sixe hundred foot, and eightie horse. Wee expect your lordship's assistance, which we heartily desire, and not any further to deferre us with letters, as you respect us and the service: and, whereas you write, you have no force, your own presence, and the fruite of your comming, will much further the service, and dismay the enemy, &c.—2d September, 1600.

"Your loving Cousen,
"JAMES DESMOND."

But the situation of the Sugan earl was too replete with danger to admit of open assistance from one so cautious as M'Carthy who satisfied his affection to the cause, with temporizing messages, and perhaps vague intentions. The earl, closely pressed by Wilmot, was driven out of Kerry. His allies and associates began to perceive the ruin which was coming so fast upon his cause; yet reluctant to desert him, strongly urged his flight from the south, promising to support him when he should return with an army sufficient to make resistance practicable. So strongly, indeed, was the necessity of submission beginning to be felt, and so fiercely at the same time did the fire of rebellion burn under its embers, that the chiefs sent an ambassador to Rome to purchase absolution for their feigned submission to the queen,* and a dispensation for their further continuance in a course so inconsistent with their profession of faith.†

The Sugan earl, having left Kerry, was on his way to the fortress of Arlogh, when the report of his approach reached Kilmallock; several companies stationed in this place hastened out to meet him: and unfortunately for the earl, his troops were seen and intercepted before they were able to gain the covert of a wood, near which they were marching. They were instantly charged by captain Graeme's company, who obtained possession of their baggage, and killed all those who guarded it. A spirited rally was made by the Irish for the recovery of their baggage; but a few more charges threw them into confusion. Flight and slaughter began to fill the plain: 120 of the earl's men were killed, and 80 wounded. Among other things, three hundred horses laden with baggage, with a large prey of cattle, were secured by the English party. In this battle captain Graeme had sixteen of his men slain, and a few horses wounded.

From this moment the fortunes of the Sugan earl became hopeless. His friends departed to their homes—his followers deserted—and he could no longer collect a hundred men. With his brother John, the knight of the Glyn, and two other gentlemen, he left the county of Cork, and made the best of his way into Tipperary and Ormonde: from whence his companions retired from a field of enterprise which now presented no hope of retrieve, and took refuge in Ulster; where under the earl of Tyrone's command, the cause of insurrection still held its precarious existence. The rebellion in Ireland had not in fact, at any time, assumed its most formidable aspect in the south; it was rather a perplexed tissue of intrigues, murders, and tumults, than

* Pac. Hiber.   † Camden.

a contest of military operations. Sir George Carew has been condemned by some of our historians, for the means which he sometimes adopted to obtain his ends; were it worth while, and could we allow ourselves space, it would be easy to show that he had no better means than to avail himself of the character of the allies and the enemies with whom he had to deal: their moral code was not of the strictest, and their laws of war included every crime within the broad latitude of human nature. The age itself was but doubtfully advanced in civilization: the contest was carried on with an enemy which had little idea of war without murder, robbery, breach of faith, and treachery; then there was no strict rule, either express or understood, to debar Sir George Carew from taking the occasional advantages afforded by the tactics of an enemy who, it must be recollected, stood upon the low ground of treason and rebellion in the estimate of the English government. Amongst those shocking and revolting incidents to which this monstrous state of things gave occasion, we could enumerate many. It was at the time at which we are now arrived, that Honor O Brien, sister to the earl of Thomond, and wife to lord Kerry, invited a person of the name of Stack to dine with her, and caused him to be murdered; his brother, who was a prisoner in the castle, was next day hanged by order of lord Kerry. Such was the summary justice of Irish chiefs in that age: it was evidently the maxim that every one had the right, now only recognised in fields of battle, to kill his enemy as he might; and every one whose death became in any way desirable, was an enemy.

The unfortunate earl of Desmond found little prospect of relief or aid in Ormonde; he had perhaps come thither for the purpose of escaping the attention of Carew, and with a design to return when he safely might. In October, the president obtained intelligence that he had stolen back and was lurking with a few followers about the woods of Arlogh.

In the month of October, in the same year, the queen put into execution her plan for drawing away the affections of the county of Kerry from the Sugan earl by sending over the son of the 16th earl, attainted 1582. This youth had in his infancy been detained in England, where he had been born, and kept prisoner in the Tower. He was now sent over with the title of the earl of Desmond, to the care of the lord president. For his maintenance, a captain and his company were to be dismissed, and their pay allotted to this purpose. The patent for his title was to be retained by the lord-president, until he might be enabled to judge of the success of the plan. From the reception of the young lord by the people this was soon decided.

To bring this matter to the test, the president gave the young lord permission to travel into Limerick, under the care of the archbishop of Cashel and Master Boyle, clerk of the council, (afterwards first earl of Cork.) On a Saturday evening the party entered Kilmallock. The report of their coming had reached this town before them; and the effect was such as might seem to warrant the most sanguine expectations. The streets were thronged to the utmost with the people from the surrounding country—every window was full of earnest and eager faces—the roofs were alive with a shouting and cheering rabble—and every "projecting buttress and coigne of vantage" bore its share of acclamation and loyalty to the heir of the old earl. He was invited to dine at Sir George Thornton's, and so dense was the crowd, that it was half-an-hour before a lane of soldiers could enable him to reach his mansion. After supper the same press retarded his return to his own lodging.

All this enthusiasm was easily dispelled. If the young lord had drawn favourable hopes, or high notions of the loyalty of the Limerick people to the house of his fathers, a few hours more were to enlighten him on this head. The next day was Sunday, and he was, as was his wont, proceeding to church, when he was surrounded by a multitude, whose language he did not understand, but who, by their tones and gestures, were evidently endeavouring to dissuade him from entering the church. The young earl went on and entered. On coming out after service he was met with abuse and execration: and from that moment no one came near him. It was also quickly ascertained, that the numerous persons who had possession of the Desmond estates under the crown, looked with natural apprehension on the chance so detrimental to their interests, of the restoration which would transfer them from the lax management of the English plantations, to the gripe of the exacting and despotic earl of Desmond.

This unfortunate youth, the rightful heritor of the house of Desmond, having been thus painfully held for a few days in a position of high and flattering expectation, was restored to an obscurity rendered doubly painful by disappointment. If his long state of depression had not eradicated in his breast all the spirit of his race, his misfortune, to which education and the habits of life must have reconciled him, was aggravated; and the penalty of his father's crimes, revived to be inflicted afresh on him. What had been a privation hardly felt, was thus become an insult and a wrong. And such we should infer from his brief remaining history was the manner in which this reckless act of despotism affected its unhappy object. Having been found of no use in Ireland; and after having exerted himself to the utmost to meet the wishes of the queen, he was brought back to England, where he died in a few months, and with him the honours of the house of Desmond.

The Sugan earl was become a fugitive, and with two or three persons led a life of fear and hardship, skulking from forest to forest, and from desert to desert among the savage glens and defiles of Arlogh, in Drumfinnin, and in the county of Tipperary. In the latter place his maternal relations were ready to attend to his wants, but personal safety was become a principal object, and no place could long be safe for a fugitive, from the vigilance and activity of lord president Carew. Of his allies some had been more successful; Lacy had got together a small body of men and awaited the return of John of Desmond, who went to Ulster to apply to the earl of Tyrone for aid. Tyrone had, however, to mind his own defence, which, against the skilful and efficient conduct of the able and spirited Mountjoy, more than tasked his whole means and force.

In the month of November, most of the few remaining castles which were held against the queen were taken. The strong castle of Connilough was surprised—Castlemagne was surrendered from regard to the young earl of Desmond—Listowel was taken after a short but desperate siege. Of this latter the incidents have too much interest to be omitted here.

The castle of Listowel belonged to Fitz-Maurice, lord of Lixnaw, who was one of the most inveterate opponents of the president's government. Being the only one of his castles which had not been taken, Sir C. Wilmot was determined to seize it. On the fifth of November he besieged it, and ordered the wall to be undermined. After nearly a week's hard work, his men had opened a deep mine under the foundation; but they had hardly finished the chamber in which the powder was to be lodged, when a spring gushed out upon the cavity and entirely frustrated the attempt. The labour was therefore renewed on another part of the foundation; and the miners were successful in reaching far under the middle of the cellar. An application was at this period made by the garrison for leave to depart from the castle; but as they had first done all the mischief in their power—nine of the besiegers having fallen, and had now no longer a choice—Sir Charles did not think it fit or expedient to grant such terms. They were therefore compelled to surrender at discretion; and the women and children were suffered to depart. Among the latter was the eldest son of the lord of Lixnaw: the people of the castle, aware, that if recognised, its seizure must ensue, disguised it by changing its attire, and having smeared it with mud, placed it over the back of an old woman who bore it away without being questioned. It was not long before Sir Charles became aware of the circumstance; and a pursuit was immediately commanded. All was vain, until he thought of questioning a priest, who had been taken among the prisoners. The following is the account given by Sir G. Carew himself of the conversation between Sir C. Wilmot and MacBrodie the priest:—MacBrodie admitted "that he could best resolve him, for that he himselfe had given direction to the woman where shee should bestow the child till shee might deliver him to his father. 'Why then,' saith Sir Charles, 'will you not conduct me to him? Know you not that it is in my power to hang you or to save you? Yes; and I assure you if you will not guide me to the place where he lieth hidden, I will cause you to be instantly hanged.' The priest answered, That it was all one to him whether he died this day or to-morrow; but yet, if he might have his word, for the sparing of his owne life and the childes, hee might reveale his knowledge; otherwayes the governor might do his pleasure. Sir Charles, though very unwilling to grant the priest his life, yet the earnest desire hee had to gett the child into his hands, caused him to agree thereto. The priest, being put into a band-locke, is sent with a captaine and a good guard of souldiers about this businesse, who guided them to a wood, sixe miles from the castle, by reason of thicke bryers and thorns, almost unpassable, in the middest whereof there is a hollow cave within the ground, not much unlike by description, to *Cacus* his denne; or the mouth of *Avernus*, in which desolate place they found that old woman and this young childe, whom they brought to the governor, and the priest and childe were shortly after sent to the president."*

* Pacata Hib.

While the lord-president was at Clonmel, whither he had gone to confer with the earl of Ormonde, he received information that the fugitive lords were lurking in the vicinity, where they had already committed many extensive depredations. He therefore undertook a strict search. While he was thus engaged, a youth was brought before him, who had been in the Sugan earl's service; and, on being questioned, undertook to conduct a party to where his master lay. For some time there had been a close pursuit, of which we regret not being able to present the reader with any authorized details, but which can easily be followed up by his imagination, into the variety of romantic escapes and emergencies, of which every day must have had its share. The deep and rugged glens and mountain hollows, the marshy vales, and the broad wildernesses of dark forest and tangled thicket, were now all explored by human fear and misfortune, and traced through their recesses and leafy mazes, by the stern activity of military pursuit. Enmity guided by treachery, dogged the fallen earl from den to den, and from hut to hut, nor could he in this forlorn condition reckon on the fidelity of any one of those whose aid, guidance, or hospitality, his utter necessity required. The actual proof that this description is something more than imaginary, may be found in the brief statement of Sir George Carew, who mentions that they frequently reached the place of his concealment just a little after he had escaped from it. The earl of Thomond, Sir G. Thornton, and other officers, were now sent with their companies, along with this guide, who conducted them to the woods of Drumfinnan; but as they approached the border of the woods a cry was raised, and a tumult ran through the forest depth, as from persons in flight, while the soldiers, dashing aside the thick boughs, rushed in to give chase. The Sugan earl made his escape; he ran without waiting to put on his shoes. His companion, (a Romish priest,) was overtaken by the soldiers; but his "simple mantle," and "torn trowsers" deceived them—seeing but a poor old man, unable to bear a weapon, they left him unmolested. Thus were the Sugan earl and his companions reduced to the condition of hunted beasts, in daily alarm for their lives, without the commonest necessaries, and compelled mostly to conceal themselves in places selected for their very discomfort. The province was, however, reduced to order and peaceful subjection. No castle was in the hands of an enemy to the queen's government. No hostile army levied contributions, seized or plundered, or kept the country in terror; but every one was enabled securely to leave his cattle in the fields. And the lord-president, having dismissed five hundred men, was enabled to offer to send a thousand to serve in Leinster.

On the 13th of January, 1601, the lord-president was enabled to give intelligence to the English council of the approaching invasion of the Spaniards. His information was avouched by a variety of documents, which left little doubt on the subject, and confirmed strongly, by the appearance in the country of numerous foreign ecclesiastics, the accuracy of this intelligence. Enough has been already seen in our notice of O'Donell, and has also been more fully confirmed by the history of the earl of Tyrone's rebellion, which may be said to have comprised as the acts of a drama, all these lesser parts.

The Munster rebels were also ascertained to be chiefly maintained by the earl of Tyrone, and even the precise allowances in money or military stores were communicated to the lord-president, who amongst other statements mentions the following sums: to the lord of Lixnaw, L.14; to the Sugan earl, L.10; to Pierce Lacie, L.8; to M'Donough, L.12; to Redmonde Burke, L.500; to Teague O'Rouke, L.500. By which it may seem that these two last alone were in such a condition as to give the earl any hope of service from them.

The Sugan earl was, at the close of the year, reduced to such extremities, that it was little likely he could continue much longer to find refuge in the protection or connivance of those who perpetually saw fresh reason to be cautious in their movements. One day the lord-president had notice that he was at the time remaining with Dermond O'Dogan, a harper, by whom he was frequently received. A party of soldiers entered the wood where O'Dogan lived, but on reaching the house, discovered that the inmates had been on the point of sitting down to supper, but had on their approach taken flight into the woods; a mantle which they recognized, apprized them that Desmond was surely of the party. They instantly went in pursuit, but had not gone far when O'Dogan, and two others, having concealed the Sugan earl among the thickets, showed themselves in a distant open of the trees, until they attracted the soldiers' notice, and then took to flight, " with the Lapwings police."* They were readily pursued by the soldiers, who began to approach them after a long chase, as they reached the white knight's country, where a crowd of people rose in arms to their rescue. For this the pursuers were quite unprepared, and were compelled to leave them. On this pretence the lord Barry was loud in complaint against the white knight, against whom he entertained a violent enmity, and in consequence the knight was called before the president, who spoke to him so strongly, and with such decided effect, that the knight promised to exert himself for the capture of Desmond, engaging that in a few days he would give a good account of him, alive or dead, if he should be found in his country.

The white knight returning home, collected a few of his most faithful friends and followers, and informed them of his pledge. One of these asked if he would really seize the Sugan earl if he could find him. The knight assured him it was his sincere design, and the man undertook to guide him. On the 20th day of May, 1601, this party took horse and rode to the mountain of Slieve Gort. Here, in a deep cavern, among the mountain cliffs, the Sugan earl lurked with his little party. At the entrance of the cavern, the white knight, in a loud voice called on Desmond to come forth and surrender himself. But the earl, not believing that the knight's companions would seize him, and supposing that on sight of him they would rather take his part, came stoutly forth to the mouth of the cavern: as he was seen emerging from the darkness of the interior, he assumed a commanding manner, and called out to the party to seize on the white knight and secure him. As the knight and all his party were the subjects of

* Pacata Hib.

Desmond, this expedient was not without some hope of success; it was indeed his last chance of escape, and it entirely failed. Without condescending to make even a reply, the party at once surrounded their pretended lord, and in despite of his peremptory voice and looks they disarmed and bound himself and his foster-brother, and brought them away to the white knight's castle of Kilvenny, from whence a messenger was dispatched to the lord-president. On receiving this message a party from Kilmallock was sent to escort the prisoner. He was secured in Shandon castle, until he should be sent to England, and his custody was committed to captain Slingsby. The captain, considering that there was no hope for the prisoner, and that therefore nothing of a consolatory kind could be said, felt disposed to avoid all conversation with him, but Desmond, who was not inclined to be silent, or to let pass any occasion of making an impression which might be afterwards useful, of himself accosted the captain, and spent the night in extenuations to which it is probable little heed was seriously given. He represented that he had been an unwilling instrument of rebellion, and throughout urged on by the influence of others; that had he withstood the motives for taking the title of Desmond, it would have been taken by his brother John. He also pleaded his having ever avoided the shedding of English blood. He asserted his own prior title to the earldom, of which his father had been unfairly disinherited by the influence of his stepmother. With these and such topics he entertained captain Slingsby during the night. On the next morning an order came that he should be conveyed to Cork, where he was to be tried. At Cork his trial took place: he was indicted, arraigned, convicted, and condemned to be executed as a traitor. But the lord president wrote to advise that he should be confined to the Tower of London, as while he lived his brother could lay no claim to the earldom.

While a prisoner in Cork, the Sugan earl wrote the following representation to the president, which was forwarded with a letter from the lord-president, both of which may interest the reader:—

"*The relation of James of Desmond, to the Right Honourable* Sir George Carew, *lord president of Mounster, most humbly beseeching your honour to certifie her majesty, and the lords of her most honourable councell of the same: hoping in the Almighty, that her highness of her accustomed clemencie and mercy, by your intercession will take most gratious and mercifull consideration thereof, to the end that her majesties realme of Ireland shall be better planted and maintained in good government by his release.* The third of June 1601.

"First, it may please your honour, to consider that this action at the beginning was never pretended, intended, nor drawen by mee, nor my consent; but by my brother John, and Pierce Lacy, having the oaths and promises of divers noblemen, and gentlemen of this province, to maintaine the same, and not even consented unto by me, untill Sir Thomas Norris left Kilmallock, and the Irish forces camped at Rekeloe in Connologh, where they staid five or sixe dayes; the most of the country combining and adjoyning with them, and undertooke to hold with my brother John, if I had not come to them. The next sessions (before these proceedings,) at Corke. Sir Thomas Norris arrested me (in person), therefore my brother, he being then suspected by him, and intending to keep me in perpetuall prison for him, untill I made my escape; by this the intent of Sir Thomas Norris being knowen, the feare and terrification thereof drew me into this action, and had I been assured of my liberty, and not clapt into prison for my brother's offence, I had never entered into this action; further, I was bordered with most English neighbours, of the gentlemen of this province; I defie any English that can charge me with hindring of them, either in body or goods; but as many as ever came in my presence, I conveyed them away from time to time.

"Also it is to be expected, that the Spanish forces are to come into Ireland this summer, and O'Neale will send up the strongest army of northern men into Mounster, with my brother John, the lord of Lixnaw, and Pierce Lacy, and when they are footed in Mounster, the most part of the countrey will joyne with them: preventing this and many other circumstances of service, the saving of my life is more beneficiall for her majestie then my death: for it may please her majestie to be gratious unto me, I will reclaime my brother, the lord of Lixnaw, and Pierce Lacy, if it please her majestie to bee gratious unto them, or else so diligently worke againste them with her majesties forces, and your directions, that they shall not be able to make head, or stirre in Mounster at all; for by the saving of my life, her highnesse will winne the hearts in generall of all her subjects, and people in Ireland, my owne service, and continuance of my alliance in dutifull sort, all the dayes of their lives.

"Farther, I most humbly beseech your honour to forsee, that there are three others of my sept and race alive. The one is in England, my uncle Garrets sonne, James, set at liberty by her majestie, and in hope to obtaine her majesties favour, my brother in Ulster, and my cosen Maurice Fitz-John in Spaine, wherewith it may be expected, that either of these (if I were gone) by her majesties favour might be brought in credit, and restored to the house, it may therefore please her majestie to bee gratious unto me, assuring to God and the world, that I will bee true and faithful to her majestie during life, by which meanes her majesties government may bee the better setled, myselfe and all others my alliance, for ever bound to pray for her majesties life long to continue."

But afterward being examined by the president, and the provincial council, he added some other reasons for his taking of arms against her majesty, which in its due place shall be mentioned. In the dispatch which the president made into England upon his apprehension, he wrote a letter to her majesty as followeth:—

The Lord President's letter to Her Majesty.

" SACRED AND DREAD SOVEREIGN,

"To my unspeakable joy, I have received your majesties letters signed with your royall hand, and blessed with an extraordinarie addition to the same, which although it cannot increase my faith and zeale in your majesties service, which from my cradle (I thanke God) for it was ingrafted in my heart, yet it infinitely multiplies my comforts in the same, and wherein my endeavours and poore merites shall appeare to bee short of such inestimable favours, my never dying prayers for your majesties eternall prosperitie shall never faile to the last day of life, but when I compare the felicities which other men enjoy, with my unfortunate destinie, to be deprived from the sight of your royall person, which my heart with all loyall affection (inferior to none) evermore attends, I live like one lost to himselfe, and wither out my dayes in torment of minde, untill it shall please your sacred majestie to redeeme mee from this exile, which unlesse it bee for my sinnes, (upon the knees of my heart) I doe humbly beseech your majestie to commiserate, and to shorten the same, as speedily as may bee since my time of banishment in this rebellious kingdome (for better than a banishment I cannot esteeme my fortune, that deprives me from beholding your majesties person) although I have not done as much as I desire in the charge I undergoe, yet to make it appeare that I have not been idle, (I thanke God for it) I have now by the means of the white knight, gotten into my hands the bodie of James Fits-Thomas, that arch traytour, and usurping earle, whom for a present with the best conveniencie and safetie which I may finde, I will by some trustie gentleman send unto your majestie, whereby I hope this province is made sure from any present defection. And now that my taske is ended, I doe in all humilitie beseech, that in your princely commiseration my exile may end, protesting the same to bee a greater affliction to me than I can well endure; for as my faith is undivided, and onely professed (as by divine and human lawes the same is bound) in vassalage to your majestie; so doth my heart covet nothing so much, as to bee evermore attendant on your sacred person, accounting it a happinesse unto mee to dye at your feet; not doubting but that your majestie out of your princely and royall bountie, will enable me by some means or other to sustaine the rest of my dayes in your service, and that my fortune shall not be the worse, in that I am not any importunate craver, or yet in not using other arguments to move your majestie there unto, then this, assai dimandi qui ben serve e face. So humbly beseeching your majesties pardon in troubling you with these lines, unworthy your divine eyes, doe kisse the shadows of your royall feet. From your majesties citie of Corke, this third of June, 1601.*

From this letter Sir G. Carew goes on to remark, "He was within one year before his apprehension, the most potent and mightie Geraldine that had been of any of the earles of Desmond, his predecessors. For it is certainly reported that he had eight thousand men well armed under his command at one time, all which he employed against his lawful soveraigne; and secondly, a notorious traytour, because hee sought to bring a most infamous slander upon a most vertuous and renowned prince, (his queen and mistress) with his false suggestions into forraine princes; and notwithstanding that her name was eternised with the shrill sounding trumpet of fame, for the meekest and mildest prince that ever raigned, yet was not hee ashamed, (so farre had the rancour of malice corrupted his venemous heart) to inculcate into the ears of the Pope and Spanish king, that she was more tyrannical than Pharooh, and more blood-thirstie than Nero. But because I may be

* Pacata Hib. vol. i. p. 251.

thought to fain these allegations, to aggravate his treason, I will, therefore (for satisfaction of the reader), set downe the very wordes of two of his letters bearing one date, which he sent to the king of Spaine.

A letter from James Fitz-Thomas to the king of Spain.

"Most mighty monarch, I humbly salute your imperiall majesty, giving your highness to understand of our great misery, and violent order, wherewith wee are of long time opprest by the English nation. Their government is such as Pharoah himself never used the like; for they content not themselves with all temporall superiority, but by cruelty desire our blood, and perpetuall destruction to blot out the whole remembrance of our posterity; as also our old Catholike religion, and to sweare that the queene of England is supreame of the church. I referre the consideration hereof to your majestie's high judgment, for that Nero in his time was farre inferior to that queen in cruelty. Wherefore, and for the respects thereof, high, mighty potentate, myselfe, with my followers and retainers, and being also requested by the bishops, prelates, and religious men of my country, have drawn my sword, and proclaimed warres against them, for the recovery first of Christ's Catholike religion, and next for the maintenance of my own right, which of long time hath been wrongfully detained from mee and my father, who, by right succession, was lawful heire to the carledome of Desmond; for he was eldest sonne to James, my grandfather, who was earle of Desmond; and for that, uncle Gerald (being the younger brother) tooke part with the wicked proceedings of the queene of England, to further the unlawfull claime of supremacie, usurped the name of earle of Desmond, in my father's true title; yet notwithstanding, hee had not long enjoyed his name of earle, when the wicked English annoyed him, and prosecuted wars, that hee with the most part of those that held of side, was slaine, and his country thereby planted with Englishmen: and now by the just judgment and providence of God, I have utterly rooted those malepert bowes out of the orchard of my country, and have profited so much in my proceedings, that my dastardly enemies dare not show their faces in any part of my countrey, but having taken my towns and cities for their refuge and strength, where they doe remaine, (as yet were prisoners) for want of means to assaile them, as cannon and powder, which my countrey doth not yeeld. Having these wants, most noble potentate, I have presumed, with all humility, to address these my letters to your high majestie, craving the same of your gratious clemencie and goodnesse, to assist mee in this godly enterprise, with some help of such necessaries for the warres, as your majestie shall think requisite; and after the quiet of my countrey, satisfaction shall be truly made for the same, and myselfe in person, with all my forces, shall be ready to serve your highnesse, in any countrey your majesty may command me.

"And if your majestie will vouchsafe to send me a competent number of souldiers, I will place them in some of townes and cities, to remaine in your gratious disposition, till such time as my ability shall make good, what your majestie shall lend me in money and munition; and also your majestie's high commission, under the broad seal for leading and conducting of these souldiers, according to the prescript order and articles of marshall discipline, as your majestie shall appoint me, and as the service of the land shall require. I praise the Almighty God, I have done by his goodnesse, more than all my predecessors; for I have reclaimed all the nobility of this part, under the dutifull obedience of Christ's church, and mine own authority, and accordingly have taken pledges and corporall oathes, never to swarve from the same; and would have sent them to your majestie, by this bearer, but that the ship was not of sufficiency and strength to carry so noble personages, and will send them whensoever your highnesses please. So there resteth nothing to quiet this part of the world, but your majestie's assistance, which I daily expect. Thus, most mighty monarch, I humbly take my leave, and doe kisse your royall hands, beseeching the Almighty of your majesties health and happinesse. From my campe, the fourteenth day of March, 1599.

"Your majesties most humble at all command,
"JAMES DESMOND."

Another letter from James Fitz-Thomas to the king of Spain.

"Your majestie shall understand that the bearer hereof, Captain Andrew Roche, hath been always in the service of the queene of England, and hath performed her manifold services at sea; whereby he had great preferment and credit, and being of late time conversant with Catholikes, and teachers of divine instructions, that were sorry for his lewd life, made known unto him the danger wherein his soul was, so that, by their godly persuasions, he was at that time reclaimed, and subverted to bee a good Catholike, and to spend the residue of his life in the defence and service of the church; since which time of reconcilement, bee was to repaire to your majestie with his ship and goods, as is well known to your highness' councell, who confiscated that ship to your majestie's use; himself being at that time struken with extreame sicknesse, that he was not able to proceed in the voyage; and when his company returned into Ireland, they reported that the Santado wished rather his person than his ship, which made him fearefull ever since to repaire thither, till hee should deserve his freedome by some worthy service to your majestie.

"The heire apparent to the crowne of England had been carried by him to your highness, but that he was bewrayed by some of his owne men, and thereby was intercepted, and himself taken prisoner, where he remained of long, till by the providence of God, and the help of good friends, hee was conveyed into Ireland to me in a small boat; and leaving these occasions to your imperial majestie, and being assured of his trust, faith, and confidence towards mee, have committed this charge into his hands; the rather for that I understand your royall fleete is directed for England this yeare, to the end he may be a leader and conductor to them in the coast of England and Ireland, being very expert in the knowledge thereof, and in the whole art of navigation. And thus, with all humility, I commit your highnesse to the Almighty. From my campe, the fourteenth of March, 1599.*

"Your majesties most humble at all command,
"JAMES DESMOND."

* Pacata Hib. p. 252.

While he remained a prisoner in Shandon castle, the president caused him to be frequently brought before him, and examined him minutely to ascertain the true causes of the Munster rebellion; he thus obtained some statements which were confirmed by circumstances, all of which are specially mentioned by the president of Munster as exhibiting in a clear light how trifling were the pretexts of this rebellion. Many of these reasons will not appear now so trifling, but we shall, however, reserve them for an occasion further on, when we shall be enabled to give them a more full and satisfactory discussion. We shall here be content to state, that religion was the main and principal pretext— while the remainder were grievances which, though affording far more justifiable ground for discontent, were put forward as matters of less comparative moment.

Among these revelations of the Sugan earl, the most immediately important were those which gave the fullest and clearest light upon the intercourse of the Irish insurgents with the king of Spain, and left little doubt that a Spanish expedition into Ireland was in preparation, and ere long to be looked for. And next the circumstantial crimination of Florence MacCarthy, as having taken a very leading part in this design. It was on this information, that the lord-president ordered the arrest of MacCarthy, which was the easier to effect, as the double part which he had throughout acted prevented his taking much precaution. When he was arrested, his house was searched, and various letters were found, amply serving to confirm all the charges of the Sugan earl.

On the 14th of August, 1601, both the Sugan earl and MacCarthy were conveyed to London, and committed to the Tower. There the Sugan earl continued for the remainder of his life, and died in 1608. He was interred in the Tower chapel.

THE BUTLERS OF ORMONDE.

JOHN, SIXTH EARL OF ORMONDE.

DIED A. D. 1478.

This earl was attainted for his faithful adherence to the Lancastrian monarch. Edward IV., however, restored him in blood. He is memorable as the most finished gentleman of his day. Edward IV., himself eminent for manners and accomplishments beyond the rudeness of his age, said of him, "that he was the goodliest knight he ever beheld, and the finest gentleman in Christendom; and that if good-breeding, good-nature, and liberal qualities were lost in the world, they might all be found in John, earl of Ormond." He was master of most living languages of Europe, and had been employed by Edward IV. as his ambassador to every court.

He did not marry. He made a pilgrimage to the Holy Land, where he died, 1478.

PIERCE, EIGHTH EARL OF ORMONDE.

DIED A. D. 1539.

WE have already stated how this nobleman and his lady, a sister of the ninth earl of Kildare, were reduced to a condition of the most deplorable privation, and compelled to conceal themselves in some lowly dwelling among the woods, till, driven by the complaints of his wife, and his sense of wrong, he surprised and slew the usurper, and thus regained his estates and honours.

His family had, by the result of a series of political events, most of which have been noticed under their proper heads, been depressed in power and party importance in Ireland. This disadvantage was to some extent counterbalanced by court favour, and that social importance which results from polished manners and liberal accomplishments; in which respect, the members of this illustrious race appear constantly in advance of their times, and seem to have transmitted through many descents, a vein of more refined humanity than the historian may otherwise trace in the 15th and 16th centuries. The earls of Ormonde were in these ages more frequently to be found high in the councils and favour of the English monarchs, while the two great branches of the Geraldines, present, on the other hand, a uniform affinity for the Irish habits, and a strong tendency to factious movements. Their position and vast possessions in part account for these tendencies; but on a lengthened comparison carried through many generations, the singular uniformity becomes observable; the immense pride—the reckless activity—the love of popularity—the insubordinate temper, breaking out with nearly similar results in each successive generation, and ripening into the same successes and disasters, appear to assume the character of family features.

When lord Surrey was sent over as lieutenant, the earl of Ormonde was active, efficient, and distinguished in promoting the success of his various expeditions against the O'Tooles, O'Carrol, and other native chiefs. His character is set in a strong point of view by the friendship of Surrey, who appears to have relied on his counsel in all important matters, and to have set high value on his conversation. This is made evident by his many letters to the king, and to Wolsey, in which he freely praises his conduct, and shows anxiety for his interests. In a letter to Wolsey in 1520, he writes, "beseeching your grace to cause thankful letters to be sent from the king's grace to the earl of Ormonde, as well for his diligence showed unto me at all times, as also for that he showeth himself ever, with his good advice and strength, to bring the king's intended purpose to good effect. Undoubtedly he is not only a wise man, and hath a true English heart, but he is the man of most experience in the feats in war of this country, of whom I have at all times the best counsel of any in this land. I would the earl of Desmond were of like wisdom and order." It is stated on strong authority, that although bearing the title of Ormonde, he was not fully recognised as such until 1528, although in the patent by which he was appointed lord deputy of Ireland, dated 6th March, 1522, he was denominated "Petrus Butteler comes Ormonde," without qualification.

He was, during the time of Surrey's administration, involved in a party war with the earl of Desmond, and great efforts were made by government for their reconciliation.

The most remarkable incident to be noticed in the life of this earl, is perhaps the treaty which was for some time in agitation for the marriage of his son with Anna Boleyn, the daughter of Sir Thomas Boleyn, and afterwards the unfortunate queen of Henry VIII., and mother of queen Elizabeth. Happy had it been for the lady, at least, had this treaty been carried into effect. The subject appears to have occupied considerable attention; it is thus mentioned in a communication to Wolsey, from Surrey and his council: " And where, at our being with your grace, divers of us moved you to cause a marriage to be solemnized between the earl of Ormonde's son, being with your grace and Sir Thomas Boleyn's daughter. We think, if your grace caused that to be done, and a final end to be made between them, for the title of lands depending in variance, it should cause the said earl be better willed to see this land brought to good order."* The variance here alluded to, was one of long standing, and arose from the circumstance of Thomas, seventh earl of Ormonde, having had two daughters, and no male issue; in consequence of this, his large English estates, £30,000 a-year, according to the present value of lands, went to his two daughters, while his Irish estates went with his title to the male heir. The parties were not, however, themselves, satisfied about their rights; one of the co-heirs married Sir William Boleyn, who seems to have thought himself entitled to the Irish properties and honours. The marriage was approved by the earl; but did not, as the reader is aware, take place. The dispute was shortly after settled by a compromise. Sir Thomas Boleyn was created earl of Ormonde, and earl Pierce received the title of Ossory. About ten years after, on the death of Sir Thomas without issue, the title of Ormonde was restored to the earl of Ossory.

When Surrey, after remaining two years in the Irish government, was recalled, the earl of Ossory was, by his recommendation, appointed lord deputy. His conduct was such as to obtain for him in 1524 the office of lord treasurer, in Ireland. In 1528, he was again elected lord deputy by the council, and received many valuable testimonies of approbation also from the king. In 1537, he received a grant in confirmation of his extensive Irish estates to himself and heirs. The estates mentioned in this give some notion of his wealth. Among other estates, were the names of Gowran, Knockfert, Knocktopher, Kilkenny, Glashan, Carrick, Thurles, Nenagh, Roscrea, &c. &c.†

This earl was distinguished for his manly and honourable dispositions, which were generally respected; he was sagacious, and firm in council; a pleasing companion in private society, and a brave warrior in the field. He deserved the high praise of having exerted himself successfully for the improvement of the manners and condition of his people about Kilkenny, at a time when other eminent lords only thought of augmenting their estates and retaining power by unprincipled faction and sanguinary wars. In conformity with this good disposition,

* State Papers. † Lodge.

the earl of Ormonde was exemplary for the zeal and devotion of his religious observances. It is told of him, that every year, for a fortnight previous to Easter, he retired for the purpose of self-examination and holy exercise, to prepare himself for the reception of the sacrament at that festival.

It must be admitted, that in the long and angry contests between him and the earl of Kildare, he was not behind that earl in hostility; but it was a time when there was no choice between these fierce, and not very elevated contests of faction, and the total abandonment of every right. The following letter to his son, lord Butler, then with the king, may convey some notion of his own view of his position, and is otherwise of interest:—

"Ormonde to lord Butler.

"In my loving maner I recommende me unto you, and lately hath had relacion, that certain of the counsaill, by the deputies meanes, have written over thider, to have the kinges letters addressed to me, prohibiting me to take any Irishe mens part. Whereupon, ye most ever have good, secret, and diligent espyall, lest the kinges letters be so optayned, whiche then wold not oonly bee grete prejudice to me, and to you in tyme commyng, but also great discorage to all myne adherentes to continue any amytie to me, or you herafter. Now, ye may perceive the parcialitie of theym, that so certified, being ordred and conducted therin, as the deputie wolde have theym; and during my being in thauctoritie, they never certified any of therl of Kildares apparaunt mysorder, or transgression, in any maner. Shewe the kinges grace, and my lord cardynall, of the soden wilfull invasion doon by the deputie upon O'Kerole, long after the date of the kinges letters now directed; wherof I have rather certified you by a frere of mowskery. Wherupon ye must devise in my name, to the king and my lord cardinall, as my trusty servaunt, Robert Couley, shall penn and endite.

"As for thindentures, they bee enfrenged by the deputie, and in maner no point observed; and as for my parte, I will justifie, I have truly observed theym, to my gret losses, in suffring my adherentes and servauntes distruccions. The deputie, now afore Ester, did set suche coyn and liverey in the 3 obedyent sheres, that mervaile it were to here two litell townes of myne, called Castell Warning, and Oghterarde, with any other towne, did bere 420 galloglas. For 4 myles the poor tenauntes be so empoverysshed, that they cannot paye my rentes, and the landes like to bee clere wast. Now, lately he hath sente out of the eschequier a writ to Waterforde, that all maires and bailliffes, that were there sens the furst yere of our souverain lord that now is, shold appere in 15 Pā* to geve accompt, before the barons, for al maner the king duties, revenues, and poundage there; whiche is doon for a cantell to put me to losses and my heires. For Waterford hath a sufficient discharge, but oonly for my halff of the prises, and the £10 annuite, with the 20 markes to the churche; and as for the price, and £10 of annuite, I must see theym discharged. Wherfore, ye must

* Quindena Puscha.

labour to gette an especiall patent of the king of all the prises in this land, according to my graunte, made to myne anncesters by his most noble progenitours, and specially in Waterford, and the £10 of annuitie, without any accompt-making; with this clause, "absque aliquo compoto," &c. If it bee not had, it will be moche prejudice to you in tyme commying; for this is doon to dryve you ever from the principall wynes, and the said annuitie, and not to have your prises till ye have a discharge out of theschequer, from tyme. In any wise, slepe not this matier, and if ye do, the most losses and trouble wil be yours in tyme commying. Immediat upon the receipt herof sende for Robert Couly, and cause hym to seche remedies for the same; and, if James White bee not commying, let hym endeavor hymself to obteigne it. Furthermore, I desire you to make diligent hast hyther with the kinges licence; for surely, onles I see your tyme better employed in attendance of my great busynes, then ye have doon hither, I wolbe well avised, or I do sende you any more to your costes.

"Written at Kilkenny, the 22d daye of April.

(Superscribed) "To my son, James Butler, with the kings grace in England."

This illustrious earl died in 1539, and was buried in St Canice's church, Kilkenny.

JAMES, NINTH EARL OF ORMONDE.

DIED A. D. 1546.

The ninth earl of Ormonde took a prominent part in the Irish affairs of his time, long before the death of his father, in whose memoir we have already had occasion to notice him. He was, for many years, the great support and prop of his father's declining age, whom we can ascertain by his letters, recently published in the *State Papers*, to have placed much reliance on his zeal and judgment.

We have already mentioned his spirited and noble answer to a letter from his unfortunate and guilty cousin. We have also mentioned, that in 1532, seven years before his accession to his father's honours, he was appointed lord high treasurer of Ireland for life. In 1535, he was appointed admiral of the kingdom, and the same year was created viscount Thurles. He was also appointed joint governor with his father, over Kilkenny, Waterford, and Tipperary; and in the following year distinguished himself by the suppression of disturbances raised in Munster by James, the young earl of Desmond, whose father having died the same year, he was led by inexperience, inordinate ambition and evil counsel, to launch into the rebellious course so native to his family, and so fatal to many of them. Lord Butler, then lord Thurles, was sent against him, and proceeded with the spirit and prudence of his character, to the attack of his territories about Limerick; he also seized his castle at Lough Gur, and converted it into a fortress against him. We here give the reader one of his own letters on this occasion, which has been preserved in the chapter-house, and recently published:—

"Lord Butler to Cromwell.

"Please it your goodness to be advertised, that I have of late addressed mine other letters to you, containing my proceedings in the west parts of this land, immediately after the winning of Dungarvon, to which my journey, if the lord deputy had spared me one of the battering pieces (God being my leader) undoubtedly such service might have been done with so little charge, that the king's highness should have been therewith pleased and well contented. But as it chanced, with such company as I then had of my own, with the good assistance of Stephen Appany, captain of 100 spears, I rode forth to Youghal, Cork, and Limerick, and had, of the young pretended earl of Desmond, such reasonable offers at his coming in, that I suppose these many days the lords and captains of that country were not so testable to good order, like as more amply appeareth in my former letters. Sir, of truth, the lord deputy* minding to have his service and proceedings the better advanced, and blowen out by the report of my lords, my father and me, instantly desired us to put our hands to a letter (devised by himself) in his recommendation [commendation]; which letter, I suppose, is sent forth by him unto the king's grace. And albeit, my lord, my father's service or mine was never much commended by his advertisement, yet partly of courtesy, and also trusting he would then with better will have lent me one of the said battering pieces, I put to my hand, and so did my lord, my father, at his return from Waterford, trusting also to have had the said piece to serve against the Breenys. I reckon it no great wisdom, nor yet matter of honour, where any man procureth another to be his herald. And for my part, God and the king knowith my true heart, to whom I humbly commit the construction of my poor service. And since there now repaireth unto his grace, Sir John Saintlaw, who never spared for pain of art and charge to do his grace good service worthy of remuneration, I commit unto his breast the report of my proceedings, and shall most heartily desire you to thank him for the loving approved kindness I have always found in him towards my lord, my father, and me. The king's grace, and he himself, being so pleased, my desire is that he may return hither again, since I have at full perceived his diligent service to be such, as if he return not, I shall have great lack of him, as knowith God who ever preserve you. At Waterford, 17 day of October, 1535.

"Your assured kinsman,

(Signed) "JAMES BUTLER."

(Superscribed.) "To my right honourable cousin, and most loving friend, master Cromwell, the king's secretary."

Lord Butler's patent, by which he was created lord Thurles, had not yet passed. But it is remarked in a note on this letter, that neither he, nor Grey, or viscount Grane, who were ennobled, or advanced at the same time, seem to have assumed their titles "either in their signatures, or in the style by which they were addressed."†

* Skeffington. † Note to paper cxl. p. 249.

In consideration of his many and great services, large grants were made to lord Butler in the years 1539 and 1542; of these several were manors which had belonged to the earl of Kildare. In 1539, his father died, and he succeeded to his honours, &c. in the same year he was sent against the Connaught insurgents. In 1543, he had a commission along with his cousin and Desmond, to make levies through Tipperary, Waterford, Cork, Kerry, to take, imprison, or protect, according to his judgment and the purposes of his commission. Among other commissions, in this busy period of his life, he was sent into Scotland in command of the Irish forces sent over to join the earl of Lenox, and others, in prosecution of a war which had various parties and purposes, but had been promoted and joined by king Henry for views of his own in the year before when he had a considerable force at his disposal. In this year the invasion languished, and the English and Irish were withdrawn without having effected any important service. On this occasion, lord Butler, then ninth earl of Ormonde, is mentioned to have levied 1500 of his own followers—being a number equal to that levied by the deputy, St Leger, for the king.

In 1546, this illustrious nobleman was lost to his time and country in the flower of his age. Having publicly accused the deputy, St Leger, of high treason, the deputy retorted the charge, and both were summoned to England. While residing there he was poisoned, with several of his servants, at Ely house in Holborn. The entertainment is said, by Ware, to have been given him by his own people—the poison was, in all probability, accidental. The number who were poisoned is mentioned by Lodge to have been thirty-five; Ware says, his steward and sixteen servants. The earl was buried in the church of St Thomas of Acres: but his heart was brought over and buried in the cathedral of St Canice, Kilkenny. We add an extract of his will, which has interest. After the directions concerning his burial, he devises that "My sonne and heyre, being in the prince's graces court, shall have my basin and ewer, which I have here, a silver pot, a salt, a new boll, a trencher, and a spoon of silver. Item, my wife (Joan, daughter to the 11th earl of Desmond), to have my best bracelet of gold sent her for a token. Item, to my lord chancellor of England, my new gilded goblet with the cover, for a token. Item, master Fitz-William, to have a new boll of them that were lately made, for a token, &c., &c."

He was succeeded by his eldest son, Thomas, viscount Thurles.

THOMAS, TENTH EARL OF ORMONDE.

BORN A. D. 1532—DIED A. D. 1614.

IN placing the life of this illustrious Irishman in the present period, it becomes necessary to explain a disposition which may otherwise seem to be a violation of the arrangement which we have adopted; viz., to place our notices according to the death of the persons noticed. We should, however, here observe, that this most convenient general rule has been, all through the previous portion of our work, subject to another more important, though less definite principle of arrangement. We have endeavoured, in all the more extended and strictly historical memoirs of contemporary persons, to place them according to the order of the events in which they were mainly concerned; as it is evident that, by this means, the historical order would be best preserved. Thus our arrangement has been in reality one compounded on both these considerations; and, we may observe, adopted more as a convenience than as a restriction. In the present instance, as in a few more which follow in the close of the period, it will be accordingly observed, that although this earl, together with the first earl of Cork, &c., continue to live into the reign of James I., yet all the great events of their lives fall within the reign of queen Elizabeth, in such a manner that, were we to place them in our next period, we should have to travel back into the history of this—a violation of order which would be something more than formal.

The tenth earl of Ormonde was born some time about 1532; and, as he was thus but fourteen years old in 1546—the time of his father's death—great precautions were taken to preserve his property against the encroaching and freebooting spirit of the age. For this purpose it was ordered that the lord justice should draw the English army, at his command, towards the counties of Kilkenny and Tipperary; and it was also ordered that the government of these counties should be committed to his family. He was himself brought up in the English court, and was one of the most favoured companions of the young prince Edward, with whom he was educated. At the age of fourteen, he was made a knight of the Bath, at the coronation of this king. It is also mentioned that the king ordered the lord deputy to increase his allowance to the sum of 200 marks.* When he attained his nineteenth year, he obtained by the same favour a year's release of his wardship. He begun his military career at the same time with distinguished honour. It is briefly mentioned, after these incidents, by the antiquarians, that he accompanied the duke of Somerset in his expedition against the Scots. This requires some explanation; for though the Scottish war alluded to certainly was continued in the same year, yet it is as certain that it was not commanded by the duke of Somerset, who first declared war, and led an expedition into Scotland, in 1547, when Ormonde was but fifteen years of age. In the following years, the command of the armies sent against the Scots was intrusted to the earls of Shrewsbury and Northampton. But military training, at that period, formed so principal a part in education, that there is no improbability in supposing the military career of this earl to have commenced even so early. These conjectures are confirmed by the mention that he distinguished himself by his bravery in the battle of Musselburgh; better known in history as the battle of Pinkey, which took place 10th September, 1547. In this battle the Scots were defeated by the English, under the duke of Somerset, with the loss of 14,000 men, of whom 800 were gentlemen. The war was engaged in to compel the Scots to deliver up their young queen, who had been contracted to Edward VI. when they were both children.

* Collins, Lodge.

He obtained still higher distinction in his twenty-second year, when he commanded a troop of horse against the rebels headed by Sir Thomas Wyatt. This rebellion is supposed to have been caused by the discontent of the English at the marriage then on foot between Philip and Mary. The chief conspirators were the duke of Suffolk, Sir Thomas Wyatt, and Sir Peter Carew, who agreed with each other to raise their several counties of Cornwall, Kent, and Warwickshire. Through the indiscretion of Carew, the plot was soon detected. Carew escaped into France; the duke was seized before he could stir to any purpose; and Wyatt was left to pursue his desperate course alone. Of this course we shall only mention the terminating circumstances.

Wyatt approached London at the head of a force sufficient to cause great alarm in the court, and to give him high hopes of success. To the queen's messengers, who desired to know his demands, he replied that he demanded to have the Tower and the queen delivered into his hands, with such changes in the council as he should prescribe. Of course these demands were rejected, and Wyatt pursued his march toward London. When he had reached the borough of Southwark, he found the bridge so well fortified that, contrary to his expectations, he could not effect a passage. He was, therefore, obliged to continue his march to Kingston, ten miles higher up the river. Here, too, he met with another dangerous delay—the bridge was broken down, and he could not pass without having it first repaired. Having effected this, he passed over with his men, now increased to six thousand. He then set forward on his march to London; but a gun-carriage having broken on his way, he lost more time in repairing it. Two days were thus consumed when he reached London, at nine in the morning of the 3d February, 1554. The captain of the train bands who had joined him deserted, and gave information that it was his plan to enter the city by Ludgate. The earl of Pembroke and lord Clinton at first came to the resolution to attack him while entering the city, and a partial attack took place.

It was at this period of the affair, that the only occasion occurs in which the young earl could have displayed his valour. Hollinshed, who gives the detail at greater length than we can afford to follow, describes two skirmishes which took place near Hyde Park, and in Charing Cross. In the first of these it was mentioned that while Wyat was marching on the "nether way," towards St James's, "which being perceived by the queen's horsemen, who laie on either side of him, they gave a sudden charge, and divided his battel [army, marching in column] asunder hard behind Wyatt's ensigns, whereby so many as were not passed before with Wyatt, were forced to fly back towards Brainford." It was in this charge that the young earl must have taken part. The body thus separated, after a vain attack on St James's, Westminster, attempted to rejoin their leader, and were again assailed in Charing Cross, and scattered after a short resistance and a loss of twenty men. In the course of this affair, it became apparent that he was entangling his army in the streets and lanes which lay on his way towards Ludgate, so that it became impossible for his troops to extend their front, or in any way act in concert. Sending orders to have Ludgate closed, the queen's commanders contented themselves with fortifying and placing strong detachments in the streets through which he passed, so as to render all retreat impossible. In the meantime, Wyatt went on anticipating no obstruction, and imagining the whole of his remaining course sure, until he came to the gate. There his entrance was impeded, and he was forced to halt; and it was not long before he learned that he was strongly barricaded in on every side. His artillery he had in his confidence left under a guard in Hyde Park, and was now completely entrapped in the midst of enemies, who possessed every advantage they could devise for his extermination. In this dreadful emergency he was accidentally met by Sir Maurice Barkleic, who was riding unarmed near London, and entered into conversation with him. Barkleie advised him to surrender. Wyatt saw the necessity; and, resolved to seize on the occasion, he mounted behind his adviser, and, so says Hollinshed, rode to the court voluntarily to yield himself prisoner. He was sent to prison; and, after an attempt to implicate the princess Elizabeth, which he subsequently retracted, he was executed in two months after on Towerhill.

Thus early distinguished, this earl came over to Ireland, where his own affairs demanded his presence, and, having attained his twenty-second year, it was time for him to take possession of his estates, and assume the place appertaining to his family and rank in the councils of his country. He was not long settled in his possessions, before an occasion arose for his military spirit to obtain fresh distinction. In 1556, the province of Ulster was disturbed by a party of Scots, who besieged Carrick Fergus; and, although they failed in their design upon this town, obtained advantages in different quarters by associating themselves with the O'Donells, and other chiefs who in these party wars had gathered power, and were beginning to assume a dangerous attitude. In July, the lord deputy, Ratcliff, marched against them. He was accompanied by Ormonde, who commanded 200 horse, and 500 foot, raised by himself and maintained at his own cost. On the 18th of the same month, the lord deputy's army came up with the Scots, and a sharp conflict ensued, in which the Scots and the insurgents were defeated with a loss of 200 slain. In this engagement the earl of Ormonde and Sir John Stanley have obtained the principal honour from all historians by whom this affair is mentioned. The three following years were distinguished by great military activity; and, through the whole course of the marches and encounters during this period, this earl supported the same conspicuous character among the foremost in every bold and difficult enterprise.

These occasions are too numerous and too little detailed by historical writers to be here dwelt upon. The uniform distinction of the earl through the whole, is amply testified by the strong indications of the approbation of the English government. In each year his rise is marked by some honourable mark of the royal favour. In 1555, his patent was confirmed for the royalties and liberties of Tipperary—as also his hereditary patent for the prize wines. In 1557, he received a grant of the religious houses of Athassil, Jerpoint, Callan, Thurles, Carrick, &c., with all their hereditaments in the counties of Tipperary, Kilkenny, and Waterford; the manor of Kilrush in the county of Kildare, &c., &c., to hold by the service of a single knight's fee, reserving a rent of £49 3s. 9d., afterwards remitted by Elizabeth. The subsequent grants which he received from Elizabeth, fill more than a closely printed page of Collins and Archdall, from which the above are abridged.

Queen Elizabeth, in the first year of her reign, appointed this earl lord treasurer of Ireland, a post which he retained through his life. There is not a year in the first years of this queen's reign so eventful in Ireland, in which he did not bear a distinguished part, which amply maintain his claim to the foremost place in the councils and confidence of the government. To dwell on the most interesting of these events, would hereafter involve us in much repetition, as they form the material for the curious and striking history of the memorable insurgent chiefs of this reign, the Desmonds, O'Donell, and Shane O'Niall. But through the whole stormy tissue of rebellion, party war, and provincial disturbance, which seems in his time to be fast attaining its height of violence and frequency; whether as military commander or diplomatic pacificator, the earl's character appears alike eminently bright through the obscurity of the time. After being successively appointed to the most important offices of trust in every trying and difficult occasion, from 1559 to 1578, he was in the latter year made governor of the province of Munster, when he brought O'Sullivan More into subjection by force of arms, subdued Pierce Grace, Rory Oge, and the MacSwiney's, and took the earl of Desmond prisoner, with a slaughter of four thousand men and forty-six officers.

In 1581, his honourable career was rewarded by the high office of lord high marshall of England. He did not long continue in this exalted station; but his voluntary resignation is ennobled by the high and patriotic motive. He could not reconcile it to his sense of duty to retain a post of which the arduous and engrossing duties were such as imply an entire separation from his own country. He was allowed, upon his earnest suit, to resign; and in 1582, he returned with the appointment of general of Munster, and a supply of men. He, at the same time, obtained an addition of twopence a-day to the pay of soldiers employed in the Irish service, and by this means, much increased his popularity among the soldiers.

In Ireland his services were still called into action on each occasion, where activity, fidelity, and talent were required; and many instances occur in which these conspicuous qualities of his character are placed under requisition by the absence of the deputy, or by some occasion of unexpected emergency. In 1596, he was made a knight companion of the garter. He was appointed general of Leinster in 1597, when Tyrone's rebellion had assumed a formidable character; and subsequently in the same year, was made general of all her majesty's forces in Ireland. Nor was he long at the head of the military operations, when Tyrone applied to obtain a commission to treat with him, which was appointed; and a meeting having accordingly taken place at Dundalk, a truce for eight weeks was agreed upon, for the purpose of settling the terms of this great rebel's submission, by communication with the English government. These particulars we shall hereafter detail.

In January, 1600, the earl obtained a considerable victory over the Bourkes, whom he drove out of Ormonde. Redmond Bourke was forced, with many of his men, into the Nore, where they were lost. On the following April, he went with the lord president of Munster to hold a parley with Owen Mac Rory O'More, who treacherously seized upon him; the lord president Carew escaped by the swiftness of his horse. Ormonde gave hostages for the payment of £3000, in case he should seek revenge.

After this, his conduct was not less distinguished by unremitting efficiency in his high station, until the death of the queen. She had ever retained the highest regard for him, and professed to consider him as her kinsman. King James, on his accession, renewed his commission as commander of the Irish army.

His biographers mention, that a little before this period he had lost his sight—a fact which, according to the dates of some of the enterprises above mentioned, compared with that assigned for his personal misfortune, would seem to imply, that he must, when blind, have continued to take the field against the rebels: as the period of about fifteen years before his death, assigned as the time of his blindness by Collins, Lodge, &c., would make it to have occurred in 1599. He died in 1614, in the 82d year of his age, and was buried in the choir of St Canice's church, Kilkenny. His monument cost £400.

DANIEL O'SULLIVAN BEARE.

FLOURISHED A. D. 1601.

THE chiefs of Beare and Bantry claim the interesting distinction which belongs to the most romantic localities in this island, the scenes of their ancient crimes and honours. Where the broad waves of the Atlantic rush fiercest among the deep and rock-bound bays of the wild promontories of Kerry, there stand the ruins of the O'Sullivans' dwellings. Turbulent and warlike, in common with their ancient peers, the chiefs and princes of the island, barbarous with the age, they were, by the accident of position, more fierce, lawless, and independent, than their territorial pretensions would otherwise seem to imply. In the harbours of their sterile and isolated domain, the pirate and the smuggler found the surest anchorage, and the readiest mart or storehouse for his lawless cargo; nor did the spirit of the time attach dishonour to an alliance which the advance of civilization has converted into crime. Still more important was the influence and distinction which the O'Sullivans must have acquired from the advantage of possessing the main entrance of that communication with Spain, which was actively maintained during the 15th and 16th centuries. During these ages of turbulence, when enterprise and adventure were among the ordinary events of life, many are the wild romances and deep tragedies which were realized among those wild and savage sites—in which the tyrant's fortress and the plunderer's cave were nothing different; and here, as Otway tells us in his book of pictures, we can hardly call them sketches, "every man is an O'Sullivan." Bearhaven and Bantry, and all the still wild districts around, are peopled by the same ancient sept, and retain the traces of their ancient lords; and many ruins still preserve the remembrances of their history.

The composition by which the castles in the possession of the Spaniards were surrendered to the English general, could not fail to be highly offensive to the Irish chiefs by whom they had been placed in their hands; but; most of all, to O'Sullivan Beare, whose chief castle of Dunboy being among the ceded places, he was thereby, in a manner, himself delivered up to the mercy of the English governor. He, consequently, resolved to regain it, as he might, before this surrender should occur. Accordingly, in the dead of the night, he caused a hole to be made in the wall, through which eighty of his own people stole into the castle. Outside he had stationed a strong party, among whom are mentioned Archer the Jesuit, the lord of Lixnaw, Donell M'Carthy, captain Tyrrel, &c., with 1000 men. All the while, O'Sullivan himself, who lodged within the castle, was quietly sleeping in his bed. Early in the morning the Spanish commander discovered how he was circumstanced; but, by the intervention of Archer, who led him to O'Sullivan, he was prevented from making the resistance he could yet have easily made. They had some difficulty in restraining the Spanish soldiery, who slew three men before they could be pacified; but order was soon restored, and O'Sullivan took the command of Dunboy castle. Having disarmed the Spaniards, and sent off the common men to Baltimore to be shipped for Spain, he took possession of their ordnance and stores, and sent a letter to the king of Spain excusing his violent seizure of the castle, professing his intention to retain it for the use of the king, and adding, " not only my castle and haven, called Bearhaven, but also my wife, my children, my country, lordships, and all my possessions for ever, to be disposed of at your pleasure." He then, in very strong terms, complains of the injustice of Don Juan's conduct, in having surrendered by treaty his castle of Dunboy, which he describes "the only key of mine inheritance, whereupon the living of many thousand persons doth rest that live some twenty leagues upon the sea-coast." Among other things, in this epistle we learn, that with the letter O'Sullivan sent his son, a child of five years old, as a pledge for the performance of his promises. This letter, with others from the same chief, were intercepted between Kinsale and Cork.* In another letter of the same packet and date to the " earl of Carracena," there occurs a brief version of the above transaction, in which he says, that although the Spaniards killed three of his best gentlemen, that he would not suffer them to be molested, but, "without harm, forced them out of my said castle, saving their captain, with five or six, unto whom I have allowed certain roomes in my house to look to the king's munition and artillerie;" he then urges speedy relief, or else a small ship to be sent to carry away himself and his family into Spain. In another letter, deprecating the ruin of his own family, he describes them, " whose ancestors maintained the credit and calling of great gentlemen these two thousand and six hundred years, sithence their first coming out of Spaine."

To maintain this deed and those pretensions, O'Sullivan made active

* Pac. Hiber.

and energetic preparations; but his main dependance was upon the hired bands of Tyrrel and Burke.

On hearing of this obstacle to the fulfilment of his treaty with the lord-deputy, Don Juan immediately volunteered to reduce Dunboy, but the offer was civilly declined; and instructions were given to the earl of Thomond to assemble an army and draw towards the place. He was instructed to burn the country of Carbery, Beare, and Bantry; to protect the chiefs who had submitted; to take a view of the castle; to relieve captain Flower, who was in these districts with a small party, and to make other usual preparations for the attack of Dunboy.

The earl of Thomond marched to the abbey of Bantry, where he gained intelligence that Daniel O'Sullivan was engaged in strengthening his works at Dunboy, and that Tyrrel had so judiciously placed himself among the mountains, that he could not with his present force attempt to pass farther. On this the earl of Thomond left his troops with captain Flower, the lord Barry, and other eminent officers, in the Isle of Whiddy, and went to Cork, to give an account to Sir G. Carew of the position of the enemy. Carew decided on instantly assembling all the force within his reach and marching into Kerry.

The expedition was attended with great peril, both from the nature of the country, and the strength of a fortress which was thought to be impregnable; and Sir George Carew's friends and counsellors strongly dissuaded him from an attempt unlikely to succeed, and of which the failure would be injurious to the English cause, and hazardous to himself. Such fears had no place in the heart of the brave Carew, whose courage was not inferior to his prudence, or his military genius to either. To the strong dissuasion of those friends who described to him the tremendous obstacles and perils of the march, he replied, " That neither bays nor rocks should forbid the draught of the cannon: the one he would make passable by faggots and timber—the other he would break and smooth with pioneers' tools." On the 20th April, 1602, he drew out his army from Cork, amounting to 1500 men, and began his march, and in seven days came to Carew castle, anciently built by his ancestors, at a place now well known to the visitor of Glengariffe under the name of Dunemarc. He was joined by captain Flower, who had been stationed in the vicinity by the earl of Thomond. Here the army continued for some time with an occasional skirmish; they also contrived to collect considerable spoil in cows, sheep, and horses. Fifty cows were brought into the camp by Owen O'Sullivan, son to Sir Owen O'Sullivan, who continued faithful to the queen's government.

Sir G. Carew, hearing that the Spanish artillerymen were yet in Dunboy, wrote them a letter in Spanish desiring them to come out; it was delivered by means of Owen O'Sullivan, but had not the desired effect. During this time Sir Charles Wilmot, who had been made governor of Kerry, had performed many important services, seizing on several castles in the country, and obtaining the victory in three or four small battles. He was now sent for to join the president.

On the 14th of May a consultation was held to consider the best means of bringing the army to Bearhaven; and, as the difficulties of the way were fully described to the lord-president by Owen O'Sullivan and other Kerry gentlemen, it was decided to transport the army across the arm of the sea which lay between, to Bear Island, on the other side of which, on the opposite shore, stood the castle of Dunboy. But, from the roughness of the weather, it was not till the last day of May the army could be moved from Carew castle. The sick were then placed with a strong guard in the Island of Whiddy; and on the first and second of June the army crossed Bantry bay.

On the 4th, the castle of Dunmanus was surprized by Owen O'Sullivan; and on the next day intelligence reached the camp that a Spanish vessel had put into the bay of Camnara, near Ardee. The rebel party seem at this period to have conceived the notion that the English might be discouraged by the dangers and difficulties of their undertaking. Richard MacGeoghegan, constable of the fort, was sent to obtain a parley with the earl of Thomond, to whom he pretended great affection, and warned him of the dangers to which he was about to be exposed by the useless attack of so strong a place. He advised him not to risk his valuable life by landing on the main land, "For I know," he said, "that you must land at yonder sandy bay, where before your coming the place will be so trenched and gabioned as you must runne upon assured death."

Such, in fact, was the contrivance and expectation of the rebels. A low sandy beach presented the only obvious point at which an enemy's attempt might be expected, and it was strongly defended in the manner described by MacGeoghegan. But the circumspection of Carew overreached the tactics of his antagonists. He first contrived, with a small party, to get possession of a little island close to the sandy bay; on this he placed a couple of falconets and landed two regiments, so as to lead the enemy to believe that from that position he intended to attack their works and effect a landing on the beach. But, in the mean time, moving about in a small pinnace, Carew discovered a very convenient landing-place on the main land, which was concealed from the Irish party by a small eminence, and, though within a few hundred yards, separated from them by a deep rocky cleft which reached in for half a mile. Having made this observation a few hours before, he was enabled to conduct the operation in a most unsuspicious manner. While his men on the lesser island were making all preparations for an attack, and the whole attention of O'Sullivan's party on the shore was engrossed by watchful and anxious expectation, Carew stood on the further side of the island to direct his own captains, who were sailing up for the purpose of effecting a landing. To these he pointed out the unsuspected and unguarded spot, and the vessels again stood out from the bay, and, tacking short, reached it without notice, and landed their troops to the amount of two regiments under Sir C. Wilmot and Sir Richard Percy. When Carew saw that they were disembarked, he immediately ordered his own regiment and the earl of Thomond's into their boats, and they were all quickly under sail and out toward the same spot. This could not of course escape the notice of the enemy, who watched with all their eyes; and the nature of the movement was at once conjectured. Away they all rushed at their utmost speed; but they had a long circuit to perform, and before they could be half round the cleft, the lord-president with his whole party were landed and drawn up to meet them on good firm ground. A skirmish not worth detail was the result, and the Irish party were put to flight.

About two hours after this incident, the Irish received the cheering intelligence of the Spanish vessel, already mentioned, having landed in Ardee; and as the lord-president was afterwards informed by some of those who were then among the Irish, the account confirmed their courage, at a moment when they were beginning to waver. At Ardee, the ammunition and treasure were delivered to O'Sullivan Beare himself, who forwarded a supply of ammunition to Dunboy. The treasure amounted to £12,000, and was sent in shares to different Irish chiefs, £1500 being the share of O'Sullivan Beare; some letters from Ardee also were sent to different persons. One of these from the Jesuit Archer to Dominick Colling, a friar in Dunboy, is worthy of notice.

Letter from James Archer, Jesuit, to Dominick Collins, Jesuit, at Dunboy.

"Your letters of Thursday last came to our hands, but our disagreeing in some matters, makes to bee slacke in performing your desire, yet you must take better order for the premises; in the meane while, however becomes of our delayes or insufficiencies, bee yee of heroical minds, (for of such consequence is the keeping of that castle, that every one there shall surpasse in deserts any of us here; and for noble valiant souldiers shall passe immortall throughout all ages to come;) for the better encouraging, let these words be read in their hearing: out of Spaine we are in a vehement expectation, and for powder, lead, and money, furnished. Now to come to more particular matters; understand, that there are but two wayes to attempt you, that is scaling with ladders, or battery: for scaling, I doubt not but your owne wits neede no direction; and for battery, you may make up the breach by night. The higher you rayse your workes, every way the better, but let it bee thick and substantiall: raise of a greater height that worke captaine Tirrell made, betwixt the house and the cornell, make plaine the broken house on the south side: for fire work direction doe this, prime the holes and stop in the balls, with powder mixt through the materiall well, and some powder that shall take fire; the rest you know, as you have heard me declare there. By all meanes possible send me one ball, and the rest of the saltpeeter. This is in haste till better leasure. Campe this Thursday.

"Your loving Cousen,
"JAMES ARCHER."*

" To Father Dominicke Collins, these in haste."

The following letter is also valuable for the distinct view it will give the reader of the operations which the writer describes:—

A letter from John Anias, to Dominick Collins, Jesuit, at Dunboy.

"Be carefull of your fortifying continually; with a most speciall care rayse in height the west side of your port; fill your chambers on the south and north side with hides and earth; what battery is made

* Pacata Hib.

suddenly repayre it like valiant souldiers; make plaine in the south side the remnant of the broken houses; make wayes out of the hall to scowes and cast stones upon the port, and if the enemy would attempt the like, dig deepe that place wee first begun, and a trench above to defend the same, as I have sayd unto you. Although wee expect speedie reliefe out of Spaine, yet bee you wise to preserve the store of victualls discreetly. Devise yourselves all the invention possible to hold out this siege, which is the greatest honour in this kingdome. With the next I shall prepare shoes for you; send me the cord as long line, add the rest of the saltpeter, withall the yron borriers, seven peeces in all. Salute in my name Richard Magoghegune, praying God to have of his speciall grace that care of your successe. From the campe, the   of June, 1602.

"Your loving Cousen,
"JOHN ANIAS."*

"*To Father Dominick, Beerehaven, these.*"

This John Anias was very soon after taken prisoner by John Berry, the constable of Castlemagne, and condemned to die by the sentence of court-martial. While under sentence of death, he wrote the following characteristic letter to the baron of Lisnaw:—

A letter from John Anias to the Baron of Lisnaw, a little before his execution.

"In trust is treason; so Wingfield betrayed me. My death satisfies former suspicions, and gives occasion hereafter to remember mee; and as ever I aspire to immortallize my name upon the earth, so I would request you by vertue of that ardent affection I had toward you in my life, that you would honour my death, in making mention of my name in the register of your countray. Let not my servant Cormack want, as a faithfull servant unto me; let my funerall and service of the Catholique church bee observed for the soule. Heere I send you the passe and letter of that faithlesse Wingfield, having charged the bearer upon his dutie to God, to deliver this into your hands. O'Sullivan was strange to mee, but inures himselfe to want mee. Commend mee to captaine Tirrell, O'Connor, your sister Gerode Oge. This the night before my execution, the eighth day of November, 1602, and upon this sudden I cannot write largely,

"†Your loving bedfellow,
"Sometimes,
"ISMARITO.*

The next day after the landing, Carew having led out the army to a narrow isthmus within a mile of the castle, stole out of the camp shortly after to view the ground in its immediate vicinity. Proceeding on horseback with Sir C. Wilmot, until they approached within small shot of the castle, they were soon discovered and saluted with a few discharges from the soldiers upon the walls; but with the exception of Sir Charles' horse which was wounded in the foot, they suffered no injury. Within "twelve score" of the castle, an unsuspected posi-

* Pacata Hib.   † Ibid.

tion, most curiously adapted for their purpose, was discovered by the prompt perception and military eye of Carew. A slight rise in the ground concealed the spot from the castle, but was not high enough to interrupt the range of a small platform among the rocks, which seemed to have been cut out by the hand of nature for a battery. Neither the owner of the castle, nor one of his countrymen in the English camp, were aware of the treacherous recess which had so long awaited the guns of an enemy to render it fatal. When the lord-president returned to his officers and explained his design to plant a battery among the rocks on the other side of the castle, Owen O'Sullivan and other Irish gentlemen insisted that it would be impossible to find space among the rocks for cannon to be placed so as to command the castle. Carew assured them that he would plant his battery without the loss of a man, and in seven days make himself master of the place. In the castle, no apprehension was entertained of their danger; they attempted to annoy the army by a cannonade, but their balls fell near or in the camp without force to do any mischief.

The castle of Dunboy was a square pile of building enclosed with a strong wall sixteen feet in height, and faced with turf, faggots, and pieces of timber to the thickness of twenty-four feet. A low platform was sunk on the point from which any attack was considered likely to be made; and the entire skill of its defenders was exhausted in foreseeing and providing against every possible danger. Their knowledge was nevertheless but rude, and all these precautions were neutralized by the oversights they committed, the disadvantages of the structure they had to defend, and the rapid judgment of Carew.

Several days elapsed before the president could bring his plan into effect. The landing of the cannon was found to be an operation of great difficulty. The only landing-place which had the necessary advantages of being near the projected position, and accessible without the risk of interruption, was upon examination found to present insurmountable obstacles to the conveyance of the guns, as the way was broken by marshy and rocky passages. There was another still more convenient spot, but to reach it, a narrow creek close to the castle walls was to be entered; and this at last was resolved on. The mouth of this creek was within forty yards of the castle, and Carew therefore sent in the greater part of his stores and lesser ordnance in boats, which stole in undiscovered in the dead hours of a dark night; but their boats were unequal to the weight of the cannon and culverins, and no one "durst adventure in the hoy to carry them by night."*
To meet this difficulty, captain Slingsby volunteered to enter in the hoy by daylight, with thirty musqueteers. Disposing these men so that with the least possible exposure they could when required keep up a fire upon the castle gunners, captain Slingsby took advantage of a very favourable breeze, and the castle only succeeded in making two discharges upon him before he swept full sail into the creek, when he was instantly out of range of its guns.

While these operations were in progress, other important points

* Pacata Hib.

were also carried; the Irish had fortified the little island of the Dorsies, with three pieces of Spanish artillery, and forty chosen men. Carew, considering that it might easily be taken while the attention of the castle was kept in play by his approaches, then fairly in progress, sent Owen O'Sullivan, and captain Bostock, in a pinnace and four boats, with a hundred and sixty men to attack the island. They succeeded in taking the fort after a smart opposition; there Owen O'Sullivan had the fortune to recover his wife, who had been a prisoner' for the last eight months. The spoil was large, five hundred milch cows being taken on the island; the fort they razed to the ground.

On the same night a bullet from the castle wall entered the circle of officers who stood in conference with Carew in the midst of their camp, and smashed several bones of captain Slingsby's hand. On the following night about midnight, captain Tyrrel gave them an alarm, having approached so near as to pour a volley into the camp which riddled the tents well, but hurt nobody; a very slight resistance was sufficient to compel this active partizan to retire. Many other slight accidents occurred daily, while the gabions, trenches, and platforms, were in course of execution, until the 16th, when they were finished. One of these days, Sir G. Carew was with the earl of Thomond and Sir C. Wilmot, taking a ride along the shore, when Carew espied one of the artillery-men on the castle wall traversing a gun; "this fellow," said the president, "will have a shot at us," as he quickly reined in his horse and watched the event. He had scarcely spoken the last word, when the gun was fired, and the ball struck the earth between him and his companions, who had spurred on, and just cleared the spot with their horses' heels, when the earth was thrown up about them. Carew, glad to see them safe, told them laughing, that if they were as good "cannoneers as they were commanders, they would have stood firm as he did," and explained that "the gunners ever shoot before a moving mark."

At five o'clock in the morning of the 17th, the whole of Carew's preparations were made, and his battery began to play. He wasted none of his fire on the strong barbican, but ordered the guns to be levelled at the castle which stood unprotected at a dangerous height above; and about nine, a south-western tower, the fire from which had been very troublesome, came with its falcon, thundering to the ground, burying under it many of the garrison, and filling up the injudiciously narrow space of six or seven feet between the castle and the outer wall. The English guns were next turned upon the west front of the castle, which soon in like manner encumbered the court with ruin. The garrison on this sent out an offer of surrender on condition; but as they did not discontinue their fire, their proposal was not received.

An assault was then commanded, and its details having been fully arranged, the barbican was quickly scaled by the companies appointed, who were bravely seconded by the remainder of Carew's and the earl of Thomond's regiment, and a long, desperate, and confused fight of several hours began, of which no description can give any adequate idea. Whenever the hostile parties met hand to hand, the advantage lay with the besiegers who were superior both in number and in quality; but there was no flinching on the part of the garrison, who knowing that they were to receive no quarter, fought with the fury of desperation; and every floor or landing-place, or corner of advantage, was the scene of a bloody encounter, or a fierce and fatal siege. Doors were barricaded and forced, falcons and culverins, loaded with ball and bullet, seized on and discharged by either party; and every court, passage, or rampart, filled with the din, smoke, havoc and uproar of this fierce and protracted struggle for victory or life. The south and southwest turrets for a little time continued to cannonade each other, until the Irish gunner on the former was killed by a shot. The gun being disabled, and the English on the opposite turret pouring in an incessant and well-directed fire, the Irish were compelled to dislodge; they retreated to the narrow space between the east front and the curtain of the barbican which lay within a few feet of it, so that they were for a while enabled to make a gallant defence against those repeated charges of the English. Here the conflict became long and furious, for the place was too narrow for the use of fire-arms; and it became a fierce trial of physical strength and endurance between the two parties. In this, the English for a while were exposed to a very severe disadvantage: for besides the desperate party who stood at bay before them in the narrow space between two enclosing walls, they had to sustain a fierce attack from the tower overhead, whose numerous loop-holes and staircase windows looked down upon the strife; from these shot and large stones came pouring so as to kill and wound many. At last, when the endurance of the assailants must have begun to give way, a fortunate accident gave them a key to this apparently impracticable position. A sergeant of captain Slingsby's, by clearing away some rubbish in the tower from which the English had been firing immediately previous to the attack then going on, discovered a window from which, by means of the heap of ruins that filled the narrow court, he saw at once that they could command the passage defended by the Irish. This important ruin was quickly seized and occupied by the assailants, who thus charged down from the breach, and soon scattered those who had made so long a defence in the narrow passage thus laid open. Of these, all fell save eight, who escaping up the breach sprang out into the sea, where their hapless fate awaited them from the enemy's boats, which were stationed there to let none escape.

The fight was not yet ended. A party of Irish held a strong vault beneath the same tower, and when this was cannonaded from the broken wall which slanted down upon it so near that it was battered from the mouth of falcon and saker, the garrison (then reduced to seventy-seven men,) escaped to the cellars underneath, to which the only entrance was a narrow perpendicular stair. This put an end to the conflict—attack and defence were equally out of the question, and it became a trial of a more tranquil but far more dreadful kind— how long the famine and cold of the dreary dungeons beneath could be endured by the unfortunate wretches, who having done all that bravery could do, at the end of a bloody day were now reduced to a choice of deaths from which humanity must always shrink. They had, on discovering the hopelessness of their condition, offered to surrender on terms; but this was sternly rejected, and Dominick Collins alone came out and gave himself up. The night passed thus; and early in the morning twenty-three more Irish, with two Spanish gunners and an Italian, came out. It was not long till a message was sent from beneath to inform the lord-president that they had nine barrels of powder beneath, with which they would instantly blow up the castle, unless he would promise to spare their lives; Carew refused. He therefore ordered a battery to be prepared to fire downward on the vaults of the castle, and the bullets soon made their way into the crowded cellar; on this, forty-eight men compelled their captain, Taylor, to surrender. On receiving this intimation, several English officers descended to receive them: when they reached the cellars, captain Power by good fortune caught a sight of MacGeoghegan the constable, who lay desperately mangled with mortal wounds, slowly raising himself from the floor; and having snatched a lighted candle, he was dragging himself over to an open barrel of powder. As his purpose could not be for a moment doubted, the captain sprung forward and seized him in his arms, and he was slain by one of the men who also had observed the whole. There was no further resistance, and Taylor with his men were led prisoners to the camp. In this affair the English lost two officers, and many were wounded; of the privates, sixty-two were wounded, of whom many died within a few days: it was the most desperate defence ever made by the insurgents. As it was considered that the castle could not without great delay be put again into a defensible condition, the nine barrels of powder which had been discovered in the cellars, were employed to blow it up. This castle was the most important support of O'Sullivan's power; commanding Bantry bay, which was a source of considerable profit to him, both as the best fishery in Ireland, and as a well-frequented port for the fishermen of all those nations from whom the chief received a small addition to his revenue in the shape of duties.

It was presently ascertained that the capture of Dunboy was a decisive blow; as it had the effect of interrupting and terminating the formidable preparations which, at the instance of O'Donell, the court of Spain had ordered for a fresh invasion. In this island there was now remaining but little reliance on any means of resistance, but the long-desired and tenaciously-held expectations from Spain; and only in proportion as this feeling became weakened by repeated disappointment, the mind of the country showed any settled indications of a disposition to subside. These hopes, though now broken by severe disappointment, long indeed continued to delude many of the less reflecting and more restless spirits, too barbarous to be taught by the evidence of the most disastrous events, and too sanguine for experience to cool down.

Some were indeed impelled by the desperation of their circumstances. Among these was O'Sullivan Beare; he had carried resistance to a length which now left him nothing to give up. The stern and uncompromising spirit of Carew was too well known to admit of any hope that he would relent in favour of one whom it was his policy to consider simply as a rebel. The fierce old chief was taught to feel, that however desperate might be the hope of resistance, that his life or liberty at least, was involved in the dishonour of submission. His castles had been taken—the stronghold of Dunboy was no more—Carriganass, his own dwelling on the banks of the river Ouvane, was in the hands of the enemy. A happy change might he thought arrive, when O'Donell should return with a powerful fleet and army, to draw away and to defeat the cruel and powerful foe against which the castles and arms of the island seemed as nothing. To these desperate resolutions, the mountain ramparts of Kerry presented a welcome retreat of impregnable strength. In this vast and formidable wilderness of rugged defiles and dangerous precipices, the heart of resistance might be kept alive for better days; the arms and discipline of the stranger would little avail in the dangers and intricacies of the morass and hollow ravine; the fatal enginery against which the ancient towers of Dunboy had been found weak, would make no impression on the unscaleable and firm-built ramparts of the Slievelogher chain. There the brave and skilful partizan Tyrrel, still kept together his band of hardy mercenaries, every one a chosen man, and by dexterously maintaining a central movement among this broad chain of natural fortifications, contrived in security to overlook the war in Munster, and to be present whenever mischief could be done to the enemy. To join this light-heeled warfare, O'Sullivan now retreated; but the heights and hiding-places of Slievelogher were of little avail against the active pertinacity of Wilmot. This last struggle, without losing any thing of the fierceness and inveteracy which it derived from the respective situation of the parties, acquired new horrors from the manner in which it was carried on: the animosity of contention was heightened by the romantic and fiery interest of a wild, difficult, and perilous pursuit—concealment combined with resistance to give defence the anxious character of escape and surprize—suspense, anxious search, and the deepening interest of active pursuit, gave to war the animation of the chase. But here, in their native fastnesses, the activity and skill of Tyrrel and his bonnoghs were overmatched by the knowledge of the English leader and the unflagging bravery of his men: they were compelled to retreat from post to post along these mountains, at every step becoming more weak and destitute of resources, until they were driven from their last stand. We forbear entering upon the incidents of this mountain war, of which the particulars are too indistinctly related in the *Pacata Hibernia*, and other contemporary records, for the purpose of distinct historical detail. The rebels had formed a distinct plan, in which O'Sullivan, Tyrrel, M'Carthy, and O'Conor Kerry, had their allotted parts. They were first deserted by Tyrrel, who had in the course of the operations following the capture of Dunboy, suffered one or two very severe reverses, and was deprived of the greater part of his provisions and accumulated plunder; so that notwithstanding his agreements with O'Sullivan, he suddenly changed his course, and leaving behind his sick, with baggage and every thing that could retard a hasty march, he drew off sixty miles in the country of O'Carrol.

Under these circumstances it was, that Wilmot with the lord Barry and Sir George Thornton, encamped in Glengariffe, on a small space of firm ground, on all sides surrounded with bogs and forests. The spot was so narrow that their small party was partly encamped on the boggy ground, neither was there another spot so large of tenable ground, within five miles, on any side. Nevertheless, within two miles, O'Sullivan and William Burke, who like Tyrrel was a captain of bonnoghs, were encamped. Here some furious night attacks were repelled with little loss, and on the 31st December, Wilmot ordered their fastnesses to be beaten up by six hundred men, on which a "bitter fight" took place, and continued for six hours.* In this the English were repelled; but being reinforced by a small reserve, the balance of the fight was restored, and it raged on with great bloodshed until night. Many were slain on both sides, but as usual the heavy loss of life fell on the Irish. The great advantages under which they fought, in reality only served to delude them into the error of an imaginary equality, and by keeping up resistance, vastly aggravated their loss. By this fight they lost 2000 cows, 6000 sheep, and 1000 garrans, which latter we presume to have consisted wholly or chiefly of those small ponies which are to be found in Kerry, Wales, and other mountain regions.

This event was nearly decisive, it caused many of the chiefs and captains of the rebel party to sue for grace. O'Sullivan's last captain, William Burke, who had on that day commanded the Irish army, made great exertions to stop this defection, but in vain; even O'Sullivan appeared disheartened, and Burke himself began to think of following on the steps of Tyrrel. Against this O'Sullivan strongly protested, appealing to their agreement and the benefits he had conferred. The mountain bandit (for this best describes him), was fired by the remonstrance, he swore the game was over in Kerry, that he had lost more valuable men than the treasures of Spain could repay, and with violent curses accused himself of folly for having remained so long in Munster. He made no further delay, but fled with 200 men into O'Carrol's country. O'Sullivan, thus abandoned, was not subdued in spirit; but seeming to gather "resolution from despair," he now determined to make his way as he might to Ulster, where the fate of Tyrone was yet suspended in fearful uncertainty, after a reverse which turned his hostile movements into a desperate and wavering defence. With O'Conor Kerry, and a small party of those desperadoes, known by the name of bonnoghs, and best conceived as a sort of military "spalpeens," they commenced a dangerous retreat along the borders of Muskerry. As they went on their way they were attacked by Feague Owen M'Carthy, and lost most of their carts and many men. A little further on John Barry, brother to viscount Barry, made a charge upon them at the ford of Belaghan, with a small party of eight horse and forty foot, and with the loss of one man, dealt slaughter and confusion among their enfeebled ranks. Again they were met on the banks of the Shannon, while they were effecting a most difficult passage, by the sheriff of Tipperary, who having received an intimation of their approach, was prepared with his *posse comitatus* to resist their passage. Their position was then one of trying emergency—one which might have brought to mind the famous lament of

* Pacata Hibernia.

the Britons, when their Saxon invaders were driving them to the sea. O'Sullivan and O'Conor with their bold and desperate companions felt neither the terror nor the want of resource of these primitive savages; while the din of an irregular pursuit came over the hills upon their ears, and the scattered groups of the pursuers appeared at no great distance rushing out from woods or crossing the green hills, they hastily killed and flayed a number of their horses, and constructing rude little boats of their skins they managed to escape over the flood with much of their baggage. This was not effected without some loss, as their embarkation was not entirely complete when the sheriff's men came up and slew several. From this, however, they were enabled to cross a considerable tract of Connaught without interruption, till they reached the coast of Galway, where they were again attacked in the O'Kelly's country, by Sir Thomas Burke, brother to the earl of Clanricarde, and captain Malby. The attack was conducted with most unaccountable rashness. O'Conor and O'Sullivan, practised in the prompt use of all available positions, occupied a well-protected pass, rendered impracticable to assailants by its rocky barrier, and covered from their fire by the branching copse which crested the low chain of cliffs behind which they lay. Burke and Malby only consulting their impetuous valour, and scorning a fugitive enemy which had been beaten across the country from post to post, charged fiercely into the ravine, and were received by a deadly, deliberate, and unerring fire, which was followed by a sudden charge, that left many of the brave assailants on the ground. Among these was captain Malby. His fall decided the affair. Burke and his people were discouraged and fled; on which O'Sullivan and O'Conor were enabled to pursue their way to the desired land of refuge in O'Rourke's country. Their victory, an effort of desperation favoured by accident, had no other result.

In the mean time, O'Sullivan's warders in Kerry, were so pressed by Wilmot, and disheartened by the desertion of their lord, that they gave up whatever forts and castles yet remained uncaptured. In the country of O'Rourke, a district more rude and unexplored than any other in Ireland, the last sparks of rebellion maintained their ineffectual life, O'Sullivan and O'Rourke being the only persons of any name or authority who still held out, and this as the noble writer of the *Pacata Hibernia* observes, more from fear than daring—" obstinate only out of their diffidence to be safe in any forgiveness."*

From this we have no very satisfactory account of O'Sullivan Beare. But as his name disappears from history, we may assume his death to have soon after occurred.

FLORENCE M'CARTHY.

FLOURISHED A. D. 1601.

FLORENCE M'CARTHY's name is of too frequent recurrence in the civil wars of this period to be passed without some notice further than

* Pacata Hibernia.

he may have appeared to have received at our hands, in a few preceeding memoirs; but in truth we have little if any thing to add to these casual notices. M'Carthy's title to notice is more due to station and circumstance, than to any personal distinction. We shall as briefly as possible offer a summary of all that we find any account of in his history.

When the earl of Tyrone visited Munster to organize the rebellion in that quarter, it was at the pressing instance of this Florence M'Carthy, who had his own interests in view. The M'Carthys of Desmond had at the time raised Donald, an illegitimate son of the earl of Clancare, to the title of M'Carthy More. Tyrone displaced him, and without opposition set up his friend Florence in his room. The speciousness of this hollow intriguer had in like manner already won him the favour of the English government; and he made use of the importance thus obtained to court the favour of the Irish chief. His first demonstration was not, it is true, altogether consistent with the trimming and shuffling caution for which his subsequent career is so remarkable; but he was for a little while imposed upon by appearances, which were beyond his sagacity to penetrate. The slackness and remissness of the English court in providing against the growing storm and the increasing power of the Irish insurgents, which was thus inadequately opposed, gave a universal impulse to Irish disaffection. Nor can the charge be confined to Florence M'Carthy, which seems at the time to have amounted to a national characteristic, of taking part with the strongest. At the period of Carew's first arrival in Munster, all seemed to favour the cause of the insurrection; and M'Carthy, like many others, rushed forward under a press of sail before the prosperous wind.

It was in the latter end of April, that he contrived an ambuscade, at a ford between Cork and Kinsale, to intercept a party of English which had been detached into Carbery, under captains Flower and Bostock. Fortunately the ambush was detected in time, as the English party were advancing without the least apprehension of an enemy, scarcely in order, and having but a few matches burning, it happened that captain Bostock who rode before espied the glancing sunbeam from some of the steel morions of the soldiers, who were lurking in the low glen towards which he was riding; he instantly turned back, but without any appearance of haste or alarm, and gave the word to the soldiers to be ready: the time was not quite sufficient for preparation, when the rebels perceiving themselves to be discovered, sprung up with a shout from the neighbouring stones and brushwood, and came on with great impetuosity. The English were for a few minutes overwhelmed, both by the violence of the charge and the numbers of the enemy. But the real strength of the steady English was then, as now, the firmness of nerve, that resists the impulse of a first disorder, and renders them capable of that most difficult of efforts—a rally from the shock that overpowers resistance. In despite of the surprize, the broken rank, and the overbearing torrent of enemies, they stood sternly to their arms, and made fight until the impetus of their foes began to waste itself away. The skill of their leaders was thus brought into action, and the enemy were fairly caught in their own device. Commanding lieutenant Lane to lie down in an old ditch behind them, with a strong company of musketeers, captain Flower directed a retreat. The enemy led by Carbery O'Conor, confidently pressed in their rear, until he came on the line of the flank fire from Lane's party, when a volley from the ditch arrested their advance, and slew their leader with many other officers as well as soldiers. Sudden amazement suspended their steps, and while they hesitated the battle was lost. A charge from the English horse, at this critical moment, scattered them like chaff, and in a moment the party they had been pursuing was in the midst of them, slaughtering right and left without resistance: 98 fell on the spot, and multitudes went off with mortal wounds.

M'Carthy, not long after, entered into a treaty with Carew. There was at the time a favourable disposition towards him among the English lords; but the president of Munster was still more actuated by the state of the country, in his desire to draw M'Carthy from the rebels. It was to be apprehended that the English force, which was far below the demand of the occasion, must otherwise require to be further weakened by the division and extension of its operations which a war with this chief would render necessary; nor was the infirmity of purpose or the uncertainty of conduct, which soon appeared to neutralize his hostility, yet fully understood. A conference was therefore appointed, to which M'Carthy came, was reproved in the severe manner of Carew, pardoned, and swore allegiance and future obedience and duty on his knees. In his account of this scene, the writer of the *Pacata Hibernia* mentions, " These speeches being finished, the president bade him to stand up, when as both he and the earl of Thomond, Sir Nicholas Welsh, and John Fitz-Edmund, did every one of them very feelingly preach obedience to him." After this pretty schooling, M'Carthy made an eloquent answer, in which he probably showed himself a better orator at least than his advisers, using such general terms as to pledge him to nothing, while he delivered himself with so much appearance of warmth and good feeling, that even Carew could not help thinking him a very loyal man. After a repetition of the same comic drama on the following day, he was desired to send his eldest son as a pledge. At this critical demand his speciousness was a little shaken aside. He pleaded the difficulties in which such a pledge must involve him, as he would thus be deprived of the power of keeping appearances with Desmond and his own people; "adding, moreover, that it was needless in them to exact any such thing at his hands, who was in his soule so wholly addicted and devoted to her majestie's service."* These absurd subterfuges were necessarily ineffectual. Other conditions were next proposed by M'Carthy and rejected; and the conference ended in a promise to preserve a strict neutrality, and that he would from time to time send intelligence of the rebels' proceedings to the president, and " doe him the best underhand service he possibly could." It is needless to observe that such a promise, whether sincere or insincere, equally betrays the unprincipled character of this unworthy descendant of an illustrious race. With this promise Carew was satisfied, for he only desired to keep him

* Pac. Hib.

quiet for a time, until the war with Desmond should be brought to an end.

Afterwards, when the army of the sugan earl was dispersed and himself a fugitive in Kerry, M'Carthy followed the example of others; and having through the war contrived to amuse both parties and keep himself out of danger's way, he came to the president's camp, "in the midst of his troope, (like the great Turke among his janissaries,) drew towards the house like Saul, higher by the head and shoulders than any of his followers." He was courteously received by the lord-president, and gave pledges, which he desired to have received for the O'Sullivans, the O'Donoghues, the O'Crowlies, and O'Mahon Carbery. This was of course rejected; Carew wished to cut the links between him and these dependent chiefs, and intended to compel them to put in hostages for themselves.

At this period it was that a violent and deadly feud took place among the M'Carthys of Muskerry and Carbery, in which some leading persons were slain. The lord of Muskerry, grieved at the slaughter of the O'Learies his followers, applied to the council for leave to make war on Carbery; but the application was not acceded to.

We already have had occasion to exemplify and illustrate the conduct and character of Florence M·Carthy in our memoir of the Sugan earl. The correspondence which was intercepted exposes the weakness and duplicity of his character by the testimony of his own hand. It is therefore unnecessary to glean further the scanty materials before us. We have already mentioned his fate; he was in the end sent a captive into England, thus meeting the reward of a course of conduct which rendered him an object of distrust.

We have only to add a remark which has often pressed itself upon us in the course of this work. The conduct of every distinguished person who figures in the political proceedings of the period of which we have been writing, indicates so very loose and defective a system of political morality, that when we have been by any chance led to take an unfavourable view of any person of illustrious name and descent, we have ever done so with some consciousness of a disagreeable nature, and an indication to recoil, like fear in Collins' ode, "even from the sound itself hath made." We have felt the injustice of making any *one* an unhappy example of the sins of all. The best and wisest men who came forward on that tragic stage, seem to have been ignorant of the higher principles of truth, honour, and justice, which the meanest and basest who seek mob-favour in our own day think it essential to swear by. And again, when we look on the practice of our own refined age, and see many who are honourable gentlemen, and most estimable in every relation of private life, so false, hollow, and perjured in their public capacities, we are inclined to the charitable conclusion, that there is something in the game itself which none but the very noblest hearts and heads can resist; and that there is some *arcanum* in state affairs, which causes a temporary transformation, so that the same person may be a man of honour in the hall and field, while he is a knave *malgré soi* on the hustings and in the senate. We have therefore assuredly no right to affect a stern elevation of public principle, when we look back on the ways of persons whom we call unenlightened, because they did not play their game as knowingly as the gamesters of our own day, who have the wisdom to know that they are wrong, and the hardihood to act in defiance of the principles to which they pretend. Florence M'Carthy deceived, with all the dignity of virtue, because he thought it all fair ; and Sir G. Carew did not know much better. The president thought it not amiss to bargain with those who sought his favour, to murder one another; it may be said perhaps that he knew his men; but the person who employed them for such purposes, must have forgotten the spirit of the proud chivalry of England in the very day of Sidney.

With this weak apology we must take our leave of M'Carthy: he lived in an evil day, and defended himself by the only weapon of which prudence warranted the use by an Irish chief. And if it can be truly asserted that the only alternative was submission, we are inclined to suspect that the mind of his own time may rather have applauded his persevering spirit, than condemned the hollow manœuvring by which he persevered. Unhappily history, with all its boasted impartiality, can hardly try its great delinquents by their peers. We cannot guess from their public statements and letters what would Fitz-William say—what would Perrot say—what would Carew say; but must look to their policy and their acts, and with one who knew something of men, denounce the great " unwhipped of justice."

CORMACK M'CARTHY, LORD OF MUSKERRY.

FLOURISHED A. D. 1601.

DURING the events which we have largely detailed in several of our preceding memoirs, there appear occasional glimpses of persons whose names have obtained notice in Irish history, but whose part in the events of their generation was but sufficient to give them a doubtful title to present notice. Among these was Cormack M'Dermond M'Carthy, lord of Muskerry, a branch of the same illustrious parent stem from which was also descended the subject of our last previous memoir.

We shall here briefly relate such passages of his life as have sufficient interest to demand a passing notice.

Before the lord-deputy Mountjoy marched to the siege of Kinsale, orders had been issued by Sir G. Carew, to the cities and towns of Munster, to send their contingents of force to join the queen's army; and the Irish chiefs who were at the time understood to be loyally affected, were generally apprized that they were expected in like manner to prove their profession by their actions. Among the chief of those who came forward on the occasion, was the lord of Muskerry. He was immediately employed by lord Mountjoy to make an attack on the Spanish trenches, in order to let them see that the English were supported in the war by the principal Irish lords. The Irish made a stout assault, but were repelled; but the lord-deputy was prepared for this, and the attack was followed up by one from his own troop of horse, which drove the Spaniards from the position which they had begun to entrench.

Not long after, a near relative of his, Feague M'Cormack M'Carthy, with whom he had been for some time at variance on a question of property, had been induced to desert from the lord-president's troop; but finding the rebel cause unprosperous, he sought a reconciliation by offering information of the private correspondence between the lord of Muskerry and the Spaniards. He excused his desertion on the ground that it was not "malicious," "but in the hope to recover against my coson M'Dermody, some means to maintain my decayed estate, and still likely to be suppressed by his greatness, who will by no means give me a portion of land to live upon." His excuse was considered insufficient by Carew, to whom his letter was addressed, and he was given to understand that his reconciliation was only to be looked for by some signal service. On which, having sought and obtained a safe conduct, he came to the president and gave him information that the lord of Muskerry was carrying on a private negotiation with the Spaniards; that he received letters from the king of Spain, and from some foreign bishop; that he had held a secret conference with the rebel Owen MacEggan, who had given him 800 ducats, for which he had agreed to yield Blarney castle, his chief castle, within two miles of Cork, into the hands of the Spanish. The information tallied but too well with several other informations and grounds of suspicion.

The lord-president immediately gave order to the judge of session, for the apprehension and commitment to prison of M'Carthy, and at the same time sent Sir Charles Wilmot and captain Harvie to obtain possession of Blarney castle. This castle is described as being at the time one of the strongest in that part of Ireland, as it consisted of four piles of building contained within one strong wall of eighteen feet in thickness, and built upon a rock, which made it alike proof against the mine and battery. The president therefore directed that they should proceed by stratagem, and try to gain admission on the pretext of buck-hunting in the neighbourhood. But the warders were on their guard, and the stratagem failed.

The prisoner was soon after brought up for trial; and as he pleaded his innocence, it was proposed to him to maintain his plea, by giving up his castles to be held by the queen, on the condition that they should be safely returned when his innocence should be confirmed by the failure of the proof against him. M'Carthy consented, and his castles of Blarney and Kilcrea were on these conditions placed in the lord-president's hands. An army was at the same time sent against Macroome, as it lay in the very wildest and most dangerous part of Muskerry, and was not likely to be surrendered on the order of M'Carthy.

While these transactions were in their course, the lord-president received secret intimation that contrivances were going on for the escape of his prisoner. He likewise was informed, that O'Healy, a servant of M'Carthy, was prepared to embark for England, to steal away young M'Carthy from the University of Oxford, and take him into Spain. O'Healy was allowed to embark, and then suddenly seized, but contrived to throw his letters into the sea, so that nothing against his master was thus elicited. The president in the mean time was warned by the bishop of Cork, and by Sarsfield, the queen's attorney for

Munster, who had severally received information of the meditated escape; and on each occasion, Hammon, the gaoler of M'Carthy, was impressively lectured on the importance of his charge.

All precautions turned out to be in vain. Two days did not elapse when M'Carthy's servant, Owen O'Synn, contrived to loosen and break the sash of a window that looked out into the street. The night was very dark, and few were abroad but those of M'Carthy's own people who had been apprized that the attempt was then to be made, and were watching for him outside. When all was ready, and the hour was judged to be dark and lonely enough for their security, M'Carthy stripped off his clothes, which might easily be recognised, and crept out of the window into the street. In this moment, an accident had nearly disconcerted his attempt: a young woman was passing up the street, and seeing a person in his shirt escaping from the prison window, she instantly raised a cry of alarm. The keepers within leaped up at once, and rushed straight to the prisoner's room, and finding it deserted and the window open, they bolted forth and began a search along the street and surrounding country; but the measures of the fugitive had been too well contrived, and they returned without their errand.

On the 21st October, 1602, M'Carthy came before the president and council, and humbly besought the queen's mercy, acknowledging his offences, and only pleading the loyalty of his affections toward her majesty. He was then pardoned in consideration of the severe losses he had sustained, both by the burning of his castle and the destruction of the harvest of Muskerry that autumn by the queen's army and the rebels, of which the loss was computed to be £5,000 at the least.

SIR GEORGE CAREW.

BORN A. D. 1557.—DIED A. D. 1629.

OF the personal history of this great man little can be satisfactorily ascertained; the main events of his life belong to history, and have been already detailed under several heads.

His family was early settled in Ireland. On the death of Robert Fitz-Stephen, the kingdom of Cork descended by marriage to the Carews and De Courcys.* The Carews were ennobled, and handed down their possessions with the dignity of Marquis of Cork till the time of the wars of the Roses in England, when they appear to have abandoned their Irish possessions, which were soon usurped by the surrounding chiefs, with some inconsiderable exceptions. They built the castles of Ardtullagh, Dunkeran, and Dunemare; the last of which we find in the possession of Sir George Carew, while he commanded the queen's army as president of Munster.* Sir George was the son of George Carew, dean of Christ's church, Oxford: he was born in 1557, and entered a gentleman commoner in Broadgate's Hall in Oxford university, in 1572. His first military services were in Ireland, where he

* Cox.

was early promoted, and became one of the council, and master of the ordnance. His uncle, Sir Peter Carew, a military officer, slain in 1580 at the pass of Glendalough, seems to have been the representative in Ireland of this ancient family. In 1582 we find him in relations with the followers of the chief O'Byrne, who commanded against the English on this occasion, showing his early acquaintance with the faithless character of the natives,—a knowledge which he subsequently turned to account in his dealings with them.* In common with most of the eminent military characters of his day, he served with distinguished honour on the continent, and gained especial notice in the expedition against Cadiz.

In the year 1599, there had been an increased activity on the part of the English government. The queen, alarmed by intelligence that the king of Spain, with whom she was at war, was preparing for the invasion of England, and that an army of 12,000 men was destined for Ireland, became seriously and justly alarmed for the safety of the latter. Under these impressions she had yielded to the specious persuasions of the earl of Essex: and, listening rather to partiality than to sound judgment, she sent him over to mismanage the affairs of a nation where prudence, caution, moderation, and sound discretion, as well as firmness and sagacity, were indispensably required. At the time the actual state of the Irish chiefs was this:—The earl of Tyrone, who was in reality at the head of the insurrection, occupied the north with a well-disciplined and appointed army of six thousand men, while O'Donell, with an army not inferior in arms and training, was prepared to maintain the war in Connaught. Both were aided by many chiefs, of whom some were not much less formidable than themselves; while those who opposed them, and took part with the English, were chiefs of far less power and influence, who were mostly maintained in their authority and possessions by the protection of the government. There was at the time a general impression in favour of the insurgents, their cause and prospects, which was a main source of their strength. It was known to what an extent the Irish soldiery had profited by the lessons of their enemies. There was a universal reliance on Spain, and the rebellion had assumed a serious character.

The brief but misguided career of errors which Essex ran soon led to a change of administration.

In the latter end of 1599 Lord Mountjoy was sent over as deputy, and Sir George Carew, the subject of this notice, as president of Munster, and early in the following year advantages were gained by these able commanders which struck misgiving and dismay through the hearts of the national leaders.

While Mountjoy directed the operations in the north, Sir George Carew in person engaged in the re-conquest of the south. His masterly and successful campaign against the Sugan earl, the head of the southern Geraldines, has been detailed in the life of this last of the Desmonds.† Its termination, with the capture and conviction of the earl in May, 1601, left the president with one enemy the less, when the great invasion of the Spanish forces, imperfectly carried out, called

* Page 510. † Page 452.

him to aid Lord Mountjoy in expelling them from Kinsale, and at same time defending themselves from the powerful Irish army under the earl of Tyrone. The manner in which this was done is detailed in the life of that great rebel.*

After the capitulation of the Spanish general, Sir George Carew had to deal with the chief of the O'Sullivans, whose strong castle of Dunboy, having been garrisoned by them, was ceded with the other places, was resolved to regain it, and succeeding by stratagem, broke out into rebellion. The reduction of this stronghold, under circumstances the most discouraging and perilous, was the most remarkable event in this eventful period, and is fully narrated in the memoir of that chief.† This was the closing event in the great rebellion of Tyrone, who thereupon made an entire and humble submission.

After these memorable achievements Sir George Carew returned to England, where in the first year of King James, he was appointed to the government of Guernsey, and two years after, raised to the peerage by the title of Baron Carew of Clopton, near Stratford-upon-Avon in Warwickshire. He was next preferred to the high post of master of the ordnance in England, and appointed one of the privy council. He was afterwards created earl of Totnes by Charles I.,‡ His subsequent life was chiefly employed in writing the history of those events of which, in the earlier period, he had been the witness or principal actor. Among these writings, the most important and the best known is the "Pacata Hibernia," which gives the most full and minute detail of the Munster and Ulster wars above mentioned. To this work we have been chiefly indebted for our details of these transactions. It is mentioned by Bishop Nicholson, that he wrote other works on the affairs of Ireland, "whereof forty-two volumes are in the archbishop of Canterbury's library at Lambeth, and four volumes more of collections, from the originals in the Cotton library." §

These, with several other MS. volumes, all of which were read through and noted by Archbishop Usher, exhibit in a very strong and interesting point of view, the intellectual activity and untiring energy and industry of this extraordinary man. A folio edition of the *Pacata Hibernia*, published in 1633, contained his picture, under which these lines were written:—

> "Talis erat vultu, sed lingua, mente manuque
> Qualis erat, qui vult dicere, scripta legat
> Consulat aut famam, qui lingua, mente, manuque
> Vincere hunc, fama judice, rarus erat."

Sir George Carew died in 1629, "in the Savoy,"‖ and left no heir male. His only daughter married Sir Allen Apsley. ¶

---

* Page 511.   † Page 485.   ‡ Nicholson's Irish Hist. Library.
§ Page 53.   ‖ Nicholson.   ¶ Walpole's Letters. Note, vol. i. p. 157.

FEAGH MACHUGH O'BYRNE.

SLAIN A. D. 1597.

AMONGST the multitude of lesser chiefs who may be said to have taken part in the tumultuous proceedings of Ireland in the 16th century, we can select but a few. Of these Feagh MacHugh is entitled to notice, by reason of the persevering energy which gives prominence to his character—the territorial position which rendered his motions important to the inhabitants of Dublin and the surrounding lands of the English pale, but most of all for the dark interest which connects itself with the memory of one event; to which, the rest being comparatively of little interest, we shall pass as briefly as we can.

The country of the O'Byrnes, in an ancient map, lately published by the State Paper Committee, is marked in that part of the county of Wicklow, east of the river Avon, which runs from Lough-Dan to Arklow. The O'Byrnes and O'Tooles, always mentioned together as belonging to the same sept, occupied this region of the Wicklow mountains. Spenser, who collected his account from the people themselves, and improved his knowledge by extensive study of such documents as were to be then had, affirms their descent from the ancient Britons, and observes that this descent is evidenced by their names, as *Brin* signifies woody, and *Tool* hilly, in the ancient British. It is not improbable, that a hardy race had, at an early period, when driven from their native woods in Britain, taken possession of a district which, considering its coldness, dampness, and barrenness, was little likely to be disputed with them. Amid this wild district, these septs spread and built many castles, of which the ruins were abundant in the 16th century. They were subjects to the MacMurroughs; but after the English settlement, when by the subjection of Leinster to the English, they were set free from the strong control of the paramount lord, they began by degrees to assume independence, and to make themselves very conspicuous by inroads to which their near propinquity to the pale, and the difficulty of access into their steep and marshy fastnesses, rendered resistance or retaliation difficult and dangerous.

Spenser mentions, we should presume on the authority of the Byrnes of MacHugh's own time, that Shane MacTirlogh, the grandfather of Feagh MacHugh, " was a man of meanest regard among them [the O'Byrnes] neither having wealth nor power! But his father, Hugh MacShane, first began to lift up his head, and through the strength and great fastness of Glanmalur, which adjoineth to his house of Ballinacor, drew unto him many thieves and outlaws, which flew unto the succour of that glen as to a sanctuary, and brought unto him part of the spoil of all the country, through which he grew strong, and in short space got unto himself a great name, thereby, among the Irish."* Such is the account given by Spenser; and, if there is any strength in the testimony of position, this account is well attested by the rude and cliffy chains of steep hills which run parallel to each other

---

* Spenser's View.

at a quarter of a mile distance along the narrow vale, through which the Avon runs in a south-easterly direction towards Ballinacor. It was one of the three passes by which the surrounding mountain-country could be entered; and was, so late as the rebellion of 1798, a formidable pass, and the scene of many bloody deeds, when a military road was made through the glen, and a barrack built at Drumgoff.

In this well-known fastness of rebellion, Byrne held a position of power which, in the great struggle then fast rising to its height, gave him personal importance among the surrounding opponents of the English. The Kavanaghs, the O'Mores, and the Butlers, swelled his wealth and force, and drew protection from his mountains and ramparts and forest coverts. Some miles north, near Annamoe, and a little to the east of Glendalough, stood castle Kevin, the stronghold of the chief of his allied and kindred clan the O'Tooles.

From this place of strength, Feagh MacHugh made himself so formidable to the English governor, that it became at length an object of urgent necessity to expel him, and obtain possession of a place of such importance to the security of the pale.

In the year 1580, lord Grey de Wilton was sent over with instructions such as were not uncalled-for by the state of the country. In England there prevailed the utmost ignorance of the real difficulties which prolonged an interminable strife between foes whose utter disparity in all by which civilized nations are accustomed to estimate power, made the unsatisfactory and uncertain war seem quite unaccountable. In their ignorance of the real character of this warfare, conjecture but too often supplied accusations against the deputies and lords-lieutenant, whose seeming remissness allowed a barbarous, untrained, and almost naked enemy, to keep the field against a British army. Thus lord Grey was ignorant alike of the affairs of the country, and of the difficulties he should have to encounter. Looking no further than the prepossessions and prejudices of the English court, and rudely estimating the defensive resources of the Irish chiefs by the known inferiority of their armies in the field, he could conceive no reason for the failure of the queen's former deputies in reducing the country to tranquillity, but the absence of a sufficient promptness and determination to sweep all opposition from the field by force of arms. Thinking too lowly of the claims of the Irish chiefs to consideration, and neglecting to consider that amongst the causes of their disaffection, there were some just grounds of complaint, and many wise reasons for tempering force (for this was still the main desideratum) with conciliatory moderation, he resolved to bear down all resistance by unhesitating and unrepressed exertions of military strength. An occasion but too soon occurred to let him into the secret of Irish resistance. Shortly after his landing in Dublin, he received intelligence that captain Fitz-Gerald, an officer of a company in the queen's pay, had revolted with lord Baltinglas, and joined Feagh MacHugh, and that they were encamped within twenty-five miles of Dublin, and daily increasing in numbers. Grey was naturally enough indignant that the power of queen Elizabeth should be held in defiance within so short a distance of the seat of government; and, without delay, ordered off such forces as could be brought together to attack them. The veterans who received these orders were fully aware of the dangerous and difficult nature of the service on which they were sent. They knew that the enemy they were peremptorily commanded to rout, was secure in the same impenetrable fastnesses which had already for nearly 400 years enabled them to hang over the pale like a thunder cloud, ever ready to scatter waste and devastation from its unassailable position and desultory explosion; and that to encounter a strong force, in positions so peculiarly framed for their mode both of attack and retreat, and so unsuited to the tactics of the English, must be attended with the utmost risk. When they arrived at the pass into the valley of Glendalough, the danger became more apparent; and here it is said that captain Cosby, a veteran officer of considerable experience in the wars of Ireland, remonstrated with lord Grey. The remonstrance must appear to have been needless to any one who is aware of the nature of the ground. A long, winding, and deep marsh terminating in lakes, and thickly masked with copse and stunted forest, which has since disappeared, ran between two ranges of wild precipitous mountains, which overhung it with their projecting sides, or here and there retreated in secret and shaded outlets, so as to present the most complete model of an ambuscade contrived by nature. In this position, which a little military knowledge might have seen to be inaccessible, an invisible enemy was prepared to receive them. Cosby's remonstrance was disregarded; and it now seems like infatuation that no precaution appears to have been taken to ascertain the position of the enemy, or the securest mode and points of attack. Lord Grey stood on a neighbouring height, and ordered his troops to march into the valley; and it is nearly certain, that the leaders and foremost companies of that gallant and devoted band, as they entered the still and ominous hollows of the swampy vale, knew that they were not to return. All was for some time still; and lord Grey, from the hill on which he stood, saw his veterans tread on unobstructed into the dangerous maze: he probably thought that the enemy whom he held in ignorant contempt, had sculked away from the approach of the queen's representative and his army. His error was not of long duration; scarcely was the last of the English column secure within the fatal defile, when wood, and craggy cavern, and all the dark steeps above its marshy and tangled hollows echoed with a yell of deadly defiance. It was followed by the roar of musketry, which poured thick, incessant, and unreturned from the enclosing heights on every side. There was no battle, for there was no resistance. Every thicket, and each projecting steep, as the devoted victims of Grey's precipitation came within its range, sent forth its vollied thunder, and poured its deadly shower upon the defenceless victims. Discipline and valour were impotent, and retreat as dangerous as advance. Some, desiring at least to grapple with a foe, attempted to rush up the steeps: these, however, were only pervious to an accurate local experience: they who thus attempted, soon came to some fatal stop, and were butchered in detail. Others became more deeply entangled in the morass, and presented sure marks for the ambushed foe, who took them down with cool deliberation from the nearest heights. Lord Grey perceived his error when it was too late: his men could not be extricated from a position so fatal; the soldiers were slain in heaps as their efforts, either to find an enemy or to effect their escape, chanced to throw them into parties. The most active of the officers fell in the vain attempt to extricate their men. Captains Dudley, Moore, and Sir Peter Carew, were among the slain.

The next noticeable trace we find of Feagh MacHugh occurs about two years later. The tale is curious enough, but not very distinct. It is first mentioned that one of the Byrnes offered captain George Carew to bring him the head of his leader Fitz-Gerald, already mentioned as an ally of MacHugh's. Before Byrne could effect his traitorous purpose, he was himself hanged by Fitz-Gerald, who received some intimation of what was going on; but immediately after, alarmed at the summary justice he had executed, or as we should suspect, himself tempted by some report of the reward to be received by his own murderer, he made overtures to Carew, for the delivery of the much more valuable head of Feagh MacHugh, He was, however, caught in the same trap with Byrne; Feagh was informed of the intended favour, and hanged Fitz-Gerald; or as Cox tells the story, "fairly hanged his friend Fitz-Gerald in his stead."

In 1584, he seems to have found the expediency of entering into amicable terms with the government, or was led by the wise and equitable character of Sir John Perrot, and the general tranquillity which made its transient appearance, to deliver pledges for his conduct. During the following ten years he is not very distinctly to be traced; but it is quite sufficiently apparent, that he continued through that interval to be as troublesome to the inhabitants of the Wicklow side of the pale as his force and safety admitted. In 1594, we read of an order of council ordering the lord-deputy on some important service, in which a provision is made for the defence of the pale against Feagh MacHugh, during his absence. At this time the Irish rebellions, for a time partially extinguished, had begun to increase, and assume a character of method, concert, and military discipline, till then unknown. The celebrated Red Hugh O'Donell, whom a few years before O'Byrne had succoured in his flight from Dublin castle, and entertained at his castle of Ballinacor, was sweeping like a torrent over the western counties; and the emissaries of Spain and Rome were with secret influence awakening and combining the scattered fires that were so soon to burst forth under the command of that able and powerful leader, Hugh, earl of Tyrone. In the beginning of 1595, the lord-deputy entered MacHugh's own territory, and, driving him and his people into the Glenmalur, took possession of Ballinacor, in which he placed a garrison. In the same year Feagh came into Dublin castle, and made his submission on his knees, on which he received the queen's pardon; nevertheless, while under solemn engagements, and having a protection, he continued to correspond with the northern rebels, and watching his opportunity, surprised and took Ballinacor, which he razed to the foundation. On this the lord-deputy marched into Wicklow, and encamped for a few days at Rathdrum, where he took several preys of cattle and many prisoners. It was probably his expectation, that MacHugh would have come into terms; but finding this hope vain, he ended by hanging two of his pledges—a proceeding which surely stamps the barbarity of the time, yet which was nevertheless difficult to be evaded. Without such a severe equity, the system of pledges, the firmest security of the period, must have been absolutely null, and more valuable interests, both in life and property, must have been sacrificed to the absolute want of any security. The pursuit of MacHugh, was pleaded as an injury, and as an excuse for rebellion, by Tyrone.

At the close of 1596, Feagh was brought to an action by captain Lea, and defeated with a loss of upwards of 80 men; and in a few months after, May 1597, the lord-deputy again overtook him with a strong party, when he was slain in the skirmish which took place.

THE LAST OF THE O'NIALLS OF TIR OWEN.

HUGH O'NEALE, EARL OF TYRONE.

CON O'NIALL, commonly called Con Mor, had two sons, Con Boccagh, the first earl of Tyrone, and Tirlogh Lynnogh, whose name frequently occurs in the history of the time. Con Boccagh was the father of Shane O'Neale and others, his legitimate sons, and of Matthew who was admitted to be illegitimate, and was further affirmed to be by another father of the name of O'Kelly, a smith, whose son he was publicly reputed to be until his fifteenth year, when by a disclosure of his mother's, the old earl was led to believe him to be his own. This person was set up by the earl as his successor, and created baron of Dungannon by queen Elizabeth. He was slain by the followers of Shane O'Neale, and left three sons, of whom the second was Hugh, the person here to be commemorated.

On the death of Shane O'Neale, his uncle Tirlogh Lynnogh was, by the law of tanistry, entitled to become the O'Neale, which title he accordingly assumed; but by the law of English descent, and by the disposition of King Henry, Hugh was the immediate successor of his father Matthew, and entitled to the earldom of Tyrone.

He was brought up in England, and early received employment in the queen's service, in which he repeatedly distinguished himself, especially in the wars against Gerald the sixteenth earl of Desmond, in which he had the command of a troop of horse. At this time his reputation stood high with every party; while his valour and military talent recommended him to the English, the other party, accustomed to temporizing submissions, put the most indulgent construction on his adhesion to their enemies. Moryson describes his person and character with the authority of a contemporary and an eye-witness:—
"He was of mean stature, but of a strong body, as able to endure watchings, labour, hard fare; being withal industrious and active, valiant, affable, and apt to manage great affairs, and of a high dissembling subtile and profound wit."

An important change was then working in the stormy elements of

Irish contention. The wave of the reformation had flowed in, and the resistance of the Roman see gave new force, bitterness, and unity to the strife of four centuries. The enmity of Philip the Second, king of Spain, added its portion of fuel to the same flame. Ireland was too obviously the assailable side of the queen's dominions to be neglected, and the Irish chiefs were long cajoled by great promises and small aids, which were yet enough to give the excitement of hope to their ambition and hate.

Still Hugh O'Neale was looked on with an invidious eye by many of the chiefs. It was felt that he was an intruder on the territorial possessions of Tyrone; his father's illegitimacy; and a still deeper disqualification, more than suspected, caused him to be slighted by some. His adherence to the English government excited the dislike of many, and a grasping and tyrannical disposition not peculiar to him, raised numerous enemies. To these O'Neale turned a front of subtile and profound dissimulation, which ended like all indirect courses in determining his course to the baser side. While he professed, and we believe truly, his attachment to the queen, he was compelled to dissemble with his fellow-countrymen. This conduct, which Irish authorities place beyond doubt, led in two ways to the determination of his conduct: it supplied in no small abundance material for misrepresentation, betraying him from time to time into positions of an equivocal nature; and it placed him under the occasional necessity of committing himself by acting in his assumed character.

He was as yet little affected by these embarrassments of position, when in 1587 he petitioned the parliament, then sitting in Dublin under Sir John Perrot, that he might be allowed to take the title and possessions of Tyrone. The rank and title were conceded, but for the possessions he was told that the question must depend on the queen's pleasure, on which he applied for Sir John's recommendatory letters to the queen, and represented that a large rent might be reserved to the crown, with his free consent. Perrot was reluctant,* but at the pressing entreaty of his Irish friends, gave him the required letters. Thus authorized, he straightway repaired to England to plead for himself, and put the best face on his own pretensions. O'Neale's address and practised suppleness eminently fitted him for such an occasion, and in Elizabeth he had a fair object for the exercise of such qualities. She received him graciously as an old acquaintance, and suffered herself to be pleased by his wily admiration, and the well-assumed simplicity which did not prevent his exhibiting his claims and enforcing their expediency, with all the dexterity of a sagacious statesman. He warmly expressed his regret at the slowness of his countrymen to receive the improvement of English manners and laws; was particularly earnest and pathetic in his representation of the afflictions of Tyrone; and with much force of argument, convinced the queen, that nothing could proceed rightly until she had put down the barbarous title of O'Neale. On the strength of these arguments, he urged his personal pretensions, and so won upon the queen that she complied with his demands; he thus obtained the princely inheritance of his

* Ware.

family free from any reservation of rent. The conditions were few and easy. It was stipulated that the bounds of Tyrone should be accurately limited; that 240 acres, bordering on the Blackwater, should be ceded for an English fort; that the earl should claim no authority over the surrounding chiefs of Ulster; that the sons of Shane and of Tirlough* O'Neale should be provided for. Some writers add a strange stipulation : that old Tirlogh should still be continued the O'Neale or chief of the sept. This arrangement, though seemingly subversive of the main principle of the agreement, was in fact recommended by an obvious policy, as no great mischief was to be apprehended from Tirlogh, who besides his age, was without the means of any extensive disturbance, and he was thus made to occupy that position in which the ambition of the powerful earl might become dangerous.

Sir John Perrot was very much offended by this arrangement and by the mode of its completion. The patent he felt should have been drawn by his own authority, and the conditions arranged with his privity and consent. He felt the slight, and disapproved of the remission of the heavy rent which he supposed himself to have secured. Notwithstanding this discontent, when the earl came over to Dublin, he was received with all courtesy by Sir John. He then proceeded to Tyrone, and easily prevailed on Tirlogh to give up a territorial claim which he could by no possibility reduce to possession.

O'Neale had not long been thus invested with the possession of his country, before the inauspicious chain of circumstances which we have described as the main causes of his ruin, had their commencement. Among the first was his quarrel with Tirlogh Lynnogh, and many other quarrels and discontents of the same nature, which arose between him and the surrounding chiefs and proprietors. Of these the immediate consequence was, a succession of complaints, which soon placed his conduct in a questionable point of view, and raised a host of watchful and acrimonious enemies who let nothing pass unobserved and unreported, that could injure him with government. On some quarrel between himself and Tirlogh Lynnogh, he made an incursion upon his property, and drove away two thousand cows; and when ordered by the lord-deputy to restore them, instead of complying he took offence at the interposition, and made a second attack on his enemy at Strabane. Tirlogh Lynnogh was, however, supported by two companies of English soldiers, with which the deputy had prudently supplied him, immediately on receiving his complaint, and the earl was compelled to fly. It was at the same time that he had the imprudence to allow himself to be led into an intercourse with the Scots, which, though not in all likelihood carried on with any disloyal purpose, was manifestly in a very high degree questionable. The temptations to assume the privileges of an independent chief, (to which he possessed no shadow of title,) were very considerable. Being in the place and position of the chief of Tyrone, he soon began to be recognised as such, by the surrounding chiefs; they addressed him as a prince, the representative of that ancient house, and as an influential leader on whom

---

* Shane's sons were Henry, Con, and Tirlogh. Tirlogh's son, Arthur who served in the English army in the following rebellion.

the hopes of his country were mainly fixed. These dangerous assumptions were not easy to repel, and his pride concurred with his fears to warp him towards a compliance not less unsafe. There were many reasons of a more cogent nature why he should aim to strengthen himself against his numerous surrounding enemies, and thus a very narrow-sighted policy combined with other motives to lead him to enter into alliances, which could only be maintained by acts capable of receiving a criminal construction. It was in consequence of these circumstances, that in the year 1587, many questionable reports were transmitted to the lord-deputy; among which was that of a treasonable alliance with the Scots, by which he sent them aid in men, on the condition of receiving the same from them against his enemies. These errors in policy have since received from most historians the same unfavourable construction, but we cannot help thinking, that in this there is a great neglect of allowance for human nature, and the spirit of the age. A more patient and therefore more distinct contemplation exhibits Tyrone carried on by a chain of controlling circumstances; although it must be admitted, that if such be the unfavourable construction of many undoubtedly able writers, their very error seems to justify the severe constructions of those governors whose harshness assisted in precipitating the earl in his ill-advised course.

The same constructions apply with still more force to a subsequent incident. In 1588, the Spanish Armada, so well known in English history, was dispersed by a storm and seventeen of the ships were wrecked on the Ulster coast. The prepossessions of the Irish in favour of the Spanish were strong, and had, of late years, been assiduously, though secretly, cultivated. The earl could not, without offending every prejudice of the surrounding districts, notice them otherwise than as friends: it was in the spirit of his nation and character to show hospitality; and an obvious, though near-sighted reasoning, pointed out the future advantages which were likely to follow. The report of his favourable reception of the queen's enemies could not fail to be in a high degree prejudicial to the earl. Yet, so far as any fair inference was to be drawn from the general tenour of his conduct, there was in all this little to support the extreme constructions to which he soon became subjected. To suppose that one, pretending to the authority and dignity which at that period was ostensibly claimed by his ancient house, could at once altogether throw off the weight of ancient manners, prejudices, and obligations, the privileges immemorially preserved, and all considerations by which he was bound by a thousand links of opinion and custom, with the whole of his Irish connexions, dependents, and friends, was, in point of fact, to assume the extinction of his whole nature; and it is evident that any reasonable government, at whatever changes it aimed—and great changes were wanting to make Ireland a civilized country—should have proceeded on the principle of much toleration, and used much caution to avoid driving consequences more rapidly than there were means provided to ensure success, on any ground equitable or inequitable. While, here too, on the other hand, it cannot fairly be denied, that a person of Tyrone's clear perceptions must have seen and contemplated, as they arose, events and indications, which might soon render it a course of necessity or safety to take a part against the English government.

Tyrone neglected no means of increasing his own power and authority. He was authorized by the queen, or rather bound by an explicit stipulation, to maintain six companies for the defence of Ulster; of this he availed himself for the increase of his military force, by changing the men in such a manner as to train his whole county to arms—an expedient which was afterwards made a subject of accusation, but which, according to the view here taken, only affords a very gross instance of slackness in the government which permitted the growth of a power so thoroughly at variance with the whole of its recognized policy.

Under all these circumstances, the recall of Sir John Perrot was exceedingly unfortunate. In the want of a sufficient application of controlling force, the next best course was that of a moderate and conciliatory government; though, in that vicious state of civil existence, the latter course implied much connivance at abuse, and much toleration of evil doing; there was no other alternative. Sir John was mild, just, and as firm as good policy permitted; he had won the good-will of the native chiefs, and thus materially fostered a disposition to submit and to perceive the real advantages of the English laws. But violent and grasping spirits were offended at a moderation which restricted the field of confiscation and attainder, and the queen, who did not supply the requisite means, was discontented at the slow progress of Irish affairs: the general sense of those who were unacquainted with Irish policy was that more might be effected by greater energy, and more violent and sweeping measures. Under these and such impressions, Sir John was recalled, and the government committed to Sir William Fitz-William.

Previous to his departure Sir John committed an act of injustice, which throws disgrace on his character, and which had the most pernicious consequences. This was the seizure of Red Hugh O'Donell, and of the two sons of Shane O'Neale, by an act of treachery not to be mentioned without disgust. Although the historian of O'Donell, and subsequent writers, make it seem that the capture of O'Donell was the chief object of that most disgraceful expedition,* yet we think it obvious enough that its design was far more indiscriminate.† The possession of the O'Neales was thought to afford a useful curb over the proceedings of the earl, as, while they were alive, their claim could if necessary, be set up in opposition to him. This unjust and oppressive step was, however, not sufficient to repress the good-will generally won from the native Irish by the mild and equitable tenor of Perrot's administration, or to counterbalance the good effects it had produced. There was a disposition to peace, order, and submission to authority, which had been hitherto unprecedented; the most powerful of the chiefs and noblemen were ready to come on the summons of the governor, and all sorts of provisions were plenty and cheap. Fitz-William's conduct was such as to unsettle the favourable dispositions of the country. The chief cause of every disaffected tendency was one which lay tacitly under a heap of pretended or fictitious

* O'Donell's Life.   † See Cox.

grievances; the fear of oppression, and the insecurity of rights: the chiefs had long been taught to feel themselves insecure in their possessions. Compared with this pervading sense, all other discontents were slight, being mostly in their nature local or personal. Rebellion demands a common cause, the only principle of popular union. Then indeed, as since, the moving principle has been ever something different, and wholly different, from the spurious convention which inflames and rallies round a common standard the passions of the ignorant and lawless multitude: and if there be any truth in this position, it is of material importance so to direct the remedial course as to meet the *real evil*, either by fair concession, or decisive and effectual resistance. It was the misfortune of the country that both were at the time required, and both neglected. Fitz-William's first course of conduct was to awaken the reasonable fears of the Irish chiefs, both for their property and personal liberty. If the seizure of O'Donell, for which there was reasonable ground, though the artifice was base and revolting, communicated a shock, the seizure of MacToole, Tyrone's father-in-law, and of O'Doherty, both persons of the most peaceable demeanour and the highest reputation for loyalty, without the pretext of any accusation, or of the shadow even of state necessity, struck fire through the whole of Ulster. The pride and fear of every one who had any thing to lose, or any sense of self-respect, was offended by an action so unwarranted and arbitrary as to convey the dangerous sense that no person or property was safe from such a power used in such a spirit. In the year 1589, Fitz-William having received information that the Spaniards, who were the preceding year wrecked on the northern and western coasts, had left behind them much treasure, first endeavoured to secure it by a commission; this failing, he travelled into the north at great expense in quest of the supposed riches. Irritated by not finding these, he seized the two gentlemen already named, on the report of their having a large part of them in their possession. The prisoners refusing to ransom themselves were imprisoned, and detained in captivity for a long time.*

In the meantime, Hugh Na'Gaveloch, an illegitimate son of Shane O'Neale, brought information to Fitz-William that Tyrone had entered into a secret alliance with the Spaniards. Tyrone was not long in discovering the informer, whom he caused to be hanged. It is said that it was difficult to find one to hang this offender on account of the name of O'Neale.

This, with the other circumstance related, and the general impression produced by all the various rumours in circulation to the prejudice of Fitz-William's character and motives, alarmed Tyrone. He knew himself to be a fair and tempting object for suspicion and cupidity, and resolved to anticipate the accusations which he feared by a personal appeal to the favour and justice of the queen. He went over to England in May, 1590. Owing to this journey having been taken without the lord-deputy's permission, he was at first placed under arrest. On submission he was liberated, and had a satisfactory audience from the queen, after which he agreed to enter into bonds for the secu-

* Moryson.

rity of the pale, and to keep the peace with Tirlogh Lynnogh. He also agreed to put in pledges to be chosen by the lord-deputy, it being provided that these pledges should not lie in the castle, but be committed to the keeping of some gentlemen within the pale, and that they might be exchanged every three months—a provision remarkable for its fairness and humanity; but if looked on further, not less sagaciously adapted to the purpose of eluding the consequences of any violation of the terms on his part, or of the suspicions of government, which were at least as likely to occur. The articles of his former agreement were also, at the same time, confirmed by fresh engagements to the same effect.

On his return to Dublin, he came before the council, and confirmed the articles which had been transmitted from England. He, nevertheless, continued to defer their fulfilment, excusing himself by letters to the English and Irish councils, in which he entreated that Tirlogh Lynnogh, and other neighbouring lords, should be rendered subject to the same engagements.

In the same year occurred the most unjust and impolitic execution of the chief of Monaghan, MacMahon, upon no ostensible plea of justice, and for which the only appearance of excuse was the false asseveration that the whole country seemed glad of his execution. The actual charge was as absurdly made, as the whole proceeding was treacherous and undignified; and the effect was a very violent aggravation of the discontents of Ulster. The story is worth telling. Some time before MacMahon had surrendered his property, which he held under tanistry, and received it in English tenure by a grant under the broad seal, in which the inheritance was limited to himself and his heirs male, and in failure of these to his brother, Hugh Roe MacMahon. In the year 1590, MacMahon died without heirs of his body, and the succession was claimed by his brother according to the patent. He was first put off on the excuse of a certain fee of six hundred cows, for, according to Moryson, " such and no other were the Irish bribes." He was then seized and imprisoned, but after a few days released, with a promise that the lord-deputy would himself go and settle him in the county of Monaghan. Accordingly, in a few days, Fitz-William made a journey to that country with MacMahon in his company. Immediately, however, on their arrival MacMahon was seized, shut up in his own house, tried by a jury composed of soldiers and Irish kernes, which latter were shut up and denied all food until they found him guilty of a pretended misdemeanour, for which he was at once executed. His country was then divided among several persons, both English and Irish, all of whom, it was alleged, and may fairly be presumed, paid well for their shares. The whole of these facts, if truly stated, place beyond doubt that the design was preconceived and planned by the deputy, and that the journey was a contrivance to get the victim entirely into his own hands, by a removal from the constraint of the civil authorities before whom he should otherwise have been tried, and who would have treated as vexatious the charge that this person, two years before, had entered a neighbouring district, and levied a distress for rent due to him. Considering the general laxity of construction which prevailed at the time, and the far more serious offences which were daily connived at or compromised—the arrest by a most fraudulent manœuvre—the clandestine and illegal trial and execution, and the division of the spoil—it would be setting at naught the ordinary laws of equitable construction to deny that an aggravated outrage was thus committed against right. The whole of this iniquitous proceeding was at once and universally understood. It struck at the root of all confidence—the wide-spread and deeply-seated elements of disaffection and hate were aggravated and apparently justified by a well-grounded distrust; and there were at the time active agents at work, by whom nothing was let fall inoperative that could awaken and concentrate hostility to the English. On the report of this execution, the chiefs of Ulster were not slow to express their sense by their language and actions. They showed the utmost unwillingness to admit any English sheriffs, or admit of any channel for the entrance of laws which they saw could thus easily be made the weapon of rapine and murder.

These transactions, whatever may have been their influence in determining the after-course of Tyrone, had the immediate effect of rendering his conduct cautious and watchful in an increased degree. He had a fray with his neighbour, Tirlogh Lynnogh, in which Tirlogh was wounded: Tyrone anticipated his complaint by a representation that the occurrence was caused by his neighbour's attempt to take a prey in his lands, from which he repelled him by force. He also, immediately after, permitted the county of Tyrone to be made shire ground. In July, 1591, the bounds of this county were defined by commissioners appointed for the purpose; who divided it into eight baronies, and made Dungannon the shire town.

One act of Tyrone, of which we only know the fact from its consequences, was perhaps more decisive of his fate than any other cause. It was that in the same year a complaint was preferred against him by Sir Henry Bagnal, for having carried off his sister and married her, his former wife being still alive. Tyrone defended himself by alleging that the lady was taken away and married by her own consent, and that his former wife had been previously divorced.

Amidst all these occasions of offence and fear, it is not improbable that a great change may have grown over the temper of the earl; yet his overt conduct, at least, still manifested a disposition to adhere to the English government. In the English council also there was a disposition to trust him: the main occasions of his irregular proceedings were understood, or met with a favourable construction; his reputation for sagacity also stood in his favour, for as his best interest lay in the shelter of the English government, he was allowed the credit of understanding this fact; while every charge which had hitherto been advanced against him met with a fair excuse, many services of an unquestionable nature ascertained his fidelity, or disarmed accusation of its pretext. Such, indeed, both in historical or political construction of the characters of public men, is the case which constantly recurs, and renders judgment difficult and fairness itself a risk. In their overt acts, fair appearances, honest motives, and universal principles, are kept on the surface, however base, dangerous, or dishonest, may be the motives and designs of the actors. There can be no

course of public conduct maintained in the public eye, that is not
capable of being defended upon the ground of principle; while the
more refined and less popular reasoning by which the secret can be
traced, depends on facts and assumptions which, though plain to all
thinking persons, are not so capable of being substantiated to the
coarse perception and prejudiced sense of the public mind—so generally just in its practical maxims, and so inapt beyond them.

Judging by his public acts, by his fair professions, or by a due allowance for the just sense of his own interests, it is to be inferred that the
earl of Tyrone was still at this period of our narrative sincere in his
professions of loyalty. But it is impossible to make these allowances,
without also insisting upon some allowance of an opposite value, for
other facts of which he must have been fully cognizant, and in no
small degree influenced by. We are made aware, by several statements
of a very authoritative nature, that he maintained an intimate understanding with the Irish, who were at the same time entering into a
most formidable conspiracy against the English pale.

While the state of English affairs seemed to be approaching to a
steady and settled aspect of prosperity, a strong and dangerous underworking had set in, which menaced the very existence of the pale.
O'Donell, whose capture and well-grounded hate to the English government we have related, had escaped from his cruel, impolitic captivity, and, after many romantic adventures, found refuge and friendship with Tyrone; and from this moment the latter was in fact a
consenting party to all the machinations of the insurgents. This
consent may be affirmed to have been insincere, but cannot be reasonably denied. If the defence be considered worth any thing, there is
indeed ample ground for questioning his sincerity to either party;
and it will, after all, be the best that can be said, that his deportment
to either was the stern dictate of circumstance. It was the result of
his position, that the contingencies belonging to whatever course he
might take wore a formidable aspect; and his best excuse must be
found in the conduct of the English government. The difficulties
which pressed him on either side should have been allowed for; and
while his conduct received the most indulgent construction, he should
have been firmly upheld in the course which was imposed on him by
his obligations to the queen's government.

Instead of support and allowance, on the fair principle of recogniz-
ing the difficulties of his position, these difficulties were soon indefinitely
increased by a jealous scrutiny, which began to give the worst construction to every act, and the readiest reception to every whisper
which breathed against him. It was unquestionably the duty of a
vigilant administration to keep the most jealous eye on the conduct of
one whose situation was exposed to so many varied impulses. But
judicious watchfulness is not more vigilant to detect an indication,
than cautious to avoid misconstruction; and it was, or ought to have
been known, how much enmity and how much grasping cupidity
were on the alert to hunt down so rich a victim as Tyrone.

While, then, to sum the fact in a few words, Tyrone truly or insin-
cerely asserted his loyalty to the queen, with the same respective degree of insincerity or truth, he asserted his adherence to the party of

O'Donell, to whom he pleaded the necessity of preserving appearances towards the English; and under the operation of this most fatal position, the moment was fast approaching when he must of necessity have taken his choice, and when the indulgence of the English—for this too has its limits—would have been fatuity, not fairness. Such, then, is the ground which we desire to take, on a question upon which, we think, some able writers have taken a narrow and a partial view.

As yet, however, it is manifest the public conduct of Tyrone entitled him to be considered as a loyal British subject. In 1592, among other statements, he wrote to the English council that he had brought over O'Donell to the queen's allegiance, and "that he would persuade him to loyalty, and, in case he were obstinate, that he would serve against him as an enemy."* Another circumstance—one of the many which accumulated into the serious rebellion which followed—gave Tyrone an occasion to maintain his character of questionable loyalty. In the year 1593, M'Guire, chief of Fermanagh, began to take an active part in the gathering troubles of the north. He was, in common with all the surrounding chiefs of Ulster, alarmed and irritated by the execution of MacMahon; and the feeling was chiefly indicated by a reluctance to admit of an English sheriff within these territories. It is mentioned by Davis, that, when Fitz-William first intimated to M'Guire his intention to send an English sheriff into Fermanagh, the chief replied, " Your sheriff shall be welcome; but let me know his eric, that if my people cut off his head, I may levy it on the county." The sheriff was sent, with two hundred men to support him. And not long after, he was, with his party, assailed by M'Guire, and driven to take refuge in a church, where they would have been exterminated by fire, but for the timely interposition of the earl of Tyrone. The lord-deputy, on this, sent a party of soldiers into Fermanagh, who seized M'Guire's castle of Eniskillen; the chief was proclaimed a traitor; and the lord-deputy let fall some threats against the earl of Tyrone, which soon found their way to his ear. These expressions, whatever was their import, were afterwards referred to by the earl as a justification of his subsequent conduct. From the time he was apprized of the deputy's language, he said that he began to consider his safety doubtful, and to make up his mind to join with O'Donell.

Still he thought it necessary to preserve appearances; and when M'Guire, breaking into open rebellion, made an irruption into Connaught, Tyrone joined his forces to the English and took an active part in the operations by which he was driven back. On this occasion he received a wound. But whatever were his intentions, nothing could now divert the course of the suspicion and enmity which watched and severely interpreted every thing he did. Though ready to comply with his avowed engagements, there was much to support a jealous view of all his conduct: he gave his daughter in marriage to O'Donell, and refused to deliver up the sons of Shane O'Neale, whom he had seized and cast into chains.

In the month of August, 1594, Fitz-William was recalled, and Sir William Russell sent over in his room. The complaints against

* Moryson.

Tyrone had increased, and suspicion was growing fast into certainty, when he made his appearance in the metropolis, from which he had carefully absented himself during Fitz-William's government. The step was politic, but not without risk; for the enemies of the earl were many and powerful, and (had enmity been wanting) his conduct was open to suspicion. But, above all the whispers of suspicion, or the cautious doubts of guarded policy, the bitter animosity of Bagnal made itself heard. Bagnal earnestly urged that the earl's visit to the city was but an artifice to lull the suspicions excited by his long course of double dealing, entreated that he should be arrested, and offered to make good several articles of treason against him. The accusations of Bagnal had been repeatedly proffered, and comprised all the questionable acts of the earl's past life, most of which we have mentioned in their order of occurrence. They were chiefly these: That he entertained Gauran, titular primate of Ireland, knowing him to be a traitor—this Gauran had been but recently slain in an encounter between Bingham and M'Guire in Connaught; that he corresponded with O'Donell, who was at the very time levying war against the queen; that, being allowed to keep six companies in the queen's service, he so contrived, by continued changes of the men, to discipline the entire population of Tyrone; that having engaged to build a castle for his own residence after the fashion of the English nobility, he had availed himself of the occasion as a pretence to purchase a quantity of lead as if for the roof, but which he stored in Dungannon as material for bullets. But whatever may have been Tyrone's sincerity, he was no mean proficient in the arts of speciousness: he vindicated his character and intentions before the council, to whom, in the tone of ardent gratitude, he enumerated the many honours and benefits he had received from the bounty of the queen; and renounced all mercy from the Almighty if he should ever lift his hand against her. He promised to send his son to be educated in Dublin, and to deliver sufficient pledges for his future conduct. These representations, which were accompanied with specific answers to the several charges which had been made against him, impressed the council and the lord-deputy in his favour; and they agreed to dismiss him. The queen, who had, perhaps, before this been enabled to form a more correct estimate of Tyrone's conduct, was very much displeased, and sent over a severe reprimand. She thought that her deputy should at least have used the occasion to stipulate for the relief of Eniskillen,*—an object which, in the same month, was effected by Sir William Russell, who, by a week of rapid and laborious marching over mountain and bog, entered Eniskillen without a blow; the enemy having abandoned it on his approach.

Notwithstanding the strong professions of Tyrone, his real designs were now strongly impressed on the government in both countries. An equivocal course can only deceive for a short time, and suspicious conduct long persisted in becomes the certain indication of the crime suspected. The conduct of Tyrone has been by some thought reconcilable with loyal intention—we should now judge by the event.

* Cox.

The government was decided, in some measure, by the general evidence of character and the native craft ascribed to Tyrone. He was doubtless fully bent on rebellion. We have willingly conceded to those who are inclined to take the most favourable view, that his earlier professions of loyalty were sincere; it is indeed the inference we have ourselves arrived at: we have also strongly asserted our belief that he was placed in a position which rendered perseverance in loyalty difficult in a high degree—between the accusations of those who loved his possessions, or resented his encroaching and tyrannical actions—the restless suspicions and despotic temper of lord-deputies, and the fierce remonstrances of his own countrymen. Viewing his conduct with every allowance of palliation, we think that from the commencement of 1594, he must be allowed to have engaged clandestinely in the design then openly avowed by O'Donell; and all professions to the contrary were such as could only be allowed to pass by the most blameable remissness. It is at this point of time that we think it, therefore, important to draw a line, which has been obliterated by the strong party professions of those who have written on either side: Cox, whose prejudices blind him, and Moryson who lay within the dust of the struggle, and could not be expected to see beyond it, and the numerous historians who but follow in the wake of these: or, on the other hand, the recent writers who, with a far larger grasp of facts and principles, can only be just to the cause so far as their political creed allows of justice. Totally dissenting from the spirit of each, we have neither allowed the subject of our memoir to be set down as one of the most base and crafty traitors that ever breathed; nor, on the contrary, one of the most injured victims of a base faction and tyrannical government. The government was often incompetent, often tyrannical, and in no instance administered on principles of clear-sighted and comprehensive policy or justice: but Tyrone was fairly open from the beginning to suspicion. Though sagacious, he had not discretion to resist the temptations of power: he was brave in action but he had not the firmness to preserve his consistency. The taunts and solicitations of the disaffected, the injuries and insults of the interested underlings of power, warped his course and brought him into positions, in which he met not perhaps all the allowance which these considerations might seem to claim: because, in reality, such allowance cannot in any case be made, but by the eye of omniscience. We shall not, therefore, with some contemporary writers, allow him the praise of a great man. He was, in our estimate, much sinning as well as much sinned against; and it is precisely at the period of his life at which we have now arrived, that we are anxious to impress our reader with this distinction—that having till now wavered under the operation of causes hard to resist, he at length, under the continued operation of these causes joined the struggle, and began to move heart and hand with the rebel party.

But it was among the least equivocal indications of the double play upon which Tyrone had entered, that to the native chiefs who had at this time leagued against the English, he actually professed that such was the true nature of his conduct towards the English; that his professions were intended for the purpose of deception: and that his very acts of seeming good faith were necessary to support his professions. However his deception may be excused, he was a deceiver. But O'Donell, who had, from the beginning, taken the most decided course, now conceived that the time for disguise was over. The native Irish had gained discipline and confidence; they were beginning to be united into the sense of a common cause by the efforts of the foreign ecclesiastics who were sent amongst them from Italy and Spain. From the latter country, they received the fullest assurances of liberal aid in men, money, and military supplies. The hopes of the insurgent party were high, and not without strong grounds, both in their own strength and in the weakness of the English, for whom no efficient protection was yielded at any time. Under these circumstances, the temporising policy of the earl rendered him an object of suspicion to the Irish as well as to the English; and O'Donell now at once snapped asunder the cobweb tissue of his transparent deceptions, by a menace that if he did not declare himself openly he would at once treat him as an enemy. In this there can be, however, little doubt, that, considered with respect to policy, the step was premature. It was the more cautious design of Tyrone to avoid awakening the government into any decided course, until the aid so liberally promised by Spain should enable them to support their pretensions. The spirit and energy of O'Donell, with all their efficacy in stirring up the spirit of the land, were by no means as available in the combination of difficulties which were now soon to arise, as the circumspect and cautious character of Tyrone.

The true state of Irish affairs began to be understood in the English council; and it was resolved to take more effectual means to put down the rising troubles which had for some time worn a menacing aspect. A fresh supply of veteran troops was ordered for Ireland, and it was resolved to suppress and overawe the malcontents of Ulster, by encompassing them on every side. It was also directed that the lord-deputy should endeavour to detach O'Donell, of whose real spirit they were ignorant, from Tyrone: it was considered that O'Donell had received severe and gratuitous ill treatment, which demanded some offer of redress, and partly justified his proceedings.

The lord-deputy wrote over to request that, with the troops, an experienced commander might be sent; from whose judgment he might receive warrant and confirmation in the conduct of his military operations. In answer to this request, the queen sent Sir John Norris, who had very much distinguished himself as a general in the low countries.

When Tyrone was apprized of the contemplated reinforcement, he became very much alarmed for the consequences, and justly fearing the design which was rumoured about, he resolved to prevent it by the seizure of the English fort which had been built, according to his former agreement, on the Blackwater; and which was the main check which the queen's government possessed over his own movements.

Pretending some frivolous quarrel with its garrison, he attacked and took this fort, and burnt down the bridge to the water. It was the passage into his country, and had he been previously engaged in a course of open hostilities, he could not have taken a better step.

Having thus plunged into rebellion, he wrote letters to the earl of Kildare, to persuade him to follow the same mad course, and sent off emissaries to Spain to apply for aid and money. His next step was to invest Monaghan, the castle of which was garrisoned by the English.

On the news of this, general Bagnal marched to the relief of the besieged town on the 24th May, with fifteen hundred foot and two hundred and fifty horse. Late in the evening, the army reached a place called Eight-mile-church, and took its quarters for the night. While this was doing, Tyrone with a large body of horse came within sight, within about half a mile, but presently retired without any further demonstration. Next morning the English marched on until they reached a pass, when they were attacked; but succeeded in forcing their way, and proceeded on their march till they reached the town. The siege was raised on their approach; nothing material occurred during the remainder of that day, but the English leaders soon perceived that their position was not the most advantageous. Within a mile of where they lay, on a hill by the abbey of Monaghan, they were enabled distinctly to perceive the junction of the armies of M'Guire, and other chiefs, with the formidable host of Tyrone, forming a body of eight thousand foot, and one thousand horse, as well armed and scarcely less disciplined than themselves. The English, little more than the ninth part of that army in number, were besides but ill provided for an emergency, which nothing had led them to expect, and it was quite obvious that their best success would be to make a successful retreat. On the next morning the enemy's camp was in motion at an early hour, and strong parties were seen to march out in different directions with silent celerity, but not so secretly as to escape the observation of the veteran who commanded the English party. The rebel leaders conceiving that the English were in their power, and only to be secured, had prudently enough resolved to seize on every pass, and cut off their retreat. Bagnal was not prevented by the visible danger from taking such precautions as he thought necessary, for the relief of Monaghan, into which he sent men and victuals, and then ordered a retreat. This operation was, however, become in a high degree difficult ; the rebel leaders, from their knowledge of the country, were enabled to throw themselves into a hollow through which the English must presently pass. When the English reached this place they were encountered by a severe fire, which, from the multitude of the assailants and their advantage of position, would quickly have anihilated them had it lasted; but by great good fortune the rebels were not provided with ammunition sufficient to keep up their fire which after some fierce discharges became slack. On this the English, knowing that the danger was over, prepared to encamp for the night: they had lost twenty men and had ninety wounded; of the rebels between three and four hundred had fallen. All night the English lay in the very midst of the Irish army, which occupied all the heights and posts of advantage round them. They lay in their arms and were fully prepared for any sudden irruption which might reasonably be anticipated from the known customs of the enemy with which they had to deal. This consequence was perhaps arrested by a much more prudent conduct on the part of Tyrone and his friends. Thinking to make the matter sure they sent to Dungannon for a supply of ammunition, but providentially obtained none; on the next morning, therefore, the English were allowed to pursue their way unmolested to Newry.

This bold step was followed soon by a proclamation, declaring Tyrone, O'Donell, M'Guire, and others, traitors. In the mean time, Sir John Norris had arrived with 8000 men, of which 2000 were veteran soldiers; and on the 18th of June, they marched towards Dundalk. On the 23d, O'Donell, Tyrone, and other chiefs who were of their party, were proclaimed traitors, "both in English and Irish."[*] On this the insurgent chiefs, either took alarm; or else, as is not unlikely under the circumstances in which they supposed themselves to stand, they thought it would be advisable to gain time, and by any means, avoid a premature trial of strength: and adopted the course of a pretended submission. Such expedients were indeed convenient, and easy in the highest degree, at a time when the most solemn engagements and binding pledges were entered into, and broken with a facility unintelligible in any modern state of things. The Irish chiefs were under an illusory expectation of foreign aid, and had not been enabled by any experience to calculate on the real force which England could throw into the struggle if once fairly committed to it. They were imposed on by the desultory nature of the contest, in which they played unconsciously with the arms of the sleeping giant that had, when fairly roused, been ever found an overmatch for any nation on wave or plain. Yet making all allowances for the errors of the time, it is difficult for those who look through the medium of modern conventions, to comprehend satisfactorily the entire conduct of the rebel earl: or to reconcile even to any well devised system of deception, his frequent and anxious petitions for pardons which were spurned as soon as obtained: or his specious excuses and professions, with his bold and furious outbreaks—such as the demolition of the fort of Blackwater, his attack on Monaghan, and his treasonable correspondence with the earl of Kildare, in which he proposed to that nobleman to join in rebellion.

Still more strange indeed was the course which Camden attributes to the earl. While yet engaged in the preparations for an extensive combination against the English government,[†] he addressed letters to the earl of Ormonde, and to Sir Henry Wallop, to implore for their intercession in his behalf. He also wrote to the general-in-chief Sir J. Norris, to the same purpose, immediately after his former defeat. Whatever may have been the character of Tyrone's applications, their purpose was partially frustrated by a manœuvre as dishonest, and a thousand times more base. The deceit of Tyrone was sanctioned by usage; it was a trick nearly conventional in the shuffling game of Irish politics: but the interception and suppression of his letters by marshal Bagnal was the mean and dishonourable expedient of personal

---

[*] Cox.
[†] Something in this statement is to be allowed for the exaggerations of party. All the Irish historians of Camden's age, like those of our own, were, without exception, party writers.

malice—the base resource of a base passion. The letter to Norris, falling thus into the hands of Tyrone's deadliest enemy, was carefully held back until the proclamation had gone forth. But in addition to his other crimes, it was discovered that Tyrone had written to the king of Spain, to offer him the kingdom of Ireland for a supply of 3000 men and some money.* The queen was irritated by outbreaks so repeated as to remove all confidence in professions or pledges, and declared her resolution never to pardon the earl again—a resolution which, says Cox, she kept to her dying day.

Many strong considerations, however, weighed on the other side: the strength of the English was far inferior to the exigency of circumstances; and that of the rebels was fast augmenting in numbers, combination, discipline, and the munitions of war. The Irish force in Ulster alone was rated at 7,280. The incessant efforts of Tyrone and O'Donell had brought them into a state of training scarcely inferior to that of the English, of whom the greater part were but raw recruits. Sir John Perrot had been betrayed into an expedient, which had very much tended to this result: in his desire to increase his force with less cost, by fighting the Irish against each other, he had employed and trained to arms large bodies of men, who now swelled the ranks of the insurgent chiefs.

These considerations, with the strong urgency of those English lords, who were the personal friends of Tyrone, weighed with the English government. The treachery of Bagnal had also its weight in favour of Tyrone, and the queen gave her consent that a treaty should be entered on with himself and the chiefs of his party. A truce was therefore made on the 27th October, 1595, till the first of January following, for the purpose of hearing the complaints, and receiving the submissions of the chiefs, and coming to some distinct terms for their future government. For this, Sir Henry Wallop, and chief-justice Gardiner, were appointed commissioners, and a meeting took place about the middle of January.

The particulars of the conference are given at large, both by Moryson, and by the MS. historian of O'Donell. The representations of the chiefs were specious, and their complaints for the most part just; but this constitutes the vast difficulty of the Irish history of this entire period, that nothing on either side (especially on that of the Irish chiefs,) was precisely according to the ostensible pretence of the parties. The speeches were fair, and the demands not unreasonable: but nothing was meant by the leading chiefs but to trifle; and those amongst their number who were in good earnest, were perverted by the representations of O'Donell, who addressed them apart, and set before them his view of their true prospects in the growing strength of their arms, and the promises of the king of Spain, who, he said, "should not be deceived, as he was incapable of deceiving them." Such is the true representation of one who could not have mistaken what passed before him, and is the best commentary on the statement of Moryson, which otherwise leaves the conduct of the Irish chiefs inexplicable. We extract it entire.

* Cox.

"Tyrone in this conference complained of the marshall for his usurped jurisdiction in Ulster, for depriving him of the queen's favours by slanders; for intercepting his late letters to the lord deputie, and lord generall, protesting that he never negotiated with forraine prince, till he was proclaimed traytor. His humble petitions were, that hee and his might be pardoned, and have free exercise of religion granted, (which notwithstanding had never before either been punished or inquired after.) That the marshall should pay him one thousand pounds for his dead sisters, his wives portion; that no garrisons nor sheriffes should be in his country; that his troope of fiftie horse in the queenes pay might be restored to him; and that such as had preyed his country, might make restitution.

"O'Donell, magnifying his fathers' and progenitors' services to the crowne, complained that captaine Boyne, sent by Sir John Perrot with his company into his countrey, under pretence to reduce the people to civilitie, and being well entertained by his father, had besides many other injuries raised a bastard to be O'Donell, and that Sir John Perrot, by a ship sent thither, had taken himselfe by force, and long imprisoned him at Dublin; and that Sir William Fitz-William had wrongfully kept Owen O'Toole, above mentioned, seven yeeres in prison. His petitions were for pardon to him and his, and for freedome of religion; that no garrisons or sheriffs might bee placed in his countrey, and that certain castles and lands in the county of Sligo might bee restored to him.

"Shane MacBrian, MacPhelime O'Neale, complained of an iland taken from him by the earle of Essex, and that he had been imprisoned till he surrendered to the marshall a barony, his ancient inheritance. Hugh M'Guire complained of insolencies done by garrison souldiers, and by a sheriffe, who besides killed one of his nearest kinsmen, Brian MacHugh Oge, and MacHowne, (so the Irish called the chiefe of that name surviving,) and Ever MacCooly, of the same family of MacHownes, complained of the above-mentioned unjust execution of Hugh Roe MacHowne, in the governement of Sir William Fitz-Williams."*

The commissioners admitted the fairness of many of these complaints, and frankly promised redress; but thought it necessary on the part of the queen to make such conditions as were absolutely necessary to secure the peace of the country in the interim. It was stipulated that they should lay down their arms, repair the forts they had razed, admit sheriffs into their territories and counties, restore property they had obtained by recent violence, abstain from their attacks on the garrisoned forts; that they should reveal their secret communications with the foreign enemies of the queen, ask pardon for their rebellion, and solemnly swear allegiance, and to avoid all future rebellion. As there was nothing in these demands inconsistent with the repeated promises and pretences of those who were now present, it would not be easy to assign any specious ground for a refusal; yet such was the result. The conference was held in the open fields, and in sight of the armed guards which either party thought necessary for their pro-

* Moryson.

tection. But after listening with seeming respect to the propositions of the commissioners, they adjourned to a neighbouring hill, where speeches widely different from those we have just seen were made;* and the discussion was fiercely terminated without any result but a truce most injudicious on the part of the English, and precisely no more nor less than the object which the insurgents desired, and which gave them further time till April.

In the interval the earl discovered that matters were not as ripe for war as he had anticipated; for in June, he was glad to receive terms substantially the same from Norris, who came to Dundalk with the intent of leading his army into Tyrone. On this occasion the earl signed a submission in which he agreed to separate himself from the rebels, to refrain from intermeddling with his neighbours, to admit a sheriff, to rebuild Blackwater fort, to supply the garrison for ready money, to dismiss his forces, to confess his foreign negotiations, to give in sufficient pledges, and to pay whatever fine the queen should think fit to impose. His pardon was signed on the 12th May, and he sent a letter from the king of Spain to be perused by the government, taking however care to swear his messenger not to permit a copy to be taken, as such a document would evidently have the effect of committing him with O'Donell, and the other chiefs, by the exposure of an act which they might have violently resented.

But such was the uncertainty of the earl's mind, that he had not yet completely executed the preliminaries of this agreement, when he repented. Either his pride, which apparently stood on low ground, or his fear of his Irish allies, or the influence of the frank and spirited O'Donell, or his hopes of foreign aid, or all of these motives weighed upon his mind, and deterred him from the course of honour and prudence. Sir Edward Moore, who was sent to convey to him his pardon and receive his pledges, could nowhere find him: he eluded his engagement by concealing himself. We believe the fact to be, that in the interval he received a letter from O'Donell, apprizing him of the arrival of three Spanish vessels with two hundred men, and a supply of ammunition, with the promise of more. There is sufficient evidence quoted by Cox for the assertion, that he immediately engaged in a treasonable correspondence with Feagh MacHugh. At length, on the 22d of July, he took out his pardon, and put in his pledges with strong protestations of future loyalty; but by a remissness on the part of government, which would be unaccountable if it were necessary to account for the numberless inconsistencies of this anomalous history, he was allowed to refuse taking an oath against foreign correspondence.

The next incident of this strange history is in character with the rest. A war, of which we shall elsewhere give the particulars, broke out in Leinster with Feagh MacHugh, and while it engaged the attention of the English, the earl made a descent upon Armagh, which he attempted to surprize. In this assault, thirty-five of the garrison were slain, and eight were killed in the neighbourhood where they had been sent to collect wood.† On this he was written to by the lord-deputy and council, and replied that he was induced to this action by their

* MS. Life of O'Donell. † Cox.

attack on his ally MacHugh—a reply plainly in the teeth of all engagements; so as indeed to show that with all the intelligence attributed to Tyrone, he never had a distinct conception of the real force of his agreements with the government. It was on the 30th December following, that Feagh MacHugh was killed.

In our summary of the above-mentioned particulars, we have taken the accounts most favourable to Tyrone, so far as they can be regarded as entitled to consideration. The account of Moryson in some respects presents a more unfavourable aspect of the earl's history; but unless when he happens to be an eye-witness, we must consider the report of a contemporary always to be received with no slight caution, and to be carefully tested by adverse writers. Some, however, of the particulars of the agreement last mentioned, are according to Moryson's view, such as to extenuate in some degree the conduct of Tyrone. We would not, however, be mistaken; we mean that sort of extenuation which arises from judging of men's actions from their principles of action, and their notions of right, however erroneous. Moryson mentions that Tyrone made his submission on his knees, but from the same account it appears that most of the stipulations which he thought fit to make were sternly rejected. For this it may indeed be admitted, that there was sufficient reason in the nature and design of these stipulations, some of which but too plainly exhibited that the earl was trifling, and some were inconsistent with the very principle recognized in his submission, namely, that he was a subject to the English throne. Among these, one was a petition for "liberty of religion," and was as the journalist says, " utterly rejected." This must now seem hard; at that time it was both just and expedient, for religion was the hollow pretext to concentrate under the shadow of a common cause, a rebellion originating in, and kept alive by motives of self-interest, pride, resentment, and fear. Under the sacred name of religion, it was then not uncommon to mask designs which could not safely be exhibited; but it was known that Tyrone scoffed openly at theological disputes, and in his personal conduct and private intercourse was really an irreligious person. "Hang thee," said the courtly earl of Essex in a friendly conversation, "thou talkest of a free exercise of religion—thou carest as much for religion as my horse;" the jest was taken in friendly part by the earl, who had too much tact and pride to make himself ridiculous, by an unseasonable hypocrisy. The day was yet far off when political craft involved the necessity of private dissimulation; but at the same time we must in fairness admit, that the rights of conscience may be contested by the most flagitious; and that liberty of religion, is a ground on which infidelity itself may take its stand with some degree of sincerity. Such is (or was) human nature. Among other stipulations, Tyrone demanded freedom from sheriffs and garrisons. This demand, so utterly inconsistent with the idea of submission, as well as with his station as a British earl, was of course refused.* He interceded for the pardon of O'Reilly; and it was justly answered, that being himself to be pardoned, he could not be received as the mediator for the offences of another. The whole

* Moryson.

of this portion of our narrative seems to place beyond controversy that Tyrone was treated with great forbearance, and that his notions of honour and justice, as well as his character for intelligence, sagacity, and education, are a little overstated by those writers who would raise him into a hero. Some eminent talents we must allow him, but of these the illustrations are yet to appear. We should not omit to add here, that the Irish government were at the very time of which we still speak, very much divided on his account. He had warm friends among the lords, an advantage which he well knew how to secure and make the most of, and which was no slight means of his long continuance in resisting the laws. There was even some dissension on his account between Norris and the lord-deputy, of whom the latter would be severe and the first indulgent. To this, among other circumstances, may have been due the protracted uncertainty of his conduct.

But although it is difficult to convey an adequate notion of Tyrone, without some description of the numerous repetitions of submission and revolt, which, however explained, form the main features of his history; yet to avoid extreme tediousness, it becomes necessary to pass, as lightly as our task will admit, over numerous details which with slight changes of scene and party may all be told in the same language. Indeed, so far is this true, that they are not uncommonly confounded by those who have written the history of that period.

In May, 1597, Russell was recalled, and Thomas lord Brough sent over with additional powers. It is probable that the queen was by this time grown discontented with Norris, whose successes did not keep pace with her impatience, as well as by reason of his known disposition to favour the earl of Tyrone. Among the first acts of the new lord-deputy, was an order sending Norris to his government of Munster, with a strict command not to leave it without express permission; Norris obeyed, and shortly after died, it is said, from the effects of vexation and wounded pride. The change was much to the disadvantage of Tyrone, who according to his wonted custom, immediately applied for a truce for one month. Lord Brough had resolved to disregard all such applications, which were now beginning to be clearly understood; but in this instance the truce was convenient, as it would enable him to make his own preparations.

When the truce was expired, lord Brough marched into the north and entered Tyrone. The earl attempted to intercept his passage through the woods near Armagh, by their ancient method of interlacing the boughs, but the English cut their way through without meeting any check. Arriving at the fort of Blackwater, they assaulted and won this important place; but they were yet on their knees giving thanks to God for their success, when the Irish made their appearance on the edge of the forest. Lord Brough ordered an instant attack, and the brave English rushed forward into the wood, in which a desultory and skirmishing conflict took place. The people of Tyrone soon fled, but not till some valuable lives were lost. Among the slain were two foster-brothers of Henry, earl of Kildare, who commanded a troop of horse on that occasion. Their death so grieved the earl that he did not long survive.

Lord Brough had not long quitted the north. when he heard that

Blackwater was again besieged by the earl of Tyrone, on which he turned back with a resolution to march to Dungannon, but died on the way. He was succeeded by Sir Thomas Norris, brother to the late general, but he also died on his arrival in Dublin, and the lord-chancellor Loftus, chief-justice Gardiner, with the archbishop of Dublin, were entrusted as lords justices with the civil government, and the earl of Ormonde was appointed to the command of the army, under the title of lord-lieutenant of the army. On this he was immediately applied to by the earl of Tyrone, to obtain a commission to treat with him. Lord Ormonde complied, and a truce for eight weeks was agreed on; this was followed by a general pardon under the great seal, obtained also by the strong intercession of Ormonde. But this pardon was never pleaded by Tyrone, who simply availed himself of the immediate immunity it afforded to follow the course in which he must now be regarded as decided; so that, as Moryson observes, he was afterwards, in the year 1600, outlawed on a previous indictment. The terms of this pardon were the same as those hitherto proposed, and were as usual with slight and fair exceptions agreed to by the earl.

The fort of Blackwater appears to have been a subject of constant irritation to Tyrone, although its preservation was a chief point in all his treaties for pardon: though one of his main conditions was an agreement to supply the soldiers with provisions, and to offer them no indignity or impediment, yet he never lost an opportunity to molest them; and an assault upon them was mostly his first step when by the intermission of a pardon he found all quiet. On the present occasion, he did not suffer more than two months to elapse, before he sent a party to the aid of O'Byrne, the son of Feagh MacHugh O'Byrne; and at the same time made a violent attack on the fort of Blackwater. He met on this occasion a bloody repulse; captain Williams with his small party of a hundred men, filled the earthen trench which surrounded them with the bodies of their bold assailants, so that they did not attempt to renew the assault. They then retired to a safer distance, and surrounded the fort by strong parties so as to cut off all supplies, and the condition of the brave little garrison became thus one of the most imminent peril. For about three weeks they continued in this trying situation, in the entire destitution of all ordinary means of sustaining life: fortunately for them they had a few horses in the fort, and with these they contrived to find some wild weeds in the ditch, which could be converted into food. They had eaten their horses, and were lying in the extremity of want, when lord Ormonde having heard of their condition, sent Sir Henry Bagnal to raise the siege.

The leader was unfortunately chosen. When Bagnal appeared at the head of his small force, at the entrance of the thick wood east of Armagh,* the hate of Tyrone was roused by the appearance of his deadliest enemy, and the event of the battle was suspended on the fate of Bagnal, against whom the earl directed his entire fury. The first charge decided the fight, for Bagnal fell by the hand of his enemy, and the usual effect took place. The few companies which he led were panic-

* Moryson.

struck by the fall of their leader, and gave way. The fury of their antagonists did not allow them to rally; and first falling into confusion, they were scattered into groups, and suffered the most dreadful slaughter which had hitherto been known in the Irish wars between the English and Irish: fifteen hundred soldiers with thirteen captains fell. The fort of Blackwater was surrendered in consequence at the desire of the feeble remnant of the English army, who represented by their messengers to Williams, that it was their only hope of safety.

This dreadful disaster was perhaps several ways decisive of the fate of Tyrone, and his brave companions in rebellion. It gave to himself and the chiefs of his party an impulse which fixed them in their rash and presumptuous course. It told the English queen and her council that the season for trifling was over; that if England was to rule, it should first win by force of arms.

This victory supplied the rebel earl with arms, and thus enabled him to increase his force. He was on all sides congratulated by the insurgent spirits of Ulster, Munster, and Connaught, as the deliverer of his country, while universal fear seized on the English of the pale, and the garrisons of the queen. Moryson, speaking of the Irish soldiery at the time, observes, "The Irish kerne were at first rude soldiers, so as two or three of them were employed to discharge one piece, and hitherto they have subsisted especially by treacherous tenders of submission; but now they are grown ready in managing their pieces, and bold to skirmish in bogges and woody passages, yea, this year and the next following, became so disastrous to the English, and successful in action to the Irish, as they shaked the English government in this kingdome, till it tottered and wanted little of fatal ruine."*

It was at this period that the Munster rebellion broke out with increased fury under James Fitz-Thomas, commonly nick-named the Sugan Earl. This unfortunate person, as we have already related at length, set up for the earldom and inheritance of Desmond, with strong promises of support from the earl of Tyrone, which were however very inadequately fulfilled. The Ulster chief having fully roused and encouraged the disaffected chiefs of Munster, left them to pursue the sanguinary stream into which they were thus launched, and turned back to Tyrone.

In the meantime, Tyrone maintained the same course of transparent dissembling with government. It was necessary to adapt his professions and asseverations to the alteration of circumstances; but he still continued to make applications for truces and pardons, though with conditions more exacting than before. It can however be scarcely supposed, that he looked for any further advantage than a little delay. This, it must be kept in mind, was, as it appeared to be, the main object. In common with all his countrymen, the earl was at the moment under the fatal delusion caused by the promises of Spain. He is indeed unlikely to have so far overrated the successes he had gained, as to imagine that they could have any effect on the English government, but to elicit a vast increase of force. And such was the speedy

* Moryson.

consequence, though the natural result was delayed by the indiscretion and mismanagement of the earl of Essex, who was now sent over.

The history and character of Essex are among the most popular passages of English history, and cannot need to be dwelt upon here. Brave, generous, ardent, and ambitious, with great talent and little discretion or judgment, he was in this as on other trying occasions, made the dupe of his more subtle enemies and rivals, and of his own passions. His military reputation stood high, but not on any very authoritative experience; but his personal valour was at least unquestionable, and his talents specious and imposing. His enemies in the English court were also desirous both to send him out of the way, and to entangle him in a position where honour had been seldom gained, and was least of all likely to be gained by him. It was easier to impose on the queen than on Cecil: Essex had, in his comments on the Irish insurrections, which then occupied the conversation of the English court, shown that superficial sagacity so often to be met with in critics and lookers on, and strenuously insisted upon the gross error of the Irish lieutenants, in allowing themselves to be trifled with, and not striking at once at the root of all the insurrections, by the suppression of Tyrone. This was the sentiment of the queen and generally of the English court and council. It was therefore but natural, that from the ardent and impetuous earl, with all his bravery and cheap-won military character, and with all her own womanly partiality, that the queen should form the fond hope, that he would prosecute this tedious and vexatious war to an end, by pursuing a course so apparently obvious and on which he himself so strongly insisted. Under these auspices, the earl entered on his enterprize.

On the 15th April, 1599, he landed in Dublin with greater powers and more splendid allowances than had hitherto been granted to any lord-lieutenant. Among these, which are detailed at great length by the writers of that time, we may specify the allowance of ten pounds a day for his pay.* On his arrival, he demanded and obtained from the Irish council a statement of the actual position of affairs. By this it is made clear as can be, that every part of the country was in total or partial insurréction. It was nevertheless equally apparent, that in these various instances of local rebellion, there was not one, the magnitude or importance of which was sufficient to warrant the diversion of the whole or any part of the English army, from the great northern rebellion which was the vital centre to the whole. A few days after his arrival, Essex dispatched letters to England giving an account of every thing to the queen and council. In one of these, he states, that Tyrone had in his own council declared his design to be a concentration of all the rebels into one united power, acting under himself as its head: that for this purpose he was to have an army of his own in Ulster of 6000 men, and one of 6000 under Hugh O'Donell in Connaught. He further informed the council, that in Munster large bodies of men had assembled at a public cross, to swear that they would be steadfast in rebellion. He added that the general sense of the rebels was to repel

* Moryson.

all thoughts of pardon, and that in consequence they had assumed an unprecedented insolence of deportment.

Such, we believe to be, in the main, a fair statement of the circumstances under which Essex thought fit, or as some suppose, suffered himself to be persuaded by designing persons to lay aside all his previous opinions of the conduct of the war, and instead of marching into Ulster, to waste time and means upon desultory and inconsequent hostilities. Pursuing the very course which he had so strongly censured, he marched into Munster and took Cahir Castle belonging to Edward Butler; and collected a large plunder of cattle, without having any opposition to encounter, the rebels scattering at his approach and taking refuge in the woods. While on this expedition, however, lord Essex had not been remiss in taking the most effective steps to obtain information, and the letter which he wrote to the queen, is valuable for the general sketch which it presents of the real position of both parties. It contains also much that is characteristic of both the character and circumstances of the unfortunate writer. We therefore give it at length.

" When this shall come to your majesties hands, I know not; but whensoever it hath that honour, give it leave (I humbly beseech your majesty) to tell you, that having now passed through the provinces of Leinster and Munster, and been upon the frontire of Connaught, (where the governour and the chiefe of the province were with me;) I dare begin to give your majesty some advertisement of the state of this kingdome, not as before by heare-say, but as I beheld it with mine owne eyes. The people in generall have able bodies by nature, and have gotten by custome ready use of arms, and by their late successes boldnes to fight with your majesties troopes. In their pride they value no man but themselves, in their affections they love nothing but idlenesse and licentiousnesse, in their rebellion they have no other end but to shake off the yoake of obedience to your majesty, and to root out all remembrance of the English nation in this kingdome. I say this of the people in generall; for I find not onely the greater part thus affected, but it is a generall quarrell of the Irish, and they who do not professe it, are either so few or so false, that there is no accompt to be made of them. The Irish nobility and lords of countreys, doe not onely in their hearts affect this plausible quarrell, and are divided from us in religion, but have an especiall quarrell to the English governement, because it limitteth and tieth them, who ever have been and ever would be as absolute tyrants as any are under the sunne. The townes being inhabited by men of the same religion and birth as the rest, are so carried away with the love of gain, that for it, they will furnish the rebels with all things that may arme them, or inable them against the state or against themselves. The wealth of the kingdome, which consisteth in cattle, oate-meale, and other victuals, is almost all in the rebels' hands, who in every province till my comming have been masters of the field. The expectation of all these rebels is very present, and very confident that Spaine will either so invade your majesty that you shall have no leisure to prosecute them here, or so succour them that they will get most of the townes into their hands, ere your majesty shall

HUGH, EARL OF TYRONE.   535

relieve or reinforce your army; so that now if your majesty resolve to subdue these rebels by force, they are so many, and so framed to be souldiers, that the warre of force will be great, costly, and long. If your majesty will secke to breake them by factions among themselves, they are so courteous and mercenary and must be purchased, and their jesuits and practising priests must be hunted out and taken from them, which now doe sodder them so fast and so close together. If your majesty will have a strong party in the Irish nobility, and make use of them, you must hide from them all purpose of establishing English government till the strength of the Irish be so broken, that they shall see no safety but in your majesties protection. If your majesty will be assured of the possession of your townes, and keepe them from supplying the wants of the rebels, you must have garrisons brought into them, able to command them, and make it a capital offence for any merchant in Ireland to trade with the rebels, or buy or sell any armes or munition whatsoever. For your good subjects may have for their money out of your majesties store, that which shall be appointed by order, and may serve for their necessary defence; whereas if once they be tradable, the rebels will give such extreme and excessive prices, that they will never be kept from them. If your majesty will secure this your realme from the danger of invasion, as soone as those which direct and mannage your majesties intelligences, give notice of the preparations and readinesse of the enemy, you must be as well armed and provided for your defence: which provision consists in having forces upon the coast inroled and trained; in having magazines of victuall in your majesties west and north-west parts ready to be transported; and in having ships both of warre and transportation, which may carry and waft them both upon the first allarum of a discent. The enroling and training of your subjects, is no charge to your majesties owne cofers; the providing of magazines will never be any losse, for in using them you may save a kingdome, and if you use them not you may have your old store sold (and if it be well handled) to your majesties profit. The arming of your majesties ships, when you heare your enemy armes to the sea, is agreeable to your owne provident and princely courses, and to the pollicy of all princes and states of the world. But to return to Ireland againe, as I have shewed your majesty the dangers and disadvantages, which your servants and ministers here shall and doe meete withall, in this great work of redeeming this kingdome; so I will now (as well as I can) represent to your majesty your strength and advantages. First, these rebels are neither able to force any walled towne, castle, or house of strength, nor to keepe any that they get, so that while your majesty keeps your army in strength and vigor, you are undoubtedly mistresse of all townes and holds whatsoever; by which meanes (if your majesty have good ministers) all the wealth of the land shall be drawne into the hands of your subjects; your souldiers in the winter shall be easefully lodged, and readily supplied of any wants, and we that command your majesties forces, may make the warre offensive and defensive, may fight and be in safty as occasion is offered. Secondly, your majesties horsemen are so incomparably better than the rebels, and their foot are so unwilling to fight in battle or grope, (howsoever they may be desirous to skirmish and fight loose,) that your majesty may be alwaies mistresse of the champion countries, which are the best parts of this kingdome. Thirdly, your majesty victualling your army out of England, and with your garrisons burning and spoyling the countrey in all places, shall starve the rebel in one year, because no place else can supply them. Fourthly, since no warr can be made without munition, and this munition rebell cannot have but from Spaine, Scotland, or your own townes here, if your majesty will still continue your ships and pinaces upon the coast, and be pleased to send a printed proclamation, that upon paine of death no merchant, townes-man, or other subject, doe trafficke with the rebell, or buy or sell in any sort munition or armes, I doubt not, but in a short time I shall make them bankerout of their old store, and I hope our seamen will keepe them from receiving any new. Fifthly, your majesty hath a rich store of gallant colonels, captains, and gentlemen of quality, whose example and execution is of more use than all the rest of your troopes. Whereas, the men of best qualitie among the rebels, which are their leaders and their horsemen, dare never put themselves to any hazard, but send their kerne and their hirelings to fight with your majesties troopes; so that although their common soldiers are too hard for our new men, yet are they not able to stand before such gallant men as will charge them. Sixthly, your majesties commanders being advised and exercised, know all advantages, and by the strength of their order, will in all great fights beate the rebels; for they neither march, nor lodge, nor fight in order, but only by the benefit of their footmanship, can come on and go off at their pleasure, which makes them attend a whole day, still skirmishing, and never engaging themselves; so that it hath been ever the fault and weaknesse of your majesties leaders, wheresoever you have received any blow, for the rebels doe but watch and attend upon all grosse oversights. Now, if it please your majesty to compare your advantages and disadvantages together, you shall finde, that though these rebels are more in number than your majesties army, and have (though I doe unwillingly confesse it) better bodies and perfecter use of their armes, than those men which your majesty sends over; yet your majesty, commanding the walled townes, holders, and champion countries, and having a brave nobility and gentry, a better discipline, and stronger order than they, and such meanes to keep from them the maintenance of their life, and to waste the countrie which should nourish them, your majestie may promise yourselfe that this action will (in the end) be successful, though costly, and that your victorie will be certaine, though many of us your honest servants must sacrifice ourselves in the quarrell, and that this kingdome will be reduced, though it will ask (besides cost) a great deale of care, industry, and time. But why doe I talke of victorie, or of successe? Is it not knowne that from England I receive nothing but discomforts and soules wounds? Is it not spoken in the army that your majesties favour is diverted from me, and that already you do boad ill both to me and it? Is it not beleeved by the rebels, that those whom you favour most doe more hate me out of faction, then out of dutie or conscience? Is it not lamented of your majesties faithfullest subjects both there and here, that a Cobham, or a Raleigh (I will forbeare others for their places' sake) should have such credit and favour with your majesty, when they wish the ill successe of your majesties most important action, the decay of your greatest strength, and the destruction of your faithfullest servants. Yes, yes, I see both my owne destiny, and your majesties decree, and doe willingly imbrace the one, and obey the other. Let me honestly and zealously end a wearisome life, let others live in deceitful and inconsistent pleasure; let me beare the brunt and die meritoriously, let others achive and finish the worke, and live to erect trophies. But my prayer shall be, that when my soveraigne looseth mee, her army may not loose courage, or this kingdom want phisicke, or her dearest selfe misse Essex, and then I can never goe in a better time, nor in a fairer way. Till then, I protest before God and his angels, that I am a true votarie, that is sequestered from all things but my duty and my charge: I performe the uttermost of my bodies, mindes, and fortunes abilitie, and more should, but that a constant care and labor agrees not with my inconsistent health, in an unwholesome and uncertain clymate. This is the hand of him that did live your dearest, and your majesties faithfullest servant,

"Essex."

In this letter there is a fair and just representation of the general condition of the country. It exhibits, in strong colours, the true force and weakness of either side—the growing strength of the Irish, and the incredible want of the commonest forethought and activity in the provisions and conduct of their opponents. But, like all persons of unpractical understanding, the earl theorized, observed, and wasted his thoughts on circumstances and preliminaries, while the main fire of the rebellion was allowed to gather uninterrupted force; and the queen was justly incensed, when, instead of receiving intelligence of some direct and vigorous attack on the main forces of Tyrone or O'Donell, she received a letter of general policy and counsel, of the greater part of which she was herself very sufficiently informed before she sent him over armed with unusual powers and at vast expense to bring the struggle to an issue.

Towards the end of July he returned to Leinster, leading back an army broken and exhausted by weariness and sickness, and, as Moryson says, "incredibly diminished in number," without having met an enemy, or performed any service worthy of account. During this nugatory expedition, a party of 600 men, rashly detached into the dangerous glens of Wicklow without experienced leaders, met the natural consequence of such a heedless disposition, and were routed by the O'Byrnes, headed by Phelim, the son of Feagh. On this unhappy occasion, lord Essex displayed a rigour not less pernicious than the feebleness of his former conduct. He disarmed and decimated the unfortunate men whom he should have preserved from a disgrace for which he inflicted on them a punishment more justly due to himself; and brought their officers to court-martial, for the failure of an expedition which should have been more prudently planned.

He was ere long apprized of the queen's displeasure at his remissness, on which he promised to march speedily into Ulster; but it is highly probable that at the moment he felt his force to be unequal to the undertaking. In his reply to the queen on that occasion, he threw the whole blame of his conduct upon the advice of the Irish council. Notwithstanding this, he was compelled to a nearer expedition for the defence of the pale. His own remissness had, in fact, given courage to the lesser chiefs who dwelt around the English borders; and the O'Mores and O'Conors were up in arms in Leix and Ophaly. On his return from an expedition, in which he met with not sufficient opposition to add very materially to his reputation, he found his force so much reduced that it became necessary to apply for a reinforcement of a thousand men before he could proceed further. He, nevertheless, as a preliminary movement, ordered Sir Conyers Clifford into Connaught to compel Tyrone to send a part of his troops that way. Sir Conyers, as we have already had occasion to relate, at length marched on with a small body of 1500 horse and foot until he came to the Curlew mountains, among the passes of which he was surprised, defeated, and slain, by a body of Irish under O'Ruarke.

In the meantime the necessary reinforcements arrived from England. But the winter was approaching, and lord Essex was compelled to write to the queen, that nothing more could be done that season but to draw his now small forces to the north. It was late in September when, with 1300 foot and 300 horse, he took up a position on the borders of Tyrone. The rebel earl, with his army, were in sight ranged on the opposite hills.

Tyrone, who was thoroughly aware of Essex's nature, seems to have at once decided his course of conduct, and sent him a messenger to request an interview. Lord Essex returned for answer, that if the earl of Tyrone desired to speak to him, he should be found on the morrow in arms at the head of his troop. The next day a slight skirmish took place; but one of Tyrone's men cried out, with a loud voice, that the earl of Tyrone would not fight, but meet lord Essex unarmed and alone; and on the following day, as Essex again advanced, he was met by Hagan, Tyrone's messenger, who declared his master's wish to submit to the queen, and his request that lord Essex would meet him at the ford of Ballycliach. The lord-lieutenant consented, and sent some persons forward to view the ford. They found Tyrone himself in waiting, who assured them that lord Essex and he could hear each other with perfect ease across the river. Lord Essex arrived, and the earl of Tyrone, on seeing him at the river side, spurred down the hill from his party, and, coming alone to the bank, without any hesitation, rode into the stream until the water was up to his knee, and saluting lord Essex, whose romantic spirit was captivated by this dexterous specimen of Irish frankness, they had a long conversation, which we are not enabled to detail, but which the reader of the foregoing pages may with sufficient probability conjecture. On the subject of the grievances he had endured from the Irish government, Tyrone's material for complaint and self-justification was too obvious to be neglected; many harsh measures were to be complained of; much doubtful conduct explained away, or ascribed to self-defence against those whose design it had been to drive him to extremity; much, too, could be easily distorted; and, as in all such pleadings, it was easy to omit all that could not be excused. The quick, but not profound apprehension of the rash and generous Essex could easily be won by such a tale told under such circumstances; and it is quite plain from the result that he was completely the dupe of his antagonist's speciousness and his own generosity.

The conference was for a long time carried on, to the great surprise of the English; and, as some writers relate the story, Tyrone had come up from the river, and the two hostile leaders for some time continued the conversation as they rode together on the bank. This, if true, exhibits the indiscretion of the queen's lord-lieutenant more strongly than we should venture to describe it. At length Tyrone beckoned to his party, and his brother, Cormac, came forward, accompanied by M'Guire, MacGennis, O'Quin, &c.; while lord Essex called the earl of Southampton, Sir Warham St Leger, Sir Edward Wingfield, &c., and a truce was concluded, which was to be renewed every six weeks, till the " calends of May,"* either party having the power to break it on fourteen days' notice. It was immediately after this most unfortunate and ill-managed, though, in some respects, inevitable transaction, that Essex received from the queen the following severe and highly characteristic epistle :—

" ELIZABETH REGINA.—BY THE QUEEN.

" Right trusty and right well beloved cosen and councellor, and trusty and well beloved, we greet you well. Having sufficiently declared unto you before this time, how little the manner of your proceedings hath answered either our direction or the world's expectation; and finding now by your letters, by Cuffe, a course more strange, if stranger may be, we are doubtful what to prescribe you at any time, or what to build upon by your owne writings to us in any thing. For we have clearly discerned, of late, that you have ever to this hower possessed us with expectations that you would proceede as we directed you; but your actions shew alwaies the contrary, though carried in such sort as you were sure we had no time to countermand them.

" Before your departure no man's counsell was held sound which perswaded not presently the maine prosecution in Ulster—all was nothing without that, and nothing was too much for that. This drew on the sudden transportation of so many thousands to be carried over with you, as when you arrived we were charged with more than the liste, or which wee resolved to the number of three hundred horse; also the thousand, which were onely to be in pay during the service in Ulster, have been put in charge ever since the first journey. The pretence of which voyage appeareth by your letters, was to doe some present service in the interim, whilst the season grew more commodious for the maine prosecution, for the which purpose you did importune, with great earnestnesse, that all manner of provisions might be hastened to Dublin against your returne.

" Of this resolution to deferre your going into Ulster, you may well thinke that we would have made you stay, if you had given us more time, or if we could have imagined by the contents of your owne writings that you would have spent nine weekes abroad. At your re-

* Moryson.

turne, when a third part of July was past, and that you had understood our mislike of your former course, and making your excuse of undertaking it onely in respect of your conformitie to the council's opinion, with great protestations of haste into the north, we received another letter of new reasons to suspend that journey yet a while, and to draw the army into Ophalia; the fruit whereof was no other at your comming home, but more relations of further miseries of your army, and greater difficulties to performe the Ulster warre. Then followed from you and the counsell a new demand of two thousand men, to which if we would assent, you would speedily undertake what we had so often commanded. When that was granted, and your going onward promised by divers letters, we received by this bearer now fresh advertisement, that all you can doe is to goe to the frontier, and that you have provided onely for twentie daies' victuals. In which kind of proceeding wee must deale plainly with you and that counsell, that it were more proper for them to leave troubling themselves with instructing us, by what rules our power and their obedience are limited, and to bethink them if the courses have bin onely derived from their counsells, how to answere this part of theirs, to traine us into a new expence for one end, and to employ it upon another; to which we could never have assented, if we could have suspected it would have been undertaken before we heard it was in action. And, therefore, wee doe wonder how it can be answered, seeing your attempt is not in the capitall traytor's countrey, that you have increased our list. But it is true, as wee have often said, that we are drawne on to expence by little and little, and by protestations of great resolutions in generalities, till they come to particular execution: of all which courses, whosoever shall examine any of the arguments used for excuse, shall find that your owne proceedings beget the difficulties, and that no just causes doe breed the alteration. If lack of numbers, if sicknesse of the army, be the causes, why was not the action undertaken when the army was in a better state? If winters approach, why were the summer months of July and August lost? If the spring was too severe, and the summer that followed otherwise spent—if the harvest that succeeded was so neglected, as nothing hath beene done, then surely must we conclude that none of the foure quarters of the yeere will be in season for you and that counsell to agree of Tyrone's prosecution, for which all our charge was intended. Further, we require you to consider whether we have not great cause to thinke that the purpose is not to end the warre, when yourself have so often told us, that all the petty undertakings in Leinster, Munster, and Connaught, are but loss of time, consumption of treasure, and waste of our people, until Tyrone himself be first beaten, on whom the rest depend. Doe you not see that he maketh the warre with us in all parts by his ministers, seconding all places where any attempts be offered? Who doth not see that, if this course be continued, the warres are like to spend us and our kingdome beyond all moderation, as well as the report of the successe in all parts hath blemished our honour, and encouraged others to no small proportion. We know you cannot so much fayle in judgement as not to understand that all the world seeth how time is dallied, though you think the allowance of that counsell, whose subscriptions are your echoes, should serve and satisfie us. How would you have derided any man else that should have followed your steps? How often have you told us, that others which preceded you had no intent to end the warre? How often have you resolved us, that untill Loughfoyle and Ballishannin were planted, there could be no hope of doing service upon the capitall rebels? We must, therefore, let you know, that as it cannot be ignorance, so it cannot be want of meanes, for you had your asking—you had choice of times—you had power and authority more ample than ever any had, or ever shall have. It may well be judged with how little contentment wee search out this and other errors; for who doth willingly seeke for that which they are so loth to find—but how should that be hidden which is so palpable? And, therefore, to leave that which is past, and that you may prepare to remedy matters of weight hereafter, rather than to fill your papers with many impertinent arguments, being in your generall letters, savouring still, in many points, of humours that concerne the private of you our lord-liefetenant, we doe tell you plainly, that are of that counsell, that we wonder at your indiscretion, to subscribe to letters which concerne our publike service when they are mixed with any man's private, and directed to our counsell table, which is not to handle things of small importance.

"To conclude, if you will say though the army be in list twenty thousand, that you have them not, we answer then to our treasurer, that we are ill served; and that there need not so frequent demands of full pay. If you will say the muster-master is to blame, we much muse then why he is not punished, though say we might to you our generall, if we would *ex fuere proprio judicare*, that all defects by ministers, yea though in never so remote garrisons, have been affirmed to us, to deserve to be imputed to the want of care of the generall. For the small proportion you say you carry with you of three thousand five hundred foot, when lately we augmented you two thousand more, it is to us past comprehension, except it be that you have left still too great numbers in unnecessary garrisons, which doe increase our charge, and diminish your army, which we command you to reform, especially since you, by your continual reports of the state of every province, describe them all to be in worse condition than ever they were before you set foote in that kingdom. So that whosoever shall write the story of this yeere's action, must say that we were at great charges to hazard our kingdom, and you have taken great paines to prepare for many purposes which perish without understanding. And therefore, because we see now by your own words, that the hope is spent of this year's service upon Tyrone and O'Donell, we do command you and our counsell to fall into present deliberation, and thereupon to send us over in writing a true declaration of the state to which you have brought our kingdome, and what be the effects which this journey hath produced, and why these garrisons which you will plant farre within the land in Brenny and Monaghan, as others, whereof we have written, shall have the same difficulties.

"Secondly, we looke to hear from you and them jointly, how you think the remainder of this year shall be employed; in what kind of warre, and where, and in what numbers; which being done, and sent us hither in writing with all expedition, you shall then understand our pleasure in all things fit for our service; until which time we command you to be very careful to meet with all inconveniences that may arise in that kingdom where the ill-affected will grow insolent upon our ill success, and our good subjects grow desperate when they see the best of our preserving them.

"We have seene a writing, in forme of a cartel, full of challenges that are impertinent, and of comparisons that are needless, such as hath not been before this time presented to a state, except it be done now to terrify all men from censuring your proceedings. Had it not bin enough to have sent us the testimony of the counsell, but that you must call so many of those that are of slender experience, and none of our counsell to such a form of subscription. Surely howsoever you may have warranted them, wee doubt not but to let them know what belongs to us, to you, and to themselves. And thus expecting your answer wee ende, at our manor of Nousuch, the fourteenth of September, in the one and fortieth yeere of our raigne, 1559."

The effect of this letter was the return of lord Essex to complete his tragic history in England. Of this the particulars are known to every one. He left Loftus, archbishop of Dublin, and Sir George Carew lords justices, and departed in the latter end of September.

The truce had been entered into by Tyrone, as one of those ordinary expedients by which he contrived to gain time, without sacrificing the least consideration of his own intentions, and was only, therefore, to be observed till he thought fit to break it. Nor was this powerful rebel without encouragement from the foreign enemies of England, who communicated aid or incentive, according to their characters and the nature of their designs. From the Pope he received a crown of Phœnix plumes, the worthy reward of the champion of the Roman see. The king of Spain sent him the less doubtful gift of a sum of money, and a promise of a further supply. He came in consequence to the resolution to renew the war, and easily found a pretext to evade the stipulation of notice: at the same time, he took the title of O'Niall. In January he made the expedition already noticed into Munster, to spirit up the Sugan earl of Desmond, and returned after having successfully stirred up the southern districts to insurrection.

The queen had formerly designed to send over Charles Blount, lord Mountjoy, as lord-lieutenant to Ireland; but was deterred by the representations of lord Essex, who was desirous to secure for himself a post which promised a quick and cheap-won harvest of military honour: with the usual good faith of courtiers, he represented the small military experience, the bookish character, the narrow income of his friend; and thus succeeded in his object. But in the moment of disgrace, his motives were correctly weighed, and lord Mountjoy was now selected by the queen, and landed, together with Sir George Carew, at Howth, on 14th February.

He was but a short time in the country when he perceived the errors of his predecessors, and formed a plan of operation, which though at first difficult to be carried into effect, had the merit of skilful and judicious adaptation to the nature of the country, and the habits of the enemy to be opposed. The English troops had latterly been discouraged by the successes of the Irish, as well as by their peculiar mode of warfare, which for the most part consisted in surprise, and ambuscade, and all the various stratagems of savage war, for which their wild rude confusion of morass and mountain, ravine and forest, afforded peculiar advantage: their tactics accommodated to these local circumstances, were as skilful in the bog and wood as those of the English upon the open field. Against these difficulties lord Mountjoy meditated to commence by cautious operations, of which, for some time, the object should rather be to avoid defeat than to look for victory. Another disadvantage was the desultory and scattered character of the war. The Irish chiefs marching in all directions through the kingdom, moving insurrectionary feeling wherever they came, committing depredations, and gaining advantages, which, though severally slight, were aggregately of importance, both as they were thus enabled to force the chiefs to unite with them, and also to divide the English force into detachments; and by preventing all decisive movements to draw out the war indefinitely. To counteract this, lord Mountjoy planned a circle of garrisons to confine the operations of the principal chiefs, and prevent their junctions and escapes. With this view he placed garrisons in Dundalk, Atherdee, Kells, Newry, and Carlingford, and left Sir Philip Lambert with a thousand men to watch the pale. He was himself, in the meantime, to encounter the rebellion at its head, and lead his army to watch Tyrone in the north.

When lord Mountjoy landed in Ireland, the earl of Tyrone was on his visit to Munster. Of this fact the new lord-deputy was apprized, and active steps were taken to cut off his return. Though he had with him a force of five thousand men, it was yet thought that without the Ulstermen, in whom the whole force of the rebellion consisted, he could not become seriously formidable. Under these circumstances Tyrone's position was one of more danger than he himself suspected: the laxity of precaution, the total want of plan, and the facility to enter into illusory treaties and truces, which had hitherto so fatally protracted the operations of government, had enabled this alert and sagacious partizan to do as he pleased, and almost unobstructedly to organize the scattered elements of insurrection. To have, under these circumstances, anticipated his danger, would have been to anticipate a change in the management of affairs, which as yet lay concealed in the contriver's breast. Lord Mountjoy saw at once the importance of the incident, and sent directions accordingly to the earl of Ormonde, who lost no time in making the best dispositions to shut up the roads by which the return of the rebel earl could be effected. These efforts were nevertheless frustrated by the great difficulty of obtaining intelligence and of moving the Irish barons to efficient effort. Though encompassed by the earls of Ormonde and Thomond, and by the commissions of the forces in Munster—with the mayor of Limerick on one coast, and the mayor of Galway on another, to watch their respective posts—Tyrone made his way good and conducted his followers, without obstruction, through the hostile ring; and when Mountjoy received intelligence that he was encompassed on every side, he was already on the frontier of Ulster.

The Irish chiefs through Ireland who were connected with Tyrone, received the greatest discouragement from this forced march. It manifested the weakness which hitherto had been concealed, and materially abated the confidence generally inspired by the ease with which he had till then trifled with the English administration. His escape on this occasion too much resembled the flight of a discomfited chief. At the end of a forced march, when he had just settled in his quarters for the night, he heard of the advance of the lord-deputy, on which he roused his weary soldiers and again immediately marched away, leaving behind those who could not save themselves by speed from the advanced guard of the enemy. In this incident appears another of the great advantages of the prudence of Mountjoy. He had noticed that one of the main causes of former failures was the quick intelligence by which the rebel chiefs were enabled to anticipate all the movements of the English forces; and he had already, in one of his letters, noticed that the Irish chiefs were almost all secretly disaffected, so that there was a rapid diffusion of this intelligence through the whole country : and thus it was enough to frustrate the best concerted plan if it was allowed to transpire but a few hours before execution. To the observation of this, and the strict secrecy by which it was counteracted, lord Mountjoy's successes were as much due as to any other cause.

In sending an account of Tyrone's escape, the lord-deputy transmitted also several of his intercepted dispatches, one of which may assist the reader's conception of this extraordinary person and his time.

" O'Neale commendeth him unto you Morish Fitz-Thomas. O'Neale requesteth you in God's name to take part with him, and fight for your conscience and right; and in so doing O'Neale will spend to see you righted in all your affairs, and will help you: and if you come not at O'Neale betwixt this and to-morrow at 12 of the clock and take his part, O'Neale is not beholding to you; and will do to the uttermost of his power to overthrow you, if you come not at farthest by Saturday at one. From Knock Dumayne in Calrie, the 4th of February, 1599. (P. S.) *O'Neale requesteth you to come speake with him, and doth give you his word that you shall receive no harm, neither in coming from, whether you be friend or not, and bring with you O'Neale Gerat Fitzgerald.*

Subscribed " O'NEALE."*

On the 15th of February, Tyrone reached his castle at Dungannon, and called a meeting of the lords of the north to consult how the projected settlement of the English at Loughfoyle might best be prevented.

It was at this time, in the month of April, that the earl of Ormonde was taken prisoner at a conference with MacRory, (as shall be related,) in such a manner as to lead to some unjust suspicions that he had a private understanding with the rebels.

On the 5th of May lord Mountjoy advanced into the north, both to

* Moryson.

confine the operations of Tyrone, and to protect the settlement of the garrisons of Loughfoyle. When he arrived at Newry, he learned that the rebel earl had turned from Loughfoyle on receiving information of his advance; and that, having razed the old fort at Blackwater and burned Armagh, he had occupied the strong fastness of Loughlucken, where he entrenched himself strongly, and fortified a space of nearly three miles in extent. A chief object of Tyrone was to prevent the junction of the earl of Southampton with the deputy; for which purpose he had taken means to obtain information of the time when he was expected. As this was the way by which he must needs arrive, there was every hope of his being cut off in this most dangerous pass. Mountjoy had heard of the inquiries of the rebels, and had foreseen the danger; to meet it he drew toward the pass, and detached captain Blany with 500 foot and 50 horse with orders to secure a safe position on the road, and send to hasten the movements of Southampton. Blany, leaving his foot at the Faghard, took on his horse and reached the earl, whom he informed of the nature and objects of Tyrone's position, and told him that the deputy would await him on the same day at two o'clock, at the road of Moyry, at the place where the danger lay.

In the midst of this dangerous pass there was a ford, called the Four-mile-water, surrounded on every side with woods. Here Tyrone posted a strong body of men, who filled these woods on either side. Beyond, on a neighbouring hill, lord Mountjoy lay with his troops. To reach them it was essential to clear this passage of danger. Southampton accordingly advanced, and captain Blany, dividing his men into three companies, went into the river, and crossed the ford, when they saw the enemy awaiting them, and placed to great advantage. On this the English charged, and the lord-deputy at the same moment appeared advancing from the opposite side. After a few discharges of musquetry, the Irish gave way, and, passing through the thickets, reached the other side, at the rear of Southampton's party. Captain Blany then posted himself to the right, so as to cover the passage of the carriages; and the lord-deputy, pressing into the woods on the left, occupied the rebels in a hot skirmish, till all were safely over the pass. Repelled on each side, the rebels made next an impetuous attack on lord Southampton's rear, but were soon repulsed; and the English, having thus completely cleared this dangerous pass, were ordered by the deputy to march on. It will be needless to remark to the intelligent reader, that this was one of those perilous occasions in which the English had latterly met with the most fatal repulses, by trusting too much to that superiority of arms, which had, till of late, rendered tactics a matter of less essential moment. The Irish, at all times formidable in this war of bogs and fastnesses, were now become alarmingly so, from the advantages of arms and discipline, which, under a leader like Tyrone, had seriously reduced the odds against them. During this transaction, the earl was himself stationed, with a more considerable force, at a little distance, to wait the moment of advantage, and seize on the indiscretion of the enemy; but it is one of the proofs of the skill and coolness of Mountjoy that no such occasion presented itself. Many were slain on both sides.

Lord Mountjoy now drew off his forces, and returned to Newry. Here he received intelligence which rendered his presence necessary in Leinster, and also the satisfactory information that his garrisons at Loughfoyle were settled; in that quarter, his captains, under Sir Arthur Chichester, governor of Carrickfergus, had taken possession of Newcastle from O'Doherty, whose country they wasted; he was also apprized that they were occupied in fortifying about Derry, and that great numbers of rebels had passed, with their cattle and goods, into Scotland, from whence it was their hope to obtain aid. It became also apparent that the northern rebels were beginning to be shaken in their confidence by these vigorous and systematic regulations, and were either returning, or affecting to return, to their loyalty.

In May the lord-deputy, leaving the north thus shut in, returned to Dublin, to make effectual dispositions for the security of the pale. Of the transactions in this quarter we cannot here say much without unwarrantable digression. While in Leinster, the lord-deputy had to contend with the usual confusions of petty interests—the cabals and misrepresentations of all who did not comprehend the interest of the country, or had their own to press; he wrote to the secretary a fair and full exposition of the situation of affairs, and of the progress he had made. It was indeed important. Having complained that he found it would be an easier undertaking to subdue the rebels than to govern the English subjects, he stated, that having found the army completely disorganized, he had given it form and combination; it was disheartened, and he had raised its drooping and desponding spirit into courage and military ardour; he had preserved it from all disgrace, and restored its reputation, on which so much must depend; and that it was now by these means disposed once more to undertake, and likely to perform, services of an arduous and extensive character. He also mentioned that the hope of foreign succour was the main reliance of the Irish rebels; and entreated that unless the English government had some sure information that no assistance was to be sent over from Spain, that they would strengthen his army with reinforcements, which must be necessary should the Spaniards come over, and which, should they not, would soon end the rebellion. To guard against that danger he requested that some English vessels of war should be stationed off the north-western coast; while a few small sail boats could easily intercept all attempts to bring over ammunition from Scotland.

In the meantime Tyrone was nearly reduced to inactivity by the military circle which watched his movements in the north. Several small attempts, which were probably designed to try the way, were made, and failed. Lord Mountjoy was thus enabled to give his attention to the troubles of the pale; and his efforts were much required. In the districts of Carlow and Kildare, into which he led 560 men, he met with rough resistance, and had a horse shot under him in a skirmish, in which thirty-five of the rebels were killed.

On the 14th of September, the lord-deputy again turned his face to the north. Among the many improvements he had introduced, a principal one was the disregard of weather or season. The climate of Ireland, since then ameliorated by the cutting away of its forests, the draining of marshes, and perhaps by many other causes, was then far more severe than will now be readily conceived. Against such an evil the English might be secured by expedients, but the habits of the natives were such as to admit of far less resource; neither their imperfect clothing, nor their methods of supply or of encampment were suited to afford any adequate provision to meet the hardships, privations, and exigencies of a winter campaign.

On the 15th, lord Mountjoy again put his troops into motion, he encamped on the hill of Faghard, three miles beyond Dundalk, and lay there till the 9th of October; during which time he lived in a tent which was kept wet by the continual rain, and frequently blown down by the equinoctial tempests. Not far off lay Tyrone in the fastness of the Moyrigh, strongly entrenched as well by art as by the nature of the place. The difficulty of these positions, and the skill of Tyrone's defence, are well illustrated by the pass which Mountjoy describes as "one of the most difficult passages of Ireland, fortified with good art and admirable industry." Tyrone availing himself of a natural chain of impassable heights and marshy hollows, connected them by broad and deep trenches, flanked with strong and high piles built with massive rocks, and stockaded with close and firm pallisades. These well-contrived impediments were protected by forces numerically stronger than those which could be opposed to them; and were rendered additionally effective by the great rains which flooded the streams and quagmires, and contracted the lines of defence to a few dangerous points. For some time there were almost daily skirmishes in which the English had mostly the advantage; till at last lord Mountjoy ordered an attack on their entrenchments, which being for two days successfully followed up, Tyrone evacuated the fastness, and reluctantly left a clear road for the English general, who immediately levelled the trenches, and caused the woods on each side of this dangerous pass to be cut down: and passing through with his army came on to Newry, where he was for some time detained for want of provisions; but, in the beginning of November, was enabled to proceed to Armagh. In the neighbourhood of Armagh lay Tyrone, entrenched amid the surrounding bogs with a skill not be countervailed by all the prudence and tact of his antagonist. Many skirmishes took place, but nothing of a decisive character seemed likely soon to occur.

It would be entering farther into detail than our space allows to trace with a minute pen the numerous slight encounters, the petty negotiations with minor chiefs, the captures, the cessions, or the pardons and proclamations which fill the interval of many months. If we would compare the conduct of the two eminent individuals who are prominently before us, the skill and talent of each must appear to great advantage. Each was pressed by trying difficulties of no ordinary kind in Irish warfare. Tyrone, cooped in within the mountains and marshes of the north by a system of military positions hitherto unknown in Ireland, constrained and checked on every side, could not still be hurried into any imprudence, or forced into any risk by the vigilant and skilful leader who had succeeded in thus controlling and isolating the turbulent elements of a national insurrection, which had hitherto baffled the power of England. Mountjoy had not only thus constrained the efforts of a dangerous foe; but the means by which he had effected this purpose had another equally important operation. One of the most prevailing causes of failure had hitherto arisen from the tardy, expensive, and exposed operation of marching an army from place to place, by which it was impossible to act with the secrecy necessary to prevent every movement from being foreseen and guarded against, nor to accommodate the marches of so expensive an instrument to the more rapid and unencumbered marches of an enemy that seemed to start up with an endless growth in every quarter. Instead of this, by the efficient distribution of his forces in those stationary points from which they could with facility be collected, Mountjoy was enabled to traverse the country in person by journeys comparatively rapid and with a force comparatively small; so that an expedition involved little more preparation, publicity, or expense than the journey of an individual. By this he soon contrived to pacify or awe into submission every county but Tyrone. The rebel earl still held his ground, and fencing off the operations of his antagonist with skill and courage, awaited patiently the expected aid from Spain.

The situation of Tyrone was however becoming monthly more hazardous and distressing. Governing his motions with the most consummate tact, so as to avoid the hazard of an action, he could not yet avoid a frequent repetition of skirmishes in which his men were uniformly worsted. Of these the effect was doubly hurtful to his strength; it gave confidence to the enemy, and caused an extensive falling off of the Irish chiefs, who presently began to sue for pardons and offer submissions in every quarter. A skirmish near Carlingford, in the middle of November, 1600, gradually increasing to a battle, was considered to have first given this dangerous turn to his affairs, and awakened a general conviction that he could not hold out through the winter: and this general impression is amply confirmed by all the information we have been enabled to attain. The lord-deputy was contracting the circle of his operations; he was fast reducing Tyrone's means of subsistence by laying waste his country, while, with a view to this expedient, he had arranged to be supplied from England with sustenance for the garrisons. Lastly, and most to be dreaded, another part of lord Mountjoy's plan was becoming fast apparent—the resolution not to intermit his operations during the winter. It becomes, indeed, a matter of curious and interesting speculation to witness the obstinate perseverance under such apparently hopeless circumstances, of a chief so sagacious as Tyrone; but this apparent state of things was softened by many illusory circumstances of which the entire force could not then be felt: no sagacity is equal to the full interpretation of a conjuncture wholly new. The surrounding districts had begun to show signs of weariness, and numerous chiefs despairing of the prospects of rebellion had submitted; but Tyrone was aware that the submission of an Irish chief was but a subterfuge in danger, and that the slightest gleam of a favourable change would rouse rebellion from province to province with simultaneous vigour and effect. He had seen and felt the capricious relaxation of the queen's anger, after the heaviest denunciations, on the slightest seemings of submission. Such had been the history of Ireland for centuries; and he confidently expected supplies and aid from Spain, which should be enough to turn the scale in his favour.

and, at the least, restore him to a condition to treat on more advantageous terms for pardon.

In the commencement of 1601, when M'Guire, with many other powerful Irish chiefs, had submitted, when many had taken arms for the English, and when the Munster rebellion had been completely put down; reports of the promised succour from Spain became more frequent, and various accounts were transmitted from her majesty's foreign ministers, of definite preparations on the part of Spain, for the equipment and transport of forces destined for Ireland. On this subject, the chiefs also who came in for pardon had all their facts to tell. Hugh Boy informed Sir Henry Dockwra that the king of Spain had promised to invade Ireland in the course of the year, with 6000 men, who were to be landed in some Munster port. Every week confirmed these reports with fresh intelligence from Calais and from Flanders. In Waterford some seamen made their depositions that they were recently pressed into the service of the king of Spain, and sent to Lisbon with bread for 3000 men who were lying there to be shipped for Ireland. They added the report, that an agent from Tyrone was then at the Spanish court, who represented that his master could subsist no longer without speedy aid.

Matters were still advancing by a tedious progress to a termination, which must have appeared to depend entirely on the truth of these last mentioned reports. Lord Mountjoy's operations had the purpose and intent hitherto rather of shutting in the rebel earl, of compelling him to exhaust his resources, and of drawing away all hope of assistance from the Irish chiefs, than any direct design of bringing him to action. The result of the most complete defeat could not have had the desired effect, until the resources of Tyrone should be thus broken down, so as to allow no hope of being enabled again to collect an army. It is for this reason that although this peculiar warfare was productive of numerous incidents, they are seldom such as to warrant detail. Scarcely a movement could anywhere be made, but the first wood approached poured out a sudden volley from its invisible marksmen, or the rude figures were seen rapidly appearing and disappearing among the leafy concealments. Amongst these incidents, we may select some, rather for specimens than as carrying on our narration. For this purpose we extract a page of Moryson's *Itinerary* on the 13th and 16th of July, 1601. Moryson was brother to Sir Richard Moryson, then serving under Mountjoy, and afterwards vice-president of Munster: he was himself a fellow of the University of Cambridge, from which he had leave to travel for three years; at the end of which term he resigned his fellowship to come to Ireland, where he was made secretary to lord Mountjoy, and thus became both the eye-witness and historian of this war.

"The 16th day the lord-deputy drew out a regiment of Irish, commanded by Sir Christopher St Laurence, and passing the Blackwater, marched to Benburb, the old house of Shane O'Neale, lying on the left hand of our camp, at the entrance of Great Wood. Their out men made a stand, in a faire greene meadow, having our camp and the plaines behind them, and the wood on both sides and before them. The rebels drew in great multitudes to these woods. Here we in the campe, being ourselves in safety, had the pleasure to have the full view of an hot and long skirmish, our loose wings sometimes beating the rebels on all sides into the woods, and sometimes being driven by them back to our colours in the middest of the meadow, where as soone as our horse charged, the rebels presently ran backe, this skirmish continuing with like varietie some three howers; for the lord-deputie, as he saw the numbers of the rebels encrease, so drew other regiments out of the campe to second the fight. So that at last the rebell had drawne all his men together, and we had none but the by-guards left to save-guard the campe, all the rest being drawne out. Doctor Latwar, the lord-deputies chaplaine, not content to see the fight with us in safetie, (but as he had formerly done) affecting some singularitie of forwardnesse, more than his place required, had passed into the meadow where our colours stood, and there was mortally wounded with a bullet in the head, upon which he died next day. Of the English not one more was slaine, onely captaine Thomas Williams, his legge was broken, and two other hurt, but of the Irish on our side, twenty sixe were slaine, and seventy-five were hurt. And those Irish being such as had been rebels, and were like upon the least discontent to turne rebels, and such as were kept in pay rather to keepe them from taking part with the rebels than any service they could doe us, the death of those unpeaceable swordsmen, though falling on our side, yet was rather gaine than losse to the commonwealth. Among the rebels, Tyrone's secretary, and one chiefe man of the O'Hagans, and (as we credibly heard) farre more than two hundred kerne were slaine. And lest the disparitie of losses often mentioned by me should savour of a partiall pen, the reader must know, that besides the fortune of the warre turned on our side together with the courage of the rebels abated, and our men heartened by successes, we had plentie of powder, and sparing not to shoote at randome, might well kill many more of them, than they ill-furnished of powder, and commanded to spare it, could kill of ours."*

At the time of the last incident, the lord-deputy was engaged in rebuilding the important fortress of Blackwater, which appears to have so long been a main object of contest, as it was the key to Dungannon, the hitherto inaccessible stronghold and dwelling of Tyrone. To this latter position therefore the earliest attention of both parties was at the time bent—Mountjoy to approach, and Tyrone to defend it. Meanwhile, the English were mainly engaged in cutting down the corn in every quarter round the county, and in preparing their garrisons for the winter's war. They performed these important operations in tranquillity; so much had fallen the courage of the Irish, who now began to be sensible that the skirmishes in which they had so freely indulged, were productive of no advantage save to their enemy. This desultory warfare was not however felt to lead to results as decisive as the lord-deputy looked for with considerable anxiety, at a time when his already insufficient means of prolonging the war, and the slowness and scantiness of his supplies made progress, of more than ordinary importance. There was little to be effected against an enemy which melted

* Moryson.

away like mists before the attack, yet still ever hovered round to watch for the moment of advantage, and render every movement harassing if not insecure. The principal objects were to obtain possession of their fastnesses and lurking-places, and to scatter and dissolve them by depriving them of the means of subsistence; for this, it was the immediate aim of lord Mountjoy to cut down their corn, which he took all possible means to effect. Nor was there any great obstacle to be feared, except immediately about Dungannon, to which the English could not approach. But lord Mountjoy had by considerable diligence discovered a new pass to Dungannon, to facilitate which he cut down a large wood, which opened the way over a plain at the distance of about four miles. By this means he reached a river, on which by building a bridge and fort, he expected to obtain complete possession of Tyrone's country; or, as he represents in his letter to the council, "that this would cut the archtraytor's throat;" and in another letter to Cecil, "that if we can but build a fort, and make a passage over the river, we shall make Dungannon a centre, whither we may from all parts draw together all of her Majesty's forces."

The progress of this desultory state of affairs now became embarrassed by additional difficulties. The report of the intended invasion from Spain, while yet uncertain as to its force and destination, became an object of alarm; to meet this fear, Mountjoy was urged to draw off a large portion of his troops towards the south, where their landing was apprehended. Against such a course he strongly protested, observing that the landing-place of the Spaniards could be by no means certain, and that he might find himself as far from the point of danger wherever he should march to, as where he was then stationed. His troops he observed were not 1500 effective men, with which he might easily retain the positions of which he was then possessed, and prosecute the advantage they gave him. He thought that if he should succeed in completely breaking down Tyrone's strength, which he expected to effect during the winter, that the king of Spain should not have it in his power to cause any very dangerous disturbance in Ireland.*

But while the lord-deputy was thus industriously engaged in arrangements to prosecute to an end the war against Tyrone, the rumours of the Spanish invasion began to grow still more frequent, and to assume more the character of certainty; and as all indications seemed pointing to the south, it became a question of no small moment and perplexity to provide against the new emergency, without relinquishing the advantages which had been gained in Ulster. Should the Spaniards land in any of the harbours along the south-western coast, the motions of Tyrone would obtain increased importance; and it could not but appear in a high degree dangerous to relax the military chain, by which he was confined to the north. The real strength of the English army was hardly equal to these multiplied emergencies: the demand of numerous garrisons and the waste of war had been too much supplied by Irish soldiers. The expenses allowed for the supply of the army and forts had been exceeded, and all arrangements were carried into effect against every conceivable disadvantage.

* Mountjoy's letter to Sir Robert Cecil.

To make the best of these untoward circumstances the lord-deputy resolved to strengthen his garrisons, and provide effectually for the safety of Ulster; and then to lead the rest of his army into Connaught, and to hold a council on the way at Trim. With this view he applied to the English council to forward the necessary succours and provisions to Galway and Limerick; and to send a good supply of arms and ammunition to the garrisons of Ulster, that they might be preserved for the protection of the north, and be found in a fit condition for his summer campaign in that quarter. In the same communication, the lord-deputy informs the council, that many of his Irish captains had shown signs of wavering in consequence of the reports of the Spaniards; and that they had received from Tyrone the most urgent messages, assuring them that if they should further delay to join him, it would be too late, and he would refuse them after a very little. Notwithstanding which, some of them assured the lord-deputy of their fidelity, though their condition in his army was, in his own words, "no better than horseboys."*

On the 29th, Lord Mountjoy arrived at Trim, and a council was held, of which it was the chief object to provide for the defence of the pale, to molest which the rebel earl had sent captain Tyrrel, a partisan leader of great celebrity at the time. To meet this danger it was resolved to strengthen the Leinster troops with such forces as could be spared from the Ulster army: and the lord-deputy determined to conduct them in person, until the landing of the Spaniards should be ascertained. This event was not now long a matter of doubt.

On the third of September, letters from Sir Robert Cecil informed the lord-deputy that the Spanish fleet had appeared off Scilly, to the number of forty-five vessels, of which seventeen were men-of-war, and the remaining vessels of large burthen, containing 6000 soldiers. In the same letter, the lord-deputy was desired to demand whatsoever forces and supplies should appear to be needful, and direct the places to which they should be sent.

The full confirmation of the arrival of the Spaniards speedily followed. The lord-deputy was in Kilkenny, whither he had gone to consult with Sir George Carew and the earl of Ormonde, when he received the account that their fleet had entered the harbour of Kinsale, by letters from Sir George Wilmot and the mayor of Cork. On this information, the lord-deputy resolved to meet them with all the force he could muster from every quarter; justly considering, that on their fate must depend the entire result of the war. He accordingly sent to draw off the companies from Armagh, Navan, and the pale, into Munster: and, accompanied by the lord-president Carew, he travelled thither with all speed. He soon ascertained that the Spaniards which had taken possession of Kinsale, were 5000 men under the command of Don Juan D'Aguila; and that they had brought with them a large supply of arms, as the provision for a general rising of the people, which they had been led to expect; they had also 1500 saddles for their cavalry; and expressed an intention not to keep within their

* Lord Mountjoy's letter. Moryson.

fortifications, but to meet the English in the field. Among other steps, they sent out a friar, with bulls and indulgences from the pope, to stir up the people in every quarter. They also caused the report to be spread that their number amounted to 10,000, with 2000 more, which had been separated from the fleet, and were since landed at Baltimore.

On his arrival, the Spanish commander sent back all his ships but twelve—a step which strongly marks the confidence of his expectations. He despatched messengers to Tyrone and O'Donell, to urge their speedy approach, and demanded a supply of horses, and of cattle for provision, assuring them that he had other stores sufficient for eighteen months, and treasure in abundance. He also sent out his emissaries into every quarter to secure the assistance of mercenary bands and partisan leaders, soldiers of fortune whose entire dependence was the sword—a class then numerous in Ireland. The confidence of the English commander was no less, but he was still dependent on the speed and efficiency of the supplies and reinforcements for which he had applied. These had not yet reached him from Dublin, but it was plain that further delay was dangerous; and on the 16th October, without his artillery, ammunition, or provision, he marched from Cork, and on the 17th instant arrived at Kinsale, and encamped under the hill of Knockrobin, within half a mile of the town. Here they lay for some days, unable to execute any military operation, from the want of implements and artillery.

During this time several skirmishes took place, in all of which the Spaniards were worsted and driven within their walls. In the letter in which these circumstances are reported by the lord-deputy, it strongly appears how much anxious suspense must have attended such a situation. The seemingly premature advance of an army thus unprovided, was hurried on by the apprehension of the effect which their inaction might produce on the Irish of Munster. The rising of the uncertain multitude of the surrounding districts, who watched all that passed with no uninterested eye, the arrival of Tyrone, and what they still more feared, of fresh supplies from Spain, might any or all of them happen while the English lay at this heavy disadvantage. To these embarrassing considerations may be added, that in point of fact, the Spaniards within the town were stronger in numbers and appointments of every kind, with every advantage also that could be derived from their possession of a strong town and of the castle of Rincorran on the other side of the harbour. Were they to make one vigorous effort, and to succeed in breaking through the lines of the little army that lay before them, without any means of resistance but the personal bravery of its ranks, the odds must from that moment become incalculably great in their favour; the possession of a few towns would have raised all Ireland in their support; and it is not easy to see by what means short of an army of thirty thousand men and a re-conquest of the island, the consequences could be retrieved. The English army, besides its unarmed state, was otherwise in the lowest condition, having been sadly thinned by sickness, and the waste of continual skirmishes. The absolute necessity of maintaining so many fortified places, left but a comparatively small force at the dis-

554   HUGH, EARL OF TYRONE.

posal of lord Mountjoy. One fact appears from the list of the English army at this time, by which it appears that of sixteen thousand foot and eleven hundred and ninety-eight horse, the lord-deputy could only lead six thousand nine hundred foot, and six hundred and eleven horse against the enemy.*

The disposal of the whole army of Ireland, the seven and twentieth of October, 1601:—

Left at Loughfoyle.

Sir Henry Dockwra, 50; Sir John Bolles, 50;—horse, 100 Sir Henry Dockwra, 200; Sir Matthew Morgan, 150; captaine Badly, 150; Sir John Bolles, 150; captaine Crington, 100; captaine Vaughan, 100; captaine Bingley, 150; captaine Coath, 100; captaine Basset, 100; captaine Dutton, 100; captaine Floyd, 100; captaine Oram, 100; captaine Alford, 100; captaine Pinner, 100; captaine Winsor, 100; captaine Sydley, 100; captaine Atkinson, 100; captaine Digges, 100; captaine Brooke, 100; captaine Stafford, 100; captaine Orrell, 100; captaine Leigh, 100; captaine Sidney, 100; captaine Gower, 150; captaine Willes, 150; captaine W. N. 100;—foote 3000.

Horse left at Carrickfergus.

Sir Arthur Chichester, governour, 200; Sir Foulke Conway, 150; captaine Egerton, 100; captaine Norton, 100; captaine Billings, 150; captaine Philips, 150.—Foote 850.

Foote left in Secale.

Sir Richard Moryson, the governour's company under his lieutenant, himselfe attending the lord-deputy at Kinsale, 150.

Horse left in northern garrisons, 100.

Foote in north garrisons.

At Newrie, Sir Thomas Stafford, 200; at Dundalke, captaine Freckleton, 100; at Carlingford, captaine Hansard, 200; at Mount Norrey's, captaine Atherton, 100; at Armagh, Sir Henrie Davers, under his lieutenant, himself being at Kinsale, 150; at Blackwater, captaine Williams, 150.—Foote 800.

Horse left in the pale, and places adjoyning.

In Kilkenny, the earl of Ormonde, 50; in Kildare, the earle of Kildare, 50; in Westmeath, the lord Dunsany, 50; in Lowth, Sir Garret Moore, 25.—Horse 175.

Foote in the pale, (that is to say)

At Kilkenny, Carlogh, Nass, Leax, and Ophalia, Dublin, Kildare, O'Carrol's countrie, Kelles and Westmeath.—Foote 3150.

* The curious reader will be gratified by a more distinct view of the composition and distribution of this army, as contained in one of those old lists of which Moryson gives many. They are the more valuable, as exhibiting in a single view the principal places then garrisoned by the English. For this reason, we give one at length.

HUGH, EARL OF TYRONE. 555

Horse left in Connaught.

The earle of Clanricarde, 50; captaine Wayman, 12.—Horse 62. Foote left in Connaught, 1150.

Totall of Horse, 587. Totall of Foote, 9100.

The Lyst of the army with his lordship at Kinsale.

The Old Mounster Lyst.

Sir George Carew, lord-president, 50; Sir Anthony Cooke, 50; captaine Fleming, 25; captaine Taffe, 50.—Horse 175.

Foote of the Old Lyst.

The lord-president, 150; the earle of Thomond, 150; lord Andley, 150; Sir Charles Wilmot, 150; master treasurer, 100; captaine Roger Harvey, 150; captaine Thomas Spencer, 150; captaine George Flower, 100; captaine William Sacy, 100; captaine Garret Dillon, 100; captaine Nuse, 100; Sir Richard Percy, 150; Sir Francis Berkeley, 100; captaine Power, 100; a company for the earle of Desmonde's use, 100.

New companies sent into Mounster lately, which arrived and were put into pay the fourth of September past. The lord-president added to his company, 50; the earle of Thomond added to his company, 50; Sir George Thorncton, 100; captaine Skipwith, 100; captaine Morris, 100; captaine Kemish, 100; captaine North, 100; captaine Owstye, 100; captaine Fisher, 100; captaine Yorke, 100; captaine Hart, 100; captaine Liste, 100; captaine Ravenscroft, 100; captaine Richard Hansard, 100; captaine George Greame, 100; captaine Yelverton, 100; captaine Panton, 100; captaine Cullem, 100; captain Habby, 100; captaine Gowen Harny, 100; captaine Coote, 100.

Horse brought from the north and the pale to Kinsale.

The lord-deputie's troope, 100; Sir Henrie Davers, 100; mastermarshall, 50; Sir C. St Lawrence, 25; Sir H. Harrington, 25; Sir Edward Harbert, 12; Sir William Warren, 25; Sir Richard Greame, 50; Sir Oliver St John's, 25; Sir Francis Rush, 12; captaine G. Greame, 12.—Horse, 436.

Foote that Sir John Berkeley brought from the borders of Connaught to Kinsale, 950.

Foote brought out of the pale by master-marshall, and from the northern garrisons by Sir Henry Davers to Kinsale.

The lord-deputie's guard, 200; master-marshall, 150; Sir Benjamin Berry, 150; Sir William Fortescue, 150; Sir James Fitz-piers, 150; Sir Thomas Loftus, 100; Sir Henrie Follyot, 150; captaine Blaney, 150; captaine Bodley, 150; captaine Rotheram, 150; captaine Roper, 150; captaine Roe, 150; captaine Trevor, 100; captaine Ralph Constable, 100.—Foote 2000.

At Kinsale, Horse 611. Foote 6900.

Totall of the whole army in Ireland:—Horse 1198. Foote 16000

Providentially they escaped these perils; the Spaniards were perhaps not fully aware of their advantages in this interval, and were also discouraged by the ill success which attended their sallies. On the 27th, the English received their own artillery and a supply of ammunition, and were thus enabled to assume the offensive. The lord-deputy began by fortifying his camp, which had hitherto been exposed to the nightly attacks of the enemy. The next consideration was the great disadvantages to be apprehended from the castle of Rincorran, on the side of the harbour opposite to the town, which Don Juan had also seized and garrisoned with upwards of 150 Spaniards and as many Irish. While they continued to hold it, it was evident enough that no supplies or reinforcements from England could be received in the harbour; and it was therefore judged expedient to commence an attack upon it without delay. For this purpose a small battery of two culverins was mounted against it.

The Spaniards fully aware of the real importance of the castle, now made the most continued and energetic efforts for its relief both by sea and land. On the water, their boats were beaten back by captain Button's ship. By land several lively skirmishes began. The Spaniards brought out a small cannon, and began to fire upon the English camp: a shot entering the paymaster's tent, which lay next to that of lord Mountjoy, smashed a barrel of coin, and damaged much other property; all the balls being directed at the lord-deputy's quarter, and most of them striking close to his tent.

On the 31st, two culverins and a cannon played against the castle wall incessantly. While the attention of the English was thus engaged, the Spaniards put out a few boats from the town for a feint, and sent a party of five hundred men along the harbour, on the pretext of covering the boats, but in reality to surprise a party of the English who were stationed on the shore between the town and castle. They were first noticed by several straggling parties and groupes of English who were loitering or standing at their posts about the camp. All these scattered soldiers collected quickly of their own accord towards the enemy, and were quickly joined by an hundred men sent out by Sir Oliver St John, under captain Roe and another officer: Sir Oliver himself followed with thirty men. A spirited but short skirmish was the consequence; the Spaniards stood but for a few seconds to the charge, and retreated precipitately on their trenches, where they had placed a strong party as a reserve; here the combat was fiercely renewed, and numbers fell in the trenches. Sir Oliver received many pikes on his target, and one thrust in the thigh; but this gallant officer, one of the most distinguished in the British army for personal valour, on this occasion attracted the notice of both parties by his single exploits, bearing back and striking down his numerous opponents who broke and turned before him. Lord Audley was shot in the thigh: other officers, and about fourteen men, were wounded and slain, and about seventy of the enemy, of whom many were taken with much arms; among which were "divers good rapiers,"—a weapon of great value, for which Spain was then celebrated, being no other than the small sword, which about that time became an important part of the gentleman's costume.

About six o'clock in the evening, the effects of the little three-gunned battery began to be felt in the castle; and a treaty commenced and was kept up during the night and next day, for a surrender. The Spaniards desired to be allowed to enter Kinsale with their arms and baggage, and were peremptorily refused; and several further proposals were in like manner rejected. Late on the next day, the Spanish commander, Alfiero, proposed first that the garrison should be allowed to enter Kinsale unarmed; and when this was refused, that he alone might be allowed to enter. All conditions being refused short of surrender at discretion, Alfiero resolved to hold out to extremity; this, however, his people would not submit to, and a surrender was made on the sole condition that Alfiero should be permitted to surrender his sword to the lord-deputy himself. The Spaniards to the number of eighty-six were then disarmed in the castle, and sent off as prisoners to Cork; about thirty had been slain in the siege: the Irish had contrived to escape in the darkness of the previous night.

Lord Mountjoy was by no means in condition for an attack upon Kinsale, but thought it expedient still as much as possible to keep up some appearance of preparatory movements. He received at this time letters from the queen, with accounts of coming supplies and reinforcements to the amount of five thousand men. One of the queen's letters on this occasion is amusingly characteristic.

"Since the braineless humour of unadvised assault hath seized on the hearts of our causeless foes, We doubt not but their gaine will be their bane, and glory their shame, that ever they had thought thereof. And that your humour agrees so rightly with ours, We think it most fortunately happened in your rule, to show the better whose you are and what you be, as your own handwrit hath told us of late, and do beseech the Almighty power of the Highest so to guide your hands, so that nothing light in vain; but to prosper your heed, that nothing be left behind that might avail your praise: and that yourself, in venturing too far, make not to the foe a prey of you. Tell our army from us that they make full account that every hundred of them will beat a thousand; and every thousand, theirs doubled. I am the bolder to pronounce it in His name that hath ever prospered my righteous cause, in which I bless them all. And putting you in the first place, I end, scribbling in haste,*

"Your loving soveraine,
"Eliz. Regina."

On the 5th of November, four ships came from Dublin with supplies; and at the same time accounts were received of the approach of the confederate Irish under Tyrone and O'Donell. It was therefore determined in council to fortify the camp strongly toward the north; and on the day following the completion of that work, (the 7th,) the lord-president left the camp with two regiments, to endeavour to intercept the enemy on the borders of the province.

On the eighth, thirteen ships were seen, which were soon after ascertained to carry a reinforcement of one thousand foot and some

* Moryson.

horse under the earl of Thomond. But the Spaniards had discovered the absence of lord Mountjoy and his party, and thought to avail themselves of it by a strong *sortie*. For this, they marched out in force, and lined their trenches with strong bodies: they then sent forward a well-armed party toward the camp. The English detached a sufficient party against this, but at the same time sent out another armed with fire-arms to a bushy hill extending towards Rincorran castle, to take the trenches by a flanking fire, while they rushing out from their entrenchment, repelled the enemy before their camp; the hill detachment at the same time drove their reserve from the trenches before the town, so that when the retreating party came up and thought to make a stand, they found themselves without the expected support, and were charged with such fury by the English, that they fell into entire confusion and left numbers dead in the trenches. Don Juan was much irritated by this repulse, and praised the bravery of the English, while he reproached his own men with cowardice, and committed their leader to prison. He then issued a proclamation, that from that time no man should, on pain of death, leave his ground in any service until taken away by his officer; and that even if his musket were broken, he should fight to death with his sword.

On the 12th, the English army received the cheering and satisfactory information of the landing of the supplies and succours from England. Their transports had put in at Waterford, Youghal, Castlehaven and Cork; which latter harbour Sir R. Liveson, admiral, and vice-admiral Preston entered with ten ships of war, bearing 2000 foot, with artillery and ammunition. To these the lord-deputy sent to desire that they would sail into Kinsale harbour, as the artillery could not otherwise be easily or speedily brought into the camp. Though these supplies were far below the exigency, they yet relieved the English from a position of very great danger, in which they lay almost helpless, and quite incapable of offensive operations. The firm and resolute energy of Mountjoy appears very prominently in the active series of operations which he now commenced and conducted with the most consummate prudence, and unwearied perseverance and courage, under circumstances in every way the most disheartening. Immediately before the arrival of the English fleet, his army had been for some time reduced to every extremity of suffering, which a body of men can be conceived to bear without disorganization. During this interval, a letter of the deputy's to Cecil, enables us to catch a distant gleam of his personal character and conduct, which must gratify the reader. "Having been up most of the night, it groweth now about four o'clock in the morning, at which time I lightly chuse to visit our guards myself; and am now going about that business, in a morning as cold as a stone and as dark as pitch. And I pray, sir, think whether this be a life that I take much delight in, who heretofore in England, when I have had a suit to the queen, could not lie in a tent in the summer, nor watch at night till she had supped?"* It is observed of this nobleman by Moryson, who was about his person, that

---

* Lord Mountjoy's letter to Cecil. Moryson.

he never knew a person go so warmly clad in every season of the year. The description of Moryson gives a lively picture of the man of his time, but it is too long for our present purpose. While commanding in Ireland, besides his silk stockings, " he wore under boots, another pair, of woollen or worsted, with a pair of high linen boot hose; yea, three waistcoats in cold weather, and a thick ruffe, besides a lusset scarf about his neck thrice folded under it; so as I never observed any of his age and strength keep his body so warm." Speaking of his diet, among other circumstances he mentions, "he took tobacco abundantly, and of the best, which I think preserved him from sickness—especially in Ireland, where the foggy air of the bogs and waterish fowl, plenty of fish, and generally all meats of which the common sort always are salted and green roasted, do most prejudice the health." At his care of his person, and " his daintie fare before the wars," it was the custom of the rebel earl to laugh and observe that he would be beaten, while preparing his breakfast. But on this the secretary, justly jealous of his master's honour, remarks, "that by woful experience he found this jesting to be the laughter of Solomon's fool."*

The extreme suffering of the English at this time can imperfectly be conceived from the mere circumstance that they were living in tents, and huts less warm than tents, in the month of November, without much added allowance for the far colder state of the climate, where the country was a wild waste of damp and marshy forests and watery morasses. In one of his letters the lord-deputy mentions that the sentinels were frequently carried in dead from their posts; the officers themselves " do many of them look like spirits with toil and watching." Under such circumstances, the feeling of impatience must have been great for the occurrence of some decisive event.

The arrival of the fleet cheered the English with at least a prospect of active service; yet from the very unfavourable state of the weather, many delays were experienced. The artillery was disembarked with difficulty, and the troops so disordered in health by the long and tempestuous passage, that upwards of a thousand men were sent to Cork to " refresh" and rest themselves. On his return from a visit to the ship, lord Mountjoy was saluted by a discharge of cannon balls from the town, of which " one came so near that it did beat the earth in his face."†

It was now resolved to ply the town with a heavy fire, not so much with the design of an assault as to annoy the Spaniards, and, by breaking in the roofs, make them share in the hardships which the English had to sustain from the wet and frost. One very great disadvantage for this purpose was, the impossibility of finding a spot uncommanded by the guns of the town. The fleet was directed to batter a tower called "castle Nyparke," on an island on the side; but on account of the stormy weather, were compelled to desist. Captain Bodly was next sent with 400 men to try whether it might be carried with the pickaxe—this also failed; the Spaniards rolled down huge stones so fast and successfully, as to break the engine which protected their assailants, who were thus driven off with the loss of two men. It was, however, resolved by the

* Moryson. † Ibid.

lord-deputy and his council to persevere, as this was indeed the only service at the time to be attempted. The reader will recollect that two thousand men had been sent to wait for Tyrone upon the verge of Munster; and it would be unsafe to commence a regular siege with the force remaining, as the fatigue of the trenches would quickly exhaust the men. To invest the town, therefore, and proceed to cut off every post without, held by the enemy, was the utmost they could yet hope to effect without great risk. It should be added, that one-third of the army was composed of Irish, who were not then so effectual in open assaults as they have since become; and it was also apprehended, that on the slightest seeming of disadvantage they would join the Spaniards. Under these circumstances the firing against castle Nyparke was renewed on the 20th, with additional guns, and an impression was soon made on the walls. There was not yet a practicable breach when a flag of parley was hung out, and the Spaniards offered to surrender if their lives should be spared. The offer was promptly accepted, and they were brought prisoners to the camp. Another advantage was at the same time obtained, by the discovery of a spot halfway between Kinsale and the camp, which commanded a most important portion of the town, where the Spaniards kept their stores, and Don Juan resided. On this judiciously-chosen situation a small platform was raised and a fire opened with a single culverin on a part of the town visible from thence. It did considerable mischief, and among other lucky shots, one went through Don Juan's house.

The Spaniards, in the mean time, were not without their full share of suffering and apprehension. It was made apparent that their provision was beginning to run low; the Irish women and children were sent out of the town and came in great numbers to the camp, from which they were sent on into the country. The inference was confirmed by intelligence from the town whence an Irishman escaping came to the lord-deputy and told him, that Don Juan said privately, that the English must take the town, should it not be quickly relieved from the north. The Spaniards were reduced to rusks and water; they had but four pieces of artillery—a circumstance which may account for the small annoyance the English had all this time received from them. They had left Spain 5000 in number, and landed 3500 in Kinsale. Of these the waste of the war had been 500, so that at the time of our narration, they were 3000. To these main circumstances many other particulars were added, as to the positions of strength and weakness, and the places where ammunition and treasure were kept. Among other things it was mentioned, that six gentlemen had entered the town on Sunday, and were ready to go out again to raise the country. A messenger had been despatched nine days before to Tyrone to hasten his approach. It was also beginning to be greatly feared, that if this event should be much longer deferred, the Spaniards must be compelled to capitulate.

The battery on the platform was soon strengthened with four guns, making thus six in all; and having been informed that Don Juan especially feared a cannonade from the island, the lord-deputy had three culverins planted there. One discharge from the platform killed four men in the market place, and carried off the leg of an officer. Reports were received of great damage suffered in the town from the fire of both these batteries on the following day. On that day an incident occurred in sight of the Spaniards, which must have added in no small degree to the notions they had already been enabled to form of the English valour. A private soldier of Sir John Berkeley's company attempted to "steal a Spanish sentinel," a feat which he had often already performed: on this occasion, however, four other Spaniards whom he had not seen, came to the rescue of their comrade, and a sharp contest ensued, in which the Englishman defended himself against the five. He wounded the serjeant, and came off after some exchange of blows, with a cut in his hand, received in parrying one of the numerous pike thrusts which they made at him.

From this period the lord-deputy commenced a series of regular approaches, of which the detail, though otherwise full of interest, would occupy an undue space here. A breach was made in the town walls, which gave occasion to several fierce contests falling little short of the character of general engagements, in all of which the Spaniards were worsted with great slaughter. The town was summoned on the 28th November; but Don Juan replied that he kept it "first for Christ, and next for the king of Spain, and so would defend it *contra tanti.*" At this time six Spanish vessels arrived at Castlehaven, with 2000 men on board. The lord-deputy in consequence, drew his forces close to the town, and distributed them so as most effectually to guard every inlet. He sent a herald to Don Juan, offering him permission to bury his dead; and this brought some further communications. Among other things, the Spanish general proposed that they should decide the matter by single combat between the deputy and himself. To this amusing *fanfavonade,* lord Mountjoy replied, that they had neither of them any authority from the courts to put the war to such an arbitration; and that the council of Trent forbade the " Romanists to fight in *campo steccato.*"* The arrival of the Spanish vessels gave a temporary renovation to the waning hopes of Don Juan: the result fell far short of his expectation. The English squadron sailing out from Kinsale harbour, came on the 6th of December to Castlehaven, where opening its fire on the Spaniards, it sunk one of their largest vessels, drove their admiral a wreck on shore, and took many prisoners—the Spanish soldiers from two vessels succeeded in making their escape, and went to join the Irish under O'Donell. From the prisoners the lord-deputy learned that active steps were in course for the purpose of sending over large supplies during the spring; and that 4000 Italians were raised for the Irish service. They added, that in Spain the impression was that Ireland was already in the hands of the Spaniards; and that on their approach they had mistaken the English fleet in the harbour for that of the army under Don Juan.

Early in December the state of the war assumed an aspect of more awakening interest. Daily accounts were brought to the camp of the near approach of Tyrone: nor were they long without more sensible intimations of the presence of a powerful foe. This able and wary chief had seized on the surrounding fastnesses and bogs, and entrenched

* Moryson.

himself so as to be secure from any effort of his enemies. But the English army was thus itself hemmed in, and not only in danger of being attacked on every side; but what was really more serious, cut off from those supplies from the surrounding country, which had till now enabled them to preserve their stores. To effect the double object of investing the town and keeping off the Irish, was now become an embarrassing necessity. The lord-deputy increased the extent, the breadth, and depth of his trenches—and made the most able dispositions to cut off all communication between the Irish camp and the town. By his dispatches to the English council and secretary, we learn that the combined armies of Tyrone and O'Donell lay at the distance of six miles from the camp; and that they possessed all that had been saved from the Spanish fleet at Castlehaven, both in men and supplies. He demanded large reinforcement, and complained that the previous one had been in a measure made ineffectual by the tardiness of their arrival. Instead of arriving to increase his force, they came only to supply the losses consequent upon its weakness; so that thus his means of active operation never rose to an efficient level. The sufferings and losses from cold and privation were also daily increasing.

Meanwhile nothing was omitted that could distress Kinsale; an effective fire, though interrupted by rain and storm, dismounted the guns with which the Spaniards attempted to interrupt the works; and on the 15th, many of the castles were destroyed. On the 18th, the following letter was intercepted:—

To the Prince O'Neale and Lord O'Donell.

" I thought your excellencies would have come at Don Ricardo his going, since he had orders from you to say, that upon the Spaniards comming to you (from Castlehaven,) you would doe me that favour. And so I beseech you now you will doe it, and come as speedily and well appointed as may bee. For I assure you, that the enemies are tired, and are very few, and they cannot guard the third part of their trenches which shall not avail them; for resisting their first furie, all is ended. The manner of your comming your excellencies know better to take there, than I to give it here; for I will give them well to doe this way, being alwaies watching to give the blow all that I can, and with some resolution, that your excellencies fighting as they do alwaise, I hope in God the victorie shall be ours without doubt, for the cause is his. And I more desire that victory for the interest of your excellencies than my owne. And so there is nothing to be done, but to bring your squadrons; come well appointed and close withall, and being mingled with the enemies, their forts will doe as much harme to them as to us. I commend myself to Don Ricardo. The Lorde keep your excellencies. From Kinsale the eighth and twentieth (the new style, being the eighteenth after the old stile) of December, 1601.

" Though you be not well fitted, I beseech your excellencies to dislodge, and come toward the enemy for expedition imports. It is needfull that we all be on horsebacke at once, and the greater haste the better.*

" Signed by DON JEAN DEL AGUYLA."

* Moryson.

The desire of the lord-deputy was, to bring on a decisive battle if possible. The English were dying by dozens, and the effects of delay were more to be feared than the enemy, and his suffering troops were much more disposed to fight than to endure cold, exposure, and starvation. To draw on this desirable event new breaches were effected, and a considerable part of the town wall struck down. The Irish on this approached within a mile of the camp; but when two regiments were sent out to meet them, they retired within their lines—" a fastness of wood and water where they encamped."

On the nights of the 20th, 21st, and 22d, the weather was stormy; and on the 22d particularly, the work of war went on by almost unremitting flashes of lightning, which streamed from the low dense vault of clouds overhead, playing on the spears, and showing every object between the camp and the town with an intensity beyond that of day. In this confusion of the elements, the Spaniards made several bold but vain assaults upon the English trenches; and notwithstanding the numerous obstacles opposed, both by the depth and continuity of these, and the incessant vigilance of the English who now lay under arms all night, still they contrived to communicate by frequent messengers with the camp of Tyrone and O'Donell. On this very night, it is mentioned upon the authority of Don Juan, that he dispatched three messengers to Tyrone and received answers. It was decided on the next night to attack the English camp on both sides; and there is every reason to believe, that if this design had been effected, it would have gone hard with the English. But, strange to say, by some mischance, seemingly inconsistent with the near position of the Irish (about six miles), they were led astray during the night, and did not come within sight of the enemy until morning light. The lord-deputy was fully prepared. Sir G. Carew had received on the previous evening a message from MacMahon, one of the leaders in the rebel camp, to beg for a bottle of usquebaugh, and desiring him to expect this assault. Early on the morning of the 24th, lord Mountjoy called a council, and it was their opinion that some accident had prevented the expected attack; but while they were engaged in debate, a person called Sir George Carew to the door, and told him that Tyrone's army was very close to the camp. This report was quickly confirmed, and the lord-deputy made prompt arrangements to attack the Irish army.

At this important moment, the whole effective force of the English army was 5840 English soldiers in eleven regiments, with 767 Irish. The army of Tyrone and O'Donell, cannot be estimated on any satisfactory authority; but the Spanish commander, Alonzo de Campo, assured the lords Mountjoy and Sir G. Carew, that the Irish amounted to 6000 foot and 500 horse—a number far below any estimate otherwise to be formed from other data. In the Irish host captain Tyrrel led the vanguard, in which were the 2000 Spaniards who had landed in Castlehaven; the earl of Tyrone commanded the main body, then commonly called the battle, and O'Donell the rear.

This moment was one of the most critical that has ever occurred in the history of Ireland. The whole chance of the English army, and consequently of the preservation of the pale, depended upon their success in bringing the enemy to an engagement. They were themselves completely shut in, and out of condition to preserve their very existence against the destructive effects of cold, sickness, and want; so that a few weeks must have reduced them without any effort on the part of the enemy. Fortunately for them, one alone of the hostile leaders had formed any just notion of their respective strength and weakness: the earl of Tyrone, whose sagacious mind had been well instructed by severe experience, had exerted all his influence to moderate the impatience of his allies, and to retain the advantages of his position by avoiding all temptations to engage the enemy. If left to his own discretion, he would have kept securely within his lines, and confined his operations to the prevention of intercourse between the English and the surrounding country—trusting to the progress of those causes which could scarcely fail to place them in his power. But Don Juan was impatient of a siege which had become extremely distressing, and his urgency was backed by the confidence of the Spaniards under Tyrrel, and the impetuosity of O'Donell.

If the reader will conceive himself to stand at some distance with his face toward the town and harbour of Kinsale,* with the river Bandon on his right, he will then have the whole encampment of the English in view; the position of the lord-deputy and the president Carew being before him, in the centre of the semi-circumference, of which the castle of Rincorrad occupies the extreme left, and the lesser camp under lord Thomond the right extremity, so as to form a semicircle round the town. On the 24th of December, the combined army under Tyrone occupied a position inclining to the right, or in a line drawn from the central camp towards Dunderrow on the north-west.

To prevent the fatal consequence of a *sortie* from Kinsale, Sir George Carew was directed to take the command of the camp, and to proceed as usual with the siege. By this able commander the guards were doubled at every point, from which the Spaniards could come out, and so effective were these precautions that the battle was over before Don Juan had any distinct intimation of its commencement.

Lord Mountjoy led out two regiments amounting to 1100 men to meet the enemy. The marshall Wingfield, with 600 horse and Sir Henry Power's regiment, had already been in the field all night. On their approach the Irish retired across a ford; but as they showed evident signs of disorder, the lord-marshal sent for leave to attack, to the lord-deputy, who took his stand on a near eminence; on which Mountjoy—having first inquired as to the nature of the ground on the other side, and learned that it was a fair wide field, ordered the attack. At or about the same time, the earl of Clanricarde, whose regiment was occupied in the camp, came up also to urge the attack. The difficulty to be overcome was considerable. A bog and a deep ford lay between them and the rising-ground on which the Irish stood, and as it was plain they could only pass in detail, a very little skill would have prevented their passage. The marshal first passed over with the brave earl of Clanricarde, and advanced with 100 horse, to cover the passage

---

* We have chiefly taken our description of this memorable battle from a very confused and unsatisfactory map in the *Hibernia Pacata*.

of Sir Henry Power, who led two regiments across the ford. A hundred harquebusiers, led by lieutenant Cowel, began the fight by a fire, which was returned by a strong skirmishing party sent out to meet them along the bogside. The English skirmishers were driven in upon the ranks, but being strengthened they returned and repulsed those of the Irish. The marshal with his party next charged an Irish division of about 1800 men, on which they failed to make any impression. On this the lord-deputy sent down Sir Henry Davers with the rest of the horse, and Sir William Godolphin with two other regiments of foot. Marshal Wingfield once more charged them, and the Irish were broken and began to fly in all directions. The explosion of a bag of powder in the midst of their rout added to its terror and confusion, and produced on both parties a momentary suspense. The circumstance most discouraging to the Irish was the flight of their horse, which being chiefly composed of the chiefs of septs or their kindred, were looked on with reliance.* In consequence a great slaughter took place. But the two other bodies of Irish and Spanish seeing this, came on to their assistance. To meet this danger, lord Mountjoy sent Sir Francis Roe with his regiment, and also the regiment of St John, to charge the Irish vanguard in flank, which retired in disorder from the charge. The Spaniards which formed part of this body, however, rallied, and separating themselves from the Irish, made a stand; they were charged a second time and broken by the lord-deputy's troop, led by Godolphin. In this second charge they were nearly all cut to pieces, and the remnant made prisoners with Don Alonzo del Campo, their commander. From this no further stand was attempted, but the Irish army began to fly on every side, and their flight was facilitated by the resolute resistance of the Spaniards. A chase commenced and was continued for two miles, in which great numbers were slain without any effort at resistance. On the field of battle lay 1200 Irish, besides the greater part of the Spaniards. Tyrone, who afterwards said that he was beaten by an army less than one-sixth of his own, added that besides the number slain he had 800 wounded.†

According to Moryson's account, lord Mountjoy, "in the midst of the dead bodies, caused thanks to be given to God for this victory." And never, indeed, was there an occasion on which the impression of providential deliverance was better warranted: whether the magnitude of the consequences be looked at, or the almost singular circumstance of such a formidable preparation being thus set at nought; and upwards of 3000 slain or wounded, with the loss of one cornet and seven common soldiers.

A note given by one of Tyrone's followers, of his loss at this overthrow.

"Tirlogh O'Hag, sonne to Art O'Hagan, commanded of five hundred, slaine himselfe with all his company, except twenty, where eleven were hurt, and of them seven died the eighteenth day after their returne.

" Kedagh MacDonnell, captaine of three hundred, slaine with all his men, except threescore; whereof there were hurt five and twenty.

* Moryson. † Moryson. *Hibernia Pacata.*

"Donell Groome MacDonnell, captaine of a hundred, slaine himselfe and his whole company.

"Rory MacDonnell, captaine of a hundred, slaine himselfe and his company.

"Five of the Clancans, captaines of five hundred, themselves slaine and their companies, except threescore and eighteene, whereof threescore were hurt.

"Sorly Boyes sones had followers in three hundred, under the leading of captaine Mulmore O'Heagarty, all slaine with the said Mulmore saving one and thirty, whereof twenty were hurt.

"Colle Duff MacDonnell, captaine of one hundred, lost with all his company.

"Three of the Neales, captaines of three hundred sent by Cormack MacBarron, all lost saving eighteene, whereof there were nine hurt.

"Captaines slaine 14; soldiers slaine 1995; soldiers hurt 76."

The earl of Clanricarde was knighted on the field for his distinguished services that day, having slain twenty Irish, hand to hand, and had his clothes torn in pieces with their pikes.

The English were marching back to their camp a little before noon, and on reaching it a general volley was fired to celebrate their success. This the garrison in Kinsale mistook for the approach of the Irish, whom they imagined to have driven in the English and to be now engaged in an assault upon their camp. On this supposition they made a sally but were as usual quickly driven in. They were at the same time shocked and disheartened by the sight of the Spanish colours in possession of the enemy's horse, who were waving them on a hill in sight. The position of Don Juan now afforded little hope; but he continued to hold out, and on the night after the battle the conquerors had to maintain an action of two hours' continuance against a fierce sally. A similar attempt was made on the following night.

On the 29th of December, accounts came that Tyrone had crossed the Blackwater with the loss of many carriages and 140 men, who were drowned in their hurry, having attempted to pass before the waters were fallen. Tyrone was said to be wounded and compelled to travel in a litter. O'Donell embarked for Spain, with Pedro Zubuiar, one of the commanders of the Spanish ships.

Don Juan now saw that it was necessary to save his little garrison by capitulation; having, in fact, committed every oversight, that the circumstances made possible, he still considered that his military character was to be preserved. He had by the unaccountable blunder of landing in the south, to strengthen a rebellion of which the whole efficient strength lay in the north, first thrown himself and his army into a position in which their isolation and danger were a matter of course, and thus compelled his ally to give up the advantages he possessed, and meet all the dangers and distresses of a winter march through the forests, morasses, tempests, and enemies, over 300 miles of country. He then, when this desperate point was gained, with an entire disregard of the constitution and quality of his allies, their habits of warfare, and all the obvious advantages and disadvan-

tages on either side, precipitated his friends into the hazard of an
engagement: he failed to recollect that a few weeks must needs bring
succours both to himself and Tyrone, and reduce the English as
much: for they were really sinking fast, although it is suspected that
the policy of Mountjoy made him believe matters worse than they
really were. Then, when the fatal step was thus hurried on by
his inconsiderate pride and impatience, he suffered himself to be reduced to inaction, by a small part of the army which he affected to
despise, and lay still while his ally was cut to pieces by a handful of
his besiegers.

Notwithstanding this catalogue of blunders his indignation was
roused, he spoke as one betrayed by those he came to save; and
sent a message to lord Mountjoy, proposing that a negotiation should
be opened between them for the surrender of the town. In this communication he did not fail to insist that his own honour, and that of
the Spanish arms were safe; that having come to give assistance to
the arms of the Condes, O'Neale, and O'Donell, these two Condes,
were it appeared no longer "in *rerum natura*," but had run away,
leaving him, the Spanish commander, to fight the battle alone. Lord
Mountjoy knew too well the difficulties he should have to encounter
in maintaining the siege even for a few days more with his scanty resources and shattered army. Indeed, the last sally of the Spaniards
had cost him far more men than the victory of the morning. He
therefore most willingly consented, and sent Sir W. Godolphin into
Kinsale. It is unnecessary here to detail the circumstances of the
negotiation. One point only occasioned a momentary disagreement.
Lord Mountjoy stipulated for the surrender of the Spanish stores,
ordnance, and treasure: Don Juan took fire at the proposal, which
he considered as an insult, and declared that if such an article were
insisted upon further, he would break off all further treaty, and bury
himself and his men in the ruins of the town before he would yield.
Lord Mountjoy knew that he would keep his word; for however incapable as a commander, he was resolute and punctilious. It was
therefore agreed, that the Spaniards should surrender Kinsale, and all
the other forts and towns belonging to her Majesty, which were in
their possession, and stand pledged not to take arms for her enemies,
or commit any hostile act until they had been first disembarked in a
Spanish port. On the part of the English government, it was agreed
that they should be allowed to depart for Spain, with all their property
and friends, and while the preparations were making, they were to be
sustained by the English government. These were the principal
articles of the treaty, which was with some slight interruptions, hereafter to be noticed, carried into effect.

Don Juan, in the mean time, accompanied the lords-deputy and
president into Cork, where they lived on those terms of friendly
intercourse which mark the cessation of hostility between civilized
nations and honourable enemies. During this time, however, a despatch from Spain was intercepted, containing numerous letters from
the king of Spain, and his minister the duke of Lerma, to Don Juan;
they are preserved in the *Pacata Hibernia*, and plainly manifest the
extensive preparations then in progress, to send over formidable rein-

forcements—a result which providentially was set aside by the victory of Kinsale, which for the first time made clear to the Spanish court the real military character of their brave but barbarian allies. Shortly after his return to Spain, Don Juan was disgraced by his court, and died of vexation and disappointment. He seems to have possessed the proud and punctilious honour for which Spanish gentlemen have always been distinguished. His defence of Kinsale proves him a good soldier, and not destitute of military knowledge and talent; while his entire conduct was such as to exhibit still more unquestionably, that he wanted the sagacity, prudence, and the comprehensive calculating and observing tact, so necessary when difficulties on a large scale are to be encountered. A short correspondence with Sir G. Carew, after his arrival in Spain, seems to warrant an inference that he was a proficient in the art of fortification, and on still more probable grounds that his disposition was generous and noble.

To return to the earl: there is no further occurrence of his life, which demands any minuteness of detail. His fate for some time trembled on the wavering resentment and dotage of the queen, whose long and brilliant reign was just in its last feeble expiring flashes. He had made a futile and ineffectual effort to prolong a rebellion, of which the country was wearied. He had been taught that success alone, now less probable than ever, could purchase the alliance of his uncertain and time-serving countrymen. He nevertheless had continued to maintain a specious attitude of hostility, though in reality it was no more than a succession of flights and escapes through the whole of the following summer, until the month of November. When—learning that the obstinate resentment of the queen had given way to the desire of preventing increased expenses, by terminating all further prosecution of this rebellion—he sent his proposals of submission: but as it was apparent from intercepted letters, that while he was endeavouring to gain terms for himself, he still continued his endeavours to excite other chiefs to continued rebellion, his overtures, for a time, were doubtfully received. The expectation of some great effort from Spain, for a while continued to deceive both parties. These illusions slowly cleared away, and on the 3d of March, 1603, Tyrone made the most entire submission which it was possible for discretionary power to dictate,* and received a full pardon. He then received a promise of the restoration of his lands, with certain reserves in favour of Henry Oge O'Neale, and Tirlogh MacHenry, to whom promises of land had been made; also of 600 acres for the new forts Mountjoy and Charlemont. Certain rents or compositions to the crown, were at the same time reserved.

On the 6th of April he arrived in Dublin, in company with the lord-deputy, and the next day an account arrived of the queen's death, on which it is said the earl of Tyrone burst into a violent fit of tears.

Tyrone formally repeated his submission to king James, and according to stipulation, wrote for his son to Spain, where he had been sent to be brought up at the Spanish court. In the mean time he had permission to return to the north for the settlement of his affairs, and

* The terms are preserved in Moryson, l. 3, cap. 2.

lord Mountjoy sent over a full detail of all the particulars of his submission, and the powers on which it had been received, and demanded the king's confirmation of his pardon.

Shortly after lord Mountjoy, having been made lord-lieutenant, with permission to leave Sir G. Carew as his deputy, returned to England with the earl of Tyrone. Tyrone was received graciously at court, but his presence in the streets roused the animosity of the English mob, and he was everywhere encountered with reviling and popular violence, so that he was obliged to travel with a guard until he was again embarked for Ireland.

Lord Mountjoy was created earl of Devonshire, but did not live long to enjoy the honour, as he died in the spring of 1606, without leaving any heirs, so that the title again became extinct. Many persons of much ability had preceded him in the government of this country; yet, with the best intentions, none before him appear to have been competent to the mastery of the great and manifold disorders which had for six centuries continued to embroil its people, until long-continued war had reduced them to a state not superior to barbarism, and produced a moral and political disorganization not to be so perfectly exemplified in the history of modern states. By a consummate union of caution, perseverance, firmness, and native military tact, he met and arrested a dangerous rebellion, at a moment when its chances of success were at the highest, and when it was in the hands of the ablest and best-supported leaders that had yet entered the field of Irish insurrection. Of both these affirmations the best proof will be found in the whole of the operations in the north before the siege of Kinsale.

The country was now reduced to a state of comparative tranquillity, and the earl of Tyrone might have run out the remainder of his course, and transmitted his honours and estates without interruption. But, although rebellion was stilled, a spirit of disaffection survived; and it cannot, with any probability, be said that the more turbulent chiefs of the north had ever entirely laid aside the hope of times more favourable to the assertion of their independence. In place of the ordinary motives of human pride, ambition, and interest, the more safe and popular excitement of religion began to be assumed, as the disguise of designs which grew and were cherished in secret. By the efficacy of this stimulant, fierce impulses were from time to time transmitted through the country; and though matters were by no means ripe for any considerable impulse arising from religious fanaticism, yet a degree of popular feeling was sufficiently excited, to encourage the restless earl of Tyrone in the hope of a coming occasion once more to try the chance of open rebellion with better prospects. Such a sentiment could not be long entertained, without numerous acts and words, which, if brought to the test of inquiry, would endanger his head. Such an occasion soon occurred, and produced consequences which historians have thought fit to call mysterious.

The archbishop of Armagh had a contest with the earl for lands alleged to be usurped from his see. A suit was commenced, and Tyrone was summoned to appear before the privy council. He had, however, heard that O'Caban, a confidential servant of his own, had enlisted himself on the primate's part; and concluded that the summons was a pretext to lay hold on him. His fears were communicated to others, and, according to a report stated by Cox, they seem to have not been groundless. On the 7th May, 1607, a letter, directed to Sir William Fisher, clerk of the council, was dropped in the council chamber, accusing the earl of Tyrone and Rory O'Donell, who had been created earl of Tyrconnel in 1603, with lord M'Guire and others, of a conspiracy to surprize the castle of Dublin. However this question may be decided, it is certain at least that both Tyrone and the earl of Tyrconnel took the alarm, and fled to Spain, leaving all that they had intrigued or contended for to the mercy of the English government. From this there is no certain notice of Tyrone in history.

THOMAS, SIXTEENTH EARL OF KERRY.

BORN A. D. 1502—DIED A. D. 1590.

This eminent lord succeeded his brother, Gerald, in the earldom. His youth was spent in Italy. He was bred in Milan, and early entered the German service. On his brother's death, the inheritance was seized by one of the family, who was next heir, on the failure of next of kin in the direct line. The matter might have remained thus, and the wrongful possessor allowed to obtain that protection which time must ever give to possession, but most of all in that age of unsettled rights; but fortunately for him, he was timely remembered by his nurse, Joan Harman, who was not prevented by the infirmities of old age from proceeding with her daughter in search of her foster-child. Having embarked at Dingle, she landed in France, and went from thence to Italy. After overcoming the many difficulties of so long a journey, with her imperfect means and ignorance of the way, she found her noble foster-son; and, having given him the needful information concerning the state of his affairs, she died on her way home.

Lord Thomas came over to take possession of his estate and honours. For two years he had to contend with the resolute opposition of the intruder who relied on the circumstance of his being less known in the country from having passed his life abroad. The intruding claimant was himself, it is likely, misled by the local character of his own acquaintance with society. In two years the claim of justice prevailed, and in or about the year 1550, in his forty-eighth year lord Thomas Fitz-Maurice obtained full possession of his rights.

He was treated with distinguishing honour and confidence by Philip and Mary; who, in a letter apprizing him of their marriage, desired his good offices in aid of the lord deputy, to assist in rectifying the disorders which had been suffered to increase for some years in their Irish dominions. His course for many years was thus one of loyal duty, and honoured by the royal favour, although its incidents were not such as to call for our special notice. Among these it may be mentioned, that in the parliament of the third year of Philip and Mary, he sat as premier baron; while in that of the fourth year of the same reign, lord Trimleston was placed above him. But in 1581, when in his 79th year, he was led into rebellion, by the example of others, and by the seeming weakness of the English. The lord deputy, supposing that the quiet of Munster was secured by the flight of the earl of Desmond and the death of John of Desmond, dismissed the larger proportion of his English forces. In consequence of this dangerous step, the earl of Kerry and his son, moved by their discontents against the deputy, broke into rebellion. They began by proceeding to dislodge the English from their garrisons, which they effected to some extent by the boldness and dexterity of their movements. First attacking the garrison of Adare, they slew the captain and most of the soldiers. They next marched to Lisconnel, in which there were only eight soldiers, as the place was supposed to be protected by its strength and difficulty of access. The entrance to this castle was secured by two gates, of which, upon the admission of any person, it was usual to make fast the outer before the inner was unbarred. Taking advantage of the circumstance, the earl bribed a woman who used every morning early to enter these gates, with a large basket of turf, wood, and other cumbrous necessaries, to let fall her basket in the outer gate, so as to prevent its being closed without delay. During the night he contrived to steal a strong party into a cabin which had very inconsiderately been allowed to stand close to the gate. All fell out favourably. The woman dropped her load, and, according to her instructions, uttered a loud cry; the men rushed in, and the porter was slain before he was aware of the nature of the incident, and in a few moments more, not a man of the garrison was alive.

Encouraged by this success, the earl marched to Adnagh, which he thought to win by another stratagem. He hired for the purpose a young girl of loose character, who was to obtain admission, and when admitted, to act according to the earl's contrivance, so as to betray the fort. The capture of Lisconnel had, however, the effect of putting the captain on his guard. He soon contrived to draw from the young woman a confession of her perfidious intent, after which he caused her to be thrown from the walls.

From this the earl proceeded to range through the counties of Waterford and Tipperary, in which he committed waste, and took spoil without meeting any resistance.

The deputy receiving an account of these outrages drew together about four hundred men, and marched into Kerry; and coming to the wood of Lisconnell, where the earl was encamped with seven hundred, an encounter took place, in which the earl's army was put to flight and scattered away, leaving their spoil behind them. The earl, with a few more, escaped into the mountains of Sleulaugher. Marching on into the estates of Fitz-Maurice, the lord deputy seized and garrisoned the forts and strong places. Another severe defeat, which soon followed, completed the fall of the earl, who found himself unable to attempt any further resistance. He then applied to the earl of Ormonde, to whom he had done all the mischief in his power, to obtain a pardon for him. The earl of Ormonde had the generosity to intercede for him, and he was pardoned.

The remaining events of his life have nothing remarkable enough to claim attention. He lived on in honour and prosperity, till the close of his eighty-eighth year, when he died at Lixnaw, on the 16th

December, 1590. He is said to have been the handsomest man of his time, and also remarkable to an advanced age for his great strength.

ROBERT, FIFTH LORD TRIMLESTON.

DIED A. D. 1573.

THE first lord Trimleston was Robert Barnewall, second son to Sir Christopher Barnewall, of Crickston, in Meath, who was chief justice of the king's bench in 1445 and 1446. The ancestors intermediate between this eminent person and the fifth lord, had most of them acted their part in the troubled politics of their respective generations with credit, and were eminent in their day. We select the fifth lord for this brief notice, as he is mentioned in terms of high eulogy by the chroniclers. In 1561, he was joined in commission with the archbishop of Dublin and other lords, for the preservation of the peace of the pale, during the absence of lord deputy Sussex. Hollinshed gives the following account of him:—" He was a rare nobleman, and endowed with sundry good gifts, who, having well wedded himself to the reformation of his miserable country, was resolved for the whetting of his wit, which nevertheless was pregnant and quick; by a short trade and method he took in his study to have sipt up the very sap of the common law, and upon this determination sailing into England, sickened shortly after at a worshipful matron's house at Combury, named Margaret Tiler, where he was, to the great grief of all his country, pursued with death, when the weal of the public had most need of his life." His death happened in 1573: he left no issue, and was succeeded by his brother Peter.

JAMES FITZ-MAURICE.

DIED CIRC. 1563.

THERE are few incidents connected with the life of James Fitz-Maurice, undetailed at length, in the later memoirs of this division of our work, as inextricably interwoven with the history of his time. And we should be enabled to compass all that may be particularly connected with his life and conduct, in a few sentences, were we not desirous to present our curious reader with some more distinct notice of a few of the more memorable characters which the incidents of the period have brought into the same field of view. That Fitz-Maurice was of the Desmond family seems agreed by historians; but how, is not so agreed. Leland assumes him to be a brother to the 16th Earl.

He first appears in active rebellion against the Queen's Government, and engaged in correspondence for aid, with the Pope and Philip of Spain. With these dispositions he repaired to Spain, where he was cordially received by Philip; finding small chance of the desired aid, he journeyed to Rome, where he met with more promise of success. The Pope contrived to secure a double advantage in his agency. Italy was then, as it since has been, infested with bands of robbers among its forests and mountain retreats. These received their pardon from Gregory, with a view to their more profitable employment in the service of the church. They were placed under the command of Fitz-Maurice, who in the meantime visited Paris, to regain his wife. During his absence this respectable band was by his desire conducted by one Stukely to await him in Spain. Stukely, landing on the coast of Portugal, was persuaded by King Sebastian to join his expedition against Morocco, with a promise on his return to accompany him to Ireland with a strong force. Both Stukely and the king were slain in the battle which followed, and the remnant of the brigand troop which came back were conducted by Fitz-Maurice to Ireland, where his further career was cut short in a private brawl.

POSTSCRIPT.

WE may now conclude these notices, so far as they are simply political, with a very few contemporaneous notices of the more eminent and influential names which grace the record of these late wars, but of which the separate notice has not been within our plan.

Among the distinguished names of this period, there is perhaps none so justly celebrated as Raleigh: his unfortunate and erratic career may in some measure be said to have commenced in Ireland. While he obtained military honour and large estates in the close of this period, his name constantly recurs among the captains of the president of Munster, having borne a marked part in the desperate siege of Dunboy castle. His enterprising temper alone changed the current of his life, and prevented his having laid the foundation of an illustrious Irish name.

Having obtained ample grants in the counties of Cork and Waterford, out of the vast estates forfeited by the earl of Desmond, he built a house for himself in the town of Youghal. Of this we are enabled to give the following interesting extract:—" The house in which Sir Walter is said to have resided, when at Youghal, is still standing, and in good preservation. It adjoins the churchyard, and is at present in the occupation of Sir Christopher Musgrave. It is a mansion of long and low proportions, not remarkable either for beauty or peculiarity of architecture, several of the apartments are of rather spacious dimensions, and finished with oaken panels and large chimney pieces well carved. In a garden attached to this residence, it is believed Raleigh planted the first potatoes grown in Ireland. According to a current tradition, the man intrusted with the care of the garden in the absence of Sir Walter, supposed that the apple or seed, was the esculent part of the novel production; and finding the taste unpleasant, bestowed no farther thought on the plantation until upon digging the ground for some other crop, the root was found to yield a wholesome and palatable species of food, of more importance to the future condition of Ireland than all the political schemes, wars, and encroaching settlements of queen Elizabeth, her councillors, and armies."[*]

To the particulars in this extract, *Lewis's Topographical Dictionary*

[* Brewer.]

enables us to add a few interesting particulars. The place of Sir Walter is now called Myrtle-grove, and is or was recently the property of the Hayman family. The panelling of the drawing-room is remarkable for its rich carving. "In removing the panelling of one of the rooms some years since, an aperture in the wall was discovered, in which were found several old books, one bound in oak and printed at Mantua, 1479, consisting of two parts, one in black-letter, a history of the Bible, with coloured initials: the other an ecclesiastical history by John Schallus, professor of physic at Hernfield, dedicated to prince Gonzales."

Sir Walter Raleigh's Irish career began under the earl of Ormonde and was pursued in the wars of Munster, where he gained more in fortune than reputation. After this, returning for a while to England, he rose in the queen's favour, and served with distinction in many enterprizes. In 1584, he is traced in England serving as M.P. for Devon, and leading a life of most intense study, cultivating and patronizing every science and liberal art. The following interval is not very distinctly traced, but we are inclined to fix upon it as the period of his residence in Ireland, we should conclude from the above-mentioned particulars, with the design of settling; and this seems confirmed by the additional fact that, in 1588, he was mayor of Youghal. But it appears that the management of his large Irish property required an exclusive attention which ill suited with his romantic and restless nature, and that the rents were far below the apparent value of the property. He returned to England with a mind filled with specious and glittering prospects, and soon after obtained an appointment from Elizabeth to the government of Jersey. He had failed in his endeavours to excite the mind of the prudent queen, by the sanguine representations of foreign discoveries of visionary realms, which lay before his imagination with the brightness and solidity of the gorgeous vapours of a glorious sunset, and his fancy tinged even realities with a dream-like aspect, which rendered them questionable to sober minds. In his account of one of his voyages he says, "Those who are desirous to discover and to see many nations, may be satisfied within this river which bringeth forth so many arms and branches, leading to several countries and provinces about two thousand miles east and west, and eight hundred north and south, and of these the most rich either in gold or other merchandizes. The common soldier shall here fight for gold, and pay himself instead of pence with plates half a foot broad, whereas, he breaketh his bones in other wars for provant and penury." During the latter years of queen Elizabeth, the name of Raleigh is illustrious among the splendid constellation of glorious names, which raise the literary glory of her reign so high. Shakspeare, Johnson, Beaumont, and Fletcher, with their contemporaries, were among his familiar acquaintance.

It was some time after the siege of Dunboy, that Sir Richard Boyle was sent into England with an account of that transaction, by Sir George Carew, who advised him to purchase Raleigh's Irish estates. A meeting for the purpose took place in England, between Boyle and Raleigh, and Cecil introduced them at Carew's request, and acted as moderator in the transaction, which ended in a bargain by which Raleigh conveyed his Irish estate to Boyle for the sum of £1500, the land being about 12.000 acres in extent. It is a curious circumstance that some years after Sir Walter obtained his liberty, after twelve years' confinement in the Tower, at the expense of the same sum, with which he purchased the intercession of the profligate Villiers. This long interval of confinement was rendered more honourable by Raleigh's genius than his years of liberty by military exploits of which the character was little chivalric or humane, and foreign enterprizes too much like buccaneering expeditions to be satisfactory to a mind like his. It was immediately after the transaction above related, that he became involved in a charge of treason, made by lord Cobham, and too well-known for detail. Of his innocence we entertain no doubts. His long confinement was mitigated by the free exercise of an unconfined imagination; the gloomy cell was peopled by his boundless fancy, and the Hesperian Isles of discovery lay between his contemplation and the grim walls which cooped him in. With much difficulty, and the exertion of considerable influence, he revived a plan which he had long entertained for the colonization of New Guiana; in an unlucky hour, surrounded by the evil influence of Spain, and the unfavourable dispositions of the king and his principal ministers, and under a sentence of death which made his life answerable for the result of a doubtful adventure, Raleigh was appointed to command an expedition for the purpose of founding a settlement in Guiana. The result of this is familiar in every English history; it failed in such a manner as to wreck the fortunes and implicate the character of the unfortunate leader. He had embarked his entire property in it; his son who sailed as one of his captains, was slain in an attack upon St Thomas; his friend and second in command shot himself in despair, and Raleigh returned to a bloody death from the axe of the executioner: he was ordered to execution on his sentence twelve years before.

Among the eminent names of this period, of whom our regular plan cannot properly be said to admit of a distinct memoir, there is none whose claim to notice stands higher than Charles Blount, lord Mountjoy, by whose distinguished services the Ulster rebellion was brought to its conclusion. Our life of Hugh, earl of Tyrone, may indeed be considered as containing the most important passages of the life of this eminent soldier, and we shall here endeavour to supply some additional particulars which we were in that article compelled to omit. Charles Blount, the second son of lord Mountjoy, was born about 1563. He was educated at Oxford, and designed for the bar. In the university, the fairest hopes were encouraged by his rapid progress in literature, as well as by the habits of intensely diligent study which became the habit of his life, and strongly marked his character. Early in his youth he professed the honourable resolution, to raise again the sinking honours of his family. His grandfather had dilapidated a good fortune in the profuse and luxurious court of Henry; his father evidently a weak man, instead of improving his impoverished estate by industry and economy, had recourse to the chimeras of alchemy, which then as for previous ages continued to impose on mankind, and to beggar thousands with the promise of visionary wealth. His elder brother's extravagance still further reduced the fortune of the family. Charles began early to manifest the indications of a wise, honourable, and aspiring temper. Moryson mentions, on his own authority, that "in his childhood, when his parents would have his picture, he chose to be drawn with a trowel in his hand, and this motto—*Ad reædificandam antiquam domum.*" Moryson also mentions that, on leaving Oxford university very young, he was still "not well grounded," but that he repaired the deficiency in London by obtaining the most skilful instructors in the languages, history, mathematics, cosmography, and natural philosophy. In these pursuits he took chief delight, spending much of his time in canvassing subjects of doubt and difficulty, and practising his memory on the most subtle objections with their solutions. But his chief delight was in theology, ever the most attractive in early youth to minds of wide and grasping range: he loved much to study both the fathers and the schoolmen. For this latter taste he accounted by mentioning that, " being in his youth much addicted to popery, so much as through prejudicate opinion no writer of our time could have diverted him from it, yet, by observing the fathers' consent, and the schoolmen's idle and absurd distinctions, he began first to distaste many of their opinions, and then by reading our authors, to be confirmed in the reform doctrine."

His introduction to court was curious. Having come to London he repaired to Whitehall to see the court. The queen chanced to be at dinner, when Blount's figure, then strikingly graceful, caught her eye, not the slowest to discern the attractions of manly beauty. She immediately inquired his name, and, on being informed who he was, called him to her, gave him her hand to kiss, and desired him to come often to court, with the assurance that she would keep his fortune in view.

The queen kept her word. After a few years' waiting, during which he was employed from time to time, he was appointed to the government of Portsmouth. In 1594 his brother's death took place, and he succeeded to the title of Mountjoy, with the remains of a wasted property, amounting to 1000 marks a-year. This, though small, was sufficient to supply the expenses of a moderate young nobleman who had no family to maintain. Two or three years after, he served under lord Essex in an expedition to the Azores. We have already mentioned in a former page, that the friendship of Essex was rendered unprofitable by the intense jealousy with which he looked on the queen's favour, which he wished entirely to engross. To this jealousy it was owing that, when the queen was afterwards desirous to send Mountjoy to Ireland, Essex, not content with obtaining the appointment for himself, endeavoured to represent Mountjoy as a bookish dreamer, unfit for that arduous and responsible charge. Nevertheless, it is mentioned by Moryson, that the high qualities of his character had so struck "two old counsellors of Ireland," that they long before pointed him out as the person most likely to suppress the rebellion of Tyrone. The history of his Irish campaign, by which the prognostication of the two old gentlemen was amply verified, we have fully given. King James, who succeeded immediately on the close of this rebellion, created him earl of Devonshire. His life is said to have been embittered by unfortunate love. In his early days he had engaged the affections of a daughter of the earl of Essex; but he was not felt by the lady's father to be a match equal to their expectations. According to the tyrannical usage of the time, she was reluctantly married to lord Rich. The consequence was unhappy, and leaves a blot, the only one, on the memory of Mountjoy; the cruel award of the tyrannical father was repaired by a crime. The divorce of lady Rich followed. After which she was married to Mountjoy, who lived but a few months after.

Moryson, from whom we have already drawn some interesting particulars of this eminent commander, enables us to add a few more of no small interest respecting his person and character:—" He was of stature tall, and of very comly proportion; his skin faire, with little haire on his body, which haire was of colour blackish, (or inclining to blacke,) and thin on his head, where he wore it short, except a locke under his left eare, which he nourished the time of this warre, and, being woven up, laid it in his necke under his ruffe. The crown of his head was in his latter days something bald, as the fore part naturelly curled; he onely used the barber for his head; for the haire on his chin (growing slowly) and that on his cheeks and throat, he used almost daily to cut it with his sizers, keeping it so low with his owne hand that it could scarce bee discerned, as likewise himselfe kept the haire of his upper lippe something short, onely suffering that under his nether lippe to grow at length and full; yet, some two or three yeeres before his death, he nourished a sharpe and short pikedenant on his chin. His forehead was broad and high; his eyes greate, blacke, and lovely; his nose something low and short, a little blunt in the end; his chin round; his cheeks full, round, and ruddy; his countenance cheareful, and amiable as ever I beheld of any man; onely some two yeeres before his death, upon discontentment, his face grew thinne, his ruddy colour failed, growing something swarthy, and his countenance was sad and dejected; his arms were longe, and of proportionable bignes; his hands longe and white; his fingers great at the endes; and his leggs somewhat little, which he gartered ever ebone the knee, wearing the garter of St George's order under his left knee, except when he was booted, and so wore not that garter, but a blue ribbon instead thereof above his knee, and hanging over his boote."

To this curious description of the man, we are enabled to add one not less so of his manners and habits:—" Further," writes his biographer, " in his nature he was a close concealer of his secrets, for which cause lest they should be reveuled, and because he loved not to be importuned with suites; a free speaker, or a popular man, could not long continue his favourite. He was sparing in speech, but when he was drawn to it most judicious therein, if not eloquent. He never used swearing, but rather hated it, which I have often seen him controll at his table with a frowning brow and an angry cast of his black eye. He was slow to anger, but, once provoked, spake home. His great temper was most seene in his wise carriage between the court factions of his time. He was a gentle enemy, easily pardoning, and calmly pursuing revenge; and a friend, if not cold, yet not to be used much out of the high way, and something too much reserved towards his dearest minions." To this admirably drawn character no comment is wanting. Judicious, refined in taste, of acute and quick understanding, unswayed by violent passions, of a kindly and mild temper, but, like many such, self-centred in his affection for others, Mountjoy was well fitted for a scene of action, which was rendered perplexed and intricate, not more by the moving chaos of forces which were to be checked and subdued, than by the various cross-currents of passion, prejudice, and opposite interests, which were to be neutralized or controled.

We shall not prolong this postscript farther than to make mention of one, who, though in no way connected either with politics or literature, has left a name rendered memorable by extreme longevity. Elinor, countess of Desmond, was daughter of the Fitz-Geralds of Drumana in the county of Waterford, and widow of James, thirteenth earl of Desmond, in the reign of Edward IV. She lived till some time in the reign of James I. The ruin of the house of Desmond reduced her to poverty, as no provision was made to save her jointure from the spoil. On this occasion she made her appearance in the court of Elizabeth, who, we presume, redressed the grievance. She was at the time 140, and seemed to retain considerable vigour and animation. She seems to have held her jointure on the Desmond estate till then. Her life, indeed, seems to have been held by some renewable tenure, as she is mentioned by Bacon to have twice renewed her teeth, each renewal having perhaps been accompanied by a renovation of vitality. It is indeed remarkable, in most persons who live to ages beyond the ordinary duration of human life, that there does not, for the most part, appear any proportional mark of the waste of time. Whether this be owing to a greater fund of the vital principle, (whatever this may be,) or to a slower progress of the changes of life, or to renovation, such as the above fact would seem to imply, such is the fact. Of this the writer of these pages has known some examples, several persons, of eighty and upwards, not seemingly advanced further in decay than others of sixty-five and seventy; and in the same way, at earlier ages, the principle is to be traced, so that some appear to be advancing faster than others to the common event of life, and all moving, as it were, with different rates of progress in periods of different duration. Mention is made of the countess of Desmond by various writers, none of whom furnish materials for the biographer. Walpole makes mention of a picture of her, which is also noticed by Pennant as a remarkable picture, in the earl of Kinnoul's collection at Dupplin Castle.

CLERICAL AND LITERARY MEMOIRS.

It will be hardly needful to account for the scanty selection to which we feel compelled, of the ecclesiastical and literary classes of the preceding period of Irish history. Though Religion, taken generally, had always more or less influence in the course of events, this cannot be truly said of the Ecclesiastical body, as holding any distinct or cognizable rank or official place. Christianity was then existing in the unsettled form in which it emanated from its first apostolic missionaries; contracting, as it spread, controversies and those heresies which at last found their common sewer in the double creed of Pius IV. In an early age the primitive faith, first found in the "Isle of Saints by Palladius and Patrick, the *Scoti in Christo Credentes*," began soon to be somewhat loosely connected with the more advanced corruptions of the English church, (already in connection with the Roman,) through the medium of their Danish and Norwegian conquerors.

But this adulteration can hardly be said to have any settled confirmation or distinct existence till late in the 12th century, when the Norman conquest may be said to have prostrated the land with its people (already prepared), at the feet of the Pope.

About 1172 the Romish church, for which the way had been long in gradual preparation by a succession of slow intrusions, was, with the more direct authority of Henry, raised to the ascendency, by a compact with Pope Adrian, in virtue of which this monarch's claim to the island was pretended. Of this revolution,—admissibly less considerable by reason of the long accumulation of growing corruptions from the purity of the earlier faith,—the effects are sufficiently traceable in the historical memoirs and statements of the following five centuries.

Of the long line of ecclesiastical dignitaries who took their parts in the dissension and political conflict of that unsettled and uncivilized period to the termination of Queen Elizabeth's reign, we cannot, without vainly loading our pages with most unprofitable notices and obscure names, offer any distinct details. We select a few of the more eminent, who either have obtained distinction by their conduct in the earlier struggles between the Romish and Reformed churches, or who, by their leading abilities and official position, came to be employed in the government of the country.

Respecting the few literary or learned characters belonging to the same period, we must observe a similar rule. Of these, most should be numbered with the ecclesiastical classes; many, with the old chroniclers, whose lives have little interest though their records are of much authority. With regard to literature in Ireland we shall, therefore, on the whole have little to swell the few remaining sheets of this first division of our work. Still, in a land which had, in earlier times, been the favoured seat of learning in Europe—there could not fail to linger many isolated gleams of mind, shedding their feeble glimmer, little observed and unappreciated in the mist and haze of surrounding barbarism. A few eminent names, in the moral and intellectual dearth of those drear times, will show that the lamp of scientific inquiry was even still burning in its lone cell, amid the clash and tumult of plundering chiefs and conspiring demagogues, kept alert and effective by the intrigues of Roman ambition or Spanish enmity.

In the few ecclesiastical personages to be noticed in the following brief division, it will appear that, while the long early struggle for the establishment of an absolute ultramontane ascendency was changing its character, by laying aside the arms of fleshly warfare and substituting the arms and weapons of spiritual intrigue and ecclesiastical domination, a new power was introduced with the entrance of the Reformation; the restoration of the lost elements of apostolical faith, fell amidst the vast undigested mass of the accumulated heresies of medieval Christianity, and instead of the warring cabinet and the strife of arms, gradually awakened sectarian rancour, and transferred the strife to human hearts. A spurious patriotism supplied fuel for spurious religion; and as, unhappily, the nominal professors of the true religion are not necessarily true to their profession, the sin of one side was reciprocated by want of charity on the other. The scale of justice was, for one sad interval balanced by indiscriminate fear and prejudice, and the seed of future trouble committed to time, for distant retribution. But these must be the burthen of a future page.

As the period under immediate notice, in both its political and ecclesiastical aspect, mainly offers a view of the conflicts for dominion between the papacy, pursued, according to the universal policy of the Roman see, in Ireland as elsewhere, against the growing ascendency of the Reformation,—it will be our simplest course, and (so far as respects this contest) the least encumbered by controversial discussion, before we enter upon our selection, to premise a brief sketch comprising a few of such of the earlier ecclesiastics whose lives offer some indication of the stages of this struggle of hostile churches. A few pages will thus dismiss the subject of many painful sheets.

Early in the seventh century we find the early apostolic faith yet lingering—as nearly first taught in Ireland—retaining its first authority from the Holy Scriptures; and only modified in a few of those earlier controversies which had obtained general possession of the Christian world. The Papacy, in its later sense, as now understood, had not yet been developed in the metropolitan see of Rome. It may therefore conduce to order, to commence with some one or two notices, taken from this earlier era. At the time thus referred to, Fursey, descendant from a royal stock, by the license of his uncle, founded a monastery in an island called Rathmat, near Lough-orbsen, in the county of Galway, with all the necessary cells and appendages belonging to it. There are now no remains of this building, but there is a parish church near this lake called, in honour of him, Kill-Fursa. He continued to preach the gospel for about twelve years in Ireland; and about the year 637 he went to England. There, by the assistance of Sigebert, king of the East Saxons, he founded a monastery in Suffolk to which he ultimately induced Sigebert to retire, and to exchange the regal for the monastic life. Sigebert afterwards being compelled to witness a battle, fought against Pendo, king of the Mercians, and holding (says Florence of Worcester) only a wand in his hand, was slain, together with his kinsman Egric, to whom he had resigned his kingdom. This monastery was afterwards adorned with magnificent buildings and valuable presents, but Fursey, to avoid the horrors and dangers of war, committed the care of his abbey to his brother, Foilan, and two other priests, and, accompanied by his other brother, Ultan, went over to France, where he founded a new abbey, in the diocese of Paris. A life of Fursey has been published in French, by a learned doctor of the Sorbonne, which has since been translated into Latin, in which he is described as having gone to Rome before the foundation of the abbey of Laigny; and the conversations which took place between him and the Pope are detailed. It is also stated, that the Pope consecrated both him and his brother, Foilan, bishops, though without appointing them to any sees. Their journey back is then described through Austrasia, Flanders, Brabant, Liege, and Namure; their meeting with St. Gertrude, who formed so strong a friendship for Fursey, that she accompanied them in their subsequent journeys, and at length founded a monastery for her fellow-travellers at Fossis, and made Ultan abbot of it. Foilan continued to travel through Flanders, boldly preaching Christianity wherever he went, and overturning the pagan altars. At length he, with three of his fellow-labourers, gained the crown of martyrdom, having perished by the swords of the infuriated pagans. Fursey fearlessly continued his labours, and induced large numbers of the courtiers of the king of Austrasia to embrace Christianity. He then proceeded to the court of Clovis, where he was received with great honour, and was highly esteemed for his uncompromising boldness in rebuking the vices of his king and his courtiers. Fursey died at Peronne, in Picardy, on the 13th of January (which day has been consecrated to his memory), in the year 650, or as others say, in the year 653. Under this year the author of the *Annals of the Abbey of Boyle* places his death according to the following passage: "Anno 653, Fursu Paruna quievit." In the year 653, Fursey went to rest at Peronne. *Miræus* states that on his death-bed "he bequeathed the care of his abbey of Laigny to St. Eloquius, an Irishman, who afterwards perceiving faction to have arisen among his disciples, retired, with a few friars, to Grimac, on the river Isarake."

Fursey wrote, according to Dempster, *De Vita Monastica*, Lib. 1. There is also a prophecy, written in the Irish language, still extant, which is ascribed to him.

Nearly at the same period Adamnanus, abbot of Hy, was sent on an embassy into Britain to Alfred, king of Northumberland, and, while he continued there, became a convert to the views of Rome respecting the true time for celebrating Easter. "After his return home," says Bede, "he used his utmost endeavours to guide the monks of Hy, and all those who were subject to the said monastery, into that beaten road of truth which he himself walked in, and of which he made a sincere profession, but was not able to prevail." He then sailed into Ireland, where he had better success. He composed, according to Ware, *Vitam St. Bathildis Clodovæi Francorum Regis Uxoris.* He also wrote *De Vita Columbæ,* Lib. iii., *Poemata Varia,* and a description of the Holy Land, which was afterwards published at Ingolstad under the following title, in 1619; *Adamnanni Scoto-Hiberni Abbatis celeberrimi de situ Ferræ Sanctæ, et Quarundam aliorum Locorum ut* Alexandriæ *et* Constantinopoleos, Lib. iii.; *Ante Annos Nonagentos et amplius conscripti, et nunc primum in lucem prolati, studio Jacobi Gretseri Soc. Jesu Theologi Ingolstadii,* 1619. Bede states the circumstances which gave rise to this work as follows:—"Arculph, a French bishop, who had travelled to Jerusalem merely to visit those holy places, and having taken a view of the whole Land of Promise, travelled to Damascus, Constantinople, Alexandria, and to many islands in the sea. Thence returning to his native country on shipboard, he was driven by a violent tempest on the western coasts of Britain, and at length came to the before-mentioned servant of Christ, Adamnanus; who, finding him well versed in the Scriptures, and of great knowledge in the Holy Land, joyfully entertained him, and with great pleasure hearkened to what he said, insomuch that everything he had affirmed to have seen in those holy places, worthy to be preserved in memory, Adamnanus committed to writing and composed a book profitable for many, and especially for such who, being at a great distance from the places where the patriarchs and apostles resided, have only a knowledge of them from books. Adamnanus also presented this book to king Alfred, by whose bounty it fell into the hands of more inferior people to be read. The writer also himself, being rewarded with many presents, was sent back into his own country." Bede gives a short abstract of the book in two chapters. Our abbot is said to have written, besides, some *Epistles, A Rule for Monks, De Paschate Legitimo,* and the *Canons of Adamnanus.* He died on the 23d of September, 704, in the 74th, or, as others say, the 80th year of his age. His remains were removed to Ireland in 727, but were conveyed back again, three years after, to the monastery of Hy.

From this ancient ecclesiastic we may pass on to a somewhat later period. Previous to the 11th century the Irish church, though far from retaining the purity of its origin, had still preserved its independence. It had been largely infested by foreign missionaries, and harassed by numerous local disorders fatal alike to religion and civilization; its condition was unregulated and fragmentary; its bishops unattached; there was a general absence of diocesan partition. All this, with a consequent laxity of profession and conduct, tended to prepare the way for the changes then enforced by the influence and authority of the English government between the second and the eighth Henry.

As a main instrument toward the approximation of the change contemplated by the Pope, we may briefly notice the conduct of the first legate, sent 1106 by Paschal II. This man, whose name was Gilbert, is mentioned as the first who laboured actively in the conversion of the Irish clergy to the customs and clergy of Rome. With this view his writings, then published extensively and partly still extant, were eloquent in the advocacy of papal supremacy, by the specious interpretations of Scripture still applied for the same purposes. In a volume entitled the "State of the Church," he adds details for the information of the Irish bishops and clergy, its correct order and constitution, according to the rules and canons of Rome, and teaches the due methods, dresses, requisites, and rites for the observance of devotion and celebration of mass.—This had at the time much influence. The decline of piety and general disorder already mentioned, favourably inclined several of the most respectable of the Irish church to the design. Nor was it less influential towards its promotion, that the same process of transition has long before set in, and fixed its ground in England, where Anselm and Lanfranc gave their aid and sanction to the Irish Prelate Gilbert.

We may now proceed to notice a few of the most conspicuous persons who had part in the religions, politics, or literature of the country in this period, classed under (1.) Ecclesiastics connected with politics; (2.) Clerical literates; and (3.) Laymen connected with literature;—giving, as by customary right, precedence to the church.

I. ECCLESIASTICAL AND POLITICAL.

LAWRENCE O'TOOLE.

DIED A. D. 1180.

HE was the youngest son of Murtogh O'Toole, chief of Imaile, in the county now called Wicklow, the territory of the celebrated septs of the Tooles and Byrnes, which are with some reason represented as of British origin.* In Lawrence the two coeval and kindred streams were united, as his mother was an O'Byrne.†

At the early age of ten, it was his fortune to be delivered by his father according to the customs of that barbarous time, as a hostage to the king of Leinster, the notorious Dermod MacMurragh. Of Dermod's savage disposition the reader is aware. Young Lawrence O'Toole was doomed to know it by experience: ever involved in hostility with the surrounding chiefs, and always actuated by the bitterest rancour in his enmities, the brutal prince of Leinster, in some moment of inflamed animosity, resolved to make the innocent boy, who was even then distinguished by early genius, the victim of his father's offence ; and with this execrable design caused him to be conveyed to a deserted and barren spot, and left to meet and suffer the horrors of want and exposure, under the care of such wretches as were fit to be the instruments of king Dermod's enmity. In such a condition, the sufferings of the tender child can easily be conceived. But the eye of a guardian providence was awake; his father quickly received intelligence of the deplorable situation of his child: Murtogh

* See the life of Feagh MacHugh O'Byrne.   † Dalton.

had the feeling to resent, and the spirit to retaliate the cruel indignity. He seized on twelve of Dermod's most noted followers, and shutting them in prison, he sent word to the tyrant that he would cut off their heads, unless they should be immediately redeemed by his son's release. The menace was effectual: however little regard Dermod might entertain for the lives of his men, yet as he chiefly relied on the favour of the populace, he could not without serious detriment to his nearest interest, hazard his low popularity by abandoning his faithful partizans to the revenge of an enemy. At the same time, as Lawrence was the pledge of a treaty, he would not give him up to his father. The matter was therefore compromised by placing him in the hands of the bishop of Glendalough.

The incident was not unfavourable to the disposition and future fortunes of the youth. The bishop received the child of his noble neighbour with benevolent hospitality, and while he remained in his hands, had him carefully instructed in the principles of the Christian religion by his chaplain; and after twelve days, he was sent back to his father. Soon after he was taken by his father on a visit to the bishop, very probably to return thanks for the kindness he had received, and revisit a spot which must needs have powerfully affected his young imagination. On this occasion it is mentioned, that his father proposed to cast lots which of his sons should adopt the ecclesiastical calling, on which young Lawrence said with a smile, "Father, there is no necessity for casting lots; if you allow me, I will embrace it with pleasure."[*] The offer gave much satisfaction both to the bishop and the father of Lawrence, who took him by the right hand and dedicated him to God and St Kevin.

The pious youth was then entirely committed to the careful tuition of the bishop and his worthy chaplain; and not often in the uncertain allotments of human character, has it occurred that the profession and the heart were so well harmonized. The temper of the youth was constitutionally pious and contemplative; he was gifted with a sensible, yet bold firm and lofty spirit, and with no small share of that ideality which gives external scenery a powerful influence over the breast: and the scene in which he was now to receive daily lessons in piety and goodness was happily adapted to such a frame of mind. Here with the mingled piety and superstition of his age, he walked the solemn mountain-vale as we explore some ancient cathedral, among the time-worn inscriptions and decaying effigies of old-world piety and virtue: its picturesque gloom was tinged with the coloured radiance of old tradition, which the broad daylight of recent ages had not yet dispelled, or the profane humour of modern showmen turned into caricature. A gleam of tender and sacred recollection invested the footsteps of the good saint who fled hither from the allurements of the world. In such a scene it was, and amid the atmosphere of such impressions and influences, that the youthful Lawrence O'Toole continued to grow in knowledge and piety as he advanced in years, until the fame of his learning and the lustre of his virtues, added grace and

* Lanigan's Eccles. Hist., Vol. iv.

sanctity to a place already so venerated for the memory of its good and holy men.

When he was twenty-five years of age, he was elected abbot of the monastery of Glendalough. Of this monastery, Dr Lanigan says, that it was distinct from the bishopric, with which it has not unfrequently been confounded. It was very rich, and had usually been placed under the government of abbots chosen for the rank and power of their families; a precaution rendered necessary for the protection of the surrounding district, by the predatory and encroaching temper of the age.

In this high and influential station, the value of his character was soon extensively manifested, his instructions were effectively diffused by that moral energy of character which appears to be his distinguishing feature in history; and his precepts were beautifully illustrated by the practice of all the Christian virtues. With a wise anxiety for the social amelioration of his country, he exerted himself with industrious zeal to civilize the manners and correct the barbarous habits of the people; and with an equally intense solicitude he watched with a paternal care over their wants and interests; and, as the people are most likely to retain the memory of those attentions which they can best comprehend, Lawrence O'Toole has ever been especially praised for his charity to the poor and needy. A famine, which lasted for four years during this period of his life, gave ample exercise to this virtue, and doubtless impressed it deeply on the hearts of thousands, to whom during so dreadful a visitation he was the dispenser of mercy.*

On the death of the bishop of Glendalough, the dignity was pressingly offered to the youthful abbot; but conscious of the immaturity of his years, and sensible of the importance of the charge, he declined the office, and continued in the faithful discharge of his duties until the death of the bishop of Dublin, in 1161, whom he then succeeded. It is at this period that his life in some measure falls into the general history of the country; and being already fully detailed so far as detail can have importance, may be more briefly noticed.

Shortly after his elevation to the see of Dublin, the bishop assumed the habit of an order of French monks famed for the severity of their discipline and the sanctity of their lives; and ever after wore under his episcopal habiliments, the hair shirt prescribed by the severe discipline of that ascetic order. He also observed its rule of keeping strict silence for certain prescribed hours, and always attended with his canons at the midnight offices in Christ Church; after which, "he often remained alone in the church, praying and singing psalms until daylight, when he used to take a round in the churchyard or cemetry, chaunting the prayers for the faithful departed." To this his historians add striking examples of austere abstinence, which, however they may be estimated by the theology of more enlightened times, cannot be erroneously referred to the sincere and devoted faith of this good Christian, who acted according to the best lights which it pleased the Father of all lights to bestow upon his age. Less doubtful was

* Lanigan, 175.

his eminent practice of those pure and holy charities which the scripture teaches us to regard as the "fruits of the Spirit;" his regard to the morals, religion, and sustenance of the poor, was only bounded by his means. Every day he took care to see fed in his presence from thirty to sixty needy persons. In the severe famines which were the consequence of the desolating wars of his time, and which on one occasion lasted for three years, he daily fed five hundred persons.

Many indeed are the accounts of beneficence and of high but rigid sanctity, which, scattered loosely among the doubtful mass of the idlest traditions, are yet in O'Toole's case authenticated by their characteristic consistency, and which combine to throw a venerable lustre round his memory. It is stated by historians, that in his day the absolution which the church assumed the power to give, had been for a time prostituted with lavish indifference to the state of the heart or the nature of the crime; archbishop O'Toole exerted himself to repress an abuse so dangerous, by refusing to give the pardon of the church in certain extreme cases unfit to be mentioned in this work.

While in the see of Dublin, the general character of his life and actions has been placed in a conspicuous light by the historical magnitude and importance of events in which his name occupies a respectable place. These events have been told already in the political series of this period. The reader has already seen, that while he was the life and spirit of his country in its efforts to resist invasion, he was no less an object of respect to the English. Above the low level of the wisdom and patriotism of that degenerate day of Irish history, the exalted sense and spirit of the archbishop rose pre-eminent. About the real character of his patriotism there can be little doubt: there is but too much justice in the casuistry which finds a large proportion of base alloy in the purest seeming course of public conduct:—

> "Whate'er of noblest and of best
> Man's soul can reach, is clogged and prest
> By low considerations, that adhere
> Inseparably."*

This doctrine may be easily pushed too far. In our day it might be referred to party or to sect, but it was then otherwise. To understand this rightly, it must be observed that archbishop O'Toole, in common with the other Irish bishops of his day, had one prominent object in view—to bring the Irish church into the jurisdiction of the Roman see. For this, the clearest and shortest way was the subjection of the country to England, of which the church acknowledged the supremacy of Rome. It was for this reason that in the course of these wars, the Irish bishops, with a large party among their clergy, are to be traced in constant negotiations favourable to the interests of the settlement. O'Toole, who worked more than all of them for their common purpose, alone spurned the unworthy means; and rejecting the fiendish illusion of doing evil that good might come, he boldly put himself forward in behalf of his own country, and by his spirited exertions organized at least the show of resistance. It was, however, in vain, in the absence of all national spirit and of all sense

* Faust, p. 42.

of common cause, that this patriotic archbishop endeavoured to infuse life and unity into that senseless chaos of provincial feuds, interests, and tyrannies; as among the evil "πολυκοιρανιη," the aristocracy of squabbling thrones, principalities, and powers, one breast only was found to catch a gleam of the patriot's spirit—the ill-fated Roderic; and Lawrence O'Toole, when the hopes of the warrior's arm were found unavailing, still found a duty not unworthy in the office of a mediator between the conqueror and the fallen foe. It should not indeed be left unmentioned in proof of his eminent and conspicuous virtues, that Giraldus, who looked on every thing native with a prejudiced eye, calls him "a just and good man;" nor is it less to his honour, that Henry, who was known to dislike him for his bold and uncompromising patriotism, could not help respecting his person. He was indeed so much employed as the medium of the most difficult and delicate negotiations with the hostile powers during the struggle, and with the English court afterwards, that, considering the looseness of public faith, and the capricious and arbitrary deviations which mark the conduct of the tyrants of that age, one cannot help pausing to wonder and to conceive more distinctly the state of circumstances, and the assemblage of impressive virtues which seemed as with a charmed influence to carry the worthy archbishop unharmed, uninsulted, and without fear, through hostile camps and courts. On one occasion, when Dublin was exposed to the horrors and revolting atrocities of a stormed city, some of our readers will recollect the conduct of the archbishop, equally characteristic of the saint, the hero, and the patriot. While all was devastation, fury and terror, flight and helpless panic, while the streets rung with the hurried step of trembling citizens, and the gutters ran red with life-blood, "in the midst of all the confusion and massacre," says Mr Moore, "the good St Lawrence was seen exposing himself to every danger, and even as his biographer describes him, dragging from the enemies hands the palpitating bodies of the slain, to have them decently interred. He also succeeded at great risk, in prevailing upon the new authorities to retain most of the clergy in their situations, and recovered from the plunderers the books and ornaments which had belonged to the different churches."

Henry, it has been mentioned, disliked him; but his dislike was of that pardonable description which kings or parties may be permitted to feel (for such is the law of human feeling,) against those whose virtues are unfavourable to their partial aims. St Lawrence, whatever duties he acknowledged to king Henry, did not consider himself exempt from the prior and paramount duty which he owed to the King of kings and Lord of lords, whose servant he was. The immunities of the Irish church, for which he always held out firmly, and for which he had the honour to plead at the council of Lateran, which he attended with other Irish bishops, gave offence to Henry, whose construction of those privileges placed them at variance with his prerogative. But the upright Lawrence, incapable of subserviency, knew that all temporal duties must be limited by the superior and more important duties to God, so far as they are clearly and authentically known, and acted as all, whether rightly or erroneously, should act, according to the dictates of conscience; a law which however latitudinarian it will seem to those who rightly contemplate the vast and multiform tendencies of human error, will, after all deductions, keep its ground as the most universal and compendious normal, on which all duty stands, and all virtue consists. It is indeed the principle which gives so much profound importance to the question of Pilate, awful when it cannot be answered with the utmost clearness—" What is truth ?"

When he was attending king Henry at Canterbury, he had a most providential escape from being assassinated by a lunatic. We can do no better than tell the story as we find it in *Hanmer's Chronicle*. " He came to the king at Canterbury, where the monks received him with solemn procession, and hee gave himself one whole night to prayers before St Thomas his shrine, for good success in his affairs with the king. A fool espied him in his pontifical weed, wholly devoted to St Thomas Becket, and said, ' I can do no better deed than make him equal with St Thomas,' with that he took a club, ranne through the throng, and gave him such a blow upon the pate, that the blood ran down his ears. The man was so sore wounded, that it was thought he would yield up the ghost. The cry was up, the fool ranne away, the bishop taking breath, called for water, and in a short time was healed."

After a life of indefatigable zeal and goodness, in 1180, revered by his countrymen, respected by their enemies, trusted by the church, and though feared yet honoured by the king, this good and truly pious prelate resigned his breath and died of a fever at the monastery of Eu, in Normandy. When reminded of the propriety of making a will, he answered, "God knows I have not this moment so much as a penny under the sun." He was interred in the centre of the church of Eu, in Normandy. He was canonized by pope Honorius in 1226, when his remains were placed in a silver shrine over the altar.

Among the various notices which remain of the life of Lawrence O'Toole, there is a common agreement which cannot be misinterpreted as to the main incidents which fix his character as most illustriously exempt from the vices and common infirmities which are the main colouring of history, and as nobly endowed with knowledge and public spirit beyond his countrymen in that unenlightened age. In awarding with the most cordial sincerity the still higher praise of sanctity, we must not be so far misunderstood as to be supposed to acquiesce in the errors of his darkened age; these he held honestly in common with the best and wisest of his time, when the chair of philosophy was hung with the cobwebs of the schoolmen, and a despotic superstition whose foundations rested in the depths of earth, while its towers and battlements concealed amid the clouds of heaven, overshadowed the mind of the world. But if St Lawrence worshipped at the shrine of Canterbury, he was what can with the same certainty be said of few, in an hour of triple darkness, according to his lights—the faithful servant of God; he was a pious Christian, a worthy and upright citizen, a patriot *sans peur, et sans reproche:* acting through the whole of his long life in the higher and earlier sense of this motto, debased in its applications by the degeneracy of modern times.

Of O'Toole's personal appearance, Mr Dalton's research enables us to give some account, which may best be offered in his own language. "St Lawrence is represented as having been tall, and graceful in stature, of a comely presence, and in his outward habit grave though rich."

Among the characteristic recollections which often help to give their beautiful and softened tone to the colouring of the sterner lines of the characters of great men, the heroes of virtue, none diffuse a glow so chastely pure as those which indicate the freshness and wholeness with which the uncontaminated heart retains to the last the fond and almost sacred impressions of earliest years—indications which while they affect us with the soft force of tender feeling, contrasted with stern and lofty strength, also never fail to convey a profound and sensible impression of the deep corruption that mingles in the current of social existence. To find peace unembittered, purity unsullied, spirit unchilled, it is necessary to go back to the scenes where remain for ever fixed, the bright, pure, fresh associations of those early years before life began to unfold those fatal poison seeds in man's nature, which undeveloped—

"Men were children still,
In all but life's delusive wisdom, wise."

In the leisure intervals of his busy life the archbishop was wont to retire to Glendalough, where among the scenes of his youth, he might recal many peaceful and blessed recollections of hours of heaven-seeking meditation, and hear the old monastery's familiar bell (if bell it had) echoing from St Kevin's hollow cliff, with the same feeling which the German poet puts into the lips of a far different character.

"Oh once in boyhood's time, the love of heaven
Came down upon me with mysterious kiss,
Hallowing the stillness of the Sabbath-day!
Then did the voices of these bells melodious
Mingle with hopes and feelings mystical;
And prayer was then indeed a burning joy!
Feelings resistless, incommunicable,
Drove me a wand'rer through fields and woods;
Then tears rush'd hot and fast—then was the birth
Of a new life and a new world for me."*

* Faust, p. 52.

MALACHY, ARCHBISHOP OF ARMAGH.

DIED A. D. 1148.

MALACHY, called by the Irish, Maelmedoic O'Morgair, was abbot of Bangor, and afterwards bishop of Connor. He was appointed by Celsus (archbishop of Armagh), on his death-bed, as his successor, but did not obtain the see for some years; for "one Maurice, son of Donald, a person of noble birth, for five years held that see in possession, not as a bishop, but as a tyrant, for the ambition of some in power had at that time introduced a diabolical custom, of pretending to ecclesiastical sees by hereditary succession, not suffering any bishops but the descendants of their own families."* Nor was this kind of execrable succession of short continuance: for fifteen generations the system was persevered in, and great abuses were its natural consequence. Malachy did not retain the archbishopric for more than about three years, when he resigned it to Gelasy, about 1137, and retired to Down, where he founded a monastery. He went to Rome for the purpose of obtaining two palls from Innocent the second, one for Armagh, and the other for Dublin, but was dismissed with the answer, "That a matter of so great concern ought to be done with solemnity, and by the general approbation of the council of Ireland." He afterwards undertook another journey to Rome, but was taken ill on the road, and died at the monastery of Clarevall, on the 2d of November, 1148, in the 54th year of his age.

GREGORY, FIRST ARCHBISHOP OF DUBLIN.

CONSECRATED BISHOP A. D. 1121.—DIED A. D. 1161.

THIS ecclesiastic, with those immediately preceding, may be considered as a link between the former period and that with which we are at present occupied: as in point of time he may be considered as belonging to the one while his station implies a change by which he is connected with the succeeding order.

Gregory succeeded Samuel O'Haingly in the see of Dublin, and was consecrated at Lambeth, October 2d, 1121, by Ralph, archbishop of Canterbury, assisted by the bishops of London, Salisbury, Lincoln, Norwich, and Bangor. Augustin Magraidan, calls him "a wise man, and one well-skilled in languages," and he was highly esteemed both by the clergy and people of Dublin. He presided over this see about thirty-one years, when he was invested with the pall by John Paparo, and Christian O'Conarchy (O'Conor), bishop of Lismore, both legates from the pope, at a synod convened at Kells, A. D. 1152. About this period many of the bishops of Ireland, and particularly Maurice M'Donald, of Armagh, evinced great jealousy against the clergy and people of Dublin, for their preference of and adherence to the jurisdiction of Canterbury, (established for about a century,) in opposition to the practice of all the other sees, which were subjected to the control

* Bernard.

of their own hierarchy. Limerick and Waterford had adopted
the same practice, had been placed by the decree of the synod of
Rathbreasil, under the archbishop of Cashel. Ireland was about
this time divided into ecclesiastical provinces, and four archbishops
were appointed to preside over them; while the number of bishoprics
were reduced, and a certain proportion of them subjected to the control of each archbishop. Gelasius was appointed to the diocese of
Armagh, Gregory to that of Dublin, Donatus to Cashel, and Edanus
to Tuam. The bishoprics placed under the government of the archbishop of Dublin were, Glendalough, Ferns, Leighlin, Ossory, and
Kildare. A number of minor ecclesiastical arrangements were also
made, and the collection of tithes established by the cardinal. Princes,
bishops, abbots, and chiefs, were collected at this synod, and besides
the prelates, there were, according to the *Annals of the Four Masters*,
three thousand other ecclesiastics present. Gregory continued to
govern this see until 1161, when he died on the 8th of October, after
an incumbency of forty years.

JOHN COMYN.

SUCCEEDED A. D. 1181.—DIED A. D. 1212.

JOHN COMYN, a native of England, who was a particular favourite
of Henry II. and his chaplain, was recommended by him for the archbishopric of Dublin, and was accordingly elected to it on the 6th of
September, 1181. He was afterwards ordained priest at Velletri, and
on Palm-sunday, March 21st, was consecrated at the same place archbishop, by pope Lucius III. He there obtained a bull from the pope,
dated April 13th, 1182, in which there is the following passage :—
" In pursuance also of the authority of the holy canons, we order and
decree that no archbishop or bishop, shall, without the assent of the
archbishop of Dublin, (if in a bishopric within his province,) presume
to celebrate any synod, or to handle any causes or ecclesiastical matters
of the same diocese, unless enjoined thereto by the Roman pontiff or
his legate." The copy of this bull may be seen in an ancient registry
of the archbishop of Dublin, called *Crede Mihi*. A very sharp controversy arose afterwards between the archbishops of Armagh and
Dublin, on the subject of this privilege, which did not terminate for
centuries. *Cambrensis*, who knew the archbishop, states, that he was
at the time of his consecration, created cardinal priest at Velletri; but
Ware disputes this, as it is not alluded to, either in the bull of pope
Lucius, in Comyn's characters, or in Onuphrius, or Ciacorims, who
have published a catalogue of the cardinals. Comyn came to his see,
September, 1184, to prepare for the reception of earl John, whom
Henry II. was sending over as governor of Ireland. John gave him
in 1185, the reversion of the bishopric of Glendalough, when it should
become vacant, and also granted him a remarkable charter, which entitled him and his successors to hold courts, and administer justice
throughout Ireland; but it does not appear that any of his successors

exercised either civil or ecclesiastical jurisdiction beyond the dioceses of their own archbishopric. Comyn assisted at the coronation of Richard I., on the 3d of September, 1189, and was a witness to that monarch's letters patent, for surrendering to William, king of Scotland, the castles of Rockbork and Berwick, which he acknowledged to have been his hereditary right. He was also present at the council which appointed the regency during the king's absence in the Holy Land. Roger Hoveden gives an account of the various injuries inflicted on this prelate, by Hamo de Valonis, lord-justice of Ireland, which made the archbishop determine to leave the kingdom rather than be subjected to a continuance of them. He first, however, excommunicated all those who had done him wrong, and laid an interdict upon his archbishopric. He then went to earl John to obtain redress of his grievances, and to demand restitution of what had been forcibly taken from him. Not receiving the prompt and efficient aid that he expected, he fled to France, and appealed to pope Innocent III., who wrote a remonstrance to John upon the occasion, and also complained of the archbishop having been unreasonably detained in Normandy. This appeal, although it effected Comyn's present purposes, and that Hamo was in consequence recalled from the government, caused a long and bitter enmity against the archbishop on the part of John, which does not seem to have been removed until 1206, when the king again received him into favour, and commanded the lord-justice in Ireland both to protect him from all injuries, and also to make every possible restitution to him for the losses he had sustained. Hamo also, who had greatly enriched himself before leaving Ireland, seems to have at length become conscious of his own injustice, and to expiate his crime, gave to the archbishop and his successors (in free alms,) twenty plough-lands in the territory of Ucunil. The account of this is given by John Alan, a subsequent archbishop, in his registry, which is called the *Black Book of the Archbishop of Dublin*, a copy of which is in Marsh's library. Comyn is described as a man of learning, gravity, and eloquence, and a very munificent benefactor to the church. He built and endowed as a collegiate church, St Patrick's cathedral in Dublin, about the year 1190, and in part repaired and enlarged the choir of Christ's church. He also founded and endowed a convent of nuns in Dublin, which took its name *a Gratia Dei*, and was commonly called *Grace Dieu*. Dempster asserts Comyn to have been a Scotchman, born at Banff, and descended from the earls of Buchan, but there does not seem to be any good authority for this statement. The constitutions and canons made by this prelate, and confirmed under the leaden seal of pope Urban III., are yet extant among the archives preserved in Christ's church, Dublin. His mortal remains are also deposited there, where there is a marble monument erected to his memory on the south side of the choir. His death took place in Dublin, on the 25th of October, 1212.

As the regulations and canons made by this prelate are curious in themselves, and many of them still binding, we subjoin them. The synod at which they were agreed to was held in the year 1186 in Dublin, in the church of the Holy Trinity:—

" The 1st. Prohibits priests from celebrating mass on a wooden table according to the usage of Ireland; and enjoins that, in all monasteries and baptismal churches, altars should be made of stone; and if a stone of sufficient size to cover the whole surface of the altar cannot be had, that in such a case a square entire and polished stone be fixed in the middle of the altar, where Christ's body is consecrated, and of a compass broad enough to contain five crosses, and also to bear the foot of the largest chalice. But in chapels, chauntries, or oratories, if they are necessarily obliged to use wooden altars, let the mass be celebrated upon plates of stone of the before-mentioned size, firmly fixed in the wood.

"2d. Provides that the coverings of the holy mysteries may spread over the whole upper part of the altar; and that a cloth may cover the front of the same, and reach to the ground. These coverings to be always whole and clean.

"3d. That in monasteries and rich churches chalices be provided of gold and silver; but in poorer churches, where such cannot he afforded, that then pewter chalices may serve the purpose, which must be always kept whole and clean.

"4th. That the host, which represents the Lamb without spot, the alpha and omega, be made so white and pure, that the partakers thereof may thereby understand the purifying and feeding of their souls rather than their bodies.

"5th. That the wine in the sacrament be so tempered with water, that it be not deprived either of the natural taste and colour.

"6th. That all the vestments and coverings belonging to the church, be clean, fine, and white.

"7th. That a lavatory of stone or wood be set up, and so contrived with a hollow, that whatever is poured into it may pass through, and lodge in the earth; through which also the last washing of the priests' hands after the holy communion may pass.

"8th. Provides that an immoveable font be fixed in the middle of every baptismal church, or in such other part of it as the paschal procession may conveniently pass round. That it be made of stone, or of wood lined with lead for cleanness, wide and large above, bored through to the bottom, and so contrived that after the ceremony of baptism be ended, a secret pipe be so contrived therein as to convey the holy water down to mother earth.

"9th. That the coverings of the altar, and other vestments dedicated to God, when injured by age, be burnt within the inclosure of the church, and the ashes of them transmitted through the aforesaid pipe of the font to be buried in the bowels of the earth.

"10th. Prohibits any vessel used in baptism to be applied ever after to any of the common uses of man.

"11th. Prohibits, under the pain of an anathema, any person to bury in a churchyard, unless he can show by an authentic writing, or undeniable evidence, that it was consecrated by a bishop, not only as a sanctuary or place of refuge, but also for a place of sepulture; and that no laymen shall presume to bury their dead in such a consecrated place without the presence of a priest.

"12th. Prohibits the celebration of divine service in chapels built by laymen to the detriment of the mother churches.

"13th. Since the clergy of Ireland, among other virtues, have been always remarkably eminent for their chastity, and that it would be ignominious, if they should be corrupted through his (the archbishop's) negligence, by the foul contagion of strangers, and the example of a few incontinent men, he therefore forbids, under the penalty of losing both office and benefice, that priest, deacon, or subdeacon, should keep any woman in their houses, either under the pretence of necessary service, or any other colour whatsoever; unless a mother, own sister, or such a person whose age should remove any suspicion of unlawful commerce.

" 14th. Contains an interdict against simony, under the before-mentioned penalty of losing both office and benefice.

" 15th. Appoints that if any clerk should receive an ecclesiastical benefice from a lay-hand, unless, after a third monition, he renounce that possession which he obtained by intrusion, that he should be anathematized, and for ever deprived of the said benefice.

" 16th. Prohibits a bishop from ordaining the inhabitant of any other diocese, without commendary letters of his proper bishop, or of the archdeacon ; nor that any one be promoted to holy orders without a certain title to a benefice assigned to him.

" 17th. Prohibits the conferring on one person two holy orders in one day.

" 18th. Provides that all fornicators shall be compelled to celebrate a lawful marriage, and also that no person born in fornication should be promoted to holy orders, nor should be esteemed heir to either father or mother, unless they be afterwards joined in lawful matrimony.

" 19th. Provides that tythes be paid to the mother churches out of provisions, hay, the young animals, flax, wool, gardens, orchards, and out of all things that grow and renew yearly, under the pain of an anathema, after the third monition; and that those who continue obstinate in refusing to pay, shall be obliged to pay more punctually in future.

" 20th. Provides that all archers, and all others who carry arms, not for the defence of the people, but for plunder and sordid lucre, shall on every Lord's day be excommunicated by bell, book, and candle, and at last be refused christian burial."*

HENRY DE LOUNDRES.

CONSECRATED A. D. 1213—DIED A. D. 1228.

HENRY DE LOUNDRES, or the Londoner, archdeacon of Strafford, was elected to the archiepiscopal see of Dublin, immediately on the death of Comyn. He was consecrated early in the following year, and was present in the year 1213 when king John executed his degrading charter, surrendering the crowns of England and Ireland to Pandulph the pope's legate. Henry resolutely protested against it, and refused to subscribe to it as a witness, or as in any degree sanc-

* Harris's Ware.

tioning the proceeding. It concludes, *Teste rege, coram Henrico archiepiscopo Dublinensi et aliis*, and not *his testibus*. He seems to have stood high in the favour of John, and to have proved himself a very faithful servant to him. In the July of this year he was appointed lord-justice of Ireland, and continued to fill this office until the year 1215, when he was summoned to Rome to assist at a general council. He appointed Jeffry de Mariscis to conduct the affairs of the kingdom in his absence, under the title of Custos of Ireland;* and, making England his way to Rome, he was present, and of the council, together with the archbishop of Canterbury, and other bishops, and barons of England, when the king executed the *Magna Charta*, and charter of the forests at *Runnemede;* and his name is mentioned in the said charters, as one of the persons by whose advice the king granted these liberties to his subjects. Some historians assert that Henry built the castle of Dublin at his own cost, but this, at all events, is certain, that it was erected by his exertions. He expended large sums for John, not only when he was lord-justice of Ireland, but when he went to Rome—as much to solicit aid† for John against the barons as to attend at the general council. While he was lord-justice of Ireland he had to supply the kings of Ireland, and others of the king's liege subjects, with scarlet cloth for their robes at his own expense; and John's short and troubled reign prevented his ever being reimbursed by him. He was personally engaged in many of the most important occurrences of this reign, and was selected to conduct Stephen Langton, archbishop of Canterbury, and the rest of the exiled bishops, into the king's presence. Henry III. did not forget the archbishop's services to his father; and accordingly we find that in the twelfth year of his reign he issued a writ to the lord-justice, reciting his obligations to this prelate, and stating that he had granted him the custodium to all vacant archbishoprics and bishoprics in Ireland, the profits to be received by John St John, bishop of Ferns and treasurer of Ireland, and G. de Theurville, archdeacon of Dublin, until the debts due by the crown to the archbishop should be paid. The king also in the same year issued another writ to Richard de Burgo, lord-justice, letting him know that he had assigned one hundred pounds out of the farm rent of the city of Limerick, and fifty marks a-year out of the farm rent of the city of Dublin, toward the payment of debts due by the late king to the archbishop. In the year 1219, the archbishop again took the reins of government into his hands, and for five years faithfully discharged the trust committed to him, but was afterwards accused of trenching on the rights of the crown for the benefit of the church; by which he both offended the king, and irritated the people committed to his charge. So far back as the year 1217, he had been appointed legate by pope Honorius III.; and in 1225 the pope sent a bull to this prelate, authorizing him to excommunicate all such as detained the king's castles in Ireland from him. The see of Glendalough was first united to the see of Dublin under this archbishop, at the distance of about six centuries from the death of St Kevin, its first bishop. He augmented the revenues of *Grace*

* Mathew Paris. † Cox.

Dieu, erected the collegiate church of St Patrick, built by his predecessors, into a cathedral, and neglected no opportunity of advancing the interests of the church. There is a story told, not very creditable to him, by which he obtained the nick-name of *Scorch-villein.* He summoned his tenants, according to the statement in the *Black Book of the Archbishop of Dublin,* to give an account by what title they held lands, and immediately, on getting the deeds into his hands, he flung them all into the fire. He held the archbishopric for fifteen years, and died about the beginning of July, 1228, and is said to be buried at the north wall of Christ's Church, opposite to Comyn, where there had been a wooden monument; but there is at present nothing to mark the spot.

FULK DE SAUNDFORD.

CONSECRATED, A. D. 1256.—DIED, A. D. 1271.

FULK DE SAUNDFORD, a native of England, an archdeacon of Middlesex, and a treasurer of St Paul's, London, was appointed archbishop of Dublin, July 20, 1256. In the interval between the death of archbishop Luke and this appointment, Ralph of Norwich, a canon of St Patrick's, had been elected by both chapters to the vacant see, but this nomination was set aside by the pope; and, according to the statements of Mathew Paris, it would appear, on just grounds. He describes him as being "witty and pleasant, and one who loved good cheer," and from being chancellor of Ireland, he was necessarily engrossed in secular occupations. Ware states, on an ancient authority, that he lost his election by the treachery of his own people, "by whom he was betrayed" in the court of Rome. Fulk obtained a license from the pope to retain his treasurership and other benefices, and by subsequent bulls gained many additional privileges and preferments, amongst which was the deanery of St Michael of Penkeriz, in the diocese of Coventry, which had before been granted to Henry de Loundres, and which was now annexed to the see of Dublin for ever. In 1261 he visited Rome, when he complained of the illegal interferences of the king's justiciaries in ecclesiastical matters, and their wresting from the clergy their established rights; sheltering offenders, and restraining the due collection of sums appropriated to religious purposes. On this representation, pope Urban issued a bull condemnatory of such practices, and threatening excommunication if persevered in. During the absence of De Saundford, the bishops of Lismore and Waterford superintended and transacted the business of the see. After his return from Rome he visited England, where he remained for a long period; but was sent by king Henry to Ireland in 1265, along with the bishop of Meath, Lords William de Burgo, and Fitz-Maurice Fitz-Gerald, in the capacity of commissioners, to quiet the contentions of that kingdom.

The archbishop found on his return that the mayor and citizens of Dublin had been interfering with the revenues of the church, and had resorted to very arbitrary means to limit his power and diminish his finances. Finding all threats and admonitions ineffectual, he excommunicated the offenders, and put the city under an interdict; sending at the same time to desire the bishops of Lismore and Waterford to denounce them as excommunicated persons through the province of Dublin. In the year following, the contending parties were reconciled through the interposition of Sir Robert de Ufford, lord-justice, and the privy council, when the citizens made all just concessions. It would appear, however, that their rebellious and contumelious spirit had been merely curbed, not quelled; for in 1270 prince Edward, to whom his father had given the sovereignty of Ireland, received information of an attempt made on the life of De Saundford and his companions, which, though then unsuccessful, would probably be repeated in a more determined manner, and with fatal results. He accordingly ordered that every protection should be extended to him, that he should be granted whatever aids or powers he might require for the establishment of his ecclesiastical authority, and commanded the government steadily to repress all infringement on the rights or liberties of the church.

Archbishop Fulk did not long survive. He was attacked with his last illness at Finglass, and died in his own manor, May 6th, 1271, having governed the see about fifteen years. His body was taken to St Patrick's church, and buried in Mary's chapel, which Ware thinks had been founded by himself. The archbishopric remained unfilled for seven years, owing to the opposing elections of individuals, combined with other less prominent causes. In the month following the archbishop's death the king granted a license for the election of William de la Comer, chaplain to the pope, who was subsequently promoted to the see of Salisbury, but on the same day the dean and chapter of St Patrick's appointed Fromun le Brun, who was then chancellor of Ireland. This led to long and virulent controversies, which remained unsettled until 1279, when the pope rejected the claims of both, and appointed John de Derlington to the vacant see. On the death of Fulk, Henry III. granted the chief profits of this see to prince Edward, to aid in the expense of his expedition to the Holy Land, and issued a writ to John de Saundford, his eschcator of Ireland, to prevent any interference from him in this appropriation. He also ordered, if any of the funds had been collected, that they should be at once paid back to the attorneys of the prince. In the year 1272, when Edward the first ascended the throne, he entrusted the management of the temporalities of this see to Thomas Chedworth, and directed the chief-justice of Ireland to present to the vacant benefices, as in the right of the crown. In some of the records of this period, Robert de Provend is mentioned as bishop of Dublin, but he evidently could only have been entitled to this denomination by having been an assistant, or deputy, to Fulk during his various absences, as he did not either receive the revenues, or exercise the privileges or functions of an archbishop. In 1275, the prior of the chapter to the convent of the Holy Trinity asserted that he had the right, during the vacancy of the see, to appoint to the archdeaconry of Dublin, which the king and his justices steadily resisted; and this dispute remained unsettled until the elevation of John de Derlington took from both parties any further claim to the appointment.

RICHARD DE FERINGS.

DIED A. D. 1306.

ON the death of William de Hothum, there was a contest between Christ's church and that of St Patrick's, as to the nomination of an archbishop of Dublin—the former selecting Adam de Balsham their prior, and the latter Thomas de Chatsworth, dean of St Patrick's, and also chief-justice of the King's Bench, to the vacant see; to which he had been on a former occasion elected by the king and clergy, but was set aside by the authority of the pope. Neither of these elections, however, at this time pleased the king; and an interval occurring, the pope asserted his title to nominate, and appointed Richard de Ferings, who had been for a long period archdeacon of Canterbury, and who was consecrated in 1299. This prelate made a large conveyance of church lands to Theobald Fitz-Walter, butler of Ireland, with the sanction of the chapters of the Holy Trinity and St Patrick's. He also, says Ware, "took a great deal of pains to reconcile the differences between the two cathedrals, the heads of which composition are in the register of Alan (archbishop of Dublin), whereof these are the chief:—" That the archbishops of Dublin should be consecrated and enthroned in Christ's church; that each church should be called cathedral and metropolitan; that Christ's church as being the greater, the mother and elder church, should take place in all church rights and concerns; that the cross, mitre, and ring of the archbishop, wherever he should die, be deposited in Christ's church; and that the body of every archbishop that died for the future be buried in either church, by turns, unless he disposed of it otherwise by his will." These articles were written and agreed to in 1300; and after having thus established peace in his diocese, he went to England, and subsequently to the continent, where he remained for many years. He at length determined on returning to Ireland, but was attacked with a sudden illness in the course of his journey, of which he died the 18th of October, 1306.

ALEXANDER DE BICKNOR.

SUCCEEDED A. D. 1317.—DIED A. D. 1349.

NOTWITHSTANDING the articles of agreement formally entered into between the two cathedral churches of Dublin, and confirmed by the seal of each chapter, with a penalty annexed to their infringement, the usual contests commenced on the death of archbishop Lech, respecting the appointment of a successor: one party declared for Walter Thornbury, chanter of St Patrick's and chancellor of Ireland; while the other nominated Alexander de Bicknor, or Bignor, the descendant of a distinguished English family, and treasurer of Ireland. Walter, thinking to secure his election at once, took shipping for France, where the pope then resided, but was overtaken by a violent storm, and he with the entire of the crew and passengers, amounting to 150 persons, perished. Alexander was accordingly elected without opposition, but his consecration was delayed in consequence of his personal services being required by the king. He was sent by Edward II. along with Raymond Subirani, and Andrew Sapiti, to transact some business of importance, relative to his foreign dominions with the cardinals attending on the pope, at Avignon; to twenty-four of whom the king wrote special letters.* He was three years afterwards consecrated in this place, July 22d, 1317, by Nicholas de Prato, cardinal of Ostium. Edward, who appears to have held him in high estimation, appointed him lord-justice of Ireland, in 1318, and he arrived there on the 9th of October, in the joint character of archbishop, and governor of the kingdom, and was received both by the clergy and people with great demonstrations of joy. He had been previously directed by pope John XXII., to excommunicate Robert Bruce and his brother Edward, with all their followers, unless restitution was made for their destructive and sacrilegious ravages throughout the kingdom. He attended several parliaments in England, was present in the palace of Westminster when the bishop of Winchester surrendered the great seal, and was also a party with the king in the treaty made with the earl of Lancaster.

In 1320, he founded or rather renewed the university founded by his predecessor John Lech, and procured a confirmation of it from Pope John XXII. It had doctors of divinity, a doctor of the canon law, and a chancellor, besides inferior officers. There were public lectures established, and at a later period a divinity lecture by Edward III.; but from want of proper aid for the maintenance of the scholars it gradually declined, though Ware says, "there remained some footsteps of an academy in the time of Henry VII." According to the same writer, Bicknor was sent ambassador to France by the English parliament in 1323, along with Edmund de Woodstock, earl of Kent, younger brother of Edward II.; but this embassy proved unsuccessful. He was also afterwards joined in a commission with the same earl, to reform the government of Acquitaine, but ultimately fell under the king's heavy displeasure for consenting to the surrender of the town and castle of La Royalle, in that duchy, to the French. He was one of the accusers of Hugh de Spencer, which so irritated the king that he wrote a letter to the pope, entreating that he might be banished from his kingdom, and that another might be appointed to the see. The application of this weak and vindictive monarch was however disregarded at Rome; and we find him again taking his place among the prelates and barons of England in 1326, when prince Edward was appointed guardian of the kingdom. The king, however, found means to punish the archbishop by seizing on the revenues of his see, on the pretence of arrears being due to him from the time of Bicknor having been treasurer of Ireland; this money was appropriated to the expenses of his army. The archbishop took a strong and creditable part against Ledred, bishop of Ossory, who prosecuted several persons accused of heresy. These persons boldly seized Ledred, and kept him in confinement until they were enabled to escape

* Dalton's Archbishops.

beyond his jurisdiction, and seek the protection of Bicknor. He not only saved them from all further persecution, but when Ledred sought to appeal to Rome, he took means to prevent his journey thither; and when he ultimately succeeded in leaving Ireland, Edward's power arrested him in France, and he was there detained an exile for nine years. During this period, the archbishop exerted his power as metropolitan, and seized on the profits and jurisdiction of the diocese of Ossory. In 1331, Edward III. wrote to the pope to counteract the impressions likely to be made by the representations of Ledred against Bicknor; but his interference does not appear to have been very effectual, for the pope suspended his power over the diocese of Ossory immediately after his holding a visitation there, and the interdict continued in force during the remainder of Bicknor's life. Edward granted him a royal license in 1336, for annexing additional lands to the see, to the amount of £200 yearly.

In the following year he had a contest with David O'Hiraghty, archbishop of Armagh, who was summoned to attend a parliament in Dublin, held by Sir John Charleton, lord-justice of Ireland; when as Ware states, O'Hiraghty "made procession in St Mary's near Dublin, but was hindered by the archbishop of Dublin and clergy, because he would have the cross carried before him, which they would not permit," and this contest was carried on with more or less violence during the remainder of Bicknor's life. In 1348, the king appears to have taken part with Bicknor, as he wrote to cardinal Audomar, urging his being exempted from any subjection to Armagh; while in the year following he seems to have favoured the pretensions of Richard Fitz-Ralph, who, by asserting that he had royal authority, triumphantly entered Dublin with the cross borne erect before him. Ware, however, thinks this assertion false, and that he had received no permission from Edward on the subject; and this opinion seems confirmed by the lord-justice and others in authority sending him hastily back to Drogheda, where he was accompanied by those who supported his pretensions. Edward had always shown him particular favour, and in 1347, had extended to him a formal pardon for the charges that were against him, whether true or false, respecting the inaccuracy of his accompts when treasurer in the reign of his father. Bicknor's life was now drawing fast to a close. He died on the 14th of July, 1249, having governed the see of Dublin for nearly thirty-two years. He was remarkable for learning, wisdom, sound judgment, and exemplary morals; and in that age of civil strife, was entrusted with the management of secular as well as spiritual affairs of great importance, and managed them with a dexterity and discretion which proved that his sovereign's confidence in him was well founded. He built the Bishop's House at Tallagh, and considerably improved the lands belonging to the see. He is said to have been buried in St Patrick's cathedral, but no monument remains to mark the spot.

THOMAS CRANELY.

DIED A. D. 1417.

ON the death of Northall, archbishop of Dublin, Thomas Cranely was appointed as his successor, but he did not arrive in Dublin until late in the following year, when he accompanied the lord-lieutenant, Thomas Holland, duke of Surrey, at which time he was also appointed chancellor of the kingdom. In 1399, (the year of Richard's deposition,) he was empowered to treat with the Irish rebels; and in 1401, he was again appointed chancellor. Henry V. nominated him to the same office in 1413, and subsequently made him lord-justice of Ireland, while he held this situation he addressed a long and spirited epistle in verse to Henry, of which Leland the antiquary speaks in terms of high admiration. He was so impartial in the administration of justice, both in his official, legal, and spiritual character, that he not only obtained the testimony of Irish writers of his day, but he gave the utmost satisfaction to the king and council in England. Cox speaks of him as "a man of singular piety and learning," and Marlborough, who enlarges more upon his character, calls him "a very bountiful man, and full of alms-deeds, a profound clerk and doctor of divinity, an extraordinary fine preacher, a great builder and improver of places under his care: he was fair, sumptuous, of a sanguine complexion, and a princely stature." At the time that MacGenis, one of the Irish chieftains, obtained a victory over Jenico de Artois, his followers and the surrounding Irish became so daring and insolent, that the lord-justice was forced to go out against them in person, but did not proceed farther than Castle-Dermot; he then committed his army to a competent military commander, and remained with his clergy engaged in earnest prayers for its success. The result was favourable; but as the English were shortly after defeated in Meath, it was thought expedient to commit the government of Ireland to a military commander; and accordingly on the 10th of September, Sir John Talbot, lord Furnival, arrived as lord-lieutenant. He immediately made a progress round the pale in a warlike manner, and though he brought no additional forces with him from England, he induced all the surrounding chiefs to sue for peace. In 1416, when lord Furnival went to England, he appointed the archbishop as his deputy, who pursued the same mild and judicious line of conduct—repressing disorders, redressing grievances, and administering justice with an impartiality at that time little practised. He visited England in 1417, and died the 25th of May at Faringdon, "full of days and honour." His body was conveyed to Oxford, and buried there in New College of which he had been warden, and had also been for a time chancellor of that university.

RICHARD TALBOT.

DIED A. D. 1449.

RICHARD TALBOT, brother to the celebrated Sir John Talbot, lord of Furnival, was consecrated archbishop of Dublin in the year 1417.

He had the year before been elected to the primacy, but having neglected to hasten his confirmation in due time, John Swain was promoted in his place. His brother, who for his distinguished and faithful services in France, was in the succeeding reign created earl of Shrewsbury, Waterford, and Wexford, was now the lord-lieutenant; and when he was summoned to England in 1419, he appointed the archbishop as his deputy. In 1423 he was made lord-justice, and afterwards chancellor of Ireland, and had various grants of land assigned him for the purpose both of supporting his dignity, and rewarding his services. There were various contests between him and Swain on the subject of primatial jurisdiction, and Talbot was summoned to England on the complaint of the latter to answer the charges made against him on this subject. These complaints, however, do not appear to have had any prejudicial effect on his interests; as in 1431 he was granted the custody of two-thirds of the manor of Trim, and other lands being in the crown, in consequence of the minority of Richard, duke of York; he was also still continued as chancellor, and in 1436 was again appointed deputy of the kingdom, to Sir Thomas Stanley. On the primacy of Armagh becoming vacant, he was a second time elected to that see, but refused the appointment. In 1440 he was nominated lord-justice, and held a parliament in Dublin, at which it was enacted,

"1st. That no purveyor or harbenger should take any thing without payment; and if he did the proprietor might resist.

"2d. That comrick or protection of tories be treason.

"3d. That charging the king's subjects with horse or foot without consent, is treason.

"4th. That the party who desires a protection, (cum clausa volumus) shall make oath in Chancery of the truth of his suggestion.'

But to make provision for war, it was enacted that every twenty pound worth of land should be charged with the furnishing and maintaining an archer on horseback.*

James, earl of Ormonde, being shortly after sent over as lord-lieutenant, Talbot resigned his office, and in the subsequent administration of lord Wells, was sent to England by the parliament, along with John White, abbot of St Mary's, to the king, "to represent the miserable estate and condition of Ireland, whereby the public revenue was placed so low, that it was less than the necessary charge of keeping the kingdome by one thousand four hundred and fifty-six pounds per annum." In 1447, he was appointed deputy to his brother the earl of Shrewsbury, then lord-lieutenant, who, on his return to England, accused the earl of Ormonde of treason before the duke of Bedford, constable of England, in the Marshall's Court, but the king abolished the accusation. The archbishop wrote a tract this year, entitled, *De Abusu regiminis Jacobi Comitis Ormondiæ, dum Hiberniæ esset locum tenens.* And it seems that Thomas Fitz-Thomas, prior of Kilmainham was on the side of the archbishop, for he also accused the earl of Ormonde of treason, and the combat was appointed between

* Cox.

them at Smithfield in London, but the king interposed and prevented it. There were also champions on the opposite side, among whom was Jordan, bishop of Cork, and Cloyne whose epistle to Henry VI. upon this subject is still extant.

The contests for primatial sway between Talbot and the archbishops of Armagh were numerous, and were renewed by him and John Mey in 1446, and the three following years. In the last of these Talbot died, having held the archbishopric for nearly thirty-two years, during the entire of which time he was privy councillor to Henry V. and VI., and was buried under a marble tomb in St Patrick's church, which was ornamented with his figure cut in brass.

GEORGE BROWNE, ARCHBISHOP OF DUBLIN.

DIED A. D. 1556.

AMONG the most illustrious churchmen of the period in which we are engaged, none claims a higher place than George Browne. As the main agent of the Reformation in Ireland, he is justly entitled to that notice which belongs of right to the instruments of the Almighty in the working out of his plans, even when we are compelled to separate the character and motives of the agent from the tendency of the work effected by his instrumentality. Browne's life demands as little allowance of this nature as that of most men; but we make the remark, because his time and actions have placed his character in the arena of a great controversy, and the Roman Catholic historians, when writing with the greatest fairness of intention, have been led into the error of viewing his conduct through the medium of strong prejudices. There is one especial error against which it is indeed necessary to guard in all biographical notices which are to be found in the pages of controversial history—injustice done through the means of statements in themselves not untrue. Misstatements of fact can easily be coped with; but the tacit insinuation of a fallacious inference demands reflection and analysis—a labour disagreeable to the reader even when competent to the task. A few reflections on this fallacy will be here an appropriate preface.

It has been too much the custom of the popular adversaries of the reformation to make an uncandid attempt to throw discredit on it by the misrepresentations of individual character—a resource not more unfair than injudicious, from the facility with which it can be retorted with fatal effect in most instances. If it were possible, without an absurdity too glaring for ordinary discretion, for any hostile writer to tell us,—your creed is a spurious compound of human inventions, traceable to no adequate authority, opposed to revealed religion, or contrived for evil ends, we must admit the fairness of the issue, and can prove the contrary. But when the human infirmities of human teachers—their fears, their passions, or the errors of their lives, and, above all, the weakness of which they have been guilty under trying circumstances, are brought forward, and the least worthy constructions of which human nature will permit are affixed to all their actions, we must feel it a sacred duty to guard every reader, of whatever creed, against the fallacy of the appeal to prejudice. We protest, once for all, against the insinuation of a test by which no profession can be fairly tried, so long as its agents and teachers are subject to the laws of humanity. To give the slightest weight to *the inference*, the *conduct* which is to be condemned *must* be traced to the *creed*. If flagrant vice can be traced to a flagitious article of faith, we have done with the argument; our answer fails, and not till then. Otherwise, objections of more or less cogency must arise from the life of every man of every creed that ever has been taught or professed, save the *one man*, who alone was without sin. If, indeed, the articles of our creed were to be accredited from human authority, it might be fair enough to grope among the roots of error, among the failings of their inventors and promoters. But in all things appealing directly to a common admitted source, of which none (here concerned) deny the authority, we disclaim all reliance on the goodness or wisdom of any human being, and affirm that God himself governs his Church, and guides its changes according to his own purpose by the methods of his providence, and without any regard to the characters of the various agents he uses, who are moved to act, or whose acts are overruled according to circumstances. The case actually to come before us does not require extreme instances; we are not called on to illustrate the universal fact of human fallibility, by the vice of one eminent monster; we are not called on to execute that always nice and delicate task of exhibiting the course of examples by which the moral Governor of the universe often visibly elicits good from evil: we are to exhibit, with a faithful hand, that usual compound of human virtue and weakness, which, when truth is preserved, will ever appear in the proudest niches of biographical history, affording ample material for partial eulogy, or party misrepresentation.

We have thus far written to exonerate ourselves from the ungracious and disagreeable task of noticing remarks among our authorities, which have excited our sense of opposition, and against which we felt in fairness bound to protest.

On the shocking and barbarous murder of Allen, George Browne was appointed in his room, to the metropolitan see. He had been a friar of the order of St Augustin, in London, and provincial of the order. He had distinguished himself for some time, by the boldness of his preaching, in which he maintained the doctrines of the Reformation, which were then rapidly spreading in the English church. Fortunately for him, the tyrant, Henry VIII., who had commenced by the vain effort to put down the growth of opinions then by no means confined to a few in England, was led by many motives to adopt its views; and the doctrines, for which he might a little before have been led to the stake, were under providence, the means of opening to him the path to promotion and extended usefulness. Having been recommended to the fickle tyrant as a preacher of the doctrines he now meant to impose on his subjects, by the same force that he had previously exerted for the opposite doctrines; George Browne was consecrated by Cranmer, and other bishops on the 19th March, 1535: and on the 23d the lord-chancellor of Ireland was directed by writ to have the revenues of the see restored to the new bishop.

On his arrival in Ireland, his religious tenets were openly avowed. And not long after he had the satisfaction to receive a letter from Cromwell, containing the welcome information, that the king had renounced the authority of the see of Rome, "in spiritual affairs within his dominion of England: that it was his will that his Irish subjects should follow his commands as in England: and that he was appointed by the king as one of the commissioners for carrying his purpose into effect." Browne's answer is preserved by all his biographers, and is as follows:—

"MY MOST HONORED LORD,—Your most humble servant receiving your mandate, as one of his highness's commissioners, hath endeavoured almost to the danger and hazard of this temporal life, to procure the nobility and gentry of this nation to due obedience, in owning of his highness their supreme head, as well spiritual as temporal, and do find much oppugning therein, especially by my brother Ardmagh, who hath been the main oppugner, and so hath withdrawn most of his suffragans and clergy within his see and jurisdiction; he made a speech to them, laying a curse on the people whosoever should own his highness's supremacy; saying that this isle, as it is in their Irish chronicles, *Insula sacra*, belongs to none but the bishop of Rome, and that it was the bishop of Rome's predecessors gave it to the king's ancestors. There be two messengers by the priests of Ardmagh, and by that archbishop now lately sent to the bishop of Rome. Your lordship may inform his highness, that it is convenient to call a parliament in this nation to pass the supremacy by act; for they do not much matter his highness's commission which your lordship sent us over. This island hath been for a long time held in ignorance by the Romish orders, and as for their secular orders they be in a manner as ignorant as the people, being not able to say mass, or pronounce the words, they not knowing what they themselves say in the Roman tongue; the common people in this isle are more zealous in their blindness than the saints and martyrs were in the truth at the beginning of the gospel. I send you my very good lord these things, that your lordship and his highness may consult what is to be done. It is feared O'Neal will be ordered by the bishop of Rome to oppose your lordship's order from the king's highness, for the natives are much in number within his powers. I do pray the Lord Christ to defend your lordship from your enemies. Dublin, 4 Kalend Septembris, 1535."

In the following year a parliament was called in Dublin, by lord Grey, in which—among many important enactments, providing chiefly for the inheritance of the crown, in conformity with the similar provisions in the English statutes passed at the same time on the king's marriage with Anne Boleyn—it was further passed into a law, 28 Henry VIII., that the king was supreme head of the church of Ireland: appeals to Rome were declared illegal, and the first-fruits vested in the king. By a separate act he was also invested with the first-fruits of the bishopricks and other ecclesiastical temporalities of every denomination. The authority of the Roman see was abrogated, and its acknowledgment prohibited under the penalties of premunire. The oath of supremacy was imposed on every official person, and whoever should refuse to take it declared guilty of high treason. An English statute which prohibited all applications for faculties and dispensations, and the payment of pensions and other dues and impositions to the Roman see, was adapted to Ireland, and declared to be law. Another enactment suppressed twelve religious houses and vested their lands in the crown.

These important changes, though they were fully accommodated to the progress of the public mind in England, which had long been ripening for the reformation, cannot be denied to have been abrupt, arbitrary, and tyrannical, in Ireland, where no free breathing of opinion, no advance in social organization, had given birth to progress, and where after a long and fierce contest, favoured by the state of the country for the last four previous centuries, the church of Rome had at length cast its deep and widely spreading roots. It was therefore to be anticipated that a spirited opposition must have been roused by these propositions. In the house of Parliament, accordingly, the abolition of the pope's supremacy did call forth considerable excitement and opposition. On the occasion, Browne delivered a short speech which expressed his view of the argument in a few words, which, though far from conveying the real force of the argument, as it might now be stated, seems to have carried much weight: it affords some notion of the theological method of reasoning at the time.

"My lords and gentry of his majesty's realm of Ireland, behold your obedience to your king, is the observing of your God and your Saviour Christ, for he, that high priest of our souls paid tribute to Cesar (though no Christian), greater honour then is surely due to your prince, his highness the king, and a Christian one. Rome and her bishops in the fathers' days, acknowledged emperors, kings, and princes, to be supreme over their own dominions, nay Christ's own vicars; and it is much to the bishop of Rome's shame, to deny what their precedent bishops owned; therefore his highness claims but what he can justify. The bishop Elutherius gave to Lucius, the first Christian king of the Britains, so that I shall without scrupuling vote king Henry supreme over ecclesiastical matters, as well as temporal, and head thereof, even of both isles, England and Ireland, and without guilt of conscience or sin to God; and he who will not pass this act, as I do, is no true subject to his highness."

The act was passed, but the effect was not equal to the expectations of the peremptory despot who sat on the British throne. Henry made no account of the convictions or the conscience of others, but with the ferocious and irrespective decision of a selfish and arrogant man, presumed that the mind of a nation was to veer with the changes of his own. He could only attribute the recusancy of the Irish to the slackness of his ministers: and when he soon ascertained that, with its natural effect, oppression raised a fiercer zeal among the people in behalf of their church; his rage vented itself in threats on archbishop Browne, whose zeal was more sincere, and founded on purer motives

than his own. He wrote an angry letter, in which the archbishop
was reproached with the benefits which had been conferred on him
on the consideration of his known principles, and charged with a blameable slackness : with threats of removing him if his conduct should
not become more satisfactory.

The archbishop was naturally alarmed; he well knew the nature of
the tyrant, and the dangers with which he was himself environed on
either side, so that in fact no course was safe. While the course
which it was his most bounden duty to pursue, was such as to make
him the mark of general aversion, and demanded the exercise of much
moderation and caution, he was at the same time surrounded by the
rivalry and secret hostility of the party from which he should receive
the surest support, and urged on into the extremest steps, by the
blindfold tyranny at his back. The archbishop was fully sensible of
these dangers, and also of the necessity there was of conciliating and
soothing the royal breast, on the determinations of which both his
personal security and the difficult concerns committed to his agency
must entirely depend. He returned a submissive answer to the king,
and wrote another letter to Cromwell, in which he strongly states the
oppositions which he experienced, with the general contempt of his
authority; as an instance of which, he states, that he could not prevail
so far as to have the bishop of Rome's name cancelled from the church
books. He strongly and judiciously pressed for the appointment of
an ecclesiastical jurisdiction, in such authorities as might be competent
to the exigencies of church regulation and government under the
circumstances.

It is observed by Mr Dalton, in his useful and able work on the
archbishops of Dublin, that this letter, which he has cited at length,
shows how slight was the progress in Ireland of the attempted reformation. The same intelligent author observes, that this attempt
appears to have been very much limited to the assertion of the king's
supremacy in Ireland. In point of fact, Henry's own views went
nothing farther, and it would be unsafe in the most thorough reformer
to go a hair's-breadth beyond the theology of the king. Henry,
while with arbitrary decision he put down the authority of the pope,
with equal determination maintained all the doctrinal tenets of the
Roman church. For a moment, in the first ardour of opposition, he
lent an indulgent ear to those whose views though substantially different from his own, yet were such as to favour his main object. But
as this appeared to be no longer a matter of dispute, he assumed the
position of an ecclesiastical despot, and maintained it with a fierce and
peremptory authority, to which all opposition was alike useless and
perilous. Cranmer and Cromwell on the one side, and on the other
the duke of Norfolk and Gardiner, with the other peers and prelates
who adhered to the pope, felt themselves under the necessity of compromise. And while the reformers were compelled to give a seeming
acquiescence to the doctrines of the Roman church, their opponents
were, with equal reluctance, forced to renounce the pope. Each
party acted with dexterous pliability, for the furtherance of its objects,
suppressing whatever articles of faith on the one side, or discipline on
the other, they respectively held in opposition to the royal will: while

the king with more boldness, and not less vigilance, used the compliance of both for the confirmation of his own power. Had it not indeed been for the irritation caused by the violent resistance of the church of Rome, the reformers might soon have found Henry a rougher antagonist than the Pope; but decidedly, as the king was bent on checking the progress of Reform, he could not have been fully aware how much his power against the pressure of the Papacy lay in the reforming spirit of the bulk of the people. And hence it was, that he was forced to afford a doubtful countenance to a party whom he disliked. Such is the explanation of the conduct of Browne—himself decided, zealous, and disinterested, he was necessarily compelled to adopt the expedient language of subserviency, and to yield where conscientious conviction would have gone further than discretion. The English reformers though awed by the king, were supported by the people; notwithstanding which, their zeal was tempered by a due share of caution: Browne was on the other hand alike circumscribed, by the zealous opposition of the national spirit, and the limitary dictation of Henry. Under these circumstances, the conduct of the archbishop was in all respects such as the exigencies of the situation demanded, he could not be more decided without endangering his object, or less active without betraying his trust. The instructions which he sent round to the incumbents and curates of his diocese, present the doctrines of the church of Rome in the form least inconsistent with the views of the reformation; and contain some clauses not quite reconcileable with Romanism, as it existed until very recently within our own times, when under the pressure of external circumstances it has been undergoing a silent and partial reformation. We give the "form of beads," from the *State Papers*. "You shall pray for the universal catholic church, both quick and dead, and especially for the church of England and Ireland. First for our sovereign Lord the king, supreme head on earth, immediate under God, of the said church of England and Ireland. And for the declaration of the truth thereof, you shall understand, that the unlawful jurisdiction, power, and authority, of long time usurped by the bishop of Rome in England and Ireland, who then was called pope, is now by God's law, justly, lawfully, and upon good grounds, reasons, and causes, by authority of parliament, and by and with the whole consent and agreement of all the bishops, prelates, and both the universities of Oxford and Cambridge, and also the whole clergy both of England and Ireland, extinct and ceased, and ceased for ever, as of no strength, value, or effect in the church of England or Ireland. In the which church the said whole clergy, bishops, and prelates, with the universities of Oxford and Cambridge, have, according to God's law, and upon good and lawful reasons and grounds, acknowledged the king's highness to be supreme head on earth, immediately under God, of this church of England and Ireland, which their knowledge confessed, being now by parliament established, and by God's laws justifiable, to be justly executed; so ought every true christian subject of this land, not only to acknowledge and obediently recognise the king's highness to be supreme head on earth of the church of England and Ireland, but also to speak, publish, and teach their children and servants the same, and to show unto them how that the said bishop of Rome hath heretofore usurped, not only upon God, but also upon our princes. Wherefore, and to the intent that ye should the better believe me, herein, and take and receive the truth as ye ought to do, I declare this unto you. The same is certified unto me from the might of my ordinary, the archbishop of Dublin, under his seal, which I have here ready to show you, so that now it appeareth plainly, that the said bishop of Rome hath neither authority nor power in this land, nor never had by God's laws; therefore I exhort you all, that you deface him in all your primers, and other books, where he is named pope, and that you shall have from henceforth no confidence nor trust in him, nor in his bulls or letters of pardon, which before time with his juggling casts of binding, and loosing, he sold unto you for your money, promising you therefore forgiveness of your sins, when of truth no man can forgive sins but God only; and also that ye fear not his great thunder claps of excommunication or interdiction, for they cannot hurt you; but let us put all our confidence and trust in our Saviour Jesus Christ, which is gentle and loving, and requireth nothing of us when we have offended him, but that we should repent and forsake our sins, and believe steadfastly that he is Christ, the Son of the living God, and that he died for our sins, and so forth, as it is contained in the Credo; and that through him, and by him, and by none other, we shall have remission of our sins, 'a pœnâ et culpa,' according to his promises made to us in many and divers places of scripture. On this part ye shall pray also for the prosperous estate of our young prince, prince Edward, with all other the king's issue and posterity, and for all archbishops and bishops, and especially for my lord archbishop of Dublin, and for all the clergy, and namely, for all them that preacheth the word of God purely and sincerely. On the second part ye shall pray for all earls, barons, lords, and in especial for the estate of the right honourable lord Leonard Grey, lord-deputy of this land of Ireland, and for all them that be of the king's most honourable council, that God may put them in mind to give such counsel, that it may be to the pleasure of almighty God and wealth of this land. Ye shall pray also for the mayor of this city, and his brethren, with all the commonalty of the same, or for the parishioners of this parish, and generally for all the temporality. On the third part, ye shall pray for the souls that be departed out of this world in the faith of our Saviour Jesus Christ, which sleep in rest and peace, that they may rise again and reign with Christ in eternal life. For those and for grace every man may say a Pater Noster and an Ave."*

This is not the place to enter in detail upon the subject of a controversy, still raging, and to rage with a scarcely mitigated force until it shall please the Divine Ruler, in the development of his own purposes to send peace to his church. But it is plainly apparent, according to every view, that the place of the reforming archbishop of Dublin was not one to be desired by any one who sought his own tranquillity, or desired to shrink back from the turbulence and bitterness of the times, then as now keenly edged with the zeal of controversy. Among the

* State Papers. Dalton. Ware.

many trials with which Browne had to contend, the most personally vexatious arose from the opposition and the hostility of Leonard lord Grey, who, himself the object of a persecution which pursued him to the block, did not the less indulge in the gratification which his high and arbitrary temper found in heaping insult and injury upon one whom he personally disliked, and to whose exertions he was no friend. The civil and religious state of the time was such as to demand the control of stern, arbitrary, and uncompromising spirits, which alone have efficacy amid the tempests of disorganized society. Of this temper each of these persons had his due share. But the spirit of the military and civil ruler, and that of the ecclesiastic, were so placed in respect to each other, as to be too easily brought into collision, and to entertain the dislike to which arbitrary and aspiring tempers will ever mutually tend. The archbishop sat under too close and stern a control, to move in enmity towards his powerful antagonist; but Grey could admit no shadow of a rival jurisdiction in any department of the state, he probably felt that if the king was to be the arbitrary ruler of the church, the archbishop's active assumption of power would be an encroachment; but it is still more likely, that his arbitrary temper was provoked at the additional difficulties he apprehended from the exasperation of the public mind, by a controversy, to which he assigned no serious importance. Such indeed is the observable spirit of every time, the serious controversialist who has motives of conscience to direct his zeal, will still be constrained more or less by the spirit and temper of the religion he professes: the Christian will reason because it is his duty; the partisan will fight on this as he would on any other cause; the sceptic, who is alike indifferent to every creed, will treat the controversial combatant, to whom by party he is opposed, or whose views are such as to come into collision with his own, with irrespective and irreverent scorn—because he can comprehend no reason why the concerns of a *future*, in which he has neither hope nor faith, should be suffered to disturb the present, in which all his heart and understanding are centred. We cannot now pretend with any accuracy or justice to analyze the mind of lord Grey, who executed his own trust with vigour, and was ill repaid with the punishment of a traitor. But we entertain no doubt that his persecution of archbishop Browne was carried into minute and vexatious aggressions which were hard to bear. In the complaints which are to be found in Browne's letters to the king, he seems nevertheless to have exercised great moderation, as he confines himself to the plea of his own want of authority under the interference of Grey, when such a complaint is rendered necessary by the reproaches of the king; but in his other correspondence with his personal friends, the true state of the case appears more plainly. Such passages as the following extract, speak a very overbearing and persecuting spirit, and show more clearly the difficult straits in which Browne was placed between the king, his lord-deputy, and the country, or rather the Irish church. *Romanis ipsis romaniores*, if this grammatical barbarism may be allowed. "Good master Allen, it needeth not me to declare unto you what wrongs I do sustain by the lord-deputy, and I perceive it needeth not me to expect for any of his better favours; but rather the encrease of daily wrongs. It chanced me and the abbot of St Thomas court, to have bought against this time of our own tenants, two fat oxen being paid for more than two months past; that notwithstanding, my lord-deputy hath not only taken the said oxen to his own kitchen, but also doth imprison one of the tenants. Thus by high power man be here oppressed."*

But the greatest difficulties with which the zeal of Browne had to contend, was unquestionably that which he met in the direct discharge of his ecclesiastical functions, as the prelate of a divided and recusant church. From other bishops he met with a resistance the more difficult to contend with, as their recognised authority was upheld by the spirit of the Irish people and hierarchy. The bishop of Meath resisted him by open and violent opposition, and countermined him by secret intrigue. The clergy of his own immediate diocese used both evasion and resistance: his attempts to displace the images and relics from the cathedrals of Dublin were stubbornly opposed by his clergy, who dispatched a secret emissary to Rome to bear their assurances of devotion and implore for aid. Of these trials he complains with much evident bitterness in a letter to Cromwell in 1538: the letter is given in the republication of *Ware's Annals* by his son, who has an autograph letter in it from the collection made by his father. It is also printed in Mr Dalton's *Bishops*.

" *Right honourable and my singular good lord.*

" I acknowledge my bounden duty to your lordship's goodwill towards me, next to my Saviour Christ, for the place I now possess. I pray God give me his grace to execute the same to his glory and highnesses honour, with your lordship's instructions.

" The people of this nation be zealous, yet blind and unknowing; most of the clergy, as your lordship hath had from me before, being ignorant, and not able to speak right words in the mass or liturgy, as being not skilled in the Latin grammar, so that a bird may be taught to speak with as much sense as many of them do in this country. These sorts, though not scholars, yet crafty to cozen the poor common people, and to dissuade them from following his highnesses orders. George, my brother of Armagh, doth underhand occasion quarely; and is not active to execute his highnesses orders in his diocese.

" I have observed your lordship's letter of commission, and do find several of my pupils leave me for so doing. I will not put others in their livings till I know your lordship's pleasure, for it is fit I acquaint you first. The Romish relics and images of both my cathedrals of Dublin, of the Holy Trinity, and St Patrick's, took off the common people from the true worship; but the prior and the dean find them so swat for their gain that they heed not my word; therefore, send in your lordship's next to me an order more full, and a chide to them and their canons, that they might be removed. Let the order be that the chief governors may assist me in it. The prior and dean have written to Rome to be encouraged; and if it be not hindered before they have a mandate from the bishop of Rome, the people will be

*Archbishop Browne to Allen. State Papers

bold, and then tug long before his highness can submit them to his grace's orders. The country folk here much hate your lordship, and despitefully call you, in their Irish tongue, the blacksmith's son.

" The duke of Norfolk is, by Armagh [*the bishop*] and that clergy, desired to assist them not to suffer his highness to alter church rules here in Ireland. As a friend I desire your lordship to look to your noble person, for Rome hath a great kindness for that duke, (for it is so talked here,) and will reward him and his children. Rome hath great favour for this nation purposely to oppose his highness, and so have got, since the act past, great indulgences for rebellion; therefore my hope is lost, yet my zeal is to do according to your lordship's orders. God keep your lordship from your enemies here and in England. Dublin, the 3d kalends of April, 1538.

" Yr lordship's at commandment,
" GEORGE BROWNE.
" *To the Lord Privy Seal his Honourable Lordship.*"
[Ex autographo.*]

Immediately after this letter a bull was sent over which all the historians of every party have severally thought proper to preserve, and which we do not feel authorized to omit. This bull is contained in a letter from the archbishop to Cromwell, as follows:—

" RIGHT HONOURABLE,
" My duty premised, it may please your lordship to be advertised, sithence my last there has come to Ardmagh and his clergy a private commission from the bishop of Rome, prohibiting his gratious highnesses people here in this nation to own his royal supremacy, and joyning a curse to all them and theirs, who shall not within forty days confess to their confessors (after the publishing of it to them) that they shall have done amiss in so doing. The substance, as our secretary hath translated the same into English, is thus:—

" I, A. B., from this present hour forward in the presence of the holy Trinity, of the blessed Virgin Mother of God, of St. Peter, of the holy apostles, archangels, angels, saints, and of all the holy host of heaven, shall and will be always obedient to the holy see of St Peter of Rome, and to my holy lord the pope of Rome and his successors, in all things as well spiritual as temporal, not consenting in the least that his holiness shall lose the least title or dignity belonging to the papacy of our mother church of Rome, or to the regality of St Peter.

" I do vow and swear to maintain, help and assist the just laws liberties and rights of the mother church of Rome.

" I do likewise promise to confer, defend and promote, if not personally, yet willingly as in ability able, either by advice, skill, estate, money or otherwise, the Church of Rome and her laws against all whatsoever resisting the same.

" I further vow to oppugn all hereticks, either in making or setting forth edicts or commands contrary to the mother Church of Rome, and in case any such be moved or composed, to resist it to the utter-

* Ware's Annals.

most of my power, with the first convenience and opportunity I can possible.

"I count and value all acts made or to be made by heretical powers of no force or worth, or to be practised or obeyed by myself, or by any other son of the mother Church of Rome.

"I do further declare him or her, father or mother, brother or sister, son or daughter, husband or wife, uncle or aunt, nephew or niece, kinsman or kinswoman, master or mistress, and all others, nearest or dearest relations, friend or acquaintance whatsoever, accursed, that either do or shall hold for the time to come, any ecclesiastical or civil authority of the mother church, or that do or shall obey for the time to come, any of her the mother church's opposers or enemies, or contrary to the same of which I have here sworn unto: so God, the blessed Virgin, St Peter, St Paul, and the holy evangelists help, &c.

"His highness's viceroy of the nation is of little or no power with the old natives, therefore your lordship will expect of me no more than I am able; this nation is poor in wealth, and not sufficient now at present to oppose them: it is observed, that ever since his highness's ancestors had this nation in possession, the old natives have been craving foreign powers to assist and rule them; and now both English race and Irish begin to oppose your lordship's orders, and do lay aside their national old quarrels, which I fear if any thing will cause a foreigner to invade this nation, that will. I pray God I may be a false prophet, yet your good lordship must pardon mine opinion, for I write it to your lordship as a warning.

Your humble and true servant,
"GEORGE BROWNE.
"*Dublin, May,* 1538.
"*To the Lord Privy-Seal with speed.*"

We have already mentioned the letter to O'Neale* from the pope, which was found on the person of a friar who was seized by the archbishop at the same period with the last-mentioned bull and letter; in the beginning of June, Thady O'Birnie was seized and imprisoned, till orders could be received from England; but on hearing that an order had arrived for his transmission into England, this order the unfortunate friar justly looked on as the preliminary to a rough trial and a certain death, to avoid the horrors of which, he anticipated the executioner, and was found dead in his prison.

The struggles between the archbishop and his powerful and numerous opponents were at this time attended with much active and rancorous hostility, which, as either party gained the advantage, showed the extent to which the worst elements of human nature could take the lead in the zeal of sects and parties for a religion broadly opposed to the passions which were thus enlisted in its cause. Human beings, animated by the purest motives of which humanity is capable, and engaged in the holiest cause, will still act from the spirit which rules the breast of short-sighted and inferior creatures, and "call down fire from heaven" on those whom God in his long-suffering allows to brave him with impunity; nor in the energy of opposition

* Con Boccagh, first earl of Tyrone. See *ante*, p. 375.

and defence once revert to the precept and the testimony which tells how different indeed is the fight of faith to which our Lord sent forth his chosen, or the test of that divine light which shows the creature of sin what spirit he is of: but the strife was actually embittered by the infusion of mere political and party rancour; and two great and powerful parties were opposed to each other, fighting under the name of religion, and drawing excitement from the zeal of party prejudices.

We have already at some length shown how the part of Browne was rendered difficult not alone by the formidable tyranny at his back, with both the remissness and impetuosity of which he was reduced to contend, nor even by the vast weight of national prejudice and zeal which opposed him; his most truly vexatious trials arose from those to whom he might have mainly looked for support. The lord Grey, while he was ostensibly the instrument of the king's designs, was in effect their determined enemy, and omitted no occasion by which he might without suspicion impede the progress of the reformation, or embarrass the proceedings of Browne. There is a paragraph in a letter from lord Butler to Cromwell, which contains a curious account of a scene which in some degree illustrates this.

" This last week the vicar of Chester, sitting at the lord-deputies board, the archbishop of Dublin, the chief-justice, the master of the rolls, with others of the king's counsel, and I, there present, said openly before us all, that the king's majesty had commanded that images should be set up again, and honoured and worshipped as much as ever they were; and we held us all in silence in my lord-deputy's presence to see what he would say thereto. He held his peace and said nothing. Then my lord of Dublin, the master of the rolls, and I, said among other things, that if he were in any other place, out of my lord-deputy's presence, we would put him fast by the heels, and that he had deserved grievous punishment. His lordship kept his tongue and said nothing the while. Sure he hath a special zeal to the papists." This letter is dated 26th August, 1538.

Nevertheless, in the end of the same year, by a letter bearing date 6th November, the archbishop seems to have met with many circumstances of better hope. In a letter to Cromwell, he says, "that the papishe obstinate observants be here among themselves in such desperation, that where there hath been twenty in a monastery, there be now scarcely four; yea, and by your presence they think that little number too many; for their feigned holiness is so well (among the king's subjects) espied, that the people's devotion is clean withdrawn from them."* In the same letter he complains emphatically of the continual counteraction he met with from the interference of lord Grey. In the following month, a letter from the Irish council to Cromwell, mentions the following circumstances:—A little before Christmas, the writers Allen, Brabazon, and Aylmer, made a sort of progress through the "four shires" about the Barrow, for the purpose of publishing and giving effect to the king's commands and ordinances both civil and ecclesiastical; as also to hold sessions and levy first-fruits and other revenues. They resorted first to Carlow. " where the lord

* State Papers.

James Butler kept his Christmas, and these being very well entertained, from thence we went to Kilkenny, where we were no less entertained by the earl of Ormonde. There on new-year's day, the archbishop of Dublin preached the word of God, having very good audience, publishing the king's said injunctions, and the king's translation of the Paternoster, Ave Maria, the articles of faith, and ten commandments in English; divers papers whereof we delivered to the bishop and other prelates of the diocese, commanding them to do the like, through all their jurisdictions."*

Though the lord-deputy Grey had set himself in opposition to the archbishop, and frequently disconcerted his efforts to introduce the changes enjoined by the king, yet his efficient activity in the suppression of rebellion had more favourable consequences than his personal opposition could defeat. Numbers, whose religious animosity was little else than faction, were when the political motive was suppressed, ready to adopt any change for peace and favour; and much ecclesiastical zeal was subdued into acquiescence, by a sense of the idleness of holding out. The religion enforced by Henry was, it is to be remembered, far more that of Rome than England: on the Reformation in England, the tyrant looked with an eye of watchful jealousy, and whatever he had yielded to its doctrines, was rather unwilling political concession than sincere. The conquest over such opposition in Ireland, so far from being matter of surprise, must indeed on the contrary appear far below what should, under all the circumstances, be expected; and were it not that the Irish looked rather to the party than the creed, a far greater effect might have been reasonably anticipated. The defeats at this time sustained by the Irish chiefs contributed much to facilitate the objects of Browne; and the same favourable effect was forwarded by the successful vigour of De Brereton, who was deputed in the room of Grey on his return into England. Many of the monasteries were in consequence resigned to the king. The priory of the Trinity in Dublin is more especially noticed, which was changed, in 1541, into a deanery under the new appellation of Christ Church. It now consisted of a dean and chapter, with a chanter, treasurer, six vicars choral, and two singing boys. It was after extended by King James.

Soon after, Sir Anthony St Leger was sent over, and a parliament called in Dublin, in which the king's style was changed from lord of Ireland to that of king, an act to which much good is attributed. Among other immediate consequences seems to be numbered the unqualified submission of Con O'Nial, with the fullest renunciation of the papal authority, an example which was followed by the other chiefs of Ulster.

Such is nevertheless but the fair aspect of the history of the day. The concessions and submissions of the Irish were partly insincere, partly from ignorance; they were also but partial. The vindictive ferocity of Henry impelled numbers whom the thunders of the Roman see drove back; and while the chiefs were tossed back and forward by the contending sway of parties, no pains were taken to instruct the

* State Papers.

populace. For this indifference to the spiritual intent of religion, Browne and his bishops have been justly censured, nor can it be admitted as an excuse that their opponents were no less to blame. It was indeed a time, when the inferior orders were little more thought of than beasts for the ends of husbandry or war. "Hard it is," writes chancellor Cusack, "that men should know their duties to God and to the king, when they shall not hear teaching or preaching throughout the year."* The evil here complained of was indeed wide spread and fatal; and the obstacles to any remedy, perhaps, insurmountable, unless by the slow operation of time. The knowledge of the English language, a needful preliminary, can hardly be described as co-extensive with the pale; and through every other district the people were altogether dependent on such instruction as they were likely to obtain in their native tongue.

In 1542, the archbishop caused an application to be made by the council in his behalf, that he might be compensated for lands released by him to the king in favour of one of the O'Tooles; and was let off a debt of 250 pounds by the king. This debt had been originally incurred by a promise of so much to lord Rochford, and on the attainder of this lord, it fell to the king.†

In 1542, an inquisition was taken of the temporality of the see of Dublin,‡ and in the next a suit between the archbishop and lord Howth, for the inheritance of Ireland's Eye, was adjudged in favour of the archbishop.§ In the same historian we find many interesting particulars of the internal regulations and changes made about the same time by this prelate—one of which alone we shall now delay to mention :—
"By deed of the 12th July, 1545, this prelate, in consideration of £40, conveyed to trustees the town of Rathlande, being on the southern part of Thomas-Court Wood, then lately occupied by Thomas Battee; also, all the lands, &c., in Rathlande aforesaid, and the rents and reversion of the same, to hold for ever, to the use of William Brabazon, ancestor of the earl of Meath, his heirs and assigns, at the yearly rent of 13s. 4d., being the site of that wretched district of paupers, now denominated the earl of Meath's liberties."‖

It was in the following year that a commission was issued for the sequestration of St Patrick's, with its lands and revenues to the king's use. For a time the chapter refused to yield, but after some days' deliberation, the required resignation was made by the dean. They were afterwards restored in 1554, by queen Mary. Before that restoration, however, the canons had been pensioned liberally by Edward VI., their plate, jewels, and other moveables restored, and an addition of priests and singing boys is also attributed to the same occasion by Ware; which nevertheless, is placed by Mr Dalton at an earlier period.

The death of Henry and the accession of Edward VI. introduced momentous changes into the English church. The first steps of the reformation were, on the part of Henry, reluctant concessions to

---

* Leland, from MS. Trin. Col. Dub.
† State Papers, vol, ii. pp. 11, 390, 594.   ‡ Dalton.   § Ibid.
‖ Ibid.

those who acting with more sincerity, and from far other motives, were yet necessary to his purposes: these purposes were nothing more or less than the emancipation of his own actions from control, the gratification of revenge, and the assertion of an arbitrary temper. To the reforming party it was necessary to concede, and opposition alone impelled him to a certain length; but his was not a nature to be carried far with the changes of others, and he sternly turned round when his point was secured. Such institutions or doctrines of the Roman see, as when admitted must needs have rendered his usurpation impossible, and which formed the basis of its power, he willingly, and with a high and arbitrary hand, suppressed with all that disregard of opinion and conscience, which were characteristic of one who was himself little, if at all, swayed by either: and as he arbitrarily dragged his subjects to the point required by his purpose, so, with the same arbitrary will, he forbade them to go further. His creed, which was in some of its points repugnant to the faith of the Roman, and in more, irreconcileable with that of the reformer, he enforced against both with irrespective tyranny. He was content to establish a supremacy more absolute than the pope ever claimed over the faith; and when the point was (according to his opinion) gained, it was his wish to repress innovation, and the daring spirit of search and speculation, under which no tyranny could long subsist, and to reign in a new obscurity and torpor of his own creation. Accordingly, as Burnet has observed, having once reached a certain point, he began to turn back, and had his life been spared, there can be little doubt that he would have carried back the church to the same creed from which he had endeavoured violently to remove it. Among his own bishops there were few who were not fully aware of this fact: nor were there wanting many to avail themselves of it. Hence a protracted and violent struggle set in between two powerful and influential sections of the church, who each continued to temporize and triumph in its turn, with the changes of this royal autocracy. Some time previous to the period at which we are now arrived, the natural effect of this disposition of the king had begun to take place; the influence of Cranmer, whose agency had been found useful in one part of the monarch's course, began to give way to that of Gardiner, bishop of Winchester, whose opinions and instrumentality became no less important in another stage. Cranmer's views essentially differed from those of his master who had the penetration to see that they were quite inconsistent with the infallible and all-controlling supremacy he claimed: Gardiner had no objection to acknowledge the pope in the king, and the king had no opinions incompatible with Gardiner's theology.

In this state of things a royal proclamation prohibited the importation and printing of books, unless under the most strict and jealous supervision—a provision more distinctly explained by the accompanying prohibitions:—All parts of scripture not first inspected and approved of by the king—all works denying the doctrine of transubstantiation. By the same instrument, all persons were forbidden to deny this doctrine under pain of death and confiscation. Married priests were denounced, those already married to be deprived, and those who should thereafter marry, were to be imprisoned.

This retrograde movement was completed by an act of parliament for the prevention of diversity of opinion in religion; well known as the statute of the six articles, the purpose of which was to be a formidable bulwark against the further approach of the reformation. This act fixed the creed of king Henry at a standard which he maintained to the end of his life, with the sword and faggot. By this law, of which the title was "An act for the abolishing diversity of opinions in certain articles concerning the Christian religion," hanging or burning at the stake was enacted to be the punishment of whoever should—

I. By word or writing deny transubstantiation.
II. Who should maintain that communion in both kinds was necessary.
III. Or that it was lawful for priests to marry.
IV. Or that vows of charity may be broken.
V. Or that private masses are unprofitable.
VI. Or lastly, that auricular confession is not necessary to salvation.*

Such was the Protestantism of Henry VIII. The composition of Gardiner and the act of the same subservient parliament, which granted to the king the lands of the religious houses, thus exhibiting a perfect indifference to all creeds and churches, and shaping their conscience to the fashion of a despotic court. Against this law of the six articles Cranmer stood alone. And the opposition he made, would, as Rapin justly observes, "have ruined any other person but that prelate." The bishops of Salisbury, Shaxton, and Latimer bishop of Worcester, who could neither conform their consciences to the king's rule of faith, thought to escape by the resignation of their bishopricks. But they no sooner gave in their resignations, than they were committed to the Tower, as having spoken against the six articles; and an inquisitorial commission was appointed to make strict inquiry through the country for those who had spoken against them. This proceeding was, however, interrupted, by the numerous arrests in the city of London—in consequence of which the chancellor represented to the king the detrimental and dangerous consequences likely to arise from the vast numbers who were likely to be thus involved through the kingdom.

Henry maintained thus a doubtful church which in many points gave offence to all, by a dexterous accommodation of the powers he had acquired, to circumstances as they occurred; and while he still maintained a discretionary power over articles of faith, he sometimes gave a slackened rein to the reformers, and sometimes drew them up, so as to balance the two parties and preserve his power over both. But it was thoroughly understood that he was the steady enemy of the reformers on one side, and to the pope on the other; while he went heart and hand with Gardiner's party, who agreed with his theology and connived at all with which they disagreed.

This state of things was in England partly mitigated and concealed by the king's anxious fears of the German Protestants: and by his manœuvres to gain them. This topic would lead us far from our

* Rapin

object: but it is not foreign from our purpose to notice that Henry failed to impose on the German Protestants, who answered his messages, that they had seen with grief that he persecuted those of their opinions in England.

Such, then, was the Protestantism of the monster, whom it is not to be wondered if every church is willing to disclaim. Such is the blind zeal of faction, while the reflecting and independent student of history will reject with decision the absurdity of estimating the truth of God by the folly and wickedness, or wisdom and virtue of men—fallible, whatever be their creed. In the furtherance of his private objects, in the indulgence of an opinionative and arbitrary spirit, Henry VIII. unquestionably gave to the reformation, long rooted in the public mind, a form and substance in the church. But it was still in the most essential articles, resting on the sands of human corruption. The accession of Edward VI., gave a new and effectual impulse to reformation; and though soon interrupted by his death, may be said to have fixed the form of the English church, and given it a substance in the minds of men by the publication of the English liturgy in 1548. There had previously been some ineffectual changes introduced by Henry; but still there was in point of fact no liturgy, either adequate to represent the reformation, or to supply the uses of a liturgy considered as a form of prayer. There were different liturgies used through the kingdom: of these many parts had been handed down from remote and primitive antiquity, while others had been supplied according to the growth of the tenets of the church of Rome. But on the accession of Edward, a newly arranged and improved form was sent forth in an English dress—retaining all that was according to scripture, adding much that was wanting, and rejecting erroneous forms which corrupted all the Latin liturgies. The new liturgy prepared by Cranmer, was then established by parliamentary enactment; and in 1551, sent over to Sir Anthony St Leger, to promulgate and establish in Ireland.

The following is the order transmitted from king Edward to the lord-deputy:—

" Edward, by the grace of God,
" Whereas our gracious father, king Henry the VIII. of happy memory, taking into consideration the bondage and heavy yoke that his true and faithful subjects sustained under jurisdiction of the bishop of Rome, as also the ignorance the commonality were in, how several fabulous stories and lying wonders misled our subjects in both our realms of England and Ireland, grasping thereby the means thereof into their hands, although dispensing with the sins of our nations by their indulgences and pardons for gain, purposely to cherish all evil vices, as robberies, rebellions, thefts, whoredoms, blasphemy, idolatry, &c.—He, our gracious father, king Henry of happy memory, hereupon dissolved all priories, monastries, abbies, and other pretended religious houses, as being nurseries for vice and luxury, more than for sacred learning. He therefore, that it more plainly appear to the world that those orders had kept the light of the gospel from his people, he thought it most convenient for the preservation of their souls and

bodies, that the holy Scriptures should be translated, printed, and placed in all parish churches within his dominions, for his subjects to increase their knowledge of God and our Saviour Jesus Christ. We, therefore, for the general benefit of our well-beloved subjects' understandings, whenever assembled or met together in the said several parish churches, either to hear or to read prayers, that they join therein, in unity, hearts and voice, have caused the liturgy and prayers of the church to be translated into our mother tongue of this realm England, according to the assembly of divines lately met within the same for that purpose. We, therefore, will and command, as also authorise you Sir Antony St Leger, knight, our vice-roy of that our kingdom of Ireland, to give special notice to all our clergy, as well archbishops, bishops, deans, archdeacons, as other our secular parish priests within that our said kingdom of Ireland, to perfect, execute, and obey this our royal will and pleasure accordingly.

" Given at our manor of Greenwich, the 6th February, in the fifth year of our reign.

" To our trusty and well-beloved Sir Antony St Leger, knight, our chief governor of our kingdom of Ireland."

On receiving this order, St Leger convened a council of the archbishops, bishops, and clergy, to whom he communicated it with the opinions of their English brethren in its favour. When he concluded, Dowdal, the archbishop of Armagh, stood up and made a speech in which he principally objected, that if the liturgy were to be thus adopted in the English language, the consequence must be that every illiterate person would have it in his power to say mass. Dowdal's objection was adopted by most of the Irish bishops, who (we infer from Ware's statement,) many of them followed in the expression of the same objection. St Leger replied, that, the very circumstance that many of the clergy were already too illiterate to understand the Latin tongue, rendered it advisable that they should have an English liturgy, by the adoption of which the priest and people " will understand what they pray for." To this Dowdal, who seems by his whole course of objection, to have been singularly inexpert, warned Sir Anthony "to beware of the clergy's curse." " I fear no strange curse," replied Sir Anthony, " so long as I have the blessing of that church which I believe to be the true one." " Can there be a truer church," replied Dowdal, " than the *church of Saint Peter*, the mother church of Rome." " I thought," retorted Sir Anthony, " that we had been all of the *church of Christ*, for he calls all true believers in him his church, and himself the head thereof." To this Dowdal replied, " and is not St Peter's the church of Christ," and was met by the conclusive replication, "that St Peter was a member of Christ's church, but the church was not St Peter's, neither was St Peter, but Christ the head thereof."[*] On this Dowdal rose and left the assembly, and with him all the other bishops but Staples of Meath. The order was then handed to Browne, who in a brief speech of which the substance was nothing more than a state form, proposed it to the accept-

[*] Ware.

ance of the assembly, who accordingly received it. Some of the more moderate of the other bishops, joined the archbishop of Dublin immediately after, among whom were Staples of Meath, Lancaster of Kildare, and Bale of Ossory; all of whom were shortly after expelled from their sees by queen Mary. The opposition of Dowdal does not appear to have drawn upon him any severity. The title of primate was necessarily transferred from him to Browne; but his opposition was, as might well be anticipated from the zeal and firmness of his character, continued until it was found necessary to banish him. This should, however, be stated with much caution, as a matter in some dispute, and it seems not to be clearly settled whether he was banished, or went away of his own accord. Either might well be expected to happen, and the point is of slight importance. Hugh Goodacre was certainly appointed in his place in the year following.

To what extent the change now described might have been carried in Ireland, were fruitless to discuss. It was quickly arrested in the outset, and the course of after events was such as to leave little room for amelioration of any kind for another half century, in a country of which the mind was kept low by a continual succession of demoralizing wars and insurrections.

The early death of Edward placed the weak and bigoted Mary on the throne; and the hopes of England, with the dawn of a better day in Ireland, were at once overcast with the horrors of a cruel and bloody persecution.

Mary, not long after her accession, restored the primacy to Armagh, in the person of Dowdal, who deprived Browne on the ground of his being a married man. The temporalities of his see were, according to ancient custom, deposited in the custody of the dean of Christ Church, and the see continued vacant for two years, after which it was filled by Hugh Curwen. Browne did not long survive; his death is referred to the year 1556. He is thus mentioned by primate Usher, whose testimony should not be omitted in this memoir:—" George Browne was a man of cheerful countenance; in his acts and conduct, plain and direct, to the charitable and compassionate; pitying the state and condition of the souls of the people, and advising them when he was provincial of the Augustine order in England, to make their application solely to Christ; which advice coming to the ears of Henry VIII., he became a favourite and was made archbishop of Dublin. Within five years after he enjoyed that see, he caused all superstitious relics and images to be removed out of the two cathedrals in Dublin, and out of all the churches in his diocese; and caused the ten commandments, the Lord's prayer, and the creed to be placed in gilded frames, above the altars. He was the first that turned from the Romish religion of the clergy here in Ireland, to embrace the reformation of the church in England."

HUGH CURWIN, ARCHBISHOP OF DUBLIN.

DIED A. D. 1568.

CURWIN, a native of Westmoreland, a doctor of laws in Oxford, and dean of Hereford, was appointed by queen Mary to succeed Browne in 1555. He was at the same time appointed chancellor in Ireland. At the close of the year he held a synod, in which some arrangements relative to the rites and ceremonies of the church were constituted. In connexion with this Cox states, that "afterward, the church goods and ornaments were restored, and particularly those belonging to Dublin and Drogheda." "And although," says the same writer, "many glebes contained lay fees during all the reign of queen Mary; yet at the request of Cardinal Pole, her majesty restored the possessions of Kilmainham."

In 1556, we are informed by Mr Dalton, that a commission was appointed to make an account of the value and condition of church possessions in the diocese of Dublin, and that similar commissions were issued for the other dioceses. All statutes from the twentieth year of Henry, which had been against the church of Rome, were at the same time repealed, saving the authority of the British throne and laws. Former enactments against the reformers, who were included under the denomination of heretic, were revived; and other legal provisions were made for the restoration of the ancient state of things as regarded the affairs of religion.

The accession of queen Elizabeth, which happily interrupted the changes in their course, did not alter the condition of Curwin; who, with a latitude of conscience not to be commended, at once accommodated his principles to the demand of the varying hour; and in 1557, was appointed one of the lords-justices with Sir Henry Sidney, and continued in the office of chancellor. In 1559, the office of lord-keeper of the great seal of Ireland was added to his honours. He was a second time chancellor in 1563; and in 1567, feeling the rapid encroachments of old age on his personal strength, he sought and obtained his translation to the see of Oxford, where he died in the following year.

ADAM LOFTUS, ARCHBISHOP OF DUBLIN.

DIED A. D. 1605.

THIS prelate has a more than ordinary claim upon our notice as the zealous promoter, and the first provost of Trinity college near Dublin, an institution which has conferred more real and lasting benefit on Ireland, than all others taken together; and which when justly estimated by its intrinsic merits as a repository of knowledge, and a centre for the diffusion of sound learning and principle, will, in the history of learning, be hereafter considered to stand at the head of the universities of Europe—being second to none in the cultivation of every branch of profane literature, and first of all in its proper and peculiar function as the great seminary of the principles of the church of England. Such being the chief claim of Loftus on the commemoration of history, it will be needless to dwell more than lightly on those parts of his life which are nothing more than the ordinary incidents of his time; and proceed with a rapid hand to this main transaction which sheds particular honour on every name with which it is connected.

Loftus was, according to Ware, born at Swineshead in Yorkshire, of an ancient and respectable family, and received in his youth a more careful and costly education than was usual in his time. He became soon distinguished for talent and literary accomplishment; and on some public occasion had the good fortune to win the admiration of the queen, by his striking display of logical and rhetorical talent, when, with her characteristic promptitude, she marked him for distinction, and encouraged his youthful ambition to effort by promises of speedy advancement.

The queen kept her promise, and never lost sight of the distinguished youth until an opportunity occurred, when she was sending lord Sussex over as lieutenant of Ireland, on which Loftus was sent over as his chaplain; and but little time elapsed when another mark of favour indicates the favourable impression, which his early promise made on one so keen in her discernment of merit. In 1561, he was appointed by letters patent to the rectory of Painestown in Meath, and the following year, by one wide step elevated to the see of Armagh in the room of Dowdal. On this incident, Harris remarks, that "the Irish protestant bishops derive their succession through him, without any pretence to cavil, for he was consecrated by Curwin, who had been consecrated in England according to the forms of the Romish pontifical, in the third year of queen Mary."

In 1564 he was elected to the deanery of St Patrick's by royal license, on the consideration of the insufficiency of the revenues of the see of Armagh, "his archbishopric being a place of great charge, in name and title only to be taken into account, without any worldly endowment resulting from it." In 1566 he was joined by the clergy of Armagh in excommunicating Shane O'Neale, who burned "the metropolitan church of Ardmagh; saying he did it lest the English should lodge therein." In the same year he took his doctor's degree in Cambridge, and was soon after translated to Dublin.

In 1572 he obtained a dispensation from the queen to hold with his archbishopric any sinecures not exceeding £100 in annual value. In 1573 he was appointed chancellor, and held the office during his life. In 1582, and again in 1585, he was one of the lords-justices.

We pass the particulars of his unhappy quarrel with Sir John Perrot, as not essential to the main purpose of this memoir. It chiefly originated in the archbishop's determined resolution in preserving the cathedral of St. Patrick's from being converted into a university or a law court to the prejudice of certain rights of the church. That respecting the university was one, the frustration of which might well be counted a stain on the memory of Loftus, had it not been fortunately wiped away by an ample and honourable compensation. The cathedral of St. Patrick's was preserved to the church in its ancient venerable character, and the university was soon after instituted by the zealous instrumentality of the archbishop.

The full importance of this institution is too great to admit of its being discussed at the termination of this series, where it may escape the attention of the greater portion of our readers. We shall presently have an occasion to enter on the subject at length. The history of the foundation is briefly as follows:—

Such an institution had previously, at different periods of the Anglo-Irish history, been attempted, but in vain; the troubles of the country were too rife, and the want insufficiently felt: the desire of knowledge is itself a result of intellectual cultivation. This desire was one of the chief influences of the Reformation in England; of which, as we shall hereafter more fully explain, learning was soon found to be an indispensable requisite. But in Ireland the necessity of some native centre of an academical character became strongly perceptible. The necessity of looking in England for ministers for the churches, and of supplying the deficiency by the employment of illiterate persons, grew to be felt as an evil of serious magnitude. To supply the demand of a church essentially connected with knowledge, had become a necessity which at the time strongly pressed itself on every cultivated mind. The call was felt with a force which has no expression on the cramped page of the annalist. It was indeed the ripeness of time; but, like all the events of time, chiefly traceable to incidental causes, and the underworking agents, whose names are made illustrious by changes which must have occurred if they had not been born.

Loftus having effectually resisted the plan of Sir John Perrot, which was to convert St Patrick's church into law courts, and apply its revenues to the foundation of a university, applied to the queen in favour of another scheme for that desirable end. For this purpose he pitched on the ancient monastery of All-hallows, on Hoggin Green, near Dublin. It had been founded by Dermod MacMurragh for Aroasian monks in 1166, and been richly endowed, not only by the founder, but also by the illustrious Milo de Cogan. Its possessions were confirmed by the charter of Henry II. On the dissolution of the monasteries, the site of this monastery had been granted to the corporation of Dublin. From this body it was now obtained by the assiduous representations of the archbishop, who told them that the act would be " of good acceptance with God, of great reward hereafter, and of honour and advantage to yourselves, and more to your learned offspring in the future; when, by the help of learning, they may build your families some stories higher than they are, by their advancement either in the church or commonwealth." The representations of Loftus had the influence due to their truth; and the city consented to a slight sacrifice of property, which was to be compensated by advantages more important to Dublin and the country, than they or their adviser could well appreciate at the time. They granted the monastery with its precincts.

Loftus next deputed Henry Usher and Lucas Chaloner to England, to apply for a charter and license for the mortmain tenure of the lands granted by the city. This may be regarded as a matter of course, and the deputies quickly returned with the queen's warrant for letters patent under the great seal of Ireland, dated 29th December, 1591, for the incorporation of a university, with power to hold the lands granted, with other endowments, to the value of £400 per annum. The university was thus incorporated, " by the name of the provost, fellows, and scholars, of the holy and undivided Trinity of Queen Elizabeth, near Dublin," who were thus duly qualified to acquire and hold the lands, tenements, and hereditaments, to themselves and their successors for ever, with certain legal provisions now unimportant. Their privilege to teach the liberal arts in Ireland was exclusively vested in them, and the license granted to confer degrees. They were empowered to make laws for their own internal government—a privilege afterwards revoked. The number of the members was limited to a provost, three fellows, and three scholars, and their functions and privileges were fully defined and guarded.*

Loftus was appointed first provost; Henry Usher, Lucas Chaloner, and Launcelot Moyne, fellows; and Henry Lee, William Daniel, and Stephen White, scholars;—the first representatives of a body, which was in the course of time to produce James Usher, King, Berkely, Young, Hamilton, as its members, with a host of other not inferior names, which shed the honours of literature and science around their country's name.

The erection of the college was next to be effected. To obtain the necessary fund, circular letters were issued by the lord-deputy (Fitz-William) and the council to the Irish nobility and gentry, representing the importance of the foundation to literature and the reformed church. A contribution was thus obtained; and in 1593 the building was finished for the reception of its inmates. The Ulster rebellion, under Hugh, earl of Tyrone, had an unfavourable influence on its growth, as its principal endowments lay in the north. But the zeal and bounty of Elizabeth, under Providence, carried it through this severe trial which menaced ruin to its infant state; and, in the language of Leland, himself one of its illustrious ornaments, " it struck its roots securely amid the public storms, and, cultivated as it was by succeeding princes, rose to a degree of consequence and splendour disproportioned to its first beginnings."†

King James endowed this foundation with large grants in Ulster. And Charles I., distinguished among the kings of England for his love and munificent patronage of all the arts, followed liberally in the same course. By his patent the foundation was enlarged; the fellows were increased to sixteen, and the scholars to seventy; the laws improved by the repeal of some, and the enactment of other provisions. Amongst these, one has more especially struck us as a judicious change; by the charter of the queen it was provided that the fellows were to resign their fellowships at the expiration of seven years from their election. Such a regulation, by no means so inexpedient in the infant state of such a community, was obviously inconsistent with the furtherance of its interests or uses in a more advanced stage of learning.

* Letters Patent of Charles I., in which the first patent is recited.—*Coll. Stat.*
† Leland, who was a senior fellow, about 1771.

While it is to be admitted that one of the main benefits conferred on society results from the circulation of the fellowship and the multiplication of academical offspring thus produced, it is equally evident that a regulation calculated to diminish the advantages to be sought for by a most arduous course of study, must have essentially destroyed the intent, so far as the production and circulation of scholars was an object. No man, whose intellect was in sound order for any useful purpose, would sink his better days in a course of learned labour, to be thrown aside like worn-out books when their better days were spent. It would be found, save by a very few, that life is short to be consumed over the study of the arts; and most men would shrink from a sacrifice thus to be crowned by deprivation. From the consideration of this defect, remedied in the patent of Charles, will appear the consummate wisdom of the provision which secures to society the advantage contemplated in the first arrangement, without the counteracting evil, and secures the continual circulation of the fellowship, by the creation of a beneficial interest to compensate the resignation of a functionary whose office has been hardly earned. This object is secured by benefices and professorships in the gift of the university, which, when they become vacant, are disposed of to such of the members as desire them, who thereby vacate their fellowships.

In 1637 a new charter from king Charles was accompanied by a body of statutes, which, with several modifications, are still the laws of the university. We shall, a little further on, take up this interesting subject, in its advanced and more general bearings on Irish literature and civilization. On the ecclesiastical state of Ireland its effects were rapid and decisive; and it appears, from the statements of Spencer, that the reformation in Ireland can scarcely be said to have commenced, until its influence was felt in an improvement of the education of churchmen.

We now return to the provost. In 1597 he was appointed one of the lords-justices; and again, in 1599, at the close of this year, he was appointed one of the counsellors to the president of Munster.

In 1603, he died in his palace at St Sepulchre's, and was buried in St Patrick's church. He had been forty-two years a bishop. Mr Dalton, from whose work on the *Archbishops of Dublin* we have received valuable assistance in this and some other of our ecclesiastical series, concludes his account of Loftus with the remark, " that Anne, the second daughter of this prelate, was married to Sir Henry Colley of Castle Carbery, and from that union have descended the present marquis of Wellesley and the duke of Wellington."

JOHN BALE, BISHOP OF OSSORY.

DIED A. D. 1563.

THIS ecclesiastic, famous for his many and voluminous writings in support of the Reformation, was born at Covy in Suffolk. He was for some time a Carmelite, and received his education first at Norwich, and afterwards at Cambridge. He early commenced his career as a reformer; and was imprisoned for preaching against the doctrines of the church of Rome both by Leo, archbishop of York, and again by Stokesly, bishop of London: from the latter imprisonment he was freed by Cromwell. He was, however, remarkable for an uncompromising spirit, and went beyond the progress of his leaders in the English Reformation, and in consequence was compelled to retreat from the arbitrary temper of Henry, whose ideas of reformation went little further than an usurpation of the papal authority in his own person. Bale, who little understood the secrets of court divinity, went forward in his course, simply following the guidance of facts, authority, and reason. This was not a temper to prosper long in an atmosphere where the boldest was compelled to trim his conscience by the tyrant's dictum. Bale was compelled to take refuge in Germany, where he remained for eight years, and where, it may be conjectured, his opinions lost nothing of their decision, or his zeal of its fire. The auspicious moment of Edward VI.'s accession brought him home, and by the favour of this king he was made bishop of Ossory in 1552. Again, however, the hapless event of Edward's death harshly interrupted his tenure; and he was, in six months from his consecration, compelled to fly for the preservation of his life, leaving behind him a good library. On his way to Germany he was taken by pirates, but happily ransomed by his friends, and reached Germany, where he lived for five years more in the peaceful pursuits of literature, and in the society of learned men. Among these he formed a special intimacy with Conrad Gesner, "as appears," says Ware, "by the epistles which passed between them." At the end of five years he returned into England, but wisely avoided plunging into the turbid billows of Irish politics and controversy. Instead of looking for his bishopric, he contented himself with a prebend in the cathedral of Canterbury, where he died in 1563, sixty-eight years of age.

His writings were numerous, and are remarked for their coarse and bitter humour. He was violent and satirical; but his severity is fairly to be excused, both on account of the general tone of the polemics of his age, which was rude and coarse, and of the state of controversy when its currents were fierce and high. On these currents Bale had himself been roughly tossed through his whole life. And it was a time when a conscientious writer must have felt that no resource then thought available, should be feebly or sparingly used. Among the remains of Bale's writings are several of those strange dramas which in earlier times had been invented by the monks, in imitation of the ancient drama; and used in their convents to represent the mysteries of the gospel, as understood in the papal church. The priests and doctors of the earlier reformed religion, emancipated from the more extreme and unscriptural errors of the medieval church, were neither sufficiently enlightened or refined to apprehend the incongruity of such representations which mixed a shade of burlesque with ideas too pure and solemn for the eye of flesh. It was only seen that to the gross apprehension of the age, there was in such scenes a power of religious impression. Thus the mystery plays, revived in a form somewhat less gross, are still found in the social pageants of the earlier times of the reformation. The scene was indeed for the most part changed, in place as in characteristic incident, being gradually transferred to the street, the castle, or the palace. Among the numerous records of the social life of the 13th and 16th centuries, there may be found abundant descriptions and notices of these representations, in one or other of their forms, either personifying the doctrines and characters of Scripture history, and embodying the mysteries of religion in some sensible representation; or similarly allegorizing the moral virtues and vices. As the doctrines of the reformation began to prevail, these productions obtained some change of style and use. Having in their earlier intent something of the nature and effect of religious ritual, witnessed with devotional feeling and sacred awe, they became frequently devoted to the purposes of spiritual satire. They naturally subsided into the character to which they had always had no slight adaptation; and their powers of essential burlesque were exhausted to turn popular scorn and ridicule on the tenets and ritual observances peculiar to the Roman Church. In these, ridicule was often carried beyond the bounds of discretion, and the reverence due to sacred things; but not perhaps more than was in some measure warranted by the time. "What," asks Warton, "shall we think of the state, I will not say of the stage, but of common sense, when these deplorable dramas could be endured? of an age, when the Bible was profaned and ridiculed from a principle of piety." It seems evident to our plain apprehension, that so far as reverence was felt or piety meant, there could have existed no designed or conscious purpose of ridicule. And from this axiomatic assumption, it must be the inference that those combinations of thought by which the refinement of our times is offended in its sense of propriety—conveyed nothing of the ludicrous to the rude simplicity of the days of Bale. The sense of burlesque materially depends on the extent and precision of knowledge; for, the uncouth representation, or the ill-sorted combination, can only be so by a comparison with some ascertained or imagined prototype. The prince of the air, who awes and terrifies one generation with the "horrors of his scaly tail," is in another compelled to appear as a courtier or a travelling student, to be fit company for the refined wits of posterity; and in a still later and more intellectual and less profane generation, he finds it necessary to content himself with his latent and viewless empire over human hearts. The dramas of Bale were chiefly written before he became a reformer and a bishop, though two or three were afterwards acted by the youths of Kilkenny, on a Sunday, at the Market cross. Many of them seem to have long been popular. Warton mentions that his "*Comedie of the Three Laws, of Nature, Moses and Christ, corrupted by the Sodomites, Pharisees, and Papists,*" became so popular, that it was reprinted by Colwell in 1562.

GEORGE DOWDAL, ARCHBISHOP OF ARMAGH.

DIED A. D. 1551.

This prelate lived through a time, of which the ecclesiastical history demands some detail. This, however, we have given in a memoir of George Browne, the reforming archbishop of Dublin. We shall here confine our notice of Dowdal to a brief outline. He was born in

Louth, and became official to Cromer, whom by the interest of the lord-deputy St. Leger, he succeeded. He was a staunch adherent to the Roman see, and in consequence of this and his elevated position in the Irish church, he was the constant adversary of Browne. During the short reign of Edward VI., his see was granted to Hugh Goodacre, and he lived in exile, but was recalled and restored by queen Mary to the archbishopric and primacy, which latter title king Edward had given to the see of Dublin. Dowdal was together with other bishops commissioned to deprive married bishops and priests of their livings, and amongst others they deprived the archbishop of Dublin, who after the license of the primitive bishops, and the apostolic precept, had thought fit that a bishop should be "the husband of one wife."

Dowdal went shortly after on ecclesiastical business to London, where he died 15th August, 1551.

To Ware's account of Dowdal he adds, "It is not to be omitted, that during the life of George Dowdal, who was in possession of the see of Armagh by donation of King Henry VIII., pope Paul III. conferred the same on Robert Wancop or Venautius, a Scot, who though he was blind from a boy, had yet applied himself to learning with so much assiduity, that he proceeded doctor of divinity at Paris. He was present at the council of Trent from the first session in 1545, to the eleventh in 1547. He was sent legate *a latine* from the pope to Germany, from whence came the German proverb, 'a blind legate to the sharp-sighted Germans.' By his means the Jesuits first came into Ireland. He died at Paris in a convent of Jesuits, the 10th November, 1551."*

JOHN ALLEN, ARCHBISHOP OF DUBLIN.

DIED A. D. 1594.

PREVIOUS to his succession to the diocese of Dublin, Allen had been variously engaged, and held many preferments in England. Having graduated as bachelor of laws in Cambridge, he was appointed to the church of Sundrithe in Kent in 1507. Soon after he was collated to Aldington, in the same diocese, and from thence was promoted to the deanery of Riseburgh in 1511. In 1515 he obtained the living of South Osenden in Essex. During this latter incumbency he was sent to Rome by Warham, archbishop of Canterbury, as his agent and envoy to the Pope. There he continued nine years, during which time he was incorporated doctor of laws in Oxford. On his return he became Wolsey's chaplain; but was soon removed to Ireland, as his rising character, and perhaps his ability and forward spirit, occasioned a jealousy between him and another chaplain of Wolsey's, the well-known Gardiner, afterwards bishop of Winchester.

Allen was consecrated archbishop of Dublin on 13th March, 1528. His advancement was designed partly in opposition to the wishes of Gerald, earl of Kildare, between whom and Wolsey there was a violent enmity, and Allen was deemed by his patron a fit person to resist and embarrass the earl in Ireland. It was perhaps to give additional effect to this design that Allen was immediately after his appointment made chancellor of Ireland. He brought over with him as his secretary John Allen, who became after, successively, master of the rolls and chancellor.*

In 1529 he received the confirmation of the Pope, and in 1530 held a consistory in Dublin, of which the acts are preserved in the *Black Book* of Christ Church.†

In 1532, his enemy, the earl of Kildare, rising into favour, and being appointed lord-deputy, succeeded in displacing Allen from the chancery bench in favour of Cromer, the archbishop of Armagh, a creature of his own,—a circumstance which increased the enmity that already subsisted between Allen and earl Gerald. The indiscretion of the earl was not long in placing formidable advantages in the hand of his enemy, and from the moment of this injury a strenuous cabal was formed against the Irish administration to expose or misrepresent his conduct. It happened favourably to Allen's views, though not quite so fortunately for his safety—for the desires and true interests of men are often wide asunder—that Kildare's arrogant and ambitious conduct involved him in many suspicious proceedings, and gave offence to many. Allen's faction, in consequence, rapidly increased in numbers, and in the means of annoyance. In our life of the earl we have already had occasion to relate the particulars of this proceeding, and the *State Paper* correspondence affords full and detailed evidence both of its nature and means. The council itself became, in fact, what might well be termed a conspiracy, if the substantial justice of their complaints did not necessitate and excuse the course they adopted.

In 1533 Allen entered into a dispute for precedence with Cromer, who had been made chancellor in his room. The controversy appears to have been decided in favour of Cromer. Subsequent events, as Mr. Dalton observes, put an end to "all controversies concerning bearing the cross." An arrangement of a very different nature, also mentioned from the *State Papers* by the same author, affords the only probable inference on the subject of the contest. Among the provisions made for the defence of the country, it was appointed that "all lords, and persons of the spirituality, shall send companies to hostings and journeys in the manner and form following:—

"The archbishop of Armagh, 16 able archers or gunners, appointed for the war. The archbishop of Dublin, 20, &c., &c., &c."‡

The consequences of the hostility of Allen's party now began to be rapidly and fatally developed. The earl of Kildare having continued for some time to plunge deeper and deeper in the embarrassments brought on by his own rashness and his enemies' contrivance, went, for the last time, to England, leaving the government to his son, lord Thomas Fitz-Gerald, in whose memoir we have fully related the event —the disgrace of the earl—the fatal course of infatuation which led his son to an early death—and the most foul and inhuman murder of Allen. This last-mentioned event took place on the 28th of July, 1534. On the preceding evening Allen, reasonably fearful of the enmity he had excited, and apprehending the siege of Dublin castle, resolved to save himself by a flight into England, and embarked with this intent.

---

* Ware's An.   † Dalton.   ‡ State Papers.

In the night his vessel was stranded near Clontarf—most probably by the treachery of the pilot, who was a follower of the Geraldines. Finding his danger, the archbishop took refuge in the "mansion of Mr. Hollywood of Artane, whose extensive hospitality he commemorates in his *Repertorium Ovide*." The hospitality of his friend could not, however, reprieve him from his cruel fate. His retreat was reported to Lord Thomas, and the next morning his fell and blood-thirsty foes were at the door. In his shirt he was dragged out, and beaten to death. The wretches who committed the crime shortly after came to violent deaths.

II. CLERICAL AND LITERARY.

ROBERT DE WIKEFORD.

DIED A. D. 1390.

SHORTLY after the death of Thomas de Minot, archbishop of Dublin, Robert de Wikeford was appointed to the vacant see. He was born at Wikeford Hall in Essex, was a man of learning and ability, archdeacon of Winchester, doctor both of the civil and canon law in the University of Oxford, and was held in high estimation by Edward III., who, on frequent occasions, both employed and rewarded his services. Previous to his elevation he was for some time constable of Bourdeaux, and assisted in the management of the affairs at Acquitaine, on the Black Prince surrendering that province to his father. He removed to Ireland immediately after his appointment to the archbishopric, and the following year was made chancellor of that kingdom. In 1377, on the death of Edward III., he received the writ to alter the great seal, and substitute the name of Richard for that of Edward, and he was allowed £20 from the treasury for his own expenses. He was active and judicious in his management of the see, and was permitted to make many valuable additions to it. In 1381, he was employed in promoting the collection of a clerical subsidy for Richard, and in 1385 he was again appointed chancellor. At a meeting of the prelates and nobles in Naas, he received orders not to leave Ireland, where his presence was of much importance, without a special licence; but this he obtained early in 1390, when he removed to England, where he intended to remain for a year; but while there, was seized with his last illness, and died August 29th, 1390.

ROBERT WALDBY.

DIED A. D. 1397.

ROBERT WALDBY, a man of great learning and natural endowments, accompanied Edward the Black Prince to France, and was appointed professor of divinity at Toulouse, "where," says Bale, "he arrived to such a pitch of excellence, as to be esteemed the first among the learned for eloquence and skill in the languages." He was promoted to the bishopric of Ayre in Gascony, through the influence of his patron Edward, and was some years after translated to the see of Dublin. Edward II. continued to him the same consideration and regard shown by his father, and about 1392, appointed him chancellor of Ireland. He at the same time appointed Richard Metford, the bishop of Chichester, treasurer of Ireland; and on his promotion to Sarum, in 1395, Waldby successfully used his interest at court to be removed to Chichester, from which he was the following year translated to the archbishopric of York. He did not long enjoy this new dignity, being attacked with a severe illness early in 1397, and dying on the 29th of May in that year. He is buried in the middle of St. Edmond's chapel in Westminster Abbey under a marble tomb which bore the following inscription, though from some of the brass plates being torn off it is now defaced:—

> Hic, fuit expertus in quovis jure Robertus;
> De Walby dictus: nunc est sub marmore strictus
> Sacræ Scripturæ Doctor fuit et Gentiureæ
> Ingenuus medicus, et Plebis semper amicus;
> Consultor Regis optabat prospera Legis,
> Ecclesiæ Choris fuit unus, bis quoque honoris
> Præsul advensis, post Archos Dubliniensis;
> Hinc Cicestrensis. tandem Primas Eboracensis,
> Quarto Calendas Junii migravit, cursibus anni
> Septem milleni ter C. nonies quoque deni.
> Vos precor Orate ut sint sibi dona beatæ,
> Cum sanctis vitæ requiescat et sic sine lite.

He was brother to the learned John Waldby.

WALTER FITZ-SIMONS.

DIED A. D. 1511.

WALTER FITZ-SIMONS was consecrated archbishop of Dublin in 1484. Ware calls him "a learned divine and philosopher;" and he was bachelor both of the civil and canon law. His knowledge and learning, however, did not secure him from deception; and he became a strenuous supporter of the absurd pretensions of Lambert Simnel, at whose coronation he assisted in Christ's Church in 1487, when John Payn, bishop of Meath, preached a sermon in the presence of the lord-deputy, the chancellor, treasurer, and other great officers of state, and they placed on the head of Simnel a crown taken from the statue of the Virgin Mary. This strange delusion being, however, quickly dissipated by the capture and degradation of Simnel, the archbishop renewed his allegiance, and received his pardon the year following, from Sir Richard Edgecombe, the king's commissioner, who, in the great chamber in Thomas Court, received the oaths and recognizances of the earl of Kildare, then lord-deputy, and all the nobility who had been involved in the late rebellion. In 1492, Fitz-Simons was made deputy to Jaspar, duke of Bedford, and while he held this office Perkin Warbeck made his appearance in Ireland, but from the shortness of his stay there at that time, the lord-deputy was not compelled to take any part either for or against him. He held a parliament in Dublin in 1493, and having resigned his office to Viscount

Gormanstown, he went to England, both to give the king an account of his own administration, and also to make him aware of the general state of the kingdom. After remaining there about three months, during which time he appears to have made a most favourable impression on the mind of Henry, he returned to Ireland with ample instructions respecting the management of that country. It is stated by Stanihurst that the archbishop being with the king when a highly laudatory speech was made in his presence, he was asked by Henry his opinion of it, on which the archbishop answered, "If it pleaseth your highness it pleaseth me; I find no fault, save only that he flattered your majesty too much." "Now, in good faith," said the king, "our father of Dublin, we were minded to find the same fault ourselves." When, in 1496, the king having appointed his son Henry, duke of York, lord-lieutenant of Ireland, he put him under the guidance of the archbishop, in whose "allegiance, diligence, integrity, conscience, experience, and learning," he had the most implicit confidence; and he at the same time appointed him lord-chancellor. In a synod held by the archbishop, he ordained a yearly salary to be paid by him and his suffragans to a divinity reader. In the same year the see of Glendalough, which had been united to Dublin from the reign of king John, but the government of which had been usurped by friar Denis White, was re-united to that of Dublin by the voluntary surrender of it by White, whose conscience became oppressed towards the end of his life by his illegal tenure of it. Fitz-Simons, having held the archbishopric for twenty-seven years, died at Finglass, on the 14th of May, 1511, and was buried in St. Patrick's Church. He was a man of a very just mind, of high principle, deep learning, and had a graceful and insinuating address, which particularly qualified him for the high sphere in which he moved, and won for him the regard and confidence of persons of opposite parties and opinions.

JOHN HALIFAX.

DIED A. D. 1255.

John Halifax, commonly designated Sacrobosco, from Holywood, his supposed birthplace in the county of Wicklow, claims a distinguished place in the history of science, to which he was a successful contributor in a period of intellectual barrenness. His labours may be in some measure regarded as closing the first early stage of astronomy, and (at some distance), heralding the brighter day of Copernicus, Kepler and Galileo. His writings were published, and received as standard in the schools, nearly 300 years before the earliest of those illustrious men.[*] And his great work *De Sphera* held its place as a chief authority during that interval of time.

With the common fortune of great men who have lived in obscure times, the personal records of his life are few, and his *euthanasia* will best be found in the darkness which he aided to dispel, and in the low contemporary state and obscure prospects of astronomical science.

[*] Copernicus died A. D. 1543, Kepler, 1630.

CLERICAL AND LITERARY.

With this view we will, according to the custom hitherto observed in this work, claim indulgence for a brief and glancing sketch of the wonderful history of a science, even in its failures, displaying the proudest monument of the human intellect.

The period of Sacrobosco may be viewed as the early dawn of that science which will hereafter be recollected as the glory of the nineteenth century. From the sixth century till the thirteenth, there lay a dull and rayless torpor over the intellectual faculties, in which the science of antiquity was lost. To estimate the advantages and disadvantages which then affected its revival, it may here be sufficient to make a few remarks upon the earlier history of science.

There is a broad interval between the geographical research which bounded the known world by the surrounding sea of darkness, whose unknown shores were peopled with the Hyperboreans, and Lestrigons, and Cimmerians, and other dire chimeras of ignorance, and the voyages of Ross and Parry. The step is wide from the gnomon of Thales to the practical science of Kater, Sabine and Roy, or to the exquisite scientific and instrumental precision of the Ordnance Survey in Ireland. Wider still is the ascent of discovery between the "fiery clouds" of Anaxagoras and his school, and the nebulæ—the "heaven of heavens" of Sir William Herschell, who has expanded the field of observation beyond the flight of the sublimest poetry. Yet astronomy had, nevertheless, been then, and through every period of which there is any record, an object of earnest and industrious inquiry. The most striking and glorious phenomena of the external world, could not fail at any period to excite the admiration, wonder, and speculative contemplation, of a being endowed with the vast grasp of reason which has since explored them with such marvellous success. They were a study to the inquiring, and a religion to the superstitious, from the first of times. The history of the human mind, perhaps, offers no succession of phenomena more illustrative, than the long variety of theories which seem to mark, as they descend, the advances of observation, or illustrate the law of action, by which the reason of man progresses towards its end. To pursue this view would require a volume to itself. It must here suffice to say, that hitherto there appears to have existed no adequate notions of the system of the heavens; neither the form or magnitude of the earth were known; or the distances, magnitudes, and motions of the other great bodies of the solar system. Of the earlier science of the Egyptians, the objects were confined to the measurement of time; and if we knew no farther, the error of their ancient year would sufficiently fix the limit of their knowledge. The Greek philosophers, Pythagoras and his cotemporaries, whose knowledge is referred to Egypt, were evidently further advanced, but have left the landmarks of their progress in the curious absurdity of their theoretical views. It is sufficient that they had no notion, even approaching the truth, on the true magnitude and frame of the solar system. Yet it is not to be passed over, that even at that early period, the surprising sagacity of Pythagoras attained to some just fundamental notions which there were then no sufficient means to verify, and which were destined to sleep for many ages, till taken up by the Italian geometers in the beginning of the sixteenth century. Pythagoras conceived the first idea of the true system: he supposed the sun to be at rest in the centre, and the earth with the other planets to be carried round in circular orbits. This great philosopher made even a further step, reaching by a very strange and wonderfully ingenious analogy (if the story be true) to both the principle of gravitation and the precise law of its application. He was, by an accident, led to make experiments on sound: by one of these he ascertained the force with which various degrees of tension, caused by different weights, acted on strings of different lengths, so as to produce proportional intensities of sound. This discovery, which is supposed to have been the origin of stringed instruments of music, he applied to the solar system, and conjectured that the planets were, according to the same principle, drawn to the sun, with a force proportional to their several masses and inversely as the squares of their distances. It seems to have wanted little to improve this happy thought; but that little was wanting. There can nevertheless be little doubt, that it continued to pass down the stream of ages, and to recur to the most sagacious understandings of aftertimes. The fact was veiled by the mystical spirit of the Pythagorean and Platonic philosophy, in a mythological dress: Apollo playing on his seven-stringed harp, appositely described the harmonious analogy of nature's law. It was this conception which originated the idea of the music of the spheres, as imagined by the early philosophers of Greece.

Though the geometers of ancient Greece had carried some principal branches of mathematics to an astonishing degree of perfection, their progress in physical science is chiefly memorable for its errors and the narrowness of its scope. Six hundred years before our era, Thales had invented the geometry of triangles, and measured the heights of the pyramids by their shadows. The elements of plane and solid geometry, cultivated in the long interval between, were matured by the genius of Euclid, Apollonius, and Archimedes: by this latter philosopher, whose genius finds few parallels in human history, mechanics also, and different branches of physical science, were advanced to an extent not now to be distinctly defined. But there lay around those mighty ancients a vast field of obscurity, which they had not attained the means to penetrate. Other aids, both instrumental and theoretical, were reserved for the development of future times; their knowledge was confined in its application to the operations of the rule and compass. Beyond this narrow scope lay the wide realm since fully explored by the science of Galileo and Newton, inaccessible to observation, and darkly explored by conjecture and theory, then, as now and ever the resources of human ignorance and curiosity, where knowledge cannot reach.

Nevertheless, so early as the time of Aristotle, the sounder method of observation and experiment were known: but the field of knowledge was too contracted for the range of speculation. The recognition was but partial. Yet from this period, the phenomena of astronomy were observed, registered, and submitted to mathematical computation. The visible stars were grouped and catalogued, eclipses were calculated, and attempts were made, on sound geometrical principles, to measure the circumference of the earth. Just notions of the system were even entertained, but upon inadequate grounds, and amidst a variety of theoretical systems; and it was not until the year 150 B.C. that Eratosthenes, the librarian of Alexandria, measured an arc of the meridian, and computed the earth's circumference. Among the remarkable circumstances of the interesting progress of this vast and sublime development of genius and observation, thus in (as it were) the first stage of its elevation, two are specially to be observed, for their essential connexion with the history both of astronomy and of human reason. The one, had we time and space, would lead us into the history of astrology —a wonderful combination of the great and little properties of human nature, under the towering shadows of which the science of observation was preserved and fostered in its growth. The other is the beautiful application of an expedient still employed in natural philosophy, for the same purpose of embodying and subjecting to computation the results of experience. A system purely empirical combined the observed phenomena of the known bodies of the solar system, in such a manner, that being framed so as to include all that could be observed of their motions, it was thus not only adapted for the purpose of computation within those limits, but also served to lead to a closer and more precise measure of phenomena, which, without the reference to some standard system, might easily escape the minute observation necessary for the detection of small quantities of motion or changes of position, such as might lead to further corrections. Of such a nature was the hypothesis by which Apollonius first attempted to solve the seemingly anomalous motions of the planets. This curious system, which was the faith of Europe for fourteen centuries, is worth the reader's attention, and, without any certainty that we can render it popularly intelligible, we shall here attempt to describe it.

In conformity with the universal tendency to explain phenomena by assumptions which seem the most natural, it first began to be the received opinion that the sun and planets moved in circular paths round the earth, which was supposed to be fixed in the centre. The parallel paths and circular apparent motions of the phenomena of the heavens, suggested the notion of a crystalline sphere, in which the multitude of the stars was set, and which revolved with a solemn continuity round its terrestrial centre. The observation of the unequal and contrary apparent motions of the moon and planets extended the theory, and separate spheres of hollow crystalline were devised, to account for these diverse phenomena. It was to these vast concaves, thus spinning round with complicated but harmonious times and movements, that some Eastern poets have attributed a sublime and eternal harmony, unheard in this low world, but heard we should presume, in the

"Starry mansion of Jove's court."

Such was the first rude and simple outline of the system as adopted by Aristotle and old Eudoxus. Closer and further observation, in the course of time, detected phenomena inconsistent with such a system, and for a time astronomers were content to observe. In proportion to the multiplication of phenomena, conjecture became more timid, and system more difficult. At last, the ingenuity of the geometer Apollonius contrived the first form of a theory which explained the great irregularities of those planetary motions, which most readers now understand to be the combined result of the separate motions of the earth and planets. Instead of a concave sphere having its centre of motion in the earth, Apollonius conceived each of the planets to be carried round on the circumference of a circle, which was itself carried round upon another circle, the circumference of which was the path of its centre. By this ingenious device, the planetary phenomena now so well known by the terms direct, retrograde, and stationary, seemed to be explained. The appearance of a new star, and the long and laborious course of observation into which it led Hipparchus, who undertook in the true spirit of inductive philosophy to catalogue the stars, conducted this great astronomer to the discovery of the precession of the equinoxes.

A new circle, on which the sun was moved, according to the law already explained, reduced this phenomenon to the same convenient system. To this great geometer is attributed the invention of the method of latitude and longitude, by which the position of places on the earth is ascertained: the invention of spherical trigonometry is said also to be among his discoveries.* Of these, however, the most considerable portion were lost, and the remains appear only to be known by their preservation in the Almagest of Ptolemy. Three hundred years after the great philosophers already mentioned, their system, with the addition of whatever observation had added in the interval, came into the hands of Ptolemy, whose name it has ever since borne. This great man, not undeservedly, called prince of astronomers by the ancients, may be described as the Laplace of old astronomy: he collected, combined, and completed the results of observation, and reduced the real and theoretical knowledge of his predecessor into an improved, corrected, and augmented theory. A system of empirical knowledge, even then displaying a grand and sublime aspect of the vast capability of human reason, though now chiefly valuable for its connexion with the faith, the superstition, and poetical remains of other times; unless to those who can appreciate its value as a magnificent ruin of ancient philosophy, more instructive and more sublime than Thebes or Palmyra.

Of this system, of which we have forborne to attempt a detailed description, (which would only embarrass the reader who does not already understand it,) one of the effects was, to render permanent the errors which it contained, by the seeming precision with which it explained and calculated the known phenomena of nature. The broad intelligence of Hipparchus and Ptolemy were probably not deceived: they understood the nature of the process too well: they were aware that a theory which comprised, in its first elements, the whole visible phenomena, as well as the rates of movement and times of occurrence, must necessarily, within certain limits, appear to reproduce them as results of calculation. But the very fact that a known succession of phenomena could be thus deduced from a theory, seemed to offer an unanswerable verification of its truth, to a long succession of mindless

* Laplace Systeme du Monde.

ages, whose broken recollections of ancient knowledge were simply the dreams of superstition.

A long period of ignorance followed, in which all science was lost, and human reason was engrossed in devising sophisms and subtle errors. Science, lost in Europe, found refuge in the East; and about the end of the seventh century began to be cultivated with extraordinary zeal and success by the Arabians, who invented algebra, and are also supposed to have invented trigonometry. They translated a vast number of works of Greek science, and among the rest the Almagest of Ptolemy, about the beginning of the ninth century.

At the revival of learning in Europe, astronomy, which had always more or less occupied the schools, from its connexion with astrology, as well as its essential combination with the adjustments of the calendar, began earliest to occupy attention. Among the works of science brought from Arabia, the Almagest of Ptolemy was obtained, and translated into Latin, by the patronage of Frederick III., in 1230. From this, a quick succession of astronomers and geographers began to construct anew the science of antiquity.

The progress of geographical knowledge had been far more retarded and uncertain. Being chiefly dependent on detailed and local research, it was the less likely to be advanced beyond the narrow limits occupied by civilized nations. Notwithstanding the measurement of Eratosthenes, which is supposed to have been not far from correctness, the geographers who follow for many ages were farther from any approach to the truth. The maps of various geographers of the middle ages, are still extant, to prove how restricted were the bounds of the known world; the farther extremities of Europe, Asia, and Africa, were shut out from all but conjecture: America was yet undreamed of. The knowledge which actually existed was more due to commerce and conquest than to science; and the march of the army, or the station of the caravan, were more to be relied on than the chart of science. In England, the first idea of a topographical survey originated in the distribution of the Saxon lands by the Norman conqueror, and gave rise to the celebrated compilation called *Doomsday Book.* The crusades gave some impulse to the advance of topographical knowledge. The travels of Marco Polo extended geography widely into the East. A long and improving course of maritime discovery set in, and as navigation became cultivated, far less obstructed voyages of discovery soon afforded more correct and extended notions of the compass and form of the old world. Still, however, the condition of geographical knowledge considered as a science, remained in the state in which it was left by Ptolemy.

It is in this state of the science that the great standard work of Sacrobosco finds its place. It held the schools for the following 300 years, went through numerous translations, and has been published with a commentary by Clavius. It might still have held its ground, and Sacrobosco his fame, but for the revolutions in science which the sixteenth century produced. A succession of new intellects broke from the regenerated schools of antiquity. The cycle of a long decline of scientific genius seemed to have rolled back into its renovation of youthful vigour,—the geometry of Archimedes, Apollonius, and Euclid, seemed to conduct Copernicus, Kepler and Galileo back to the era of Pythagoras. These great men discovered the inadequacy of the Ptolemaic system to account for the phenomena of the solar system. They were silenced by the despotism of ignorance; but they propagated the impulse of right reason, and the light they left never slept till it came into the school of England and the hand of Newton. Every one is aware of the main facts of the Newtonian system. But should any one who has read so far, ask the question which has been often asked—what is our security that the system of Newton is not as fallacious as the system of Ptolemy? the only answer we can give is this, that the principles of their construction are not simply different, but opposite—the one was a system devised to explain appearances, the other an undevised system, self-built, from discovered truth—the one was a theory, the other a collection of accurately ascertained facts—the one was intentionally assumed to represent what meets the eye, the other studiously rejecting both assumptions and appearances, may be regarded as the laborious work of the observation of ages, slowly falling together, until a hand of power revealed the fundamental fact which disclosed the secret system of nature. The distances, magnitudes, and motions of the system are facts, tangible to sense: the theory of gravitation rests on the most universal analogy yet discovered, and on the most varied and complex confirmation of geometrical reasoning and computation. "The terms attraction and gravity," says Mr. Woodhouse, "are not meant to signify any agency or mode of operation. They stand rather for a certain class of like effects, and are convenient modes of designating them." The law of gravity is the statement of a fact. If it were to be disproved, the vast system of facts, of which it is the combining principle, still remains the same—a symmetrical collection of calculable facts, unmixed with a single inference from mere theory.

This ancient mathematician and astronomer taught the mathematical sciences, as then known, in the university of Paris, in 1230. Besides his standard work on the sphere, he also wrote on the astrolabe, on the calendar, and an arithmetical treatise. He died in Paris, in 1235, and was buried in the church " D. Maturini." *

JOHN DUNS SCOTUS.

DIED A. D. 1308.

THE birth-place of Duns is disputed by different authorities: the English and Scotch lay claim to him; but Wadding, his biographer, adjudges him to Ireland. This conclusion is supported by the adjunct of Scotus, then unquestionably assumed as distinctive of Irish origin; and it may be observed, that it never has been (and could not have been)

---

* " Johannes à Sacro Bosco, Philosophus et Mathematicus insignus, claruit anno 1230. Hunc Balæus, ex Lelando Anglum facit, natump; Halifaxæ tradit in Agro Eboracensi, ac inde nomen accepisse, sed perperàm procul dubio. Nam *Halifax* Sacrum capillum significan, non Sacrum Boscum. Dempsterus Scotum facit. Stanihurstus et Alij Hibernum volunt et *Hollywoodæ* natum, in Agro Dubliniensi. In hâc opinionum varietate nihil definio."—*Ware.*

thus applied to any Scotchman, as it is evident that, so applied, it would have had no distinctive signification. The schools of Ireland, were at the time celebrated for a science, which was eminently adapted to the Irish genius—rather quick and ingenious than solid or profound. A remark which, to apply to the modern Irish, must, we confess, undergo some allowances and deductions, for the modifications derived perhaps from an intermixture of blood. Scotus was born about the year 1266, in the province of Ulster, according to Cavellus, Luke, and Wadding:* he was educated in the university of Oxford, and became a Franciscan friar. From Oxford he went to the university of Paris, where his logical ability quickly made him eminent, and be became a follower of Thomas Aquinas, the famous angelical doctor. During his residence in Paris, he acquired universal applause by an exploit incidental to his age.

The itinerant sophist has long disappeared with the knight errant and the travelling bard: the increase of knowledge has lessened the value of disputative skill, as the advance of civilization has somewhat cheapened the estimation of physical prowess: and the teeming profusion and facility of the press has obviated the necessity of the *viva voce* encounters of the controversialist. Some remains of this custom, may perhaps, be said to have yet a glimmering existence in Ireland; which in some respects is entitled to be called the *limbus Patrum* of antiquity: we allude to the known practice of the Irish hedge schools, of which the most distinguished scholars travel about from school to school, on a tour of disputation, in which they both add to their learning and endeavour to maintain superiority of knowledge.† This literary knight-errantry may perhaps be regarded as a monument of the time when the wandering doctors of Paris, Bologna, and Padua, and the still more subtle disciples of St Comgall's ancient university, used to travel from college to college, with the spear and shield of Aristotle—*peripatetic* in every sense—and win honours by proving black was white, in opposition to all antagonists. Duns, whose chivalry was in this at least not deficient, had early in life made a vow to support the honour of the Virgin. It was for this purpose that he presented himself to the university of Paris, and offered to maintain against all opponents, her freedom from original sin. A day was set, and the university assembled its powers and intelligence to witness this trial of dialectic skill. Many students and doctors of acknowledged reputation impugned the proposition of the Irish logician. Duns having fully stated the question, allowed his adversaries to discuss it in full detail; and for three interminable days the torrent of their logic flowed, and involved their hearers in the tangled web of scholastic distinctions. Meanwhile, Duns, nothing dismayed, sat listening with a patient and unmoved steadiness of aspect and demeanour, which puzzled all the spectators, and made every one think him a miracle of patience. They were however to be still more astonished, when—after three days of ceaseless verbosity had spun the question into two hun-

* Cited by Ware, Scriptoribus Hib. Ed. 1639.
† An ample and curious account of these worthies may be found in Carleton's Traits and Stories of the Irish peasantry.

dred elaborate arguments, and the Parisian disputants confessed there was no more to be said—Duns calmly arose and recited all their several arguments, which one after the other he unanswerably refuted. And then while the whole body were yet digesting his superiority in silent dismay, he recommenced and annihilated his already prostrate antagonists with some hundred more unanswerable arguments for the question. The university was convinced, and not only gave Duns his doctor's degree, with the well-merited title of the "subtle doctor," but also decreed that the doctrine thus affirmed should be held by the university in future. We may presume that the university kept its own law: but Duns was not to be tied by the webs of his own subtlety, and proved his claim at least to the title they conferred, by afterwards maintaining a different view of the question. The reputation of Duns grew, and his popularity increased, until it became unfit that he should any longer continue to be reputed the follower of another. To one like Duns, to whom every side of every question must have been equally conclusive, it was easy to find room to differ: and he soon found a fair field of controversy with his great Neapolitan master, Aquinas.

Of Aquinas, our reader may wish to know some particulars. He was the son of the illustrious family of Aquino, in the Terra di Lavoro, in Italy. Contrary to the wish of his parents he became a Dominican friar; and the monks were compelled for some time to remove him from place to place, to maintain their possession of a youth of such high promise. He was at one time seized during a journey by his brothers, and kept for two years in confinement; he was however found out by the Dominicans, and with their aid contrived to let himself down from a window, and escaped. At last having completed the course of study then pursued, he went to Paris and took a doctor's degree: from Paris he returned to Italy, and set up his school at Naples. He soon began to be regarded as the great light of the age, and more than any other writer contributed to the triumph of the scholastic over the ideal or mystic schools. He was among the first and greatest of those who introduced the theological method of collecting and digesting into a theory the doctrines of scripture. His system, immediately on its publication, received the most distinguished honour and acceptance—and he was ranked after death by Pius V. as the fifth doctor of the church: he was also called the angel of the church, and the angelical doctor. His death took place in 1274, and he was canonized by pope John XXII.*

Such was the mighty antagonist which Duns assailed. The nature of the co-operation between divine grace and human will, and the measure of imparted grace necessary to salvation, were among the most prominent points of difference. The Dominicans sided with their own great light: the Franciscans were no less arduous in support of their subtle doctor; and a violent division renewed the animosity of these two famous orders. Such was the origin of the two sects who are known by the names of Scotists and Thomists.†

Scotus returned from Paris to Oxford, where he for some time con-

---

* Enfield's Philosophy. † Mosheim.

tinued to preach and write, with increasing celebrity. But again, visiting Paris, he was tempted to make au effort to settle in a place which was the stage of his greatest celebrity. He continued to teach there for about one year, when he was summoned away by the general of the Franciscans to Cologne. On his approach to Cologne, he was received with all the honour due to his reputation. Here he continued his course of teaching to the numerous scholars whom his renown attracted, until his death. He was one day engaged in delivering a lecture to a crowded audience, when a sudden stroke of paralysis arrested his discourse; it proved fatal in a few hours. His works filled twelve massive folios—which remain a monument of his formidable fertility; and, considering that he died in his 42d year, present no slight illustration of the copious facility of a science which began and ended in words and verbal distinctions—a science which rejected the restraint of facts and the limits of the understanding—and with a compass beyond the grasp of Archimedes, pretended to wield infinity and omniscience without asking for a ground on which to rest the lever of the schools.

Such a state of knowledge may well awaken the interest of many readers, not conversant in the history of the period. For the benefit of such we must now attempt the performance of the promise with which we commenced this memoir; and as in the life of Sacrobosco we gave a cursory sketch of the science of the age, so we shall now offer some brief notice of the philosophy of the schools.

The earlier writers of the church had derived their system of theology from the scriptures. In the course of time, by a natural and very intelligible transition, these earlier divines themselves became the text-book of authority, and gradually began to occupy the place of the scriptures; thus in the decline of literature and philosophy, leading gradually to their disuse. Theology, thus removed from its foundations, was thrown open to the bewildering ingenuity of speculation. The corrupted Platonism of the Alexandrian school, early adopted into the theological school, and largely infused into many of the ancient writers, became in some measure the substance of opinion and controversy; and it is chiefly to the Irish schools of the middle ages that the honour is attributed of an idea which, though sadly misapplied, was yet in its principle not devoid of justness. It was proposed as a new discovery, that it was unworthy to take truths of such importance upon the opinions of fallible authorities, when they might themselves, by the exercise of reason, ascertain what was true from the original documents. But unfortunately, they were utterly devoid of any just knowledge of the use or the limits of reason. From the scripture—by the application of the most absurd system of metaphysics that ever was wiredrawn from sophistry and superstition, in the absence of common sense—they spun the sacred text into allegories and idealisms, that seem more like the ravings of delirium, than the sober interpretation of Divine truths revealed to human apprehension. Such briefly was the form taken by the ancient sect known by the name of Mystics, whose earlier history it does not suit our limits to enter upon. It is perhaps best understood to have arisen anew from the study of Augustine, whose writings it strongly tinctures, and who was a favourite in the cloisters of the middle ages.

A weak glimmer of the peripatetic logic, existing in the same periods, seems to have had little influence in correcting this abuse: the early writers of the church had condemned the writings of Aristotle as inconsistent with divine truth: and the only surviving remains of logical science seems to have been an imperfect system of dialectics ascribed to St Augustin, who was at one time an ardent follower of the Stoic philosophy. At length however an increased communication with Arabia, when about the twelfth century it became customary for learned men to travel in quest of knowledge, was the means of introducing Saracenic translations of the works of Aristotle. The immediate consequence was an infusion of new opinions into the church, founded upon new methods of reasoning.

The church, vigilant in the superintendence of opinion, soon found cause to check the growing evil. Several doctors tested by the jealous thermometer of orthodoxy, were found wanting in the standard shade of Platonism—they were cited before councils, and had their books publicly burned—fortunate in preceding by a few years the period when they might have shared a common fate with their offending volumes. A general prohibition of the writings of Aristotle quickly ensued.

At a somewhat earlier period such a prohibition would have been imperatively felt; but it was a time when a fresh impulse had been imparted to the human mind: the world was awaking from a long sleep, and men in every country of Europe began to look around for light. The orthodox bowed submission, but the schools were at the moment filled with the swarming race of a new generation, and the writings of Aristotle were zealously studied. The mind of the schools soon became largely infused with the elements of a new spirit; and the youth of the age grew up with a deeply imbued love of disputation and subtlety. The church itself felt and yielded to the strong reaction; and, when the growing evil could no longer be suppressed, with its ever admirable tact and sagacity, endeavoured to neutralize and gradually adopt the perilous instrument of human reason. Fortunately for its views, some steps of progress were still wanting to make the instrument dangerous. The love of logic grew; and it became the subject of loud complaint that disputation filled the schools with its noise, and occupied the place of all other study. Disputation became the pride and study of the scholar and the business of life—victory became the source of fame and the test of opinion. The consequence is easily inferred, for it was inevitable. Opinion thus became the end of all study, and took the place of the love of truth. The instincts of the mind were sophisticated; the subtle, word-splitting Scholastic was the fruit of this anomalous culture.

A few words must here be said on the writings, which were the foundation of this corruption of human reason. The writings of Aristotle were but imperfectly understood by their Arabian translators, and became additionally corrupt in the transfusion of a second medium. Originally obscure from the strictly scientific method of the Greek philosopher, and the total absence of those indirect artifices of style which are commonly used for illustration, an erroneous and fantastic commentary swelled the volume, and was received as the better part of its substance, so that to use the language of a historian, the students were as much indebted to Averroes as to Aristotle. A philosophy at the same time corrupt, obscure, and peculiarly unadapted to the state of human knowledge at the period, gradually filled the schools. Its effects were in no respect beneficial—a generation unacquainted with the uses of reasoning, and destitute of the first elements of real knowledge on which it must proceed, became smitten with a deep love of its forms. The syllogistic method—which accurately represents the operation of reasoning,* and offers both an excellent discipline to the intellect, and a certain test to the value of inference from ascertained premises—was mistaken for something which it did not pretend to be. It became, in the hands of subtle ignorance, a superstition of the intellect—a sort of verbal magic by which any thing could be proved. The forms of reason were substituted in the place of reason, and words took the place of things: for nearly four hundred years the just progress of the human understanding was retarded by the quibbling and interminable jargon of men like Aquinas and Scotus, and the German doctor Albertus, through whom the European schools became acquainted with the writings of the Stagyrite.†

Thus misunderstood and misapplied, Aristotle, from being first opposed by the policy of the church, soon acquired universal dominion. " And so far from falling under the censure of councils and popes, the Aristotelian and Saracenic philosophy became the main pillars of the ecclesiastical hierarchy. In the year 1366, cardinals were appointed by Urban to settle the manner in which the writings of Aristotle should be studied in the university of Paris: and in the year 1462, Charles VII. ordered the works of Aristotle to be read and publicly explained in that university. Thus the union between the peripatetic philosophy and the Christian religion was confirmed, and Aristotle became not only the interpreter, but even the judge of St Paul."‡ From this period to the Reformation, the church and the universities resounded with dispute and frothy contentions, long and difficult to specify by clear and intelligible distinction: the Thomist and Scotist, of whom we have mentioned the leading differences—the still more prolonged and vehement controversy of the Nominalists and Realists, which we shall fully state in our memoir of Bishop Berkeley, with half a dozen main shades of opinion, were contested with idle words and not idle hands, in foaming disputation and sanguinary fray.

The reformers in their turn produced a re-action, which, however salutary it must be admitted to have been in arresting the further advance of this state of philosophy, passed into the opposite extreme. Though it introduced a sound exercise of reason, and a return to the legitimate field of facts, yet by the law of opposition, so universally discernible in human opinion, they confounded the instrument with the vitiated use to which it had been applied. With the indiscriminate vigour of immature knowledge, in rejecting the doctrines they cast away all that was even accidentally in contact with them. In condemning the adversary, the house in which he lived, the garb he wore,

---

* See Whately's Logic for a satisfactory explanation on this long unnoticed fact.
† Gillies' Introduction to Aristotle's Rhetoric.
‡ Enfield's Abridgment of Brucker.

the very ground he trode on, grew criminal in their eyes. Among the many extrinsic adjuncts of Romanism thus condemned, the vast intellectual outwork of the scholastic philosophy could not hope to escape; and the works of Aristotle, unhappily confounded with this tumid and inane excrescence of human reason, were denounced.— " With the light of the gospel," writes Mr Gillies, "the champions of the Reformation dispelled the pestilent exhalations, and disparted the gorgeous but cloud-built castles with which the schoolmen had surrounded a fortress of adamant; for the genuine philosophy of Aristotle remained entire, unhurt, and alike concealed from the combatants on either side. The reformers, engaged in an infinitely greater undertaking, were not concerned in distinguishing the master from his unworthy scholars, and in separating the gold from the dross."* The violence of opposition, which was the speedy result of this indiscriminating but perfectly natural (and not unjustifiable) spirit, pursued the Stagyrite to his last retreats, the walls of colleges. The general reader of the present age will easily indeed recall the reproaches of the light-armed and superficial skirmishers of modern reviews and pamphlets discharged against the university of Oxford, on the score of the assumed worship of Aristotle. His works, only known to some of the leading writers of the very last generation, through the same impure sources from which they were presented to Scotus and his clamorous fraternity, were ignorantly assailed, and as ignorantly defended. The profound and elementary comprehension of Bacon, the perspicacious common sense of the admirable Locke, handed down the same subtle errors to the essentially scholastic intellect of Hume. Kames, Harris, Monboddo, Reid, and Stewart, all combined, in more or less specious inaccuracy and misapprehension; and it seems to have remained for the latest writings which have proceeded from the universities of Dublin and Oxford, to dispel the false medium either by strong remonstrance or clear and demonstrative exposition. To the leading writers who might be noticed at length on this subject, we have given as much notice as the summary character of our undertaking permits. We shall conclude this notice with an extract from one of the most distinguished writers of the age—an illustrious ornament of our Irish university, whose memoir must hereafter give value and interest to our pages—the late worthy and able prelate, archbishop Magee. " It has been singularly the fate of the Greek philosopher, to be at one time superstitiously venerated, and at another contemptuously ridiculed, without sufficient pains taken, either by his adversaries or his admirers, to understand his meaning. It has been too frequently his misfortune to be judged from the opinions of his followers rather than his own. Even the celebrated Locke is not to be acquitted of this unfair treatment of his illustrious predecessor in the paths of metaphysics; although, perhaps, it is not too much to say of his well known essay, that there is scarcely to be found in it one valuable and important truth concerning the operations of the understanding, which may not be traced in Aristotle's writings; whilst, at the same time, they exhibit many results of deep thinking, which have

* Preface to Aristotle's Rhetoric, p. 23.

entirely escaped Locke's perspicacity. Indeed, it may be generally pronounced of those who have, within the two last centuries, been occupied in the investigation of the intellectual powers of man, that had they studied Aristotle more, and (what would have been a necessary consequence) reviled him less, they would have been more successful in their endeavours to extend the sphere of human knowledge."*

This curious transition of human knowledge has led us on to a length of remark which we do not consider due to Scotus; unless, perhaps, it be considered, that the eminence which he attained in the sophistry of his age, must still have been the result of some highly distinguished intellectual powers. They were unhappily wasted gifts. His voluminous works, too long for the narrow period assigned to human study, repose with monumental silence and oblivion on the shelves of learned libraries—the too quiet habitations of the unmolested spider, who builds in their safe obscurity, and emulates their labours with skill as fine and less abused. If in a listless moment the student casts his wandering eye over the ponderous masses of unopened lore which seem to encumber the shelves of neglected school divines, his mind may be crossed by a reflection on the vast toil of thought and earnest stress of passion, the years of study and ambitious hope to gain distinction, which were melted down in the accumulation of those most neglected labours. He may thus be conducted by a widely different track to the same feelings, which the moral poet has expressed in the most simply just and eloquent strain which human pen ever wrote, upon the vanities of this life of wasted faculties and fleeting duration:—

"Perhaps in this neglected spot is laid,
Some mind once pregnant with celestial fire;
Hands which the rod of empires might have swayed,
Or waked to ecstasy the living lyre."

III. LITERARY.

ANNALISTS, HISTORIANS, AND POETS WRITING IN THE IRISH LANGUAGE.

THE editor begs to apologize to the Irish historical student for the omission in the following chronological summary of numerous names that might fitly be included under this class. So little is known of their personal history, that he could not avoid the consideration, that the space they must have occupied in this series would be altogether too much for a popular work, and would be regarded as objectionable by the numerous readers who cannot be assumed to look beyond the amusement of a leisure hour. A small selection has been made of those most noticed by antiquarian writers: or which are noticeable for any special circumstances. To the general reader it may be observed, that all the persons here mentioned were illustrious in their day, and have

* Magee on the Atonement.

some claim to be so still. Their writings are extant, and form a curious and unique department of national literature. Of some of these we can offer no further account than the mention of their works; and a few are withheld, because we shall have to notice their writings more at large under the general head of Irish literature.

MAL SUTHAIN O'CARROLL, is remarkable for having been the writer who commenced the Annals of Innisfallen. Of these important documents we have had occasion to give some account at an earlier period. Generally speaking, the more important portions of the literature of this and several following centuries, can only be viewed with advantage, in their collective character, and in those later times, when their record closes and the history of their transmission (the most important question in which they are concerned,) comes before us:—Of the general history of the literature of this period, we have already given some short account under the lives of Scotus and John Halifax. During the greater part of the period, literature must be considered as on the decline in Ireland. There nevertheless wanted not accomplished Irish scholars in every department then existing. The following small selection from numerous names, exhibit the fact that poetry at least was not wanting.

Of the illustrious O'Carroll, we can only add, that he was not only one of the most learned monks of the island, but of his time, and had the added distinction of high birth. He died, according to the Four Masters, in the year 1009.

IRELAND, of all countries in the world, is best entitled to the appellation of the "Land of Song," from her early writers being almost invariably poets, and verse having been selected as the easiest and simplest medium for conveying their thoughts, whether the topic was religion, war, or individual history. Among these, Mac Liag takes a very prominent place, being honoured by the title of "chief poet of Ireland," besides being the friend and chief antiquary of Brian Boroimhe. He was the son of Conkeartach, a doctor or professor of some eminence, and early became a favourite with his royal master, whose "fifty battles" he enthusiastically commemorates, and whose triumphant fall on the plains of Clontarf, he so pathetically but proudly details. His chief writings are "the Munster Book of Battles," which gives the most authentic detail of the encounters with the Danes, down to the battle of Clontarf; a life of Brian Boroimhe; a poem of an hundred and sixty verses upon the descendants of Cas, son of Conal Each Luath, king of Munster; and one of nearly the same length, on the twelve sons of Kennedy, father of Brian Boroimhe; also three separate poems, lamenting the fall of Brian, and strongly expressive of his own personal grief on the event; one beginning, "Oh Cinn-coradh, where is Brian;" another, "Westward came the fall of Brian;" and the last, which was written in the Hebrides, where Mac Liag went after the death of Brian, begins, "Long to be without delight," and bitterly mourns over his own lost happiness, and the desolation of Cinn-coradh. His death took place, according to the Four Masters, in 1015.

ERARD MAC COISI, one of the historians of Ireland, and "chief chronicler of the Gaels," carried on a literary contest of some length with Donough, son of Brian Boroimhe, in the course of which Donough asserts the superiority of his father, and the Munster troops over Maolseachlainn, in a poem of an hundred and ninety-two verses, while Erard, who was secretary to the Leinster king, contends with equal warmth for the more doubtful pre-eminence of his own master. He died in Clonmacnoise in the year 1023.

CUAN O'LOCHAIN, who was considered the most learned antiquarian and historian of his time, was made joint regent of Ireland with Corcran, a clergyman, on the death of Maolseachlainn. His virtues and talents were of a very high order, and he was the author of various poems; one of them descriptive of the splendour of the royal palace of Tarah, in the time of Cormac Mac Art, monarch of Ireland; another, on the rights and privileges of the monarch, and provincial kings of Ireland: the first of an hundred and eighty verses, and the next of an hundred and forty-eight; besides a poem of fifty-six verses, on the origin of the name of the river Shannon. The annals of Tighernach, Innisfallen, and the Four Masters state his having been killed in Teathbha, in 1024.

DUBDALETHY or DUDLEY, archbishop of Armagh, was son of Mælbury, senior lecturer of divinity in that city. He wrote annals of Ireland, beginning at 962, and ending 1021, which are quoted both in the Ulster Annals, and by the Four Masters. He was highly esteemed for his learning both in Ireland and Scotland; and when in the year 1050, he made a circuit of *Cineal Conaill*, he obtained three hundred cows from the people of that country. Colgan says, that he also wrote an account of the archbishops of Armagh down to his own time. He died the 1st of Sept., 1065.

GIOLLA CAOIMHGHIN, one of the most celebrated poets and historians of his time, has left a variety of historical and chronological writings in verse, some of them upwards of six hundred verses in length. One commences with the creation, and is carried down to the year in which he died. He divides his chronology into different eras, and gives the names of several memorable persons who lived in each period. There is a fine copy of this in the possession of Sir Wm. Betham. Another poem gives the names of the ancestors of the chief line of the Gaels, from the dispersion at Babel to their establishment in Spain. Copies of this are in the books of Ballimote and Leacan, in the library of the royal Irish academy. He has also written a poem of six hundred and thirty-two verses, which was one of the chief documents on which O'Flaherty founded his technical chronology. This poem gives an account of the first colonization of Ireland, and enumerates all the monarchs that reigned until the time of Laoghaire, A. D. 432, when St. Patrick first introduced Christianity into Ireland. Copies of this, are also in the books of Ballimote and Leacan. A poem on the Christian kings of Ireland, of an hundred and fifty-two verses, has been attributed to him, but some authorities give it to Conaing O'Maelconaire. In another poem he gives the names and number of the Milesian monarchs that reigned in Ireland, specifying from which of the sons of Golamh each king descended. In the same poem he gives the names of the kings who ruled in Ireland of the Fir-Bolg and Tuatha-de-Danan races. Giolla died 1072.

TIGERNACH, abbot of Clon-mac-noise, wrote the annals of Ireland, partly in Latin, and partly in Irish, from the reign of Cimbaeth, king of Ulster, and monarch of Ireland, A. M. 3596, to his own time. They were continued by Augustin M'Grath to the year of our Lord 1405, when he died. A copy of these annals is in the library of Trinity College, Dublin, and is amongst the most valuable of the existing materials for Irish history. Tigernach died in 1072.

GILLACHRIST UA MAEILEOIN, according to the learned editor of that work—as recently (1867) published with notes and an English translation for the British government, in that valuable series of historical works known as the "Rolls Publications," under the direction of the Master of the Rolls, by Mr. William Henessy—was the compiler of that valuable contribution to a future history of Ireland, the "*Chronicon Scottorum.*" He was abbot of that oft-levelled yet still surviving abbey of Clonmacnoise, whence the equally useful earlier "Chronicle of Tighernach," and many other works of Irish character have proceeded; and died in that office in 1127. Though by no means equal in importance to the earlier chronicle above named, or to "The Annals of the Four Masters," it is valuable alike as supplementary,—containing various matters which they omit,—and as confirmatory; giving the same accounts, but derived, to a greater or less extent, from independent sources. Singularly enough, although with only exception of a few lines in one or two places written in the Irish character, it is composed partly in Latin and partly in Irish; sentences in each language lying side by side, and intermixed continuously throughout it.

TANAIDHE O'MULCONAIRE wrote two historical poems, one giving an account of the kings of the race of Firbolg, who possessed Ireland before the arrival of the Tuatha-de-Danan, and whose descendants retained a great part of the island until after the introduction of Christianity; the other gives the names of the seven kings of the Tuatha-de-Danan race, who ruled Ireland for an hundred and ninety-seven years; it also mentions the arrival of the Milesians, A. M. 2935. There are copies of both these poems in the book of Invasions by the O'Clerys. Tanaidhe died in 1136.

GIOLLA MODHUDA O'CASSIDY, otherwise called Dall Clairineach, abbot of Ardbracean in Meath, was a very learned man, a good historian, and a poet. As usual at that time, he wrote his histories in verse. In one of them he gives a catalogue of the Christian monarchs of Ireland, with the number of years that each king reigned, from the time of Leogaire, A. D. 428, to the death of Maelseachlin II., 1022. In a poem of two hundred and forty-four verses, besides enumerating the kings, he shows how many of each name reigned; and in another, of three hundred and seventy four ranns* of irregular verses, he gives the names of the wives and mothers of the kings and chiefs of Ireland of the Milesian race. Giolla died, according to the best authorities, in 1143, though in one of the verses of the last mentioned-poem (which is to be found in the book of Leacan), it is stated that it was written in 1147.

GIOLLA O'DUNN, chief bard to the king of Leinster, wrote many poems which are preserved in the books of Leacan and Ballimote, chiefly connected with Leinster, which he calls "the province of the tombs of kings." One of his poems describes the tribes that sprung from the sons of Milesius, and from Lughaid, and the districts possessed by them; and another gives an account of the chief tribes descended from the three Collas, sons of Cairbre, monarch of Ireland, who was killed near Tara in Meath 286, after a reign of seventeen years. Giolla died 1160.

AMONGST the writers of this period, Maurice O'Regan takes a prominent place, from the importance of the events with which his life and writings are connected. He was a native of Leinster, and was employed by Dermod MacMurrough, king of that province, to whom he was secretary and interpreter, as ambassador to Strongbow, Robert Fitzstephen, and other English nobles, to entreat their aid for the recovery of his kingdom, from which, as we have before related, he was expelled by Roderick O'Connor, and other Irish chiefs, for the abduction of Devorgoil, the wife of O'Rourke. O'Regan wrote with much accuracy, a history of the affairs of Ireland during his own time, in his native tongue, and this composition was translated by a friend, into French verse. In the reign of Elizabeth it was again translated into English by Sir George Carew, president of Ireland, and afterwards earl of Totness. O'Regan was sent by Dermod and Strongbow to demand the surrender of Dublin, when they were on their way to besiege it, and all his details are given with the animation of an eyewitness. His history embraces the events of about three years, from the invasion of Strongbow, in the year 1168, to the siege of Limerick,

* Each rann consists of four verses.

in 1171, about which period it is supposed, that he either died, or was killed, as his history ends abruptly at this event.

MURRAY or MARIAN O'GORMAN, abbot of Knock, near Louth, was contemporary with Regan. He wrote a martyrology in verse, respecting which the statements of Ware and Colgan are rather at variance. The former says that he published a supplement to the martyrology of Ængus, in 1171, while Colgan states that O'Gorman wrote a martyrology in most elegant Irish verse in the time of Gelasius, archbishop of Armagh, about the year 1167, which is held in great esteem, and ever will be so, for the beauty of the style, and great fidelity of the performance. This (he continues) is, for the most part, collected out of the Ængusian martyrology, as an old scholiast, in his preface to that work, says; and further, that O'Gorman does not confine himself to the principal saints of Ireland alone, but takes in promiscuously those of other countries.

CONOR O'KELLY, who died A. D. 1220, wrote a metrical history of his own tribe, the O'Kellys, chiefs of Hy-maine, an ancient district now comprehended in the counties of Galway and Roscommon. It is preserved among the Irish manuscripts in the Marquis of Buckingham's library at Stowe.

ON the death of Matthew O'Reilly, in the year 1293, his brother, Giolla Tosa Roe O'Reilly, succeeded him in the government of the principality of East Brefny. He was learned, prudent, brave, and victorious, and he extended his territory from Drogheda to Rath Cruachan, now the county of Roscommon. In the year 1300 he built and endowed the monastery of Cavan, in which he erected a chapel and marble monument as a place of sepulture for himself and family. He was recognised by Edward the Second, as one of the chief princes of Ireland, who addressed him, "dilecto sibi Gillys O'Reilly Duce Hibernicorum de Breifeney," &c., when he wrote a circular letter to the Irish princes requesting their aid against the Scotch. Giolla appointed his nephew Maelsachlain as his successor, and resigned his principality to him in the year 1326, when he retired to the monastery of Cavan, where he continued for the remainder of his life, venerated for his wisdom and sanctity. He died in 1330.

He wrote two poems, one of them on the death of his brother Matthew, and the other, extolling the power and extent of territory possessed by his nephew and successor.

JOHN O'DUGAN, chief poet of O'Kelly of Ibh Maine, wrote a poem of five hundred and sixty-four verses, giving an account of the kings of Ireland, from Slainge of the Fir-Bolgian race, who, in conjunction with his four brothers, began to reign over Ireland, A. M. 2245, to Roderick

O'Conor, last monarch of Ireland. A copy of this poem is in the possession of Sir William Betham.

He also wrote a topographical and historical poem of nearly nine hundred verses, giving the names of the principal tribes of Ulster, Connaught, and Meath, with their chiefs at the time of Henry II.; but left this work unfinished.—It was completed by Giolla na Naomh O'Huidbrin, who wrote the entire of the history of Munster and its chieftains, and nearly the whole of that relative to Leinster. A perfect copy of this poem remains in the handwriting of Cucoigcriche O'Clery, one of the Four Masters.

He also wrote a poem recording the kings of Leinster, descended from the thirty sons of Cathaoir Mor, monarch of Ireland, and another, giving a catalogue of the kings of Cashel, from the time of Corc 380, to that of Tirlogh O'Brien, 1367. A copy of this is in the book of Ballimote. Another poem describes the actions of Cormac Mac Art, monarch of Ireland; but the most curious of all is one upon the festivals, with rules for finding the moveable feasts and fasts by the epacts and dominical letters, and its rules still regulate the practice of many who have never seen this poem. He also wrote a poetical vocabulary of obsolete words which has since been adopted into dictionaries. O'Dugan died in 1372, and O'Huidbrin survived him for nearly fifty years.

MAHON O'REILLY, lord of clan Mahon, who died A. D. 1380, wrote a poetical eulogy on his son Thomas, prince of East Brefne, who distinguished himself by the impetuosity of his valour, and his successful resistance against the English, having in a short period levelled eighteen castles belonging to the pale, and laid the country from Drogheda to Dublin under contribution.

MAGNUS O'DUIGNAN, who lived A. D. 1390, is chiefly known in connection with the book of Ballimote, on different pages of which his name is signed, but it seems uncertain what precise share he had in the composition; whether he was the compiler or merely the transcriber of those portions of that celebrated book to which his name is appended. We shall therefore, here, in the absence of all personal detail respecting O'Duignan, proceed to mention such facts respecting this book as have come to our knowledge.

It is described by O'Reilly "as a large folio volume, written on vellum of the largest size;" it contained originally 550 pages, but the two first are wanting. As usual in the history of books of this class, it passed down through the hands of numerous possessors. A portion of it appears, on the authority of the volume itself, to have been written in the reign of Tirlogh O'Conor, king of Connaught, who died 1404; and by an entry, p. 180, vol. I., "in a handwriting different from any other part of the book, it appears that Hugh *Duff*, son of Hugh Roe, son of Niall Garoe O'Donell, bought it in the year 1522, from M'Donogh of Coran, for one hundred and forty milch cows."

The matter of this volume is compiled from a great variety of ancient MSS., of which the principal are yet extant, thus receiving and imparting to these venerable documents the authority of so much importance to MS. documents.

The modern history of this valuable MS. must be regarded as especially curious and interesting. It had belonged to the library of Trinity College, Dublin, from which it was either purloined or fraudulently detained. Vallency gives an account of the book of Leacan, which, with good reason, is supposed by Mr. O'Reilly to have actual reference to the book of Ballimote. The General mentions that Doctor Raymond, about the year 1790, lent a book out of the college library to a person of the name of M'Naghten; from M'Naghten it was stolen by one Egan, from whom it came into the possession of Judge Marley, whose servant he was; and remained in the Judge's library till his death. It was then by some means conveyed to the Lombard college in Paris. That this account is mainly conjectural is apparent on its very face, and the Abbè Geoghegan states that the book of Leacan had long before been transferred to the Irish college in Paris by James II.; a fact formally attested by a notary. According to this statement, the book lent to M'Naghten could not have been the book of Leacan. There is, on the other hand, strong reason to suppose the book of Ballimote to have been that which was lent to M'Naghten—as there is among the MSS. in the college library a copy in the hand of M'Naghten. It would, then, be the high probability, that having lost the original, which he had borrowed through the interposition of Raymond for the purpose of transcription, that he, in compensation, gave his paper copy to the college.

From the mark and memoranda on the copy in the Academy, it is inferred by O'Reilly, that it was in 1769, in the hands of O'Dornin of Drogheda, " a good Irish scholar," and remained with him till 1774. It then probably came into the possession of the college. The next hand to which it seems to be traced with any certainty is that of the Chevalier O'Gorman, who presented it to the Royal Irish Academy.

Dermod O'Conor, who translated Keating, mentions having obtained the "book of Ballimore in the county of Meath by the kindness of Dr. Anthony Raymond of Trim, who entered into a bond of a thousand pounds, security for its safe return."* This statement is questioned by O'Reilly, who infers that the book in question was the book of Ballimote. He observes that no Irish scholar ever heard of a book of Ballimore in Meath; and confirms his inference by the numerous errors in O'Conor's translation, which he considers sufficient to prove that " he could make nothing" of the book of Ballimote. The conjecture that this was the book of Ballimote receives some additional probability from the circumstance that Bishop Nicholson, who mentions this book twice, calls it once "the book of Ballimore." O'Conor may have caught the word, and referred the book to the place with which he was most familiar.

One more observation we cannot avoid adding in favour of this sup-

* Preface to Keating's Ireland.

position, though personally we have no present means of verifying it. The enumeration of the contents of this book by O'Conor* is not in accordance with that of Mr. O'Reilly. For this fact, if correct, we must be content to refer to the several books, as those who choose to verify it must be already in possession of the means. Keating mentions the Psalter of Tara, and the book of Armagh.

DONOUGH BAN O'MAELCONAIRE, died A. D. 1404, chief poet of the O'Conors of Connaught, was author of a poetical catalogue of the kings of Connaught, from Tirlogh O'Conor, son of Roderick the Great, to Tirlogh O'Conor, who lived upwards of two hundred and thirty years afterwards. From this catalogue the Table given in this work showing the successors of Tirlogh O'Conor has been taken.
A copy of this poem is in the book of Leacan.

ANGUSTIN MAGRADIAN, or Austin M'Craith, continued the annals of Tigernach to his own time, and they have been since continued by another writer to the year 1571. A copy of these annals is in the library of Trinity College. He died in 1405.

MAURICE O'DALY, who, with many poets of his time, was, in 1415, cruelly plundered by Lord Furnival, revenged himself by recording in verse the defeats of the English and the signal victories of Thomas, prince of East Brefne, when he razed eighteen castles belonging to the lords of the pale, for which he was also celebrated in verse by his father, the lord of Clan Mahon.

PETER, an Irishman of great ability, who flourished A. D. 1240, and remarkable both as a philosopher and a theologian, went to Italy on the special invitation of Frederick II., who had at that time restored the university of Naples, and wished to have a man of his learning and acquirements, both as an example and instructor to the rising generation. He was tutor to Thomas Aquinas in philosophical studies, in the year 1240, and wrote *Quodlibeta Theologica*. The time and place of his death are unknown.

THOMAS HIBERNICUS, who flourished A. D. 1270, was born in the county of Kildare, at a place called Palmerstown. He left his own country, and became a fellow of the college of Sorbonne. He continued to reside for some time in Paris, and afterwards travelled into Italy. Marian of Florence writes, "That Thomas, the Irishman, flourished in the year 1270, in the convent of Aquila, in the province of Penin, now called the province of St. Bernardin, and was in great reputation for his learning and piety." He continued in this monastery until his

---

* Preface to his translation of Keating's Ireland.

death, the period of which is unknown, and was buried there. On his deathbed he bequeathed all the books he had written, with a variety of other manuscripts, to the college of Sorbonne, together with six pounds for the purpose of purchasing a rent to celebrate his anniversary. The necrology of Sorbonne states that " Master *Thomas of Ireland*, formerly a fellow of this house, died. He compiled *Manipulum Florum*, and three other small tracts, which he sent to us, and bequeathed to us many other books, and six pounds in money to buy a rent to be employed in celebrating his anniversary." Ware says that the above-mentioned treatise was begun by a Franciscan friar, of the name of *John Gualleis* or *Walleis*, and that, he dying, Thomas completed it, and gave it the title of

> Flores Doctorum penè omnium, qui tum in Theologia, tum in Philosophia, hactenus Clarnerunt, lib. ii.

He also wrote—

> De Christianâ Religione, lib. i.
> De Illusionibus Dæmonum, lib. i.
> De Tentatione Diaboli, lib. i.
> De Remediis Vitiorum, lib. i.

Ware quotes the following catalogue of his writings from the Bibliotheque of the Dominican order :—

> Tabula Originalium, sive Manipulus Florum secundum ordinem alphabeti extracta ex libris 36, Auctorum, edita a M. Thoma Hibernico, quondam Socio Domus Scholarium de Sorbona Parisiensis Civitatis.
> Liber de tribus punctis Christianæ Religionis Commendatio Theologia,

beginning " Sapientia Ædificavit fidi Domum," &c., which he explains according to the mystical, allegorical, and moral sense.

> Tractatus de tribus Hierarchiis tam Angelicis quam Ecclesiasticis.

In the college of Sorbonne there is another manuscript ascribed to him, under the title of

> In primam et secundum sententiarum.

GOTOFRID, a native of the city of Waterford, in Ireland, who flourished in the thirteenth century, was a Dominican friar, and deeply skilled in the Latin, Greek, French, and Arabic languages. He left his own country early, and it was thought that he travelled into the East to acquire a more perfect knowledge of the Arabic. He afterwards resided in France, and translated the three following treatises from the Latin, Greek, and Arabic, into French.* He dedicated, according to Harris, "this last piece to some nobleman, whose name is not mentioned in the manuscript from whence the account is taken. For he says thus in the preface—

> *A noble bers prouz et sages, &c.*

* 1. Daretis Phrygii Librum de Bello Trojano.
2. Eutropii Romanum Historiam.
3. Aristotelis ad Alexandrum librum, qui dicitur secretum secretorum, seu de regimine Regum.

which the writers of the Dominican *Bibliotheque* interpret

Nobili viro, strenuo, et prudentia—

"To a man noble, valiant and wise, Goffrid or Gotofrid, from Waterford, the least of the order of Friars preachers, wisheth health in Jesus Christ, and strength both of body and mind"———" whereas, sometimes you provide yourself with arms, and other implements necessary for war, sometimes you entertain yourself in reading books—wherefore to other good books, which you already have, you desire to add a book called *The secret of secrets, of the most wise philosopher, Aristotle, or a treatise of the government of kings and princes;* and for this end you have requested me, that I would for your sake translate the said work from Latin into French, which I have already translated from Greek into Arabic, and again from Arabic into Latin—being overcome by your entreaties, I have taken care to fulfil this task, and have used more pains in it than I am accustomed to do in my deep and profound studies. You are to observe, that the Arabians in a great circuity of words speak but few truths; whereas the Greeks are obscure in their mode of speaking: wherefore by translating from both tongues I have endeavoured to lop off the parts that are too prolix in the one language, and to illustrate what is obscure in the other, as far as the subject-matter would bear, and therein have pursued rather the sense of the words than the words themselves. You are farther to understand that I have added many other things, which, though they are not contained in that book, yet are drawn from other authentic books, and are no less profitable than what is written in that treatise; these things that are added being pertinent to the subject in hand. Lastly, you are to know, that the Latin is not without a mixture of the Arabic; and therefore I have lopped off many things, which are neither true nor profitable, in such a manner, that I have in the shortest method taken in the marrow of the subject, and what is most consonant to truth." Thus, as Harris says, the preface shows "the country of the author, of what order of religion he was, and his skill in the four languages." He also adds, that these three treatises in vellum are preserved at Paris in small folio, in the library of Monsieur Colbert, and are elegantly written in the characters of the thirteenth century; and that in the same volume are contained fourteen sermons turned into French, which in the catalogue are ascribed to *Jacobus de Boragine:* and after them follows a short exposition of the articles of faith, and of the Lord's prayer, in French; and then, other sermons on the first Sunday of advent on time, and on the gospel of all the Sundays in the year. Now as these sermons and discourses are written not only in the same handwriting with the other works before-mentioned, which are certainly Gotofrid's, but also the style and manner of orthography are the same, the authors of the said *Bibliotheque* are willing to ascribe them to him, and think, that they are either composed by him in French, or turned by him into French from some other language. The like judgment is to be made of two other treatises, in the same volume, translated from Latin into French, in the same style and handwriting. The first is entitled in Latin *Libellus mortalitatem,* and in French, *le petits livres demortalites;* and the other is called Elucidarius, being that same book

concerning the author of which there are such great disputes among
the learned—some ascribing it to Anselm of Canterbury, and others to
Honorius of Autun."* The time and place of his death are unknown.

MALACHY MAC AEDHA, or, as he was otherwise designated, Hugh's
Son, who died A. D. 1348, was consecrated archbishop of Tuam about
the year 1313, having been previously bishop of Elphin. He recovered
the see of Enaghdun, which he held for twenty years before his death,
his predecessor Bermingham having made fruitless efforts to join it to
Tuam.† Malachy was the author of a large volume of miscellaneous
writings in Irish, containing a catalogue of the Irish kings, from Neal
Nigiolach to Roderick O'Conor, and entitled "The Book of Hugh's
Son." He died at a very advanced age, and was buried at Tuam, in
the cathedral church of St. Mary's. Ware considers a prophecy, attributed to Tarlatha, as having been written by him.

ANGUS ROE O'DALY lived about 1350. Among other poems written
by O'Daly, one of four hundred and forty-eight verses is extant. The
first portion of it is devoted to Adam and the patriarchs before the
flood, and the remainder to the colonies which settled in Ireland, and
possessed the island before the arrival of the Milesians. The time of
his death is uncertain.

MAC COINMHIDE, or CONWAY, a poet of Ulster, who lived about 1350,
and a retainer of the house of O'Donell, wrote a variety of poems in
honour of that warlike race. A copy of one of them, addressed to
Brian, son of Donald O'Donell, prince of Tirconell, is preserved in a
very valuable volume of Irish historical poems, collected in the Netherlands, in the year 1656, by the Rev. Nicholas O'Gara. He also wrote
in verse, the history of Moain, grandson of Niall of the nine hostages.
From Moain are descended the Cineal Munin, one of the chief families
of which are the O'Gormlys.

GIOLLA-NA-NAOMH O'HUIDRIN, a very learned historian, who died
A. D. 1420, completed, as was before related, the topographical history
in verse, begun by John O'Dugan; adding to it the chief portion descriptive of Leinster and its kings, and the entire of that respecting
Munster. This addition consists of seven hundred and eighty verses,
and a copy of it is in the handwriting of Cucoigariche O'Clery.

FAELAN MAC A GOBHAN is remarkable for having transcribed a
great portion of that voluminous compilation called the Book of the
O'Kellys;‡ for which family it was originally collected from a great

* Harris's Ware. † Ware.
‡ See an account of this book in the "Transactions of the Iberno-Celtic Society," a valuable work, which has furnished many facts in the preceding Lives.

variety of authors, and remained in their possession until 1757. It is a large folio, written in vellum, and is at present in the possession of Sir William Betham. It contains a poem of two hundred and twenty-eight verses, composed by Faelan himself.* "It gives the names of the wives and daughters of several of the Pagan heroes and deities. This is followed (in the folio) with an account of the wives of the patriarchs, and a synchronism of the Roman emperors, with the monarchs of Ireland, to the emperor Severus, and Art the Solitary, monarch of Ireland, from A. D. 220 to 250, in which latter year he died. After this, (in immediate succession,) follows an account of the Jewish high priests and the first Christian bishops, the officers of St. Patrick's household, and different members of his family."

"We cannot say," observes our authority, "whether these latter tracts are the original productions of Faelan Mac a Gobhan or not; but by a memorandum at the bottom of the folio, it is said that they were written by Faelan Mac a Gobhan *na scel* (of the histories) for his lord and his friend, bishop Muircheartach O'Kelly. This prelate was bishop of Clonfert from 1378 to 1394, at which time he was translated by Pope Boniface IX. to the see of Tuam, over which he presided as archbishop until his death, on the 29th of September, 1447." Faelan Mac a Gobhan died in 1423.

DONOGH O'BOLGAIDH, or BOULGER, about 1468 was a physician of some eminence, and a voluminous writer of medical treatises, and also a transcriber of the writings of others on the same subject. He wrote treatises on the diseases of the head, and of the other members of the human body, and makes frequent quotations from the Arabian physicians in those works. He also wrote a tract on the medicinal virtues of herbs and minerals; and there remains in his handwriting a translation of Aristotle's treatise "On the Nature of Matter." There is a curious addition to his writings, in the form of a law tract, in which he regulates the fees or rewards to be paid to physicians by the different classes of society.

The exact year of his death is not known.

CATHALD MAC MAGNUS, died A. D. 1498, was author of those annals of Ireland called "Annals of Bally Mac Magnus," "Scuatensian Annals," and "Annals of Ulster." They commence with the reign of Feredach Fionnfactnach, monarch of Ireland, A. D. 60, and are carried down to the author's own time. They were afterwards continued to the year 1504, by Roderick O'Cassidy, archdeacon of Clogher.†

The annals of the *Four Masters* give the character, and relate the death of Cathald, in words of which the following is a literal translation:—

"Mac Magnus of Seanaigh, *i.e.* Cathal Og, son of Cathal, son of Giolla Patrick, son of Matthew, &c., was master of a house of general hospitality, and a public victualler in Seanaidh Mac Magnus; canon of the choir in Ardmach, and in the bishopric of Clogher; parson of

* Ware. † Transactions of the Iberno-Celtic Society.

Tuiscsoin, Deacon of Lough Erne; and deputy of the bishop of Clogher, for fifteen years before his death. He was an encourager and protector of learning and science in his own district; a treasured branch of the canons; a fountain of love and mercy to the poor and unprotected of God's people. It was he who collected and brought together many books of annals, from which he compiled the Annals of Bally Mac Manus, for himself. He died of the small-pox, on the 10th of the calends of April, on a Friday, in particular, in the sixtieth year of his age.

MANUS, son of Rodh, (died A. D. 1532,) of the princely house of O'Donell, was author of a life of St. Patrick, often quoted by Colgan. It is uncertain whether he was also the author of some poems, written about the same period, and attributed to a writer of the same name.

ABOUT this period, A. D. 1554, Teige Mor O'Coffey composed a poem in praise of Manus, son of Aodh Dubh O'Donell, "who gave the writer a mare of his stud for every rann contained in the poem. It consists of twenty ranns, or eighty verses."*

DONALD MAC CARTHY, who was created in 1565 first earl of Clan Carthy, was the author of several poems, chiefly on religious subjects.

AT the time, viz. 1566, that Brian na Murtha O'Rourke was chosen chief of his tribe, on the death of his brother Aodh, John O'Maolconaire wrote a poem of an hundred and thirty-six verses, in praise of Brian na Murtha, (of the bulwarks,) beginning "Breifne has obtained a prince worthy of her." This poem is stated, by Mr. O'Reilly, who had a copy of it in his own possession, to be written "in the Bearla Feine, or Phœnician dialect of the Irish," and assigns as a reason for his selecting it, that "the dialect of the plebeians was unworthy of his hero."

WHEN Feagh M'Hugh O'Byrne was elected chief of his tribe, Roderick M'Craith, A. D. 1584, wrote an ode on his inauguration, of one hundred and twenty verses, in Irish, beginning "A warning to assemble the race of Brann!" The Braun here mentioned was Brann the Black, king of Leinster, who died in the year 601, from whom the O'Brainns or O'Byrnes derive their name and lineage.† He also wrote a poem on the family of O'Byrne of Ranelagh, who so long contended against the English. Copies of these poems are in the possession of the family of O'Byrne of Cabinteely.‡

DUBHTHACH, or DUFFY O'DUIGENAN, A. D. 1588, wrote two very

* Transactions of the Iberno-Celtic Society. † O'Reilly. ‡ Ibid.

long poems, containing chronicles of the families of O'Neill and O'Donell for centuries. That addressed to Aodh, or Hugh O'Neill, embraces a period of two hundred and sixteen years; and the poem on the O'Donell family four hundred: the latter is three hundred and sixty-eight verses in length. It is written in Irish, and begins, "Let us pursue the chronicle of *Clann Dalaigh*." The O'Donells are called by the Irish, Clann Dalaigh, and Muintin Dalaigh (Daly), from Dalach, their great ancestor, and derive their name of O'Donell from his grandson Donall Mor.* This poem gives a catalogue of twenty-five kings or princes who governed Tirconnel, from Eigneachan O'Donell in 1199, to Hugh Roe O'Donell in 1600, when this poem was written.

THE MAC FIRBIS FAMILY.

At what time the Mac Firbis family began to follow the profession of historians it would now be useless to enquire. They appear to have been one of the many tribes in which the profession was hereditary, in accordance with the practice that seems to have existed since the introduction of letters into Ireland. But some individuals of the name are referred to by the annalists, at a very early period, as distinguished for learning and a knowledge of the national history; and their compilations, many of which are still in existence, have always been regarded as among the most authentic of the native Irish records.

The Annals of the Four Masters, under the year 1279, notice the death of Gilla-Isa, or Gelasius, Mac Firbis, "chief historian of Tir-Fiachrach," or Tireragh, *i. e.*, the O'Dowda's country. Harris, in his edition of the works of Sir James Ware, alludes to another person of the same name, "a learned annalist," whose death is referred to the year 1301. The obits given by the Four Masters, at the year 1362, include Auliffe and John Mac Firbis, two "intended Ollamhs," or professors of history. Under the year 1376, also, the same annalists record the death of Donogh Mac Firbis, "a historian," and three years later, that of Firbis Mac Firbis, "a learned historian."

Of the numerous compilations made by the older members of the Mac Firbis family, only two are now known to be in existence, viz.:— I., the magnificent vellum MS., called the "Book of Lecan," written before 1416, by Gilla-Isa Mor Mac Firbis, the ancestor of Duald; and II., the hardly less important volume known as the "Leabhar Buidhe Lecain," or "Yellow Book of Lecan," written about the same period, and partly by the same hand. The former of these originally belonged to Trinity College, Dublin, but was carried to France in the reign of James II., and was restored to Ireland in the year 1790; it now enriches the extensive collection of Irish MSS. in the possession of the Royal Irish Academy. The latter, or—to speak more correctly—a large fragment of it, is preserved in the Library of Trinity College, Dublin.

These manuscripts were written, as their names import, at Lecan-

* O'Reilly.

mic-Firbisy, in the county of Sligo, the residence of the compilers at the time. The Mac Firbis family seems to have previously resided in the county of Mayo; for, in the genealogical tract on the tribes of Hy-Fiachrach, contained in the Book of Lecan, the Claun Firbisigh, or sept of Mac Firbis, are stated to have resided at Ros-sere, a place still known by the same name, and situated in the barony of Tirawley, in that county. The extent of their possessions is not given; but it is certain that they were amply endowed, according to the usage of the period, by which members of the learned professions in Ireland were entitled to privileges and emoluments hardly inferior to those enjoyed by the rulers of territories. The following extract from the account of the ceremony observed at the inauguration of the O'Dowda, as prince of Hy-Fiachrach, affords a curious illustration of the nature of some of these privileges:—

"And the privilege of first drinking [at the banquet] was given to O'Caemhain by O'Dowda, and O'Caemhain was not to drink until he first presented it [the drink] to the poet, that is, to Mac Firbis. Also the weapons, battle-dress, and steed of O'Dowda, after his nomination, were given to O'Caemhain, and the weapons and battle-dress of O'Caemhain to Mac Firbis. And it is not lawful ever to nominate the O'Dowda until O'Caemhain and Mac Firbis pronounce the name, and until Mac Firbis raises the body of the wand over the head of O'Dowda. And after O'Caemhain and Mac Firbis, every clergyman and comarb of a church, and every bishop, and every chief of a district, pronounces the name."

Dubhaltach Mac Firbisigh, generally written Duald Mac Firbis, is believed to have been born about the year 1585, at Lackan, in the county of Sligo. He was the eldest of four brothers, and belonged to a junior branch of the family. According to Professor O'Curry he "appears to have been intended for the hereditary profession of an antiquarian and historian, or for that of the *Fenechas*, or ancient laws of his native country (now improperly called the Brehon Laws). To qualify him for either of these ancient and honourable professions, and to improve and perfect his education, young Mac Firbis appears, at an early age, to have passed into Munster, and to have taken up his residence in the school of law and history then kept by the Mac Egans of Lecan, in Ormond, in the present county of Tipperary. He studied also for some time, either before or after this, in Burren, in the present county of Clare, at the not less distinguished literary and legal school of the O'Davorens, where we find him, with many other young Irish gentlemen, about the year 1595, under the presidency of Donnell O'Davoren."

Duald Mac Firbis's studies were not confined to the ordinary branches of education attainable through the medium of his native language, but included also Greek and Latin. From his account of the Anglo-Norman and Welsh families settled in Ireland, he seems to have been familiar with the writings of Giraldus Cambrensis and Holingshed. He appears also to have read Verstegan's "Restitution of Decayed Intelligence," and the "Fasciculus Temporum" of Rolewinck. In his copy of Cormac's Glossary, preserved in the Library of Trinity College, Dublin, (Class H. 2, 15), he explains many Latin and Greek words in the margin, always writing the Greek in the original character. Nevertheless, the rude Latinity of some of the entries in his chronicle indicates that his knowledge of Latin was very imperfect.

We have no account of Mac Firbis's proceedings from the period when he had completed his education until the year 1645, two years after the death of his father, when he seems to have been settled in Galway, where he became acquainted with the learned Roderick O'Flaherty (then only seventeen years of age), and Dr. John Lynch, the author of "Cambrensis Eversus," to both of whom he acted as Irish tutor, affording them, besides, much valuable assistance in the prosecution of their historical studies.

During the ensuing five years Mac Firbis was occupied in compiling his important work on Irish genealogies, which he finished in 1650, as he states, in the College of St. Nicholas, Galway. In the year 1652, he lost one of his steadfast friends, Dr. Lynch, who fled to France on the surrender of Galway to the Parliamentary Forces; but he still continued, although under adverse circumstances, to apply his honest zeal and active industry to the task of transferring to a more permanent shape the contents of MSS. falling into decay. A few years later, however, his prospects assumed a brighter aspect. Sir James Ware, impressed with the importance of securing the services of one so thoroughly acquainted with the language, history, and antiquities of his country as Mac Firbis had the reputation of being, employed him, in the year 1655, to collect and translate, from the Irish Annals, materials for the composition of his learned works on the Antiquities and Ecclesiastical History of Ireland.

The death of his enlightened patron, Sir James Ware, having put a stop to his labours in Dublin, Mac Firbis appears to have returned to his native place in the county of Sligo, where he lived in great poverty during the remaining few years of his life. He had outlived many of the friends who had encouraged and assisted him in former years; others, like Dr. Lynch, had sought safety in flight from the vengeance of their successful opponents in the civil war which then distracted the country; and of those who remained behind, the majority, including the learned Roderick O'Flaherty, heir to a handsome patrimony, were reduced by confiscation to a state of poverty hardly less intense than that in which Mac Firbis was plunged.

The death of Mac Firbis was sudden and violent. In the year 1670, while travelling to Dublin, he was assassinated at Dunflin, in the county of Sligo. The circumstances attending the event, are thus narrated by Professor O'Curry.

"Mac Firbis was at that time under the ban of the penal laws, and, consequently, a marked and almost a defenceless man, in the eye of the law, whilst the friends of his murderer enjoyed the full protection of the constitution. He must have been then past his 80th year, and he was, it is believed, on his way to Dublin, probably to visit Robert, the son of Sir James Ware. He took up his lodgings for the night at a small house in the little village of Dunflin, in his native county. While sitting and resting himself in a small room off the shop, a young gentleman, of the Crofton family, came in and began to take some liberties with a young woman who had the care of the shop. She, to check his freedom, told him that he would be seen by the old gentleman in the next room; upon which, in a sudden rage, he snatched up a knife from the counter, rushed furiously into the room, and plunged it into the heart of Mac Firbis."

"Thus it was that, at the hand of a wanton assassin, this great scholar closed his long career,—the last of the regularly educated and most accomplished masters of the history, antiquities, and laws and language of ancient Erinn."

The compilations of Mac Firbis are numerous, and of the most varied nature, including works on Biography, Genealogy, Hagiology, History, Law, and Philology. He appears also to have transcribed many tracts compiled by others, and to have translated some. The following list comprises all his works that are at present known to exist, either in his own handwriting, or in authentic transcripts therefrom:—

1. The transcript of the Chronicon Scotorum.
2. His large genealogical work, completed in the year 1650, and entitled "The Branches of Relationship, and the genealogical Ramifications of every Colony that took possession of Ireland, &c.; together with a Santilogium, and a Catalogue of the Monarchs of Ireland, &c.; compiled by Dubhaltach Mac Firbisigh, of Lecan, 1650."
3. An Abridgment of the foregoing work, with some additional Pedigrees, compiled in the year 1666.
4. A Treatise on Irish authors, drawn up in the year 1656. An accurate copy of this fragment, made by Mr. W. M. Hennessy, has been placed in the royal Irish academy.
5. A catalogue of extinct Irish Bishoprics, together with a list of dignitaries anciently accounted bishops, but not so regarded in the author's time. A transcript of this catalogue, also made by the same gentleman, has been added to the collection of the R. I. Academy.
6. A List of Bishops arranged by Mac Firbis for Sir James Ware.
7. A Collection of Glossaries, including original compositions and transcripts from more ancient ones. This has been published by Mr. Whitley Stokes.
8. A Martyrology, or Litany of the Saints, in verse, a copy of which, in his own autograph, is preserved in the British Museum.
9. A transcript, or collection, from a volume of annals belonging to Nehemias Mac Egan, of Ormond, "chief professor of the old Irish or Brehon Laws." This collection has been published by the Irish Arch. and Celt. Society, from a copy made directly from Mac Firbis's MS.

Mac Firbis's translations from the Irish are believed to have been numerous, but in consequence of the wide dispersion of the MS. collection of Sir James Ware, for whom they were chiefly made, their extent cannot now be ascertained. His principal effort in this line was the translation of the Annals of Ulster, now preserved in the British Museum, and of the original Annals of Inisfallen. An important fragment, consisting of a translation of Irish Annals from the year 1443 to 1468, has been published by the Irish Archæological Society; and his English version of a curious tract called the "Registry of Clonmacnois"—believed to have been originally compiled before the year 1216—has been printed in the Transactions of the Kilkenny Archæological Society, from the translator's autograph in the British Museum.

It is unnecessary to dwell further on Mac Firbis's profound knowledge of the history, language, and literature of his native country. The opinion entertained of his abilities, honest zeal, and industry, by Irish scholars of the present day, agrees with the judgment expressed of him by his learned contemporaries. Although educated with a special view to the profession which his ancestors for centuries had followed, his association with Roderick O'Flaherty, Dr. John Lynch, Francis Kirwan, Skerrett, and the other members of the learned brotherhood which obtained for the Collegiate Institution of Galway, in the seventeenth century, a distinguished reputation for literary eminence, naturally gave a wider range to his studies; and it was probably during his residence among these remarkable men that he acquired whatever knowledge he possessed of the classic languages.

In the art—for such it may be called—of correctly interpreting the very ancient phraseology of the Irish, or "Brehon" laws, he was without an equal. It was the opinion of Charles O'Conor that all chance of rightly translating them passed away with him. He observes nearly as much himself; for in his treatise on Irish authors, he states that there were only "three or four persons" living in his time who understood a word of the subject, and they were "the sons of Ollamhs (professors) of the territory of Connaught," in which province the ancient Irish customs and system of jurisprudence continued longer than in the other divisions of Ireland. In proof of this Mac Firbis alleges, in the abridged copy of his large genealogical work, that he knew Irish Chieftains who in his own time governed their septs "according to the 'words of Fithal' and the 'Royal Precepts;'" the Fithal alluded to was Brehon, or judge, to Cormac Mac Airt, Monarch of Ireland in the third century, the reputed author of the "Royal Precepts," of which various ancient copies are in existence.

A good deal of uncertainty has hitherto been felt respecting the original from which Mac Firbis made his copy of the Chronicon Scotorum. The late eminent Celtic Scholar, Professor O'Curry, was uncertain whether to regard MS. A. as the original, or only a transcript.

The internal evidence, however, says the translator, would be sufficient to prove that it is not the original compilation of Mac Firbis. In more than one place he refers to his production as a "copy." In other places, where a difficulty apparently occurred in deciphering the original from which he copied, he ventures on conjectural emendations, without, however, affecting the integrity of his text.

On these and other grounds Mr. Hennessy decides it is a copy, in which opinion he is supported by an ancient copy in the collection of the Royal Irish Academy, in the title of which its composition is, as already stated at page 649, ascribed to *Gillachrist Ua Maeileoin*, abbot of Clonmacnois, who lived in the twelfth century.

The account of this family is taken from the Introduction by Mr. W. M. Hennessy to the edition of the *Chronicon Scotorum*, published (1867) by the authority of the British Treasury, under the direction of the Master of the Rolls.

EDMUND SPENSER.

BORN A. D. 1553—DIED A. D. 1596.

Spenser, though he, along with many of our noblest names of this period and the following, can be claimed by Ireland only by a partial interest, has yet an unquestionable claim to be commemorated by the historian of her literary worthies. If England was the country of his birth, we deny her not the claim that ranks him among the highest names of her most glorious age; but we claim a compatriot interest in the poet of Kilcolman: Ireland was the birthplace of his muse.

Like many illustrious persons, who have in those unrecording ages sprung from an humble state by the ascendant qualities of genius, the early part of Spenser's career is little known. It seems to be ascertained that he was born in London, in or about 1553; and it appears, from several passages among his dedications, that he claimed kindred with the noble house of Spenser. The claim is also said to have been recognised; but the recognition is not affirmed by any record of kind offices done, in the course of the poet's long struggles with fortune. The noble by birth will always feel some natural reluctance in admitting such claims, although native nobility of spirit, like conscious innocence, will neither fear nor find reproach where there can be no dishonour. But we apprehend that the noblest house in England would now point back to this coldly received affinity with a far different feeling, and would rejoice if it were to be found among the honourable records of its history, that the noblest of its lineage, in the estimation of time, had some nearer proof of kindred than a doubtful implication of assent. We do not indulge this reflection in the ridiculous spirit of condemnation—the claim may have been uncertain and remote, and circumstances are wholly wanting to warrant any judgment in the case. We merely express the strong suggestion arising from a circumstance, which forces a common and affecting condition of social life upon the heart:—the fact, if such, is but one among those common incidents, thick strewn in the course of every generation. The healthy and elastic sense of tender youth is not more quick to shrink from the revolting aspect of the dead, than the full-blown pride of the world to avoid the humiliating contact of a fallen or struggling relationship: bright and honourable exceptions there are, but such is the spirit of human life: *corruptus vanis rerum*. And we must in justice add, that it is not altogether from the want of beneficence, but from that species of pride which finds it essential to be separated from the humiliations of circumstance. It is still felt by the crowd which is inflated with adventitious dignity, as intensely as it was by the patrician usurers of old Rome, that there is something in the power of fortune which lowers and degrades: *quod ridiculos homines facit*. But we are led from our purpose. Spenser does not seem, at any period of his life, to have been in any way advantaged by family assistance; and the only record we can find, on any certain authority, of his youth, is his entrance as a sizar on the books of Pembroke Hall, Cambridge. Here he graduated in 1576. He is said to have sat for a fellowship in competition with Andrew, afterwards bishop of Winchester. That he was not successful is scarcely matter of regret: his subsequent career might have been more usefully and calmly secure, but we cannot doubt that after-ages are indebted rather to the vicissitude and striving with the adverse waves and winds of stern reality, which has imparted so much truth and substance to his chief writings. Instead of being permitted to indulge his dreamy spirit in the lettered trifling of the bookish cloister, he was thrown soon upon the exercise of all his senses, and compelled to infuse a large portion of corrective observation and experience with the Gothic phantasmagoria of his lofty and sequestered spirit. Spenser, however, in the instance here mentioned, was practical enough to look rather to the present good; and dreaming little of being starved or buffetted into the admiration of posterity, was as discontented as beaten candidates are very prone to be; and was encouraged, by the countenance of some of his university friends, in the complaint of having met with injustice.

Among his warmest friends was the then celebrated Gabriel Harvey, who is mentioned by Warton as being the inventor of the hexameter imitation of the Latin, and who is the "Hobbinal" of Spenser. By Harvey's advice, Spenser resolved to try his fortune in London. It was an age of literary adventure—the public favour towards poetry stood at a point to which it never again rose until the nineteenth century: but the circumstances of these two periods were wholly different. There was in the Elizabethan age, commonly called the age of poetry, no vast commercial republic of letters, of which the comprehensive and steady organization worked with the uniformity and precision of a factory; manufacturing books to the public demand, as nearly as possible, by the laws of every other produce of human labour, and with the very lowest application of mental power. Sonnet and lampoon, epigram and eulogy, it is true, like the periodical effusions of the annuals and periodicals of our time, were the universal accomplishment and affectation of the day. But few books were printed—there was no "reading public"—and no book-mill as regular as the market, and almost as needful, to pour out its vast exuberance of publications, planned, bespoken, and conducted by the trade, and wrought by operatives of every grade, from the genius and learning of Scott, Southey, and Moore, to the journeyman tinker of Brummagem books, who does his task to order, in a workmanlike way. At that interesting period, it required no small enthusiasm, and the excitement of no little genius, to brave the perils and mortifications of the tuneful avocation. Like the wayfaring harper, he had to seek fit audience. He had to meet the indifference of the vast crowd of the uneducated, the unsettled taste, or fastidious insolence of the smattering underbred, the insolence of fashion, and the want of the adventurous trade, then but in its infancy. His one resource was a patron, and it expresses the whole:—

"Toil, envy, want, the patron and the gaol."

Much of this Spenser was destined to experience; but it appears that his first introduction was smoothed by the friendship of the noble and gallant Sidney, to whom he received an introduction from the kindness of his college friend, Gabriel Harvey. Two different stories are told concerning this introduction, which might be reconciled only by a very considerable change in the order of the incidents of Spenser's early life. According to one account, we should be compelled to assume, that either his introduction to Sidney was later than the time stated, or that he received, in the first instance, a very small portion of his patron's countenance, and was soon forgotten. The story runs thus:—That when Spenser had completed the ninth canto of the first book of the Fairy Queen, he repaired to Leicester House, and sent in a copy to Sidney, who, on reading a few stanzas, was so astonished and delighted at the description of Despair, that, turning to his steward, he bade him give fifty pounds to the person who brought these verses: on reading the next stanza, he ordered him to give a hundred. The amazed steward thought fit to make some delay, in hopes that his lord might come to his senses, and estimate the verses more nearly at the current rate of scribbling; but after the next stanza, Sidney raised the sum to two hundred, and forbade any further delay, lest he might be tempted to give away his whole estate. The story must have some ground in reality; but that which it would displace is founded on a larger combination of occurrences, and occupies more space in his history. According to the more received account, Spenser's first movement on leaving college was a visit to his own family in the north of England. There he produced some minor poems, and continued in some uncertainty as to his future course, when his friend Harvey wrote to him from London, where he was himself gaining ground as a poet, strongly urging him to try his fortune in the same adventurous field. Spenser was easily persuaded; and on his arrival was introduced by his friend to Sidney, who, at once recognising his high pretension, took him into his household, and carried him with him to Penhurst, where he made use of his taste and judgment in the compositions on which he was himself engaged. This is the more probable and best sustained account: it has also the merit of offering to the reader's mind a sweet and singular picture of the high communion of the two noblest hearts and loftiest intellects of their age, in the sequestered haunts of contemplation and fancy, while the affections, and the aspirations of ambition were young in both.

In the course of his northern residence, during which some conjecture, with no small likelihood, that he was engaged in tuition, Spenser is said to have fallen in love with the lady whom, under the name of Rosalind, he celebrates in his pastorals; which are full of her cruelty and her lover's despair. But as the lady is as much the appendage of poesy as of chivalry, it is very probable that the fierceness of his despair found a full vent in the poem which first raised him to reputation, and took its permanent station in the poetry of England. These compositions were the best introduction to the favour of Sidney.

As is usual with the youthful poet, Spenser appears, during his residence with his patron, to have been engaged in wide speculations as to the adoption of a path worthy of his growing powers. The first was one highly illustrative of the age, but little worthy of the poet. The new enthusiasm for classic antiquity—the imperfection of English style, and the exquisite grace and finish of those great standard works of Greek and Roman genius, which alone seem equally attractive in every change of language, literature, and climate—most naturally suggested the adoption of the metre of Virgil and Ovid, the favourites of the age—with these, of course, the whole train of Latin harmonies would be attempted. In this curious appropriation, Spenser, with many other writers, was for a time employed; and the conception was not unworthy of the richest genius of the age: its disadvantages could only be discovered by trial.* Fortunately, Spenser, after some time, discovered a track more suited to the character and powers of his native tongue, and adapted with curious felicity to the rich Gothic solemnity of his genius. But of this we shall say more before we have done.

It seems that he soon recovered from an error which would have committed his labours to the waste-paper grave of scholastic theology; and it is thought that he then began the *Fairy Queen*. This we are, however, inclined to consider as a doubtful point. His labours, whatever was their subject, quickly met with an interruption. His patron's influence soon introduced him for a time into other scenes than the civilized and tranquil shades of Penhurst. He was sent over to Ireland with Lord Grey of Wilton, who was appointed to the government of this island in 1580. Spenser was retained as his secretary; and, in scenes of civil strife and barbarism, so uncongenial to the muse, his course is for a time lost to the eye of history. Grey returned to England in two years; but Spenser obtained a grant of three thousand acres in the county of Cork, as a compensation for his service. It is supposed that he at this time had returned to England, where he remained until the death of Sidney, who, the reader is aware, was slain in the Low Countries in 1586. This afflicting incident closed the gate of preferment, and Spenser returned to fulfil the condition of his grant by residing on his estate.

Kilcolman Castle, or rather its ruin, is still to be seen, and is described by most historians of the county of Cork. It had belonged to the earls of Desmond, the former lords of the poet's estate, and of the whole district in which it was contained. The river Awbeg, on which it stood—the "Gentle Mulla" of the poet—rises near Buttevant, and enters the river Blackwater near Bridgetown. It winded with a smooth course through the (then) wooded and romantic solitudes of a widely pastoral district, presenting along its tranquil course numerous diversities of the lone and solemn scenery which fancy loves to people with her creatures of romance. The poet's dwelling was within about four miles of the present village of Doneraile, and looked out over a far expanse of plain, bounded by the distant eastward hills of the county of Waterford. The Rathnoure mountains closed the aspect on the north, the Nagle mountains on the south, and on the west the mountains of Kerry.

"The ruins present the remains of a principal tower, in a castellated building of some extent. The outlines and vestiges of several apartments may still be distinctly traced. The lower of these rooms seems

---

* The only successful attempt we can recollect at this species of composition, is the Sapphic Ode which commences a book of the "Curse of Kehama."

to have been used as a hall or kitchen, and is arched with stone. The stairway of the tower still exists, and leads to the decayed remains of a small chamber. Little can be added concerning this interesting ruin, except that the remaining windows command extensive prospects."*

Here, then, Spenser began to reside in the year 1587, seven years from his first arrival in Ireland. And it has been observed, that the rural and scenic descriptions contained in many of his poems, and especially in the " Fairy Queen," are entirely drawn from the surrounding country: hence the "wild forests," and "wasteful woods," and the whole characteristic sylvan colouring of this poem. Nor would it be possible, without many a bold reach of conjecture, to trace the numerous latent transformations by which the incidents of time and place have become metamorphosed into the visions of poetic combination. Who that reads the opening of the twelfth canto—

" Then, when as cheerless night so covered had
Fair heaven with an universal cloud,
That every wight, dismay with darkness sad,
In silence and in sleep themselves did shroud,
She heard a shrilling trumpet sound aloud,"—

and recollects how faithfully the characteristic incident of Irish insurrection is presented, will fail to remember how often sadly familiar to the poet's ear must have been the "shrilling" horn from the nightly hills? The sudden harmony of "many bagpipes" among the thickest woods, and the "shrieking hubbubs" (an Irish word), can have no prototype in nature but the one. The scenery of the country is directly described in the following lines:—†

" Whylome, when Ireland flourished in fame
Of wealth and goodness, far above the rest
Of all that bear the British island's name,
The gods then used, for pleasure and for rest,
Oft to resort thereto, as seemed them best:
But none of all therein more pleasure found
Than Cynthia, that is sovereign queen profest
Of woods and forests which therein abound,
Sprinkled with wholesom waters, more than most on ground."

The manner in which the fawns, satyrs, and hamadryads, and all the poetical inhabitants of the woods, seem to have infested his imagination in the first portions of the " Fairy Queen," but more especially in Book I. Canto vi., appears to us decisive of the point—that it was here this poem was commenced, although the conception, and perhaps some rough sketching, may have previously existed.

It was while engaged in this retreat in the composition of his immortal work, that he was visited by Raleigh—the incident is described in " Colin Clout's come home again," in which he describes his friend who had just returned from Portugal as the " shepherd of the ocean,"

" I sate as was my trade
Under the foot of Mole, that mountain hore;

* Brewer.   † The lines are quoted by Brewer.

> Keeping my sheep amongst the cooly shade
> Of the green alders by the Mulla's shore,
> There a strange shepherd chanced to find me out;
> Whether allured with my pipe's delight
> Whose pleasing sound shrilled far about,
> Or thither led by chance, I know not right;
> Whom when I asked, from what place he came?
> And how he hight? himself he did ycleep
> The shepherd of the ocean by name,
> And said he came far from the main sea deep!

This visit was the means of drawing Spenser from his retreat: he read the three first books to his guest, whose enthusiastic spirit was fired with admiration. He conjured the poet to lose no time in its publication, and urged him so warmly to repair at once to London, that Spenser accompanied him, and the three first books were printed in the year 1590. Of his adventures on this occasion, the accounts are neither very abundant nor authentic. It is stated, with the highest probability, being in fact a matter of course, that he was introduced by Raleigh to the Queen, who appointed him Poet Laureate; but it is (with much probability) asserted by some without any pension. It is however affirmed, that the lord-treasurer, Burleigh, whose prudent parsimony exceeded his taste for verse, and his jealousy of court favour either his love of economy or his regard for merit, exerted his powerful influence to intercept the queen's favour. The fact seems ascertained by the complaints of Spenser, which with a pension of £50 would have been quite out of place. A story is told by all biographers, that the queen having read the *Fairy Queen*, ordered a gratuity of one hundred pounds to be paid to the author. Burleigh, to whom this command was addressed, with a well-feigned expression of surprise replied—"What! all this for a song?" "Then give him what is reason," answered Elizabeth, whose prudence was not less though her taste was more. Burleigh's estimate of "What is reason?" was slight indeed; and when Spenser, after an interval of suspense, discovered that he was likely to be without his expected recompense, he came to a determination to remind the queen of her promise, which he did by these lines:

> "I was promised on a time
> To have reason for my rhyme;
> From that time, unto this season,
> I received not rhyme nor reason."

The queen, who thus learned the remissness of Burleigh, peremptorily commanded the payment of her order. The patent for his pension, may perhaps have succeeded this incident. There is another passage of Spenser, which seems to be descriptive of the incident here mentioned:—

> "Full little knowest thou that hast not tried
> What ill it is in suing long to bide:
> To lose good days that might be better spent;
> To waste long nights in pensive discontent;
> To speed to-day to be put back to-morrow;

> To feed on hopes to pine with fear and sorrow :
> To have thy prince's grace, yet want her peers ;
> To have thy asking, yet wait many years ;
> To fret thy soul with crosses and with cares ;
> To eat thy heart with comfortless despairs ;
> To fawn, to crouch, to wait, to ride, to run,
> To spend, to give, to want, to be undone.
> Unhappy wight, born to disastrous end
> That doth his life in so long tendance spend."*

But the favour of courts, proverbially uncertain, and the invidious dislike of intriguing ministers, were in some degree compensated by the friendship and admiration of the higher spirits of the age. If his fortunes did not advance with the rapidity of expectation, he must have at least felt the triumph of his genius. His publisher afforded the certain proof of the success which was most to be desired, by a spirited effort to collect and publish all his other pieces at the time extant.

Not long after this event, Spenser once more sought his poetical retirement on the banks of the Mulla; and with the short interval of a visit to London in the winter of 1591, continued for many years in the assiduous composition of the remaining books of the *Fairy Queen* and other well known works. It was during this period that he formed an attachment to the beautiful daughter of a merchant of Cork. Spenser was now approaching his fortieth year: he was compelled to experience the bitter sweets of a long and of course anxious probation; and often perhaps to be painfully reminded of his youthful attachment to the perfidious and fickle Rosalind. The Irish lady was remarkable for her due sense of the dignity of her sex, and her pride is celebrated by her lover.

> " For in those lofty looks is close implied
> Scorn of base things, disdain of foul dishonour ;
> Threatening rash eyes which gaze on her so wide,
> That loose they be who dare to look upon her."†

In another sonnet he celebrates her

> " Mild humbleness mixt with awful majesty."

And again,

> " Was it the works of nature or of art
> Which tempered so the features of her face,
> That pride and meekness mixt by equal part,
> Do both appear to adorn her beauty's grace ?"

After a courtship of three years, this proud young beauty relented, and some graceful verses describe the intoxicating delight of her first smiles. He was married in Cork, in 1594, and has left the record of one day's unalloyed happiness in the epithalamium he wrote on the occasion:—

* Mother Hubbard's Tale.   † Sonnets.

> " Behold while she before the altar stands
> Hearing the holy priest that to her speaks,
> And blesses her with his two happy hands,
> How the red roses flush up in her cheeks,
> And the pure snow-white lovely vermeil stain,
> Like crimson dyed in grain!
> That even the angels, which continually
> About the sacred altar do remain,
> Forget their service, and about her fly,
> Oft peeping in her face, which seems more fair
> The more they on it stare.
> But her sad eyes, still fixed upon the ground,
> Are governed with a godly modesty
> That suffers not a look to glance away
> Which may let in a little thought unsound.
> Why blush ye love! to give to me your hand?
> The pledge of all our band."

Such was the happy commencement of a brief and troublous interval.

Not long after his marriage, Spenser paid a short visit to London, where he published three more books of the *Fairy Queen*, and presented his " View of the State of Ireland" to the queen. The next year he returned home, and for a little longer every thing wore the air of peaceful prosperity: he was happy in his wife, who had made him the father of two fair sons; and his character as a resident proprietor, as well as his reputation as a poet, began to win him golden opinions in the city and surrounding territory. He was recommended also by the crown, to the office of sheriff for Cork. But the rebellion of Tyrone broke upon these goodly prospects, and surrounded every peaceful habitation with restless disquietudes and apprehensions. The inmates of one of Desmond's castles could not sleep undisturbed by the terrors which left no home secure. Frightful rumours were the daily conversation; the quiet woods which the poet so long had peopled with the fawns, satyrs, and hamadryades in which his fancy loved to revel, teemed with no imaginary groups of wolvish kernes and ruffian bonaghts fiercely looking out upon his castle and awaiting the night: night was haunted by fearful apprehensions—evil noises mingled in the winds, and the echoing signal was heard among the hills. Hapless is their state who are under the influence of such terrors—inflicting by anticipation the sufferings which may not arrive. But this was not the good fortune of poor Spenser, of whose felicity we more lament the ruin because it was so complete. Blest in the union he had formed, a happy father, a husband much loving and much loved, admired, respected, and after a life of toil possessed of a growing fortune: one fatal hour reversed his fortunate position and sent him a houseless fugitive with his helpless family, again to try his fortune in the uncertain favour of which he had so long experience.

We cannot here offer any precise detail of the dreadful particulars of a disaster, the horror of which is perhaps better to be understood from a single incident than from any description. The poet with his family were compelled to fly with such precipitation, that their youngest infant was left behind. It was perhaps the error of the wretched parents, inexperienced in popular convulsion, to imagine that a helpless and innocent babe could not be really in any risk; and they conceived that they had provided fully for its safety, by leaving the necessary directions for its journey on the following day, in a manner more accommodated to its tender age. The castle was plundered and burned, and the infant perished in the flames. The family only escaped by the promptness of their flight. They reached London, where they took lodgings in King Street.

Spenser never recovered from the shock of this calamity. Despair and discouragement clouded his breast, and his health sunk rapidly under the combination of grief, want, and the renewal of a painful servitude upon the capricious friendship of the great. We do not believe that he was utterly deserted in this distressing condition, because we do not believe in the utter baseness of mankind it would imply: feeling, generosity, and truth, can have no existence but in fable, if they are not to be found in the ranks of a high and polished aristocracy. But a just estimate of human nature, and a precise experience of the moral workings of society, is sufficient to account for the neglect which neither high worth, nor the possession of many friends, are enough to ward off. The generosity of the world is but an impulse, which its prudence more constant, is ever trying to limit and escape from: when the effort to relieve has been made, it is an easy thing to be satisfied that enough has been done, and to lay the blame of its actual insufficiency on the imprudence of the sufferer. The kindness is for the most part accompanied by counsel, for the most part inconsiderate, because it cannot be otherwise. It cannot be expected that any one will apply to the emergency of another that clear and elaborate scrutiny into the whole combination of their advantages and disadvantages which is necessary for conduct under the pressure of difficulty: counsel is cheap and easy, and all are ready to bestow it; but sound and considerate advice few have at their disposal when they need it for themselves. Our application of these reflections, is but conjectural, and the result of our own long observation of the ways of the world. But it is certain that Spenser had many high and influential friends, and claims of no slight order upon the sympathy of the good and wise, and upon the gratitude of all—the proudest ornaments of the Elizabethan age are Spenser and Shakespeare, with either of whom (different as they are) no other can be named. Poor Spenser with a family—stripped of his estate—with the claim of service and the noble title of genius—was, if not absolutely deserted, allowed to sink into neglect and penury. It is said, and not authoritatively contradicted, that when reduced to the most abject want, lord Essex sent him a sum of money which the poet's pride induced him to refuse. The circumstance is very likely to have received the exaggerations, so commonly attendant upon all incidents which can be distorted into scandal against the upper classes. We have already in another memoir,* had occasion to examine a very similar story. We however think it sufficiently confirms the general inference of his having suffered from want; nor can we entertain any doubt that his spirit must have been shattered and

* Life of Sheridan.—*Dublin University Magazine*, June, 1837.

his pride diseased into a morbid irritability by the sufferings and mortifications ever attendant upon such misfortunes.

It is, in the midst of these painful circumstances, cheering to contemplate the fact that his wife—the haughty beauty whom he had wooed for three years, and who adorned and exalted his short interval of worldly happiness—did not wrong the deep love and the immortalizing praises of the poet; but with the attachment and constancy peculiar to her sex, walked with him like a ministering angel in the fiery furnace of affliction and bitterness: confirming her claim in sober history, to the encomium with which poesy has handed down her name.

Spenser only survived his flight from the country of his adoption, "a little more than kin and less than kind," for five years, and died at his inn in King street, in January, 1598, in the 45th year of his age. The world, which felt that he was to be no longer a burden, but thenceforth an honour, showered upon his heedless grave its most unavailing honours and distinctions. His funeral was conducted with a pomp more suited to his real merits, than to his fortunes. The earl of Essex contributed the cost, and the poets of the day came to shower their verses into his grave. He was buried in Westminster Abbey, next to Chaucer, the only other name that could yet be named with his. His wife is understood to have survived him for some years, but not to have married again. His two sons had descendants, but have left no trace in our history; they found their way to their native country, but did not recover their father's estate. Sylvanus married a Miss Nangle of Moneanymy, in the county of Cork: by her he had Edmund and William Spenser. The other son, Peregrine, left also a son, who was afterwards reinstated by the court of claims, in all that could be ascertained of the Kilcolman estate. He was however afterwards outlawed for his adherence to James II. The property was again recovered to the family by William Spenser, the grandson of Sylvanus, by means of lord Halifax. It has however long passed away, and with it all distinct traces of the family. They are not however the less likely to be still existing: property is the stem of the genealogical tree, of which the leaves and branches cannot long survive the support.

It is a part of our most especial duty to offer something more than the mere history of the *Fairy Queen*, a production of which neither the characteristic style nor the local origin can be separated from the woods and streams of the county of Cork. Milton, whose mind was more deeply imbued with the poetry of Spenser than seems to have been noticed, describes this poem with his usual graphic precision in his divine *Il Penseroso:*—

> "And if ought else great bards beside
> In sage and solemn tunes have sung
> Of turneys and of trophies hung,
> Of forests and enchantments drear,
> When more is meant than meets the ear."

Besides its intrinsic merits as a great masterpiece of English poetry, the *Fairy Queen* is a composition of peculiar interest both to the antiquary and the moral historian, on account of the fidelity with which it may be said to reflect the opinions, manners, superstitions, and the whole spirit of the age. The full evidence of this is only to be collected from a more intimate acquaintance with the numerous neglected writings, and the forgotten and exploded superstitions with which those obscure records are replete.

To attempt even a summary of this would involve us in the discussion of a variety of topics, not easily dismissed within the limits we should wish to preserve. The literature of England and that of our island, yet continued remotely apart from each other both in material and character. The literature of Ireland was, like her language, the relic of a remote civilization, for centuries on the decline and tending to no revival. English literature was just breaking fresh from the shackles, and impediments of a long but retarded progress into a fresh and glorious adolescence—under the head and heart expanding influence of the reformation. The prejudices and superstitions of earlier times rejected from the enlarging dominion of reason were delivered up to the fancy or imagination: from reality they melted into the sombre magnificence of poetry. All that was solemn, terrific, or magnificent—all that was influential over character and feeling—all that had possessed the spirit and given its whole form to the external manners of the previous age—yet held a modified power over the heart of the world, and a venerable charm in its recollections. Such is the law of moral transition—the expansion of the intellect long precedes the real alteration of the moral constitution of the breast. It is on this principle that the ghost and fairy have so long held their place in modern fiction: there is a faith of the imagination, which long outlives the stern exposures of reason. There is not indeed, when we would truly estimate the extent to which the poetry of an age reflects its actual spirit, a more essential consideration than this, that it is not in the knowledge of its books, or by the actions of its leading characters (all that history records), the world is to be truly seen: it is not so in this age of diffusive education, and was not so when knowledge was nearly confined to those who were engaged in the extension of its bounds. As the German poet, (or his translator) says—

> " To us, my friend, the times that are gone by
> Are a mysterious book, sealed with seven seals:
> That which you call the spirit of ages past
> Is but in truth the spirit of some few authors,
> In which those ages are beheld reflected
> With what distortion strange, Heaven only knows."

From the surviving lucubrations of the academy or the cloister, in which little of external life can be *felt* (the only knowledge of life,) or from history which is but an abstract of gross results, or a record of facts, connected by the webwork of the writer's art;* there is little to

---

* We have borrowed the phrase from the same writer, to whom we are indebted for the quotation above.

> " History !
> Facts dramatised say rather—action—plot—
> Sentiment, every thing the writer's own,
> As it best fits the webwork of his story."—*Faustus*, p. 39.

convey the true character of a remote age,—it is to be inferred only from an intense realization of circumstances to be laboriously gleaned from a large collation of remains and records: but the nearest approach must ever be made, by a fair allowance for the representation of the poet, and the record of transmitted customs and superstitions.

The real spirit of the public mind of the age of Elizabeth was not materially varied from the quaint and simple character of many previous generations—a few loftier pinnacles had emerged into the upward beams of morning light—but the plains and valleys lay in twilight. The fairy people played their feats and gambols on the forest glade—and the bar-ghosts and goblins of midnight were indistinctly visible. The student still endeavoured to draw responses from the stars—or brooded over the furnace and crucible, in the feverish vigil of "hope deferred." The Gothic pageantry—the chivalric spirit of all the quaint solemnities with which a long lapse of ages of growing civilization had endeavoured to refine and ornament life, held a customary sway over the mind of every class and order, and moulded the age. These features are apparent in a multitude of ancient writers now little known, and may be traced in every record of manners in the Elizabethan age. Amid the splendour of that glorious age, may be discerned the ghastly empiricism which passed for knowledge—the absurd traditions which passed for history—the quaint and scholastic, but often just and lofty ethics, stiffened with a pasteboard panoply of conceits and allegories by the taste for mysticism which is so congenial to the infancy of knowledge, as well as by the seemingly opposite but equally allied tendency to give a palpable form and representation to the invisible and spiritual. Hence indeed the gorgeous masques, moralities and mysteries, with their grotesque and cumbrous machinery of virtues, graces, and mythologic beings, the delight of that generation to which they were fraught with an intense ideal and moral interest, unintelligible to the children of our shrewd age. "In the reign of queen Elizabeth," says Warton, "a popular ballad was no sooner circulated than it was converted into a moralization." The moralization passed into a pageantry, which was but a costly improvement on the cap and bells of simpler times. In a coarse and simple age the passions are likely to occupy a prominent place in the productions of taste or fancy. "No doubt." writes an author of that period, "the cause that books of learning seem so hard, is, because such and so great a scull of amarouse pamphlets have so preoccupied the eyes and ears of men, that a multitude believe there is none other style or phrase worth gramercy. No books so rife or so friendly read, as be these books. But if the setting out of the wanton tricks of a pair of lovers, as for example, let them be called Sir Chaunticleere and Dame Partilote, to tell how their first combination of love began, how their eyes floated, and how they anchered, their beams mingled one with the other's beauty. Then, of their perplexed thoughts, their throes, their faulies, their dryric drifts, now interrupted, now unperfitted, their love days, their sugred words, and their sugred joys. Afterwards, how envious fortune, through this chop or that channer, turned their bless to bale, severing two such beautiful faces and dutiful hearts," &c. We have made so long an extract because, though much of this ridicule is equally applicable to the love tale of any age, it represents the fiction of the Elizabethan, with the precision of a general formula for practice; and will be found to have a peculiar though much refined and purified application to the *Fairy Queen*.

In a period when the scope of literature was confined and its style unfinished and unfixed; the classical writers of antiquity, then but recently revived, and having the fresh charm of novelty added to their simple unapproachable excellence, were seized upon with avidity and eager enthusiasm. They furnished a range of ideas which mingled with the Gothic associations of ancient English literature, and gave rise to those strange and monstrous mixtures of Christian and mythological personages so frequently to be met in the *Fairy Queen*, as well as other poems of the age.* An amusing example of this may be found, Book I. Cant. IV., where Pluto's daughter is described on a party of pleasure:—

"And after all upon the wagon beam
Rode Satan with a smarting whip in hand."

Still more deeply infused into the spirit of the age, were the superstitions of every various kind, whether from the corruptions of religion, or the popular notions of magic, witchcraft, judicial astrology, and alchemy. These absurdities were beginning to be displaced by the growing philosophy of a period of transition, and as they were less entertained as realities, they became more the elementary spirit of the poet. They had not yet evaporated into mere inanity before the full daylight of reason and religious truth, and had just enough of superstitious charm to give them form to the imagination.

The same might be repeated of the magnificent and gorgeous "pomp and circumstance" of chivalry: its feelings and aspirations yet mingled in the upper air of social life. It gave the law to pride and sentiment—it yet continued to elevate and inspire the hero's and the lover's breast; and could not fail to be vitally blended with poetry.

Not to exhaust a topic which would carry us too far for our immediate purpose, such are the characteristic elements of Spenser's great poem. For something he was indebted, (if it can be so termed,) to the poetry of his great patron Sydney, whose strange intermixture of Italian pastoral and Gothic romance, produced a powerful impression on the age. From these materials, was combined the lengthened tissue of romantic tales of adventure, in which religion and superstition—romance and pastoral—knights, witches, sorcerers, tourneys and enchantments, mingle in pretty equal proportions—all blended together into that medium of allegory which was the palpable poetry of the age. While we may look for the high and solemn strain of moral sentiment which is diffused throughout, to the character of the poet's own mind,

* It is curious to notice the misapplication of general facts, as well as rules, by those whose minds range within a narrow scope. The fault here noticed is little known to the generality of readers, because the writers who have committed them are not generally read. But the impression that some such thing has been found fault with, has given rise to a common charge against Milton, who has combined with singular effect and propriety the heathen and scriptural mythologies, by seizing on the real principle of relation between them.

and the general colouring of the descriptions to the scenery of Irish woods; the wild wood path of adventure—which leads or misleads the errant knight or the forlorn lady, till they light on the shepherd's hut, the robber's castle, or the wizard's cell—could nowhere else be found in such living representation.

We shall conclude these remarks with some description of the poem, the materials of which we have endeavoured to enumerate. This portion of our undertaking is done to our hand by the author himself, in a letter to Raleigh:—

To the right noble and valourous, Sir Walter Raleigh, knight, Lord Warden of the Stanneries, and her Majesty's lieutenant of the county of Cornwall.

" Sir,—Knowing how doubtfully all allegories may be construed, and this book of mine, which I have entitled the *Fairy Queen*, being a continued allegory, or dark conceit; I have thought good, as well for avoiding of zealous opinions and misconstructions, as also for your better light in reading thereof, (being so by you commanded,) to discover unto you the general intention and meaning, which in the whole course thereof I have fashioned, without expressing of any particular purposes or by-accidents therein occasioned. The general end therefore of all the book, is to fashion a gentleman or noble person, in vertuous and gentle discipline;—which for that I conceived should be most plausible and pleasing, being coloured with an historical fiction, the which the most part of men delight to read, rather for variety of matter, than for profit of the ensample: I chose the history of king Arthur as most fit for the excellency of his person; being made famous by many men's former works, and also furthest from the danger of envy and suspicion of present time: and in which I have followed all the antique poets historical. First, Homer, who in the persons of Agamemnon and Ulysses hath ensampled a good governor and a vertuous man— the one in his Iliad the other in his Odysseis; then Virgil, whose like intention was to do in the person of Æneas; after him, Ariosto comprised them both in his Orlando; and lately Tasso dissevered them again, and formed both parts in two persons; namely, that part which they, in philosophy call ethice, or vertues of a private man, coloured in his Rinaldo; the other named politice, in his Godfredo. By ensample of which excellent poets they labour to pourtraict in Arthur, before he was king, the image of a brave knight perfected in the twelve private moral virtues, as Aristotle hath devised; the which is the purpose of these twelve books: which if I find to be well excepted, I may be, perhaps encouraged to frame the other part of politick vertues in his person, after that he came to be king.

" To some, I know this method will seem to be displeasant; which had rather have good discipline plainly in way of precepts, or sermoned at large, as they use, than thus cloudly enwrapped in allegorical devices. But such me seem, should be satisfied with the use of these days, seeing all things accounted by their shows, and nothing esteemed of, that is not delightful and pleasing to common sense, for this cause is Xenophon preferred before Plato; for that the one, in the exquisite depth of his judgment formed a commonwealth, such as it should be;

but the other in the person of Syrus and the Persians fashioned a government, such as might best be; so have I laboured to do in the person of Arthur; whom I conceive, after his long education by Timon (to whom he was by Merlin, delivered to be brought up, so soon as he was born of the lady Igrane,) to have seen in a dream or vision, the fairy queen with whose excellent beauty ravished, he awaking, resolved to seek her out; and so being by Merlin armed, and by Timon thoroughly instructed he went to seek her forth in fairy. In that fairy queen, I mean glory in my general intention; but in my particular, I conceive, the most excellent and glorious person of our sovereign, the queen and her kingdom in fairy-land. And yet in some places else I do otherwise shadow her. For considering she beareth two persons, the one of a most royal queen or empress, the other of a most virtuous and beautiful lady; this latter part, in some places, I do express in Belphœbe: fashioning her name according to your own excellent conceit of Cynthia; Phœbe and Cynthia being both names of Diana. So in the person of prince Arthur, I set forth *magnificence* in particular: which vertue, for that (according to Aristotle and the rest) it is the perfection of all the rest, and containeth in it them all; therefore in the whole course, I mention the deeds of Arthur applicable to that vertue, which I write of in that book. But of the twelve other vertues, I make twelve other knights the patrons, for the more variety of the history: of which these three books contain three. The first, of the knights of the red cross, in whom I express holiness; the second, of Sir Gugon, in whom I set forth temperance; the third of Britomantis, a lady knight, in whom I picture chastity. But because the beginning of the whole work seemeth abrupt, and as depending upon other antecedents, it needs that ye know the occasion of these three knights' several adventures. For the method of a poet historical, is not such of an historiographer; for an historiographer discourseth of affairs orderly as they are done, accounting as well the times as the actions: but a poet thrusteth into the middest, even where it most concerneth him; and there recoursing to the things forepast, and devining of things to come, maketh a pleasing analysis of all. The beginning therefore of my history, if it were to be told by an historiographer, should be the twelfth book, which is the last; where I devise, that the *Fairy Queen* kept her annual feast twelve days; upon which twelve several days the occasions of the twelve several adventurers happened, which being undertaken by twelve several knights, are in these twelve books severally handled and discoursed.

"The first was this. In the beginning of the feast there presented himself a tall clownish young man; who falling before the queen of the fairies, desired a boon (as the manner then was) which during the feast, she might not refuse: which was, that he might have the atchievment of any adventure which, during that feast should happen. That being granted, he rested himself on the floor, unfit, through his rusticity, for a better place. Soon after entred a fair lady in mourning weeds, riding on a white ass with a dwarf behind her leading a warlike steed, that bore the armour of a knight, and his spear in the dwarf's hand, she falling before the queen of the fairies, complained that her father and mother, an ancient king and queen, had been by an huge dragon, many years shut up in a brazen castle; who thence suffered them not to issue; and therefore besought the fairy queen to assign her some one of her knights to take on him the exploit. Presently that clownish person upstarting, desired that adventure: whereat the queen much wondering, and the lady much gainsaying, yet he earnestly importuned his desire. In the end, the lady told him, unless that armour which she brought, would serve him, (that is the armour of a Christian man specified by St Paul, Ephes. v.) that he could not succeed in that enterprise; which being forthwith put upon him, with due furnitures thereunto, he seemed the goodliest man in all that company, and was well liked of the lady. And eftsoons taking on him knighthood, and mounting on that strange courser, he went forth with her on that adventure; where beginneth the first book, viz:—

"A gentle knight was pricking on the plain," &c.

" The second day there came in a palmer, bearing an infant, with bloody hands; whose parents he complained to have been slain by an enchantress, called Acrasia; and therefore craved of the fairy queen to appoint him some knight to perform that adventure: which being assigned to Sir Guyon, he presently went forth with that same palmer, which is the beginning of the second book, and the whole subject thereof. The third day there came in a groom, who complained before the fairy queen that a vile enchanter, called Busirane, had in hand a most fair lady, called Amoretta; whom he kept in most grievous torment, because she would not yield him the pleasure of her body. Whereupon Sir Scudamour, the lover of that lady, presently took on him that adventure. But being unable to perform it by reason of the hard enchantments, after long sorrow, in the end met with Britomantis, who succoured him, and rescued his love.

"But by occasion hereof, many other adventures are intermeddled, but rather as accidents, than intendments: as the love of Britomart, the overthrow of Marinell, the misery of Florimell, the virtuousness of Belphœbe, the lasciviousness of Hellenora, and many the like.

" This much, sir, I have briefly over-run, to direct your understanding to the well-head of the history; that from thence gathering the whole intention of the conceit, ye may as in a handful gripe all the discourse: which otherwise may haply seem tedious and confused. So humbly craving the continuance of your favour towards me, and the eternal establishment of your happiness, I humbly take leave,

"Your most humbly affectionate,
" EDMUND SPENSER.

" 23d *January*, 1589."

RICHARD STANIHURST.

DIED A. D. 1618.

THE father of Stanihurst was a lawyer, and the recorder of Dublin. He was also speaker of the Irish House of Commons, and died in 1573, aged 51.

RICHARD STANIHURST.

Richard received the first rudiments of education in Dublin, from whence he was sent to Oxford, where he was admitted in 1563, in University college. Having graduated, he entered as a student, first at Furnival's Inn, and then at Lincoln's. He next appears to have returned to Ireland, where he married a daughter of Sir Charles Barnwall, knight, with whom he returned to resume his studies in London; here his wife died in childbirth, at Knightsbridge, 1579. Having changed his religion, he left England, and went to live at Leyden, where his course is not very distinctly traceable, though it is certain that he acquired great reputation among the learned, for his scholarship and his writings. He was uncle to the celebrated Primate Usher, who was the son of his sister, and took great pains to convert his nephew to his own faith. Having entered into holy orders, he became chaplain to the archduke of Austria, and died in the Netherlands in 1618. He left one son who became a Jesuit, and died 1663.

Staniburst is now chiefly known by his "Descriptio Hiberniæ," a work in the hands of every student of Irish history and antiquity. It is described by Bishop Nicholson as "highly commendable," with the exception of some tedious and frivolous digressions. He translated four books of Virgil, in a style which has entitled him to be distinguished by critics and commentators, with unusual, but not undeserved severity. He seems to have been utterly devoid of all perception of the essential distinction between burlesque and serious poetry. A distinguished modern poet and critic sums up all that can be said in these words, "As Chaucer has been called the well of English undefiled, so might Stanihurst be called the common sewer of the language. It seems impossible that a man could have written in such a style, without intending to burlesque what he was about, and yet it is certain that Stanihurst intended to write heroic poetry. His version is exceeding rare, and deserves to be reprinted for its incomparable oddity."* To our apprehension, the burlesque of Stanihurst represents but the extreme of the defects to which there is a universal tendency among the poets of his time; the most free from burlesque, the loftiest in conception, and most harmonious in metre, seem every now and then to have a narrow escape. Stanihurst would have been burlesque at any time; he was no poet, and wrote when the distinction between different departments of literature were little understood; a person having the name of a scholar, wrote English verse for the same reasons that such persons now write Latin verse. But it must be also said, that the sense of the age was very obtuse on the subject of burlesque. More than half their representations of the solemn, terrific, or sublime, were undoubtedly burlesque. But it must be remembered, that nothing is laughable but by association. We give the following, examples from Warton. "He calls Chorebus, one of the Trojan chiefs, a *Bedlamite;* he says that old Priam girded on his sword *Morglay,* the name of a sword in the Gothic romances; that Dido would have have been glad to have been brought to bed even of a cockney, a *Dandiprate Hopthumb;* and that Jupiter, in kissing his daughter, *bussed his*

* Southey.

pretty prating parrot." Of his verse, the following specimen may suffice:—

> "With tentive listening each wight was settled in hearkening,
> Their father Aneas chronicled from loftie bed hautie;
> You bid me, O princess, to sacrifice a festered old sore,
> How that the Trojans were prest by the Grecian armie."

The reader will have noticed that the verse is a wretched imitation of the Latin hexameter. This was the fashion of his day, it was introduced by Gabriel Harvey, and adopted by Sidney, Spenser, and all the poets of the day, but soon rejected. Harvey enumerates Stanihurst, with Spenser, Sidney, and other celebrated writers, as commendably employed, and enriching their native tongue, and sounds his own glory as the inventor of the English hexameter.

Stanihurst's works are the following:—Harmonica, seu Catena Dialectica in Porphyrium; De rebus in Hibernia Gestis; Descriptio Hiberniæ, inserted in *Holinshed's Chronicle;* De Vatæ et Patricii Hibernia Apostoli; Hebdomada Mariana; Hebdomada Eucharistica; Brevis præmonitis pro futura concertatione cum Jacobo Userio; The principles of the Roman Catholic Religion; The four first books of Virgil's Æneid, in English hexameter, published with versions of the four first Psalms in Iambic metre.

SIR JAMES WARE.

BORN A.D. 1594.—DIED A D. 1666.

AMONG those to whom Ireland is indebted for the collection and preservation of the most authentic materials for her history, no name can be placed above that of Ware. And we have to express regret that we are not more fully informed in the history of his life.

He was born 26th November, 1594, in Castle Street, in the city of Dublin. His father was auditor-general, with reversion to his son. At the age of sixteen he entered as a fellow-commoner in the university of Dublin: and took bachelor's and master's degrees at the usual times. The distinction which he maintained among his fellow-students, and, above all, the taste he early began to show for the study of antiquities, attracted the notice, and gained the friendship, of Usher, who was at the time professor of divinity in the university. Ware had early commenced his collections, and Usher's collection and library were open to him; as also that of Daniel Molyneux, Ulster king-at-arms.

In 1626, he went to London, and was introduced, by Usher, to Sir Robert Cotton, who opened to him his valuable and extensive collections and library. He also made laborious researches in the Tower and other state-paper offices and repositories, from all of which he obtained large treasures of original and important records—from which he made copious extracts and copies.

On his return home, he commenced those valuable labours, by which he is now best known; and published the first parts of the History of the Irish Bishops.

His second visit to London was in 1628, when his acquaintance with Seldon, and other eminent antiquarians, enabled him to enlarge his collections very considerably. In 1629, on his return to Ireland, he was knighted by the lords justices. In 1632, his father died, and he succeeded him as auditor-general. From the lord lieutenant, Wentworth, he obtained a seat in the privy council.

Though attentive to his public duties, Sir James Ware was not remiss in the pursuit of his favourite studies. He soon after published " Spenser's View of the State of Ireland." He was at this time engaged in collecting accounts of the " Writers of Ireland." His well-known work under that title, came out in 1639.

In the troubled period which commenced in 1641, his conduct was, in the highest degree, praiseworthy. The following is the valuable testimony of the marquess of Ormonde. " Even when his majesty's affairs were most neglected, and when it was not safe for any man to show himself for them, he then appeared most zealously and stoutly for them."

In 1644, he was sent over to Oxford, as the fittest person to give the king an account of the state of Ireland, and to receive his commands on the negotiation then in progress. He availed himself of the occasion for his favourite pursuit. He was honoured by the university with a degree of doctor of laws. When returning, with despatches from the king, the packet in which he sailed was taken by a parliament ship. He was sent prisoner to London, and there committed to the Tower, where he remained for ten months—after which he was exchanged. He continued, in Dublin, to take a prominent part in the king's affairs, and was high in the confidence of the marquess of Ormonde. At the surrender of Dublin to the parliamentary commanders, in 1647, he was demanded as one of the hostages, and, as such, taken to London. On his return to Dublin his office was, of course, at an end, and he lived as a private person, until governor Jones banished him, by an order, to any place beyond seas except England. Sir James went over to France, where he resided successively at Caen and in Paris, still occupied with his antiquarian studies.

In 1651, his private affairs required his presence in England, whither he came, by parliamentary license; and, after a couple of years, went over to Ireland, to visit his estate.

During the whole of this interval, he was busy in the publication of his works, which were printed in England. The " Antiquities" came out in 1654; and four years after he published a second and improved edition.

On the Restoration, he was, at once, reinstated in his office of auditor-general, by Charles, to whom he had given a large sum of money in his necessity. At the election of parliament, he was chosen member for the university. He was, soon after, appointed one of the four commissioners for appeal in excise cases; and a commissioner for the settlement under the king's declaration.

He refused the king's offer of a title; but, according to Harris, obtained baronetcies for two of his friends.

His " Annals" were published next; and in 1665, the " History of the Irish Bishops" came out entire. But death cut short his projects of literature. He died on the 3d December, 1666, and was buried in his family vault in St Werburgh's church.

Several miscellaneous statements are given by Harris and others, of his uprightness, benevolence, and justice. He always refused his official fees from widows, the clergy, and their sons. He lived in a season of great distress, and exerted himself to the utmost for its relief. His house and table were a known refuge for the victims of reverse and spoliation; and when he was given possession of some houses and tenements, forfeited for rebellion, he instantly sent for the widow and children of the forfeitee, and made a legal conveyance of the premises in their favour.

His works are known. They have a distinguished place in every library which has its shelf for the History of Ireland. They are valuable for their brief accuracy and comprehensive extent—supplying the place of a guide and faithful sign-post to the student in a vast chaos of undigested literature. There are few of any real importance on the subject, of which the main outline will not be found among Ware's writings, with a happy freedom from theories, for which he had too little genius, yet too much common sense.

END OF VOL. I.

CONTENTS OF VOL. I.

DIVISION FIRST—EARLY.

	Page
HISTORICAL INTRODUCTION,	3—96

EARLY IRISH CHRISTIANS.

	Page
1. Pelagius,	97
2. St. Patrick,	104
3. Columbkill,	117
4. St. Columbanus,	128
5. Bridget,	132
6. Scotus-Erigena,	135

MONARCHS TO THE NORMAN INVASION.

7. Turgesius,	139
8. The Monarch O'Melaghlin,	143
9. Aodh Finliath,	147
10. Cormac, King of Cashel,	148
11. Anlaf, King of Dublin,	151
12. Bryan Boru,	155
13. Malachy,	170
14. Donchad O'Brien,	174

THE CONQUEST.

15. Dermod Macmurrough,	177

THE INVADERS.

16. Earl Strongbow,	196
17. Hugh de Lacy,	208
18. Maurice Fitz-Gerald,	210
19. Robert Fitz-Stephen,	212
20. Raymond le Gros,	213
21. De Courcy,	218
22. Sir Armorie de St. Lawrence,	231
23. Giraldus Cambrensis,	233

THE O'CONNORS OF CONNAUGHT.

24. Roderic O'Connor,	238
25. Cathal O'Connor,	247
26. Feidlim O'Connor, Prince of Connaught,	252
27. Second Feidlim O'Conuor,	254

THE DE BURGOS.

	Page
28. William Fitz-Adelm,	256
29. Richard de Burgo,	257
30. Walter de Burgo,	260
31. Richard de Burgo,	260
32. Edmund de Burgo,	261
33. William de Burgo, Earl of Ulster,	261
34. Ulick de Burgh, First Earl of Clanricarde,	263
35. Richard, Second Earl of Clanricarde,	263

THE O'BRIENS OF THOMOND.

36. Donald O'Brien, Prince of Thomond,	264
37. Murtough O'Brien,	265
38. Murrough O'Brien, First Earl of Thomond,	265

THE EARLY BUTLERS OF ORMONDE, 268

39. James, Fourth Earl of Ormonde,	270
40. James, Fifth Earl,	278
41. Sir James Ormonde,	279
42. Richard, Earl Marshall,	281

THE FITZGERALDS.—FIRST SERIES.

1. THE HOUSE OF KILDARE.

43. Maurice Fitzgerald,	286
44. Earl of Kildare,	288
45. Second Earl of Kildare,	292
46. Maurice, Fourth Earl of Kildare,	292
47. Thomas, Seventh Earl of Kildare,	296
48. Gerald, Eighth Earl of Kildare,	297

2. THE HOUSE OF DESMOND.

49. Maurice, First Earl of Desmond,	311
50. Gerald, Fourth Earl of Desmond,	317

CONTENTS.

	Page		Page
51. Thomas, Sixth Earl of Desmond,	317	78. Thomas, Tenth Earl of Ormonde,	481
52. James, Seventh Earl of Desmond,	319		
53. Thomas, Eighth Earl of Desmond,	320	MISCELLANEOUS.	
54. Maurice, Tenth Earl of Desmond,	322	79. Daniel O'Sullivan Beare,	486
		80. Florence M'Carthy,	498
		81. Cormack M'Carthy, Lord of Muskerry,	502
THE O'DONELLS OF TYRCONNEL.		82. Sir George Carew,	504
55. Donald O'Donell, chief of Tyrconnel,	323	83. Feagh Machugh O'Byrne,	507
56. Hugh Roe O'Donell,	324		
57. Hugh Roe O'Donell, last Chief of Tyrconnell,	324	THE LAST OF THE O'NIALLS OF TIR OWEN.	
		84. Hugh O'Neale, Earl of Tyrone,	511
MISCELLANEOUS.		MISCELLANEOUS.	
58. Sir Robert Savage,	348	85. Thomas, Sixteenth Earl of Kerry,	570
59. Sir John Bermingham,	352	86. Robert, Fifth Lord Trimleston,	572
60. Arnold de la Poer,	358	87. James Fitz-Maurice,	572
61. Art M'Murrough,	360		
62. Sir William Brabazon,	364	POSTSCRIPT,	573
63. Bernard Fitz-Patrick,	365		
64. Sir Anthony St. Leger,	367	CLERICAL AND LITERARY.	
		INTRODUCTORY REMARKS.	579
THE O'NIALLS OF TIR OWEN.			
65. Hugh O'Niall of Tir Owen,	371	I. ECCLESIASTICAL AND POLITICAL.	
66. Con O'Niall, First Earl of Tyrone,	373	88. Lawrence O'Toole,	583
67. John O'Neale,	379	89. Malachy, Archbishop of Armagh,	590
		90. Gregory, First Archbishop of Dublin,	590
THE FITZGERALDS—SECOND SERIES.		91. John Comyn,	591
		92. Henry de Loundres,	594
1. THE HOUSE OF KILDARE.		93. Fulk de Saundford,	596
68. Gerald, Ninth Earl of Kildare,	389	94. Richard de Feringa,	598
69. Lord Thomas Fitzgerald,	403	95. Alexander de Bicknor,	598
70. Gerald, Tenth Earl of Kildare,	416	96. Thomas Cranely,	601
		97. Richard Talbot,	601
2. THE HOUSE OF DESMOND.		98. George Brown, Archbishop of Dublin,	603
71. James, Eleventh Earl of Desmond,	421	99. Hugh Curwin, Archbishop of Dublin,	622
72. James, Fifteenth Earl of Desmond,	422	100. Adam Loftus, Archbishop of Dublin,	622
73. Gerald, Sixteenth Earl of Desmond,	423	101. John Bale, Bishop of Ossory,	626
74. James, the Sugan Earl of Desmond,	452	102. George Dowdal, Archbishop of Armagh,	628
		103. John Allen, Archbishop of Dublin,	629
THE BUTLERS OF ORMONDE.—SECOND SERIES.			
75. John, Sixth Earl of Ormonde,	475	II. CLERICAL AND LITERARY.	
76. Piere, Eighth Earl of Ormonde,	476		
77. James, Ninth Earl of Ormonde,	479	104. Robert de Wikeford,	631

www.ingramcontent.com/pod-product-compliance
Lightning Source LLC
Chambersburg PA
CBHW021158230426
43667CB00006B/455